Spiritual Contestations

Spiritual Contestations – The Violence of Peace in South Sudan

Naomi Ruth Pendle

 JAMES CURREY

First published 2023
James Currey

ISBN 978-1-84701-338-5

James Currey
is an imprint of
Boydell & Brewer Ltd
PO Box 9, Woodbridge
Suffolk IP12 3DF (GB)
www.jamescurrey.com
and of
Boydell & Brewer Inc.
668 Mt Hope Avenue
Rochester, NY 14620–2731 (US)
www.boydellandbrewer.com

It is based on research that received funding from the Economic and Social Research
Council (ESRC) for the Centre for Public Authority and International Development (grant
agreement No ES/ P00803871) and the Arts and Humanities Research Council under the
Safety of Strangers project (grant agreement No AH/T007524/1)

British Library Cataloguing in Publication Data
A CIP record for this book is available from the British Library

The publisher has no responsibility for the continued existence or accuracy of URLs for
external or third-party internet websites referred to in this book, and does not guarantee
that any content on such websites is, or will remain, accurate or appropriate

This publication is printed on acid-free paper

For Jonathan James Nhial Lam Pendle, and his grandparents (my parents) Barbara and David

Contents

Illustrations

Maps

Figures

Full credit details are provided in the captions to the images in the text. The author and publisher are grateful to all the institutions and individuals for permission to reproduce the materials in which they hold copyright. Every effort has been made to trace the copyright holders; apologies are offered for any omission, and the publisher will be pleased to add any necessary acknowledgement in subsequent editions.

Acknowledgements

The intellectual inspiration, empirical insights and time to write this book leave me filled with gratitude to a plethora of people over the last decade. My most profound thanks are owed to the people in Warrap and Unity States who generously gave their time to talk to me, to teach me, to share their stories and to respond to my questions. When I first went to South Sudan to teach in Warrap State in 2009, and when I first started learning about the material that appears in this book, I met fellow teachers and our last decade of conversations has been pivotal. Chirrilo Madut and Abraham Diing had just returned to South Sudan having lived in Kakuma Refugee Camp (Kenya). They were kind enough to include me in their conversations and daily lives. Over the last fourteen years, they have become some of my closest friends and most respected colleagues. I am looking forward to reading the books that they write, including their responses to this monograph. Chief Morris, Ajak Dit, Bol, Wol, Dut and Regina were also living nearby and helped me to learn and find a place in those villages. When I stayed in Unity State, James Gatkuoth was kind enough to welcome me to his home and to share endless ideas. He also introduced me to Latjor whose dedication to this community always humbles me. Chuol Gew has been an incredible mentor and his children are an inspiration. Gatwech has taught me so much, and Isaac and Matot continue to support my learning. South Sudan is logistically complicated, and I have spent a decade begging favours and asking advice. Tinega, Audrey, Hsiao-Wei, Glen, Chris, Ric, Pauline and Nelly have helped me in many ways at different times. Anna Rowett is also a constant rock for many of us.

Tim Allen and Sharon Hutchinson were key inspirations and mentors. Luka Biong, Zoe Cormack, Joshua Craze, Koen Vlassenroot, Jok Madut Jok, Nicki Kindersley, Alice Robinson and Glen Aronson were also particular intellectual inspirations, introducing me to new literatures or ways of thinking at key moments in ways that were often more precious than decades of formal teaching. Nicki Kindersley, Douglas Johnson and an anonymous reviewer were incredibly generous with their time in reviewing this book and giving feedback that allowed this final version. Without Nicki's encouragement, I would have given up long ago. From the inception of my research, Cherry

Leonardi has always been critically encouraging; many of us who work on South Sudan owe much to her mentorship. Lydia Tanner, Diana Felix Da Costa, Rachel Ibreck, Julia Duany, Alex de Waal, Tom Kirk, Anna MacDonald, Esther Marijnen, Ferenc 'Feri' Marko, Jok Madut Jok, Leben Moro, Sylvia Nannyonga-Tamusuza, Vicky Van Bockhaven, Tatiana Carayannis, Matt Benson, Liz Storer, Kara Blackmore and Eddie Thomas have not only been friends, but often also teachers. Plus, now, Pete Manning is fast becoming the person who keeps research (and life) exciting.

For the book itself, I am incredibly grateful to Jaqueline Mitchell (Commissioning Editor) and the editors of the 'Religion in Transforming Africa' series at James Currey. Joseph Hellweg gave me a useful nudge at a couple of crucial moments. Nicholas Jewitt also provided insightful edits at the essential, final hurdle. I am also thankful to Ben Rees, Sean McGovern, Anne Thompson, Joseph Finch and Peter Dunford for either helping with the footnotes or editing. The cartography of Jillian Luff of mapgrafix.com and the engaged cover artwork titled '*Raan aci thong kek weng* (A man is not equivalent to only one cow)' by Letaru Dralega both make a significant contribution. The book also relied on financial support from the Centre for Public Authority and International Development (ESRC-funded grant ES/ P00803871) and funding from the Arts and Humanities Research Council (AHRC) through the Safety of Strangers grant (AHRC reference number AH/T007524/1).

Writing books interrupts life. Friends and family have been patient and have kept me smiling. I am especially grateful for support over the years from Kathryn, Phil, Frankie, Meera, Tiggy, Christian, Ben, Michael and Pete, their amazing families, and my homegroup. I am also thankful to the people who supplied me coffee in The Chelsea Café.

My parents – David and Barbara Pendle – are my team and my rock, and have propped us up again and again. They have given me so much but, most preciously, a faith that encourages me to pay attention to the things unseen. In the end, it is all about Jonathan; he inspires me, spurs me on, is the biggest blessing and helps me make sense of everything else. This book is for him, as one way for him to understand part of his other homeland.

Chronology

1997	Khartoum Peace Agreement
1998	Bahr el Ghazal famine
	Riek Machar and Paulino Matip's forces fight in Unity State
	Kerubino Kuanyin temporarily takes control of Wau Town
1999	Sudan government opens oil pipeline in Unity State
	Nuer-Dinka Wunlit Peace Agreement
	Kerubino Kuanyin is killed in Mayom
2005	Comprehensive Peace Agreement between SPLA and Sudan government
2005	Death of John Garang in a helicopter crash, and appointment of Salva Kiir as SPLA leader and President of Southern Sudan
2006	Juba Declaration between SPLA and the South Sudan Defence Force
2010	The divinity MAANI seizes Nyachol in Mayendit (Unity State)
2012	Recruitment of forces in Bahr el Ghazal for defence of northern border
2013	President Kiir dismisses his cabinet
2013	Fighting erupts among the Presidential Guard in Juba and South-South wars escalate
2015	Agreement on the Resolution of Conflict in South Sudan
2018	Revitalised Agreement on the Resolution of Conflict in South Sudan
2019	The divinity TILING seizes Geng Mut in Thonyor (Unity State)
2022	Government forces carry out decisive offensives in Unity State

Introduction

It was late morning in May 2014, and I was sitting on the sofa in the lobby of a Radisson Blu Hotel. The sliding doors of the hotel opened onto a typical, international hotel lobby with marbled floors, a series of lifts, a spiralling staircase and clusters of small, hard, colourful square-shaped sofas and armchairs. If you could only see the lobby, and not the street outside, you would not have known where we were in the world. The hotel on that June morning was in the centre of Addis Ababa (Ethiopia's capital city). The hotel was hosting the negotiating teams of South Sudan's main warring parties – the South Sudan government and the still nascent Sudan People's Liberation Army – In Opposition (SPLA-IO). They had been invited by IGAD – an East African intergovernmental regional body – to Addis Ababa to continue peace negotiations. These negotiations would eventually result in the signing of the long 2015 Agreement on the Resolution of Conflict in South Sudan (ARCSS) and the 2018 Revitalised-ARCSS.

The peace negotiations had been initiated in January 2014 in response to escalating armed conflict in South Sudan. On the 15 December 2013 in Juba (South Sudan's capital city), fighting erupted between soldiers in the barracks of the Presidential Guard. The next day, soldiers divided largely based on alliances and divisions formed during the Sudan Government – Sudan People's Liberation Army (SPLA) conflicts of the 1980s, 1990s and 2000s.[1] In this 2013 moment of government anxiety, uniformed, president-aligned forces killed civilians based on crude conceptions of ethnicity.[2] In almost instantaneous response to the violence in Juba, vast swathes of soldiers in the north-eastern third of South Sudan mutinied and took up arms against the government, with many combatants and supporting communities understanding the conflict as wars of revenge for the killings in Juba.[3] Over the following three years, armed conflict would also spread to the Equatorias – the southern third of the country.

---

[1] Douglas Johnson, 'Briefing: The crisis in South Sudan', *African Affairs* 113: 451 (2014): 300–309.

[2] Skye Wheeler, 'South Sudan's New War: Abuses by Government and Opposition Forces' (2014).

[3] Naomi Pendle, 'The "Nuer of Dinka Money" and the Demands of the Dead:

By 2018, excess mortality from the conflict was over 400,000.[4] Between 2013 and 2021, there were over thirty pockets of famine-level hunger impacting hundreds of thousands of people.[5] By 2021, 3.7 million South Sudanese had fled their homes to seek safety.[6] Throughout these wars, the government and armed opposition carried out extreme and seemingly arbitrary acts of physical violence against civilians, breaking international and local norms.[7]

That late morning in May 2014, as I sat in the Radisson Blu Hotel in Addis, an eclectic combination of South Sudan's political elite walked through the sliding doors and wandered past me to access the hotel's lavish buffet lunch. It was hard not to be dazzled by this array of South Sudanese political celebrities. The day's IGAD peace negotiations on South Sudan had not yet started and there was little prospect of any significant progress. In the meantime, the opposing elites of South Sudan's warring parties could enjoy their internationally funded place of rest. The 2014 World Cup was only a couple of weeks away from starting and much time was spent watching football commentary and predicting the footballing outcomes.

If you turn to your right as you enter the Radisson Blu, the dining room is through a small opening. Tables are crowded together in a relatively small

Contesting the Moral Limits of Monetised Politics in South Sudan', *Conflict, Security & Development* 20:5 (2021): 587–605.

[4]   Francesco Checchi, Adrienne Testa, Abdihamid Warsame, Le Quach and Rachel Burns, 'Estimates of Crisis-attributable Mortality in South Sudan, December 2013–April 2018' (London School of Hygiene and Tropical Medicine, 2018), www.lshtm.ac.uk/south-sudan-full-report, accessed 7 December 2020.

[5]   Chris Newton, Bol Mawien, Chirrilo Madut, Elizabeth Gray and Naomi Pendle, 'Chiefs' Courts, Hunger, and Improving Humanitarian Programming in South Sudan' (London School of Economics and Political Science, 2021).

[6]   This includes 2.3 million refugees and 1.4 million IDPs from 'conflict and violence' but ignores IDPs caused by 'disasters'. UNHCR, 'Refugees and Asylum-Seekers from South Sudan – Total', 30 September 2021, https://data. unhcr.org/en/situations/southsudan#_ga=2.132774989.2119093081.1634396357-810602092.1634396357, accessed 16 October 2021; International Displacement Monitoring Centre, 'County Information', www.internal-displacement.org/ countries/south-sudan, accessed 16 October 2021.

[7]   Joshua Craze, 'Displaced and Immiserated: The Shilluk of Upper Nile in South Sudan's Civil War, 2014–19' (Small Arms Survey, 2019), www.smallarmssurvey.org/sites/default/files/resources/HSBA-Report-South-Sudan-Shilluk.pdf, accessed 5 April 2020; Naomi Pendle, 'Competing Authorities and Norms of Restraint: Governing Community-embedded Armed Groups in South Sudan'. *International Interactions* 47:5 (2021): 873–97; Skye Wheeler and Samer Muscati, '"They Burned It All": Destruction of Villages, Killings, and Sexual Violence in Unity State, South Sudan', Human Rights Watch, 2015.

space, and hotel guests eat from a buffet of meats, salads, cheeses, fruits, cakes and freshly prepared choices made instantly by the waiting chef. That May morning, as other mornings, the representatives of the warring parties lined up, side-by-side, irrespective of the sides of the war that their soldiers were fighting on. Although on opposing sides of the war, these negotiating elites knew each other well. Many had fought together as comrades in the 1980s and 1990s and were even in-laws through networks of politically strategic marriages.[8] They had also served together in the Southern government and army formed by the 2005 Comprehensive Peace Agreement (CPA). That May in Addis, they greeted each other and even sat with each other to eat.

Work on rituals and peace-making, such as Hennings's work on Russia and Europe in the seventeenth and eighteenth centuries, has highlighted the importance of subtle codes and ceremonial signals in making or breaking peace.[9] Eating together could be a sign of peaceful intentions, just as dancing together had been in eighteenth-century Europe.[10] However, it was not. These South Sudanese dining companions were not ready for peace; fighting between them continued unabated for many more years. One general who had been commanding battles in Bentiu (Unity State, South Sudan) only weeks before joked to me that his time at the negotiations was a gift from the opposition leadership to fatten him up before returning to the battlefields.[11] This commander, in the coming months, would go on to command further significant battles. Eating together was not a sign of peace, and the peace meeting was entangled with ongoing violence.

By 2014, international policy shifts favoured peace agreements being 'inclusive', and 'inclusive' was interpreted as inviting more categories of people to the negotiations. In a cheaper hotel a few streets away from the Radisson Blu, as part of these attempts to be inclusive, IGAD was hosting a contingent of South Sudanese chiefs. In 2013, chiefs were playing a powerful role in mobilising armed combatants to join pro-government or pro-opposition forces. Sitting between armed groups and the communities,[12] armed groups

---

8   Clemence Pinaud, 'South Sudan: Civil War, Predation and the Making of a Military Aristocracy', *African Affairs* 113:451 (2014): 192–211.

9   Jan Hennings, *Russia and Courtly Europe: Ritual and the Culture of Diplomacy, 1648–1725* (Cambridge University Press, 2016).

10   Hennings, *Russia and Courtly Europe*.

11   For discussion of the use of gifts and the application of Mauss's ideas to South Sudanese politics, see: Pinaud, 'South Sudan'.

12   Cherry Leonardi, *Dealing with Government in South Sudan: History of Chiefship, Community and State* (James Currey, 2013); Chirrilo Madut Anei and Naomi Pendle, *Wartime Trade and the Reshaping of Power in South Sudan: Learning from the Market of Mayen-Rual* (Rift Valley Institute, 2018).

relied on the chiefs to mobilise popular support and recruit military labour.[13] Chiefs also often played a significant role in governing combatant behaviour during conflict.[14] In their constituencies, these chiefs were some of the most powerful figures of the emerging wars.

Chiefs were added to the list of invitees at the last minute and a handful of senior chiefs known to an IGAD advisor were gathered from across South Sudan. They were brought directly from their home villages, including some that were close to the frontlines. This included the senior chief from the president's home region of Gogrial, a chief from the SPLA-IO headquarters in Pagak, and other chiefs from across South Sudan. Some of the chiefs who came to Addis were urban savvy and highly literate, but for others the large urban space was foreign to them. When fighting erupted in Juba in December 2013, my planned ethnographic research had been interrupted by these new uncertainties. A colleague in IGAD invited me to Addis Ababa to help support the less experienced chiefs navigate this urban setting.[15]

As I spent time with the chiefs in Addis, I was struck by the different mealtime behaviour of the chiefs compared to the politicians at the Radisson. At each mealtime, the chiefs would carefully choreograph their arrival in the dining room to avoid chiefs from areas that were from the opposing side in the war. Not all the chiefs were part of this implicit manoeuvre, but some were especially careful not to eat in the same place at the same time with those on the other side of the war. They were polite to each other. They would participate in the same meetings. Yet they would not eat together.

The chiefs described their refusal to eat together as a recognition of the spiritual and moral consequences of war. Ways of eating and not eating together are part of the rituals of life,[16] and are, as Hutchinson highlights, entrenched with moral, spiritual and political meanings.[17] The chiefs understood that legitimate armed conflict was embedded in moral and spiritual logics. Specifically, the ongoing armed conflict was seen as morally legitimate through contemporary ideas of revenge.[18] War did not only cause physical death and economic losses or gains. War also brought spiritual and moral dangers and cosmological

---

[13]   Indicative of warring parties' reliance on chiefs was Riek Machar's interest in the chiefs who came to Addis in May 2014, and his request for a meeting about their invitation.

[14]   Pendle, 'Competing Authorities and Norms of Restraint'.

[15]   In the end I failed in my mandate; one chief did go missing. A few weeks later we found out that he had gone to visit relatives.

[16]   Mary Douglas, *Implicit Meanings: Selected Essays in Anthropology* (Routledge, 1975).

[17]   Sharon Hutchinson, '"Dangerous to Eat": Rethinking Pollution States among the Nuer of Sudan,' *Africa* 62:4 (1992): 490–504.

[18]   Naomi Pendle, 'The "Nuer of Dinka Money"'.

consequences. In many of the communities where the war was being fought and from which the soldiers of the armies had been mobilised, feuds brought dangers of deadly spiritual pollution and impurity that would be made manifest by sharing food between feuding families.[19] The dangers of pollution could be useful as they could encourage parties to seek reconciliation and bring opportunities for peace-making.[20] By not eating together the chiefs avoided these spiritual dangers and upheld this cosmological understanding.[21] As they made peace, they sought to act in a way that showed a consistent moral logic to the moral logics and everyday realities of war. Peace, as war, had moral boundaries and should morally constrain all actors, including the most militarily powerful.

This book is about such spiritual and moral contestations, and the remaking of norms within the 'cultural archive', that arise from and reshape the violence of peace, protection, conflict and connected political economies.[22] The book is interested in the debates over the cosmological consequences and meanings of war and peace, and the assertions of power that are embedded in these cosmologies. After all, in the end, the warring parties in the Radisson, who ignored the spiritual consequences of eating together while at war with each other, could be understood as claiming to be immune from these moral and spiritual consequences and dangers. They could be understood as implicitly claiming to be able to step outside of cosmological restraint and moral consequence. The book explores the implications of such claims.

The arguments of this book are based on ethnographic and historic research among Nuer- and Dinka-speaking communities connected to the Bilnyang and connected river systems (contemporary Warrap and Unity States, South Sudan) from the late nineteenth century until the 2020s. The research was conducted between 2012 and 2022. The book looks at their experiences of making peace and staying safe, including everyday peace-making and peace meetings in these communities. Yet, to avoid binary distinctions between local and international peace-making, the book also explores the interactions between these communities and national and international peace-making.

---

[19] Sharon Hutchinson, *Nuer Dilemmas: Coping with Money, War, and the State* (University of California Press, 1996), pages 106–7; Sharon Hutchinson, '"Dangerous to eat": Rethinking Pollution States among the Nuer of Sudan', *Africa: Journal of the International African Institute* 62:4 (1992): 490–504.

[20] Discussions with *kuar muon*, Mayendit, August 2013.

[21] For discussions of food, see: Hutchinson, '"Dangerous to Eat": 493; Hutchinson, *Nuer Dilemmas; Douglas, Implicit Meanings.*

[22] This intentionally evokes Allen's work on the violence of healing. Tim Allen, 'The Violence of Healing', *Sociologus* 47:2 (1997): 101–28; also Adam Branch, 'The Violence of Peace: Ethnojustice in Northern Uganda', *Development and Change* 45:3 (2014): 608–30.

The book's arguments

It could easily be assumed that peace-making necessarily involves morally praise-worthy behaviour and the absence of violence. Violent conflicts need to be stopped and a lasting peace needs to be realised. Peace and violence are assumed to be opposing phenomena, with violence involving killing, displacement, uncertainty, loss and trauma, while peace-making is seen as the antithesis of these things. With these associations, peace can appear to carry unquestionable, popular moral weight.[23] Yet, histories from around the world mean that we already know that peace is rarely devoid of violence.[24] Peace-time violence is not simply a legacy of war, but is often part of the founding violence of the next political order.[25] Phenomena labelled as peace-making often include and result in incredible violence, and violence is often an intimate part of peace. The peace projects of empires in colonial and contemporary times, cementing predatory power, are obvious examples. They could be violent as they might increase physical violence through armed conflict, exploitative economies and arbitrary rule. They could also be violent by reshaping moral and cosmological norms and rituals in ways which make peace exclusive and elusive.

This book explores the violence of peace by focusing on the peace-making experiences of communities and people in a region of South Sudan. Since the mid-nineteenth century, South Sudan has experienced mercantile and colonial violence, as well as decades of war. Overlapping with these experiences have been repetitive experiences of peace-making. Between 1990 and 2020 alone there were at least seventy peace agreements in South(ern) Sudan, including peace agreements between national warring parties and between communities.[26] This book explores both these explicit peace-making activities, as well

---

23   Allen describes 'moral populism' as 'an explicit linking of notions of good and bad with assertions by individuals that they articulate the will or the best interests of the people'. Tim Allen, 'Vigilantes, Witches and Vampires: How Moral Populism Shapes Social Accountability in Northern Uganda', *International Journal on Minority and Group Rights* 22:3 (2015): 360–386, page 361.

24   Branch, 'The Violence of Peace'; 'John Darby and Roger Mac Ginty, *Contemporary Peacemaking Conflict, Violence, and Peace Processes* (Palgrave Macmillan, 2003).

25   Scholars have long observed the empirical commonplace occurrence of founding violence, and grappled with its political meaning. Arendt's work is a seminal example: Hannah Arendt, *On Revolution* (Penguin, 1990 [1963]).

26   There were definitely more. This number is the result of aggregating peace agreements or meetings that I have known about first hand or that are from online sources. These sources include: Alan Boswell, 'Do Local Peace Deals Work? Evidence from South Sudan's Civil War' (Kampala: Friedrich-Ebert-Stiftung, 2019),

as other activities by South Sudanese that attempt to make their lives more peaceful and safer. By focusing on Nuer- and Dinka-speaking communities around the Bilnyang and connected river systems, the book moves away from a focus on the peace agreements and meetings themselves, to discuss the implications of peace-making for people's lived politics. Even though peace-making often does not result in either peace nor an end to violence, it does still have significant consequences.

The central argument of this book is that to understand the real politics and violence of peace-making, we must understand how peace-making interacts with and reshapes power not only in everyday politics,[27] but also in cosmic polities. 'Human societies are hierarchically encompassed – typically above, below, and on earth – in a cosmic polity populated by beings of human attributes and metahuman powers who govern the people's fate'.[28] These cosmic polities are not solely comprised of characters that explicitly claim divinity or divine powers, such as priest, prophets and popes; governments can also be divine.

'The government is close to the divine; the government is like the divine', an elderly man described to me as we spoke in his home near Koch market (Unity State, South Sudan) in October 2022. He was living with four other elderly people in a small shelter, and children came and went, bringing them milk and food. For him, government was like the divine both because it could give and show favour, but also because it could take things away, including life itself. This book finds that South Sudanese reasoning often resonates with arguments of the famous anthropologists Graeber and Shalins in that even apparently secular governments can also be god-like, divine and part of the cosmic polity. Global histories mean that the sovereignty of governments is

https://library.fes.de/pdf-files/bueros/uganda/15872.pdf, accessed 16 October 2021; Paul Nantulya, 'Sudanese Church Commits to Promoting Peace in Sudan', *CRS Voices* 1 April 2010, http://crs-blog.org/sudanese-church-commits-to-promoting-peace-in-sudan; PA-X peace agreements databased, www.peaceagreements.org/lsearch?LocalSearchForm%5Bregion%5D=&LocalSearchForm%5Bcoun try_entity%5D=127&LocalSearchForm%5Bname%5D=&LocalSearchForm%5Bactor_mode%5D=any&LocalSearchForm%5Blink_nat_process_status%5D=all&LocalSearchForm%5Bmediator_status%5D=all&LocalSearchForm%5Bmediator_type_mode%5D=any&LocalSearchForm%5Blocale_name%5D=&LocalSearchForm%5Bcategory_mode%5D=any&LocalSearchForm%5Bagreement_text%5D=&s=Search+Database, accessed 16 October 2021.
27   Roger Mac Ginty, 'Hybrid Peace: The Interaction between Top-Down and Bottom-Up Peace', *Security Dialogue* 41:4 (2010): 391–412; Roger Mac Ginty, 'Indicators: A Proposal for Everyday Peace Indicators', *Evaluation and Program Planning* 36:1 (2013): 56–63; Oliver P. Richmond and Audra Mitchell, *Hybrid Forms of Peace from Everyday Agency to Post-liberalism* (Palgrave Macmillan, 2012).
28   David Graeber and Marshall Sahlins, *On Kings* (HAU Books, 2017), page 2.

bound up with notions of divine kingship and claims to be able to rain destruction and favour with impunity.

The god-like nature of government entangles governments in the interpretative labour of the cosmic polity; their implicit divine claims are dependent not only on brute force but also on a broad acceptance of their impunity. Even governments who have relied on the fear of force have had to engage in some interpretative labour.[29] Peace meetings and making can be a way for governments to make claims of impunity. The frequency of peace meetings means that they become regimes of governance and spaces in which power is negotiated and performed.[30] Peace is then not a rigid rupture between times of war and peace, or between old and new regimes. Instead, it is part of the continuous political negotiation of power and legitimacy.

At the same time, the regimes of governance imposed by peace-making do not always make moral and spiritual sense. For those experiencing this peace-making, it can be as illegitimate, arbitrary, spiritually dangerous, violent and exclusive as times of war. Peace agreements have often involved governments recoding violence to try to make their violence legitimate and to allow them to carry out violence with impunity. Peace also relies on '"power over", or the ability to coerce, sanction or discipline others into accepting an accord'.[31] Importantly, demands for peace amount to claims to power and legitimacy.[32] As divinity is associated with impunity, peace-making therefore often amounts to the making of divine governments and is a political act in the cosmic polity.

At the same time, if the polity is a cosmic polity, other divine authorities have unique opportunities to restrain the powers and impunity of governments. Other divine powers can contest and co-opt not only the physical power of the governments, but they can also 'creatively remake' moral and spiritual power

---

[29]   Sharon Hutchinson and Naomi Pendle, 'Violence, Legitimacy, and Prophecy: Nuer Struggles with Uncertainty in South Sudan', *American Ethnologist* 42:3 (2015): 415–430.

[30]   Cherry Leonardi, 'Points of Order? Local Government Meetings as Negotiation Tables in South Sudanese History', *Journal of Eastern African Studies* 9:4 (2015): 650–668.

[31]   P. L. Chinn and A. Falk-Rafael, 'Peace and Power: A Theory of Emancipatory Group Process'. *Journal of Nursing Scholarship* 47:1 (2015): 62–69.

[32]   Roger Mac Ginty and Oliver Richmond, 'The Local Turn in Peace Building: A Critical Agenda for Peace. *Third World Quarterly* 34:5 (2013): 763–783; Séverine Autesserre, *Peaceland: Conflict Resolution and the Everyday Politics of International Intervention* (Cambridge University Press, 2014); Mac Ginty, 'Hybrid Peace; Gearoid Millar, 'For Whom do Local Peace Processes Function? Maintaining Control through Conflict Management', *Cooperation and Conflict* 52:3 (2017): 293–308.

idioms to 'refuse' governments' interpretative labour that claims that they can step outside of moral and legal codes, and act with impunity.[33] If the contestation is cosmic, other divine powers have a significant role to play in making war or peace.

Religious ideas infuse politics around the globe, and politics is rarely secular.[34] In South Sudan, there has long been 'religiously infused political thought' and South Sudanese have long seen their difficult history as a 'spiritual chronicle'.[35] The spheres of politics and religion have not been discrete.[36] Additionally, still scattered through South Sudanese politics are acts that evoke divine authority in quests for political legitimacy. South Sudanese President Salva Kiir was compared to the biblical Joshua.[37] Vice President and sometimes armed opposition leader Riek Machar received the *dang* (ceremonial stick)[38] of the late and famous Nuer prophet, Ngundeng Bong. Both Kiir and Machar also have ancestors that wielded notable divine authority in their home areas.

However, the entanglement of the divine and politics is not simply because rulers identify themselves with supernatural beings. Graeber and Sahlins have argued that government claims of impunity to kill in themselves mean that *all* contemporary governments, anywhere in the world, invoke ideas of divine kingship. Governments 'make themselves the equivalent of gods – arbitrary, all-powerful beings beyond human morality – through the use of arbitrary violence'.[39] Globally, because of governments' claims to sovereignty, which is essentially a claim to be able to carry out arbitrary violence with impunity,

33   This invokes ideas about 'culture as creative refusal' by David Graeber: 'Culture as Creative Refusal', *Cambridge Anthropology* 31:2 (2013): 1–19.

34   Massoud describes Rule of Law in apparently secular liberal democracies as akin to a religious belief. See: Mark Fathi Massoud. 'Theology of the Rule of Law', *Hague Journal on the Rule of Law, HJRL* 11:2/3 (2019): 485–491. Colonial-era anthropological scholarship that has focused on religious belief in South Sudan could be accused of perpetuating racist, colonial distinctions and categories. However, discussion of the *hakuma* as divine in this book is about linking these South Sudanese ideas to common global patterns. The government of the UK also, implicitly, claims divine kingship, although this is not the focus of this book.

35   Christopher Tounsel, *Chosen Peoples: Christianity and Political Imagination in South Sudan* (Duke University Press, 2021), pages 3, 14.

36   Tounsel, *Chosen Peoples.*

37   Ibid.

38   Johnson has translated *dang* as 'baton', as well as 'ceremonial stick', and notes that scripturally minded Nuer translate it as 'rod'. Douglas Johnson, 'The Return of Ngundeng's *Dang*', *Sudan Studies Journal* (Sudan Studies Association, 2009).

39   Graeber and Sahlins, *On Kings,* page 81.

there is a historically contingent but globally common divine nature of sovereignty. World-over, including in Europe and the USA, the division between cosmology and politics is false, as claims of government sovereignty are claims of divinity. When governments and states execute favour, or destruction, or when they demand war or peace, with arbitrariness and impunity, they are setting themselves 'outside the confines of the human' and acting as if they were god.[40]

Such implicit claims of divine power are not based on arbitrary violence alone but a broad acceptance of impunity for this violence. Brute force and violence can be so overwhelming that this in itself makes accountability hard to fathom. At the same time, the cosmic nature of politics entangles governments in the rituals, symbols, and spiritual and moral pollution of people's cosmologies. Governments can claim impunity through engagement in the remaking of the cultural archives,[41] and the moral and spiritual order. As human societies are part of 'a cosmic polity populated by beings of human attributes and metahuman powers who govern the people's fate',[42] governments become part of the contests of the gods. Peace-making can be part of these contested claims and cosmic contestations.

Throughout this book, I borrow from Leonardi and Hutchinson in describing 'government' in South Sudan as a broad socio-political sphere, not limited to the government of the day, but including 'a bundle of influences and symbols' that encompass 'armies and the military cultures originally introduced by the Turco-Egyptian army in the 19th century', and that include contemporary government and armed opposition institutions and actors.[43] Throughout the book I use the common, Arabic-derived, South Sudanese term for government – 'hakuma' – to denote this broad government/socio-political sphere (which, for example, includes foreign traders and slavers), while 'government' is used to refer to the specific government of the time.

The hakuma came to be understood as divine in South Sudan as a result of colonial era rule, their arbitrary and unbounded violence and the global legacy of these conceptions of 'government'. In Southern Sudan, for at least a century and a half, including through colonial rule and decades of war, hakuma have inflicted predatory, arbitrary and excessive violence. This arbitrary violence has also occurred as part of the political economies in times of apparent

---

40 Graeber and Sahlins, *On Kings*.
41 Wendy James. *The Listening Ebony: Moral Knowledge, Religion and Power among the Uduk of Sudan* (Clarendon, 1988).
42 Graeber and Sahlins, *On Kings*, page 2.
43 Cherry Leonardi, '"Liberation" or Capture: Youth in between "Hakuma", and "Home" during Civil War and its Aftermath in Southern Sudan', *African Affairs* 106:424 (2007), page 394.

'peace'.[44] Therefore, *hakuma*, and the global political economies in which they are entangled, have been a considerable obstacle to peace and protection. They display a violence that most South Sudanese have little power to limit or repeat. South Sudanese histories are a brutal example of the semi-divine claims of the *hakuma*, and South Sudanese have often equated governments to other divine authorities and institutions.

In South Sudan, the last century and a half of *hakuma* violence has not only caused excessive harm, but has also been accompanied by interpretative labour that claims these *hakuma* can kill and carry out arbitrary violence with impunity. Theorists such as Agamben and Schmitt have argued that prerogatives of statehood involve claims of ability to suspend the legal and moral order,[45] and sovereignty is marked by the power to kill with impunity.[46] As Hutchinson has described, over the last century, governments in South Sudan have repeatedly claimed powers to kill with impunity, in times of war and in times of peace, and to declare their acts as 'void of all social, moral and spiritual consequences for perpetrators'.[47]

Many of the assertions of the *hakuma* to have the power to kill with impunity, without moral, spiritual or legal consequence, have taken place in legal or quasi-legal forums, such as local courts and peace meetings. Law can be a political weapon and form of social control.[48] From the early twentieth century,

44   Nicki Kindersley and Diing Majok, *Breaking Out of the Borderlands: Understanding Migrant Pathways from Northern Bahr el-Ghazal, South Sudan* (Rift Valley Institute, 2021), https://riftvalley.net/publication/breaking-out-borderlands-understanding-migrant-pathways-northern-bahr-el-ghazal-south, accessed 5 December 2020; Jovensia Uchalla, *Trading Grains in South Sudan: Stories of Opportunities, Shocks and Changing Tastes* (Rift Valley Institute, 2020), https://riftvalley.net/publication/trading-grains-south-sudan-stories-opportunities-shocks-and-changing-tastes, accessed 6 December 2020; Edward Thomas, *South Sudan: A Slow Liberation* (Zed Books, 2015); Craze, 'Displaced and Immiserated'; Joshua Craze, *The Politics of Numbers: On Security Sector Reform in South Sudan, 2005–2020* (LSE, 2021), www.lse.ac.uk/africa/assets/Documents/Politics-of-Numbers-Joshua-Craze.pdf, accessed 6 December 2020.
45   Giorgio Agamben, *Homo Sacer: Sovereign Power and Bare Life* (Stanford University Press, 1998); Carl Schmitt, *Political Theology: Four Chapters on the Concept of Sovereignty*, translated by George Schwab (University of Chicago Press, 2005 [1922]).
46   Thomas B. Hansen and Finn Stepputat (eds), *Sovereign Bodies: Citizens, Migrants, and States in the Postcolonial World* (Princeton University Press, 2005).
47   Hutchinson, *Nuer Dilemmas*, page 58.
48   Mark Fathi Massoud, *Law's Fragile State: Colonial, Authoritarian, and Humanitarian Legacies in Sudan* (Cambridge University Press, 2013). Jens

governments in South Sudan attempted to absorb into government-backed legal regimes existing religiously shaped ideas about how to make peace, such as through compensation and sacrifice. The law became an important tool of control for these colonial governments,[49] and courts and peace meetings were used to normalise governments' exception from legal restraint, including in times of war. Governments have tried to set themselves outside of the law, and have made other divine authority figures subject to the law. As Massoud writes of British colonialism in Sudan, foreign officials were conscious 'of the power of religion in people's lives and in politics' making it 'vital' in any legal reform project.[50] Based on North American and European ideas, exported through colonial rule and more contemporary international organisations, religion was something to be governed by law, and law itself was to be seen as a higher power.[51] Massoud goes as far as equating the authority of law and God as the power and legitimacy of both are based on people's faith.[52]

Importantly, the *hakuma* being supranatural is not synonymous with the distance or absence of the *hakuma*. Literature on failed states and weak governments has understood conflict as caused by the absence of the *hakuma*. However, for many South Sudanese, the *hakuma* is entangled in their daily lives and life-changing decisions, even in the most remote areas. Through chiefs' courts and taxes, the *hakuma* is part of the most intimate parts of life. Yet, this does not exclude its divinity. In the cosmic orders of many South Sudanese, the divine dwells above in the sky, but also speaks to and seizes people, and becomes entangled in everyday lives. To be divine is to be set apart and socially distinct, but this does not mean to be absent or physically distant.

Hedging in a god-like *hakuma*

In a world of god-like governments, a good strategy for seeking peace and protection against these *hakuma* involves engaging with the politics of the cosmic and divine. In South Sudan, some of the most powerful authorities capable of limiting and contesting *hakuma* power have themselves evoked their own divine nature or authority to assert that the government is still morally, legally and spiritually constrained despite its uncontested military superiority. They have used claims of supranatural power to confront the quasi-divine power of government. In our previous article, Hutchinson and I described the powerful role of two Nuer prophets in interpreting the moral limits of lethal violence by

---

Meierhenrich, *The Remnants of the Rechtsstaat: An Ethnography of Nazi Law* (Oxford University Press, 2018).

[49]   Massoud, *Law's Fragile State*.

[50]   Ibid.

[51]   Ibid., page 489.

[52]   Ibid., page 490.

government.[53] In this book I explore further how such divine authorities have played a key role in pushing back against repeated, implicit *hakuma* claims, by governments and armed opposition groups, to be able to kill and conduct arbitrary violence with impunity.

A key way in which divine authorities contested government power is the remaking of moral and ritual regimes.[54] Graeber and Sahlins argue that a way to limit the powers of the divine is to make them sacred. 'To be "sacred", in contrast [to being divine], is to be set apart, hedged about by customs and taboos'.[55] It is through subjecting governments to customs and taboos that the government becomes 'sacred' and restrained. South Sudanese have used cultural archives to assert the applicability of customs to governments.[56] Cultural archives include norms that are habitual and unremembered, alongside histories that are retold, that can be a basis for validation and 'constitutes the foundations of a moral world'.[57] In South Sudan, a major point of contestation over the last century and a half is whether governments are vulnerable to moral and spiritual pollution, or whether they can step outside these confines of custom. As Douglas has taught us, pollution can be a 'semi-judicial punishment',[58] and therefore a way to impose norm-governed regimes. By making *hakuma* subject to pollution and requiring of purity, the government can potentially be restrained.

In discussing how moral and symbolic regimes can contest power, this book draws on Graeber's ideas that cultures can be 'political projects' and a form of 'creative refusal',[59] shaped to reject other cultures and to contest economic systems which have informed them.[60] Since the 1990s, anthropologists have often described cosmologies as critiques of modernity and capitalism.[61] Paying attention to cosmologies, symbols and rituals not only allows us to

53 Hutchinson and Pendle. 'Violence, Legitimacy, and Prophecy'.
54 In South Sudan, divine authorities have been central to the remaking of moral communities. Douglas Johnson, *Nuer Prophets: A History of Prophecy from the Upper Nile in the Nineteenth and Twentieth Centuries* (Clarendon Press and Oxford University Press, 1994).
55 Graeber and Sahlins, *On Kings,* page 8.
56 James, *The Listening Ebony.*
57 Ibid., page 6.
58 Mary Douglas, *Jacob's Tears: The Priestly Work of Reconciliation* (Oxford University Press, 2004), page 163; Perri 6 and Paul Richards, *Mary Douglas: Understanding Social Thought and Conflict* (Berghahn Books, 2017).
59 Graeber, 'Culture as Creative Refusal'.
60 Ibid.
61 Jean Comaroff and John Comaroff, 'Occult Economies and the Violence of Abstraction: Notes from the South African Postcolony', *American Ethnologist* 26:2 (1990): 279–303; Peter Geschiere, *The Modernity of Witchcraft: Politics and the Occult in Postcolonial Africa* (University Press of Virginia, 1997); Luise

notice their immense physical, social, political and economic force, but also the space they can create for 'creative refusal' of predatory regimes.[62] For at least a century and a half, the political economy in South Sudan has involved the violent extraction of labour, resources and land by national and international governments and businesses.[63] While some cultures and beliefs have previously been understood as primordial, they are better understood as self-conscious political rejections of forms of cultural 'progress' that are tied to these violent economies.[64] This book documents various ways in which South Sudanese have used cultural symbols, rituals, moral norms and theology to contest predatory power and to make peace.

This book's demand to take seriously the cosmic politics of peace builds on but departs from existing work on the political economy of peace. The book recognises how cosmic polities are entangled with political economies; the divine nature of the *hakuma* is partly a creation of colonial and subsequent political economies and their violence, and key ways to refuse these political economies was through divine power. At the same time, the book pushes against ideas that meaning is determined by the material.[65] The book argues that, in South Sudan, the creative process of refusal that slowly remakes rituals, moral restraints and cosmic hierarchies is driven by empirical experiences of the divine, as well as a slow remaking of the cultural archive. Many South Sudanese who were consulted have an epistemic confidence in divine authorities based on critical analysis of empirical experiences.

Another way in which divine authorities have contested the impunity of the *hakuma* is to attempt to make the *hakuma* subject to legal norms. The legal history of South Sudan means that the cosmic politics of peace and purity have become entangled with the law. Across its empire, British colonial authorities used law to manage religions and divine claims.[66] New legal institutions allowed the government to try to make existing divine authorities sacred, and no longer divine, and through legal norms and appointments, constrain these authorities within the law. Legal institutions included chiefs' courts and

---

White, *Speaking with Vampires: Rumor and History in Colonial Africa* (University of California Press, 2000).

[62]   Graeber, 'Culture as Creative Refusal'.

[63]   Kindersley and Majok, *Breaking Out of the Borderland*; Uchalla, *Trading Grains in South Sudan*; Thomas, *South Sudan*; Craze, 'Displaced and Immiserated'; Craze, *The Politics of Numbers*.

[64]   Graeber, 'Culture as Creative Refusal', page 1.

[65]   Marshall Sahlins, *Culture and Practical Reason* (University of Chicago Press, 1976), see the final chapter.

[66]   Massoud, 'Theology of the Rule of Law'.

regular peace meetings.[67] At the same time, as law showed its power to limit the divine, the law also became a potential opportunity to limit government. In this context, making the government sacred included making the government subject to the law.

So, this book catalogues attempts by non-government divine authorities to limit the ability of the *hakuma*. Yet, crucially, these non-government divine authorities are not necessarily or consistently benign and non-violent. South Sudanese moral, legal and cosmological regimes, and the purity and peace they promote, can themselves be exclusive and violent.[68] Sometimes rituals that restrain government have also made exclusive moral communities including along ethnic lines.[69] Notions of purity can also be exclusionary and create a moral and spiritual context where conflict flourishes.[70] Such exclusive moral communities make seemingly unending war more likely. They can act as a form of violent moral populism, as Allen's work on witchcraft in South Sudan and Uganda has made abundantly clear.[71]

The politics of peace

By focusing on cosmologies, rituals and the divine, this book offers a radically different way to understand peace. Globally, in more recent decades, political scientists have argued for a recognition of the real politics of contemporary peace-making, especially internationally brokered comprehensive peace agreements, and their basis in elite bargains and political settlements.[72] De Waal's widely accepted description of armed conflict in South Sudan sees peace agreements as elite deals in the political marketplace in which

---

67 Leonardi, *Dealing with Government*.
68 Mary Douglas and Gerald Mars, 'Terrorism: A Positive Feedback Game', *Human Relations* 56:7 (2003): 763–786.
69 Hutchinson and Pendle, 'Violence, Legitimacy, and Prophecy'.
70 Tim Allen, 'Witchcraft, Sexuality and HIV/AIDS among the Azande of Sudan', *Journal of Eastern African Studies* 1:3 (2007): 359–396; Tim Allen and Kyla Reid, 'Justice at the Margins: Witches, Poisoners, and Social Accountability in Northern Uganda'. *Medical Anthropology* 34:2 (2015): 106–123; Douglas, *Jacob's Tears*, pages 85–87; Mary Douglas, *Leviticus as Literature* (Oxford University Press, 2000); Douglas and Mars, 'Terrorism'.
71 Allen, 'Vigilantes, Witches and Vampires'.
72 See discussions by: Mushtaq H. Khan, 'Political Settlements and the Analysis of Institutions', *African Affairs* 117:469 (2018): 636–655; Virginia Page Fortna, *Does Peacekeeping Work? Shaping Belligerents' Choices after Civil War* (Princeton University Press, 2008); Jan Pospíšil, *Peace in Political Unsettlement: Beyond Solving Conflict* (Palgrave Macmillan, 2019).

the loyalties of rebels are bought with money. Armed rebellions are a way to seek a place at the peace-making table and rent in this market.[73] People rebel so they can be part of a peace deal. Through these 'payroll peace' agreements, and their prescribed security sector reforms, soldiers are offered higher salaries if they agree to the peace and pledge loyalty to the government.[74] However, these accounts blame individual elites, elevate the explanatory power of rational self-interest, and ignore inequitable structures.

Alternative accounts have highlighted how peace meetings can entrench the violence of politics by elevating the power of military actors and reducing space for civil actors in politics. Srinivasan has described how competing interests at peace meetings force the simplification of understandings of conflicts and peace, resulting in the exclusion and perspectives of some actors.[75] In the Sudans, civil actors have repeatedly been left out, meaning that peace-making inadvertently increases a violent logic to politics.[76]

More Marxian interpretations of comprehensive peace agreements have instead highlighted that the neo-liberal orders created by comprehensive peace agreements produce inequalities that can lead to grievance and rebellion.[77]

---

[73]   Alex de Waal, 'When Kleptocracy Becomes Insolvent: Brute Causes of the Civil War in South Sudan', *African Affairs* 113:452 (2014): 347–369.

[74]   Alan Boswell and Alex de Waal, 'South Sudan: The Perils of Payroll Peace', Conflict Research Programme, Payroll Peace Memo, 4 March 2019.

[75]   Sharath Srinivasan, *When Peace Kills Politics: International Intervention and Unending Wars in the Sudans* (Hurst & Company, 2021).

[76]   Ibid.

[77]   Edward Newman, Roland Paris and Oliver Richmond (eds). *New Perspectives on Liberal Peace-building* (UN University Press, 2009); Oliver P. Richmond, 'The Problem of Peace: Understanding the "Liberal Peace"', *Conflict, Security & Development* 6:3 (2006): 291–314; Neil Cooper, 'Review Article: On the Crisis of the Liberal Peace', *Conflict, Security & Development* 7:4 (2007), page 605; D. Chandler, *Empire in Denial: The Politics of State-Building* (Pluto Press, 2006); Toby Dodge, 'The Ideological Roots of Failure: The Application of Kinetic Neo-Liberalism to Iraq', *International Affairs* 86:6 (2010): 1269–1286; Michael Pugh, 'Local Agency and Political Economies of Peacebuilding', *Studies in Ethnicity and Nationalism* 11:2 (2011): 308–320; Peter Uvin, *Aiding Violence: The Development Enterprise in Rwanda* (Kumarian Press, 1998); Carl-Ulrik Schierup (ed.), *Scramble for the Balkans: Nationalism, Globalism and the Political Economy of Reconstruction* (Macmillan, 1999); Susan Woodward, *Balkan Tragedy: Chaos and Dissolution after the Cold War* (Brookings Institution, 1995); Wayne Nafziger and Juha Auvinen, *Economic Development, Inequality, and War: Humanitarian Emergencies in Developing Countries* (Palgrave Macmillan, 2003).

Liberal politics and economics can produce destructive nationalisms,[78] such as the militarisation of ethnicity between the Nuer and Dinka in South Sudan.[79] As Pugh narrates, the social changes brought by these liberal orders needs new forms of social discipline to control them and this often involves government violence.[80] Moodie describes how governments can recode such violence after the civil war as 'common criminality' even when it marked a continuity with wartime violence, including agents of the state being perpetrators.[81]

Works by Craze, Kinderley, Majok, Thomas and Uchalla have highlighted South Sudanese struggles caused by the increasingly marketised and monetarised nature of the South Sudanese economy as a result of the 2005 Comprehensive Peace Agreement (CPA).[82] These new struggles build on longer patterns of political and economic inequity and change. Successive wars are 'rooted in long-established patterns of authoritarian, violent, and extractive governance of the pre-colonial, colonial and post-colonial periods, which concentrated economic and political power at the centre'.[83] Young has repeatedly highlighted how the CPA inevitably failed because it did not address the economic inequities between the centre and periphery that drove the war.[84] He criticises the international community for its refusal to be honest about the SPLA's inability to be the foundation of a liberal democracy, and blames the failed peace policies of countries such as the USA for the post-2013 violence.[85] In an important article for *African Arguments* in 2022, Joshua Craze and Feri Marko start to develop their politico-economic analysis of the 2018 Revitalised Agreement on the Resolution of Conflict in South Sudan

[78]   Dilip Parameshwar Gaonkar, 'Toward New Imaginaries: An Introduction', *Public Culture* 14:1 (2002): 1–19.

[79]   Jok Madut Jok and Sharon Hutchinson. 'Sudan's Prolonged Second Civil War and the Militarization of Nuer and Dinka Ethnic Identities', *African Studies Review* 42:2 (1999): 125–145.

[80]   Michel Foucault, *The Birth of Biopolitics: Lectures at the Collège de France 1978–79* (Palgrave Macmillan, 2010).

[81]   Ellen Moodie, *El Salvador in the Aftermath of Peace: Crime, Uncertainty, and the Transition to Democracy* (University of Pennsylvania Press, 2010).

[82]   Kindersley and Majok, *Breaking Out of the Borderlands*; Uchalla, *Trading Grains in South Sudan;* Thomas, *South Sudan;* Craze, 'Displaced and Immiserated'; Craze, *The Politics of Numbers.*

[83]   Øystein Rolandsen and Nicki Kindersley, *South Sudan: A Political Economy Analysis* (Norwegian Institute of International Affairs, 2017), page 4.

[84]   John Young, *The Fate of Sudan: Origins and Consequences of a Flawed Peace Process* (Zed Books, 2012); John Young, *South Sudan's Civil War: Violence, Insurgency, and Failed Peacemaking* (Zed Books, 2019).

[85]   Ibid.

(R-ARCSS).[86] They describe how R-ARCSS, like the CPA,[87] facilitated the making of a wealthy class of political leaders.[88] It further centralised power and created a regime in which government officials at all levels were appointed by the centre and lacked 'almost any popular legitimacy'. Armed conflict in the periphery was a result of political contestations in the centre.

This book builds on this rich, recent scholarship on the protracted inequities of South Sudan's political economy.[89] Yet, economic forces can conceal moral dynamics,[90] and there is always a danger of being pulled towards economic determinism at the cost of ignoring the way that institutions are symbolically constituted.[91] Meaning matters, and meaning is not determined by the material.[92] Even the saliency of material and economic forces can themselves be a socio-cultural product.[93] It is when we pay attention to these stories, symbols, cultural archives and imaginaries that we not only notice their immense institutional force,[94] but also the space they can create for contestation and refusal.

Class construction is part of the politico-economic dynamics that form the background of the book. Pinaud described the emergence of a 'military aristocracy'[95] and D'Agoôt the 'gun class', partly as a result of the wealth and power given to elites by 2005 CPA.[96] Pinaud more recently and controversially then claims that the class system became ethnicised resulting in

[86] Joshua Craze and Ferenc David Marko, 'Death by Peace: How South Sudan's Peace Agreement Ate the Grassroots', *Debating Ideas* (6 January 2022), https://africanarguments.org/2022/01/death-by-peace-how-south-sudans-peace-agreement-ate-the-grassroots, accessed 16 July 2022.

[87] Pinaud, 'South Sudan'.

[88] Craze and Marko, 'Death by Peace'.

[89] This includes the work discussed above by Craze, Kinderley, Majok, Thomas, Uchalla and Young.

[90] Edward Palmer Thompson, *Whigs and Hunters: The Origin of the Back Act* (Breviary Stuff Publications, 2013 [1975]); Tim Allen, 'Violent and Moral Knowledge: Observing Social Trauma in Sudan and Uganda', *Cambridge Anthropology* 13:2 (1988): 45–66; Charles Taylor, 'Modern Social Imaginaries', *Public Culture* 14:1 (2002): 91–124.

[91] Sahlins warned of these dangers long ago: Sahlins, *Culture and Practical Reason*.

[92] Ibid. see the final chapter.

[93] Ibid.

[94] Gaonkar, 'Toward New Imaginaries', page 4.

[95] Pinaud, 'South Sudan'.

[96] Majok D'Agoôt, 'Taming the Dominant Gun Class in South Sudan' (2018), https://africacenter.org/spotlight/taming-the-dominant-gun-class-in-south-sudan, accessed 10 December 2017.

ideologies of ethnic entitlement and genocidal activities.[97] Pinaud's highlighting of class as important to understandings of war and peace in South Sudan was brilliant. Yet, her claims of genocide are wrong on at least three accounts. Firstly, they misrepresent patterns of violence in South Sudan since 2013; intra-ethnic violence has been so incredibly prevalent in South Sudan, including intra-Dinka violence,[98] that any understanding of the wars must take this seriously. Secondly, the book inaccurately homogenises 'the Dinka' and itself carries the danger of contributing to the construction of the 'Dinka' identity in a way that could incite anti-Dinka violence. Thirdly, at play in the armed conflicts of South Sudan are much longer-term cultural archives and cosmologies that have shaped violence and been slowly shaped by violence, political economies, empirical experiences and creative refusal over time.

Beyond 'local' and 'international' peace and protection

For global bodies and international organisations, peace-making has become a popular pursuit; around the world since the 1990s, the UN, regional bodies and globally powerful governments have proliferated support for peace meetings and agreements. This has included internationally backed and brokered, 'comprehensive peace' agreements that have sought to create long-term peace by making politically and economically liberal states.[99] Peace agreements in Sudan and South Sudan, such as the 2005 Comprehensive Peace Agreement and the 2018 Revitalised Agreement on the Resolution of Conflict in South Sudan (R-ARCSS) are archetypal examples. When these comprehensive peace agreements have not worked, international actors have also backed local meetings and agreements, or some form of hybridity.[100] In South Sudan, supporting local peace meetings has become a common UN, NGO and church

---

[97] Clémence Pinaud, *War and Genocide in South Sudan* (Cornell University Press, 2021), page 3.

[98] Joshua Craze, '"And Everything Became War": Warrap State Since the Signing of the R-ARCSS', HSBA Briefing Paper (Small Arms Survey, 2022).

[99] Roland Paris, *At War's End: Building Peace after Civil Conflict* (Cambridge University Press, 2004); Christine Bell, *On the Law of Peace: Peace Agreements and the Lex Pacificatoria* (Oxford University Press, 2008).

[100] Kenneth Menkhaus, 'International Peacebuilding and the Dynamics of Local and National Reconciliation in Somalia', *International Peacekeeping* 3:1 (1996): 42–67; Mark Bradbury, John Ryle, Michael Medley and Kwesi Sansculotte-Greenidge, 'Local Peace Processes in Sudan: A Baseline Study' (Rift Valley Institute, 2006); Jacqueline Wilson, 'Local Peace Processes in Sudan and South Sudan', Peaceworks (US Institute for Peace, 2014); Emma Elfversson, 'Peace From Below: Governance and Peacebuilding in Kerio Valley, Kenya', *The Journal of Modern African Studies* 54:3 (2016): 469–493.

activity.[101] The 1999 Nuer-Dinka Wunlit Peace Agreement, which was mainly between chiefs, has become a classic and often-evoked example.[102]

However, this proliferation of peace-making has not resulted in 'peace'. Globally and in South Sudan, armed conflict has not stopped, with many polities apparently at 'peace' experiencing violent deaths at rates that exceed those in wartime.[103] A big part of this 'peace-time' violence results from governments imposing mass violence and excessive force against their own people.[104] For decades in South Sudan, peace agreements have not stopped protracted armed conflicts being part of life. In addition, they have not stopped physical or arbitrary violence by governing authorities whether in times of peace or war. Instead, peace has often been synonymous with increased physical violence and impunity.

Furthermore, international actors have also tried to limit governments' abilities to kill with impunity in South Sudan in times of war and peace. The international community's failure to prevent the 1994 Rwanda genocide prompted global moral outrage and panic. Since the 1990s, and the global rise of the protection agenda, international powers have been active in making state sovereignty limited or conditional, including through new norms such as the 'Responsibility to Protect' (R2P) and 'Protection of Civilians'.[105] South Sudanese lives have been saved from government violence by the inception of protection practices such as the UN Protection of Civilians sites.[106] However,

---

[101] Bradbury et al., 'Local Peace Processes'.

[102] John Ryle, Douglas Johnson, Alier Makuer Gol, Chirrilo Madut Anei, Elizabeth Nyibol Malou, James Gatkuoth Mut Gai, Jedeit Jal, Margan Riek, John Khalid Mamun, Machot Amuom Malou, Malek Henry Chuor, Mawal Marko Gatkuoth and Loes Lijnders, 'What Happened at Wunlit?: An oral history of the 1999 Wunlit Peace Conference', https://riftvalley.net/sites/default/files/publication-documents/RVI%202021.06.28%20What%20Happened%20at%20Wunlit__Pre-print.pdf, accessed September 2021.

[103] Rachel Kleinfield and Robert Muggah, 'No War, No Peace: Healing the World's Violent Societies', in Edward de Waal (ed.), *Think Peace: Essays for an Age of Disorder* (Carnegie Endowment for International Peace, 2019) https://carnegieendowment.org/files/Think_Peace_final.pdf, accessed 17 October 2021; Claire McEvoy and Gergely Hideg, 'Global Violent Deaths 2017: Time to Decide' (Small Arms Survey, 2017).

[104] Kleinfield and Muggah, 'No War, No Peace'; McEvoy and Hideg, 'Global Violent Deaths 2017'.

[105] See United Nations, 'Responsibility to Protect', United Nations, www.un.org/en/genocideprevention/about-responsibility-to-protect.shtml, accessed 1 January 2022.

[106] Caelin Briggs, 'Protection of Civilians Sites: Lessons from South Sudan for Future Operations' (Norwegian Refugee Council, 2017).

despite this rise in an agenda of human security and humanitarian protection, civilians have still been killed and the global agenda has still been primarily shaped by the focus on the building and supporting of state sovereignty.[107]

A 'local turn' in peace-making in the 1990s partly followed from failures in more international efforts.[108] With ongoing international policy support for local conflict prevention, debates about the meaning and value of the 'local' continue. Scholars like Mac Ginty and Richmond see the problem in local agency in its capture by the international and its subservience, in practice, to Western, neo-liberal logics. They have highlighted the standardisation of local conflict prevention through international support, and the lack of structural space in reality for alternative approaches.[109] The 'local turn' has captured the local for international ends, mimicking the use of local peace in colonial periods. Others, however, see more fundamental flaws in confidence in the local for conflict prevention. They highlight the dangers of romanticising the local,[110] and highlight how the local itself can be 'contested, oppressive and even violent'.[111] Support for the local is criticised for falsely perpetuating a binary, reified and essentialist understandings of local and international.[112]

This book is instead focused on the politics of peace-making however it is categorised. The book avoids making ontological distinctions between comprehensive peace agreements made in foreign capital cities and local peace-making made in South Sudan, instead focusing on how both are actually experienced and contested in specific communities. Many of the divine authorities discussed in this book would also not only claim local authority but would also claim power over different peoples and the state itself.

[107]   Autesserre, *Peaceland*; Charles T. Hunt, 'Analyzing the Co-Evolution of the Responsibility to Protect and the Protection of Civilians in UN Peace Operations', *International Peacekeeping* 26:5 (2019): 630–659; Alex J. Bellamy and Charles T. Hunt, 'Twenty-First Century UN Peace Operations: Protection, Force and the Changing Security Environment', *International Affairs* 91:6 (2015): 1,277–1,298.
[108]   Roger Mac Ginty and Oliver Richmond, 'The Local Turn in Peace Building: A Critical Agenda for Peace', *Third World Quarterly* 34:5 (2013): 763–783.
[109]   Roger Mac Ginty, 'Indigenous Peace-Making versus the Liberal Peace', *Cooperation and Conflict* 43:2 (2008): 139–163; Portia Roelofs 'Contesting Localisation in Interfaith Peacebuilding in Northern Nigeria', *Oxford Development Studies* 48:4 (2020): 373–386.
[110]   N. Džuverović, 'To Romanticise or Not to Romanticise the Local', *Conflict, Security & Development* 21:1 (2021): 21–24; T. Paffenholz, 'Unpacking the Local Turn in Peacebuilding', *Third World Quarterly* 36:5 (2015): 857–874.
[111]   Allen, 'The Violence of Healing'.
[112]   Paffenholz, 'Unpacking the Local Turn in Peacebuilding'.

Divine authorities in South Sudan

Religious thinking is changing in South Sudan, partly as people try to make sense of the brutality of war and excessive, unprecedented loss. Across Africa, Christianity and nationalism have become important as a way to make sense of the violence and social upheavals that confront people.[113] In the 1930s, Evans-Pritchard's account of Nuer prophets was already highlighting the history of religious authorities. Johnson's work on the Nuer prophets has played a seminal role in historicising religion in South Sudan.[114] Work has included sweeping histories, such as those by Werner, Anderson and Wheeler,[115] as well as intricate histories such as those of the parts of the Catholic and Protestant church, by Nikkel and Zink.[116] There have also been publications on Nuer prophets by Hutchinson, and on specific *baany e biith* (Dinka priests and masters of the fishing spear) by Mawson and Cormack. These have all highlighted the histories and politics of religious figures.[117] As governments repeatedly saw non-Christian divine authorities as anti-government figures, there has been a scholarly preoccupation with contesting any necessary propensity to violence.

Recent work has responded to the growth of churches and Christian thought in South Sudan, especially over the last four decades. Tounsel's work has described how South Sudanese used the Bible to create a lexicon of resistance, radical identities and 'potent spiritual power' through reshaping Christian thought and theology. Tounsel describes the way in which Christian worldviews, work and theology informed the ideological construction of the South Sudanese nation-state.[118] Tounsel has also documented how the Sudan People's Liberation Movement/Army (SPLM/A), including through its weekly newspaper, the *SPLM/A Update*, created a martial theology and contributed to a religious framing of the SPLA-Government of Sudan (GoS)

---

[113]   Allen. 'The Violence of Healing', page 108.

[114]   Douglas, *Nuer Prophets*; David Anderson and Douglas Johnson, *Revealing Prophets: Prophecy in East African History* (James Currey and Ohio University Press, 1995).

[115]   Roland Werner, Willian Anderson and Andrew Wheeler, *Day of Devastation, Day of Contentment* (Paulines Publications, 2000).

[116]   Jesse Zink, *Christianity and Catastrophe in South Sudan: Civil War, Migration, and the Rise of Dinka Anglicanism* (Baylor University Press, 2018).

[117]   Johnson, *Nuer Prophets*; Andrew Mawson, 'The Triumph of Life: Political Dispute and Religious Ceremonial among the Agar Dinka of the Southern Sudan' (PhD diss., Darwin College, 1989); Zoe Cormack, 'The Making and Remaking of Gogrial: Landscape, History and Memory in South Sudan' (PhD diss., Durham University, 2014).

[118]   Tounsel, *Chosen Peoples.*

wars.[119] While the SPLM/A had no formal religious affiliation, it manipulated Christian ideas to mobilise support.[120]

Zink takes a different approach and provides an account of the religious implications of the civil wars of the 1980s and 1990s, and changing modes of production, for the Anglican Church in the communities of Jonglei State. Zink argues that armed conflict, migration and economic shifts forced people to question their social existence and cosmological beliefs. Christianity offered new religious expressions and symbols that helped people navigate the shifting social relations, especially when Christian thought incorporated existing symbols and idioms.[121] Hutchinson's findings among the Nuer in the 1990s alternatively narrated how Christian norms and practice were undermining Nuer beliefs and creating confusion in how they could reconcile and come to terms with their first-hand experiences of terror and war.[122]

This book intentionally focuses on the eclectic divine and religious influences among a specific community in South Sudan – the communities around the Bilnyang River system. The book builds on this previous scholarship but focuses on how these meanings are used to contest the moral logics of government especially in a dominantly rural area of South Sudan. The book does not focus on abstract theological ideas, but instead focuses on how religion actually shapes both everyday lives and politics.[123]

The communities of the Bilnyang and connected river systems

In this book I use 'the Bilnyang and connected rivers' (or 'river system') to denote the mingled network of rivers surrounded by a permanent *toc* (swampy grazing land) that runs between contemporary Warrap and Unity States, on the western edge of the Sudd – the low lying, flat clay plains of the north-eastern third of contemporary South Sudan. In the 1950s, Howell described the river

---

[119]   Christopher Tounsel, 'Khartoum Goliath: SPLM/SPLA Update and Martial Theology during the Second Sudanese Civil War', *Journal of Africana Religions* 4:2 (2016): 129–153.

[120]   Tounsel, 'Khartoum Goliath'.

[121]   Zink, *Christianity and Catastrophe in South Sudan.*

[122]   Hutchinson, *Nuer Dilemmas*, pages 299–350; Rajech Venugopal, *Nationalism, Development and Ethnic Conflict in Sri Lanka* (Cambridge University Press, 2018).

[123]   For others in the Sudans who have encouraged a focus on the impact of religion on 'ordinary conduct', see: Godfrey Lienhardt, 'Religion', in Harry L. Shapiro (ed), *Man, Culture, and Society* (Oxford University Press, 1956), pages 310–311; Wendy James and Douglas Johnson, *Vernacular Christianity: Essays in the Social Anthropology of Religion* (Lilian Barber Press, 1988).

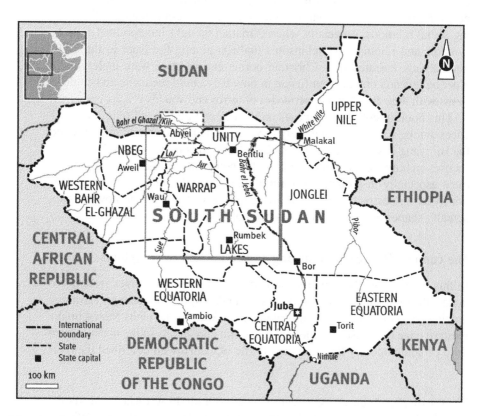

Map 1. South Sudan states according to the Comprehensive Peace Agreement (2005) (Base map data source: OpenStreetMap; © MAP*gra_x* 2022; Cartography: Jillian Luff of mapgrafix.com).

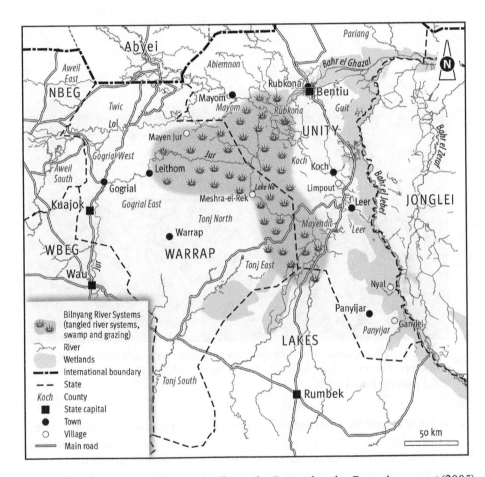

Map 2. Warrap and Unity States according to the Comprehensive Peace Agreement (2005) (Base map data source: OpenStreetMap; Cartography: Jillian Luff of mapgrafix.com).

Figure 1.   Photograph of part of the Bilnyang and connected rivers taken from a helicopter en route from Rumbek (Lakes State) to Koch (Unity State), October 2022 (Naomi Ruth Pendle).

systems around the Bilnyang as 'innumerable water courses joining in a series of large lakes'.[124] I use 'the Bilnyang and connected rivers' to refer to an area of water that is connected but not known by a common, single name. For the Dinka communities to the west, the area is better known as the generic term *toc* and not by these rivers' names. For the Nuer to the east, the name 'Bilnyang' is most commonly used for the stretch of the river as it runs through parts of contemporary Mayendit and Koch Counties; it takes on other names in other communities. The Bilnyang and surrounding river systems largely run from

---

[124]   Report by Winder on a trek from Mopair to Khor Bilnyang as part of the Jonglei Investigation Team, Sudan Archive Durham, SAD.541/2/18-23.

north to south, parallel to (but much further west of) the large Bahr el Jebel stream of the Nile, and run into the Bahr el Ghazal River to the north.[125]

The book focuses on communities tied together by rivers and *toc* in order to push against an ethno-centric lens. Despite the commonplace academic rejection of ethnic essentialism or ethnicity as a cause of conflict,[126] much research on South Sudan has still had an ethnically defined focus. Cormack implicitly challenged the focus on ethnicity by focusing on place and not ethnic identity.[127] This book follows this example and intentionally takes the step of drawing simultaneously on research from neighbouring Nuer- and Dinka-speaking communities who, in common, make use of the Bilnyang and connected rivers, including for dry-season cattle grazing.[128] The grass in these rivers – known as '*buar*' in Nuer and '*apac*' in Dinka – is rich for grazing and draws communities together. These river systems are also jointly central to the cosmological histories of the region. Kolang Ket – one of the earliest *guan kuoth* (Nuer prophets) – was seized while fishing in these waters (as described in Chapter 1). *Baany e biith* are also associated through these waters, including through the struggle of Longar (as also described in Chapter 1).

Regions discussed in this book are famous in the anthropological record, with Evans-Pritchard and Hutchinson writing on the Nuer, and Lienhardt and Jok on the Dinka.[129] While the Nuer and Dinka are famous in anthropology, the

---

[125] Some rivers in the system are fed from the Bahr el Jebel (a section of the White Nile), such as the Cier River, and others have no Nile water but are fed from the rivers coming through what are now Lakes and Warrap States, and initially from the Nile-Congo divide (Report by Winder on a trek from Mopair to Khor Bilnyang as part of the Jonglei Investigation Team, Sudan Archive Durham, SAD.541/2/18-23). They intersect and mingle as they flow north. For example, at Beeng, in what is now Mayendit County, the four rivers of the Rel, Gah, Nyathar and Thologat flow together in a lake about half a mile wide. The Bilnyang River itself starts near the boundary between contemporary Koch and Mayendit Counties. Cot-Jiok connects Mayendit and Koch Counties. The Reang and the Nyony join here and eventually flow north-west as the Bilnyang (SAD.541.2. 21) as a source for discussion and re-writing with a researcher from Mayendit). To the north, the Jur River coming from the west and through Wau is a dominant feature.

[126] de Waal, 'When Kleptocracy Becomes Insolvent'; Johnson, 'Briefing'; Thomas, *South Sudan*.

[127] Cormack, 'The Making and Remaking of Gogrial'.

[128] Report by Winder on a trek from Mopair to Khor Bilnyang as part of the Jonglei Investigation Team, Sudan Archive Durham, SAD.541/2/18-23.

[129] Evans-Pritchard, *The Nuer*; Lienhardt, *Divinity and Experience: The Religion of the Dinka* (Clarendon, 1961); Paul Philip Howell, *Manual of Nuer Law* (Oxford University Press, 1954); Jok Madut Jok, 'The Political History of South Sudan', in Timothy McKulka (ed.), *A Shared Struggle: The People and Cultures of South*

Bilnyang River system is not.[130] P. P. Howell was a British government official who became part of the team researching the likely impact of building a canal in Jonglei State (to the south-east). He went to the region of the Bilnyang in the 1950s to 'discover what happened to the spill of water from the left bank of the Bahr el Jebel and the waters of a number of rivers which, rising on the Nile-Congo Divide were largely lost in the marshes'.[131] At the time he wrote:

> It was an area of great importance to the local Nuer and Dinka tribesmen for dry weather grazing but it had never been traversed by any government official up to then, and probably has not been visited again since – it was a completely blank space on the map.[132]

This river system, despite its import to surrounding communities, continues to be largely absent from maps and written accounts of South Sudan that have been made by foreign administrators. The challenges of navigating these rivers make them useless for trade and for global economic interests.

Many communities that have economic, social and cosmological connections to these rivers do not live immediately adjacent to them, but have permanent homes days of walking away on higher, drier land, in towns such as Ler, Koch, Mayendit, Gogrial, Lietnhom, Luonyaker and Warrap. Communities across this wide expanse in contemporary central Warrap and Unity States are the focus of this book. The region is important for peace studies as it has long been significant for national politics. From the mid-nineteenth century, it was an important site for the advance of foreign governments and traders. From the 1860s, Meshra-el-Rek, to the north of the Bilnyang River itself, was a notorious transit point and *zara'ib* (Ar. 'enclosures', sing. *zeriba*) for ivory and slaves, and was a gateway from the Nile to the whole of Bahr el Ghazal (then the whole of the west of what is now South Sudan).[133] Decades later, during the Condominium rule, these rivers and swamps became administrative boundaries between districts and, at some points, provinces.[134] Administrative

---

Sudan (Kingdom of Denmark/Government of South Sudan/UN, 2013): 85–144; Andrew Mawson, 'The Triumph of Life'; Hutchinson, *Nuer Dilemmas*; Johnson, *Nuer Prophets.*

[130]   One example can be found in Howell, *Manual of Nuer Law.*

[131]   Report by Winder on a trek from Mopair to Khor Bilnyang as part of the Jonglei Investigation Team, Sudan Archive Durham, SAD.541/2/18-23).

[132]   Ibid.

[133]   Cormack, 'The Making and Remaking of Gogrial', page 64; G. E. Wickens, 'Dr. G. Schweinfurth's Journeys in the Sudan', *Kew Bulletin* 27:1 (1972): 129–146; C. H. Page, 'Inland Water Navigation of the Sudan', *Sudan Notes and Records* 2:4 (1919): 293–306.

[134]   For an important and excellent discussion of borders in these areas, see Zoe Cormack, 'Borders are Galaxies: Interpreting Contestations over Local Administrative Boundaries in South Sudan', *Africa* 86:3 (2016): 504–527.

districts separated out Dinka-speaking Gogrial to the west and the Nuer-speaking Western Nuer to the east. Now to the west of the rivers are Gogrial East, Gogrial West, Tonj North Counties (Warrap State) and to the east the counties of Mayendit, Ler, Koch and Mayom (Unity State). In the 1930s, colonial administrators prioritised what they saw as a 'modern' territorial-based identity, ignoring the importance of movement and relationships,[135] and the reality that rivers could be meeting points and not just boundaries. Between Nuer and Dinka speakers, they hardened boundaries and territorial units, and assumed ethnic homogeneity in each district.

The region is pivotal to contemporary national politics as it is the homeland of South Sudan's most powerful, contemporary *hakuma* leaders. South Sudanese President Salva Kiir, and Vice President and sometimes armed opposition leader, Riek Machar are from Warrap and Unity State respectively. In the 1970s oil was found between these rivers and the Bahr el Jebel, in what became Unity State. Armed forces of governments, eager to secure access to oil wealth, made this an epicentre of the conflict. In every decade since the 1980s, this region has seen extreme violent conflict where children have been killed, civilians have been targeted and extreme hunger has resulted. Governments have acted with brutal, arbitrary violence and with impunity.[136] This context of conflict also gave rise to the military and political leadership of Salva Kiir and Riek Machar. In addition, since 2016 and the demise of rival leaders, Warrap State has arguably also been home to South Sudan's de facto three most powerful figures (including the president and the two leaders of the most coordinated and well-armed forces in Juba), linking the region even more intimately with national politics.

Organisation of this book

This book focuses on the period since the 1980s. However, it starts with popular histories from the last century and a half that are an important part of the cultural archive that South Sudanese draw on to justify or contest the legitimacy of violence. This first section of the book focuses on early experiences of the *hakuma* as these were key decades that shaped South Sudanese

---

135 Cormack, 'Borders are Galaxies', page 508.
136 Luka Biong Deng, 'The Sudan Famine of 1998'. IDS Bulletin (Institute of Development Studies, 1984); Georgette Gagnon and John Ryle, 'Report of an Investigation into Oil Development in Western Upper Nile' (Canadian Auto Workers Union; Steelworkers Humanity Fund; Simons Foundation; United Church of Canada, Division of World Outreach; World Vision Canada, 2001); Human Rights Council, Report of the Commission on Human Rights in South Sudan, A/HRC/40/69, 25 February – 22 March 2019; Wheeler and Muscati, "'They Burnt It All'".

understanding of what the *hakuma* was, why it was often god-like, how it could claim impunity and how it fitted in to the cosmic polity.

The first chapter describes the coming of the *hakuma* in the nineteenth century and how their physical violence and implicit claims of impunity meant that they were divine. The chapter also describes how priests and other local authorities were able to carefully re-craft rituals and divine power, including through new free divinities, prophets and a dramatic elephant killing, to contest *hakuma* claims to be able to kill with impunity. The second chapter discusses the Anglo-Egyptian Condominium government's entrenching of legal logics of peace. This amounted to a new form of cosmic contestation in which the *hakuma* challenged divine authorities, not through spectacular violence, but by making them sacred by hedging them into legal institutions. The chapter highlights how the specific details of this peace reduced the divine to the sacred, entrenched government impunity and challenged the ability of peace to satisfy the demands of the dead. Divine authorities often became subordinate to *hakuma*-ordained laws.

The second section of the book turns to the more contemporary making of war and peace with discussion of the 1960s and 1970s, but with a more detailed focus on the period since the 1980s. Chapters oscillate between describing, on the one hand, the realities of *hakuma* violence against communities, including the way that *hakuma* coded their violence as legitimate through peace, and, on the other hand, the ways that the *hakuma*'s violence and impunity was contested. Chapter 3 discusses how the *baany e biith* shared with other Southerners an opposition to the Sudan government's development agenda, before describing the wars of the 1960s and 1972 Addis Ababa Peace Agreement. It illustrates how this brought new experiences of South Sudanese *hakuma* and new negotiations of the *hakuma*'s capture by moral authorities of their home communities. It ends by describing the collapse of the agreement, the 1980s to 2000s wars and the wartime violence and cosmic consequences. The chapter describes how priests pushed back against *hakuma* attempts to make wartime killing devoid of spiritual consequences by creatively refashioning their role and cosmological ideas. Chapter 4 describes the Wunlit Peace Meeting – an archetypal example of the 'local turn' in peace-making whereby international actors championed 'local' forms of peace-making. It explores its role in easing tensions and conflict, and engaging with divine authorities, but it argues that Wunlit ultimately failed to build an inclusive peace based on the norms within the cultural archive. Wunlit did not provide justice through compensation, and diminished the power of some divine authorities by hedging them in through the imposition of new peace-making rituals.

Chapter 5 focuses on South Sudan's 2005 Comprehensive Peace Agreement. The chapter argues that, for those in the communities near the Bilnyang and connected river systems, the CPA was mysterious, foreign and incomprehensible, but that it still had serious consequences for people in these rural South Sudanese communities through the way it performed power. The CPA involved significant ruptures in government-citizen power relations, including through land and local government reforms, and political leaders and diplomats drew on national and international cultural archives to make claims to have powers for such reforms. Chapter 6 describes escalations of violence in Warrap State after the CPA as a result of having an autochthonous *hakuma* alongside changing ideas of land, property, resources and cattle ownership. People in the *hakuma* both needed to be 'sons of the soil' to claim autochthonous rights, and be distinct as members of the divine *hakuma*. Those mobilising violence re-crafted the cultural archive and evoked ideas of revenge to drive conflict. The divinity MABIORDIT then seized a man and offered a combined militarised and divine means to push back against the government. Having described the proliferation of conflict, Chapter 7 focuses on the proliferation of peace meetings in Gogrial. It critically reflects both on their number and their inability to solve the feud. The peace meetings were also used to recode the violence of MABIORDIT as illegitimate and worthy of an arbitrary violent response from government. Chapter 9 then explores how the Dinka priests – the *baany e biith* – have had their legitimacy challenged by their proximity to markets and money. People have highlighted that *baany e biith* themselves potentially cannot curse and kill with impunity if they accept money for violence. These logics culturally refused the political marketplace. Chapters 9 and 10 turn to the Nuer-speaking communities to the east of these rivers. These chapters describe the cosmological crisis brought by the years of war, and then how the proliferation of prophets has sought to respond to such a crisis. Peace-making became an important part of the prophetic role, and prophets drew on the cultural archive to present their new peace-making power as continuous with previous peace-makers.

Opening the final section of the book, Chapter 11 introduces the wars in South Sudan since 2013, and argues for the prevalence of revenge in giving meaning to these armed conflicts. The wars and peace-making since 2013 have reconfigured the power of the *hakuma* and, within a decade, had centralised the politico-military power of the South Sudan government in the hands of a small cadre from Warrap State. At the same time, the war for most of those who fought it was not about centralising power. Among both government and armed opposition groups, South Sudanese drew on the cultural archive to frame a moral imperative to mobilise around ideas of revenge. This was revenge for events in December 2013, revenge for events in the 1990s and even revenge for events in the 1920s. Chapter 11 ends by highlighting how the internationally backed comprehensive peace processes failed to offer a peace that made sense if the meaning of war was of revenge. Chapter 12 then discusses the post-2013 power of the Nuer prophets. It shows how they were sometimes silenced in light of large-scale government violence, but how some prophets still built authority through peace-making. Repeatedly prophetic power was built through the prophetic power to demand a limit to the violence of the *hakuma,* through their own power to kill via the curse, and because of a continued concern with the dangers of the pollution of *nueer.* The chapter draws on examples from the Prophetess Nyachol and Prophet Gatluak, and gives an account of the emergence of Geng Mut Liah Wal as a prophet of TILING. Chapter 13 turns to the post-2013 era in Warrap State. It highlights how the growing power of the Warrap State cadre further exaggerated the dangers of having national leaders who were locally autochthonous. It describes how both war and peace often seem arbitrary and subject to marketplace logics, and also how priests continued to try to make a more meaningful peace. It draws on examples from Mayen Jur (on the Unity-Warrap states border) and from Greater Tonj.

Chapter 14 turns to the church in South Sudan. *Baany e biith* and prophets have maintained authority to make peace and contest arbitrary government violence. Yet, their rituals and morals can promote exclusive post-peace communities. The church has often promoted more inclusive communities through its moral and ritual expectations. The social separation of the church from armed young men has sometimes made it harder for it to assert its peace-making powers, and the demand for forgiveness has prompted some to suggest that church-made peace is immoral. At the same time, its proximity to the educated class of the *hakuma* has given the church power and this has sometimes been used to encourage more inclusive communities. In this chapter I draw on an example of a public debate over a wartime burial of enemy spies.

PART I

Histories and Archives of Peace and Impunity

Introduction

Cosmic battles to control violence, impunity, war and peace did not start in the mid-nineteenth century, but the physical presence of *hakuma* (governments, including foreign traders and slavers) starts at this point. While the *hakuma* did not explicitly claim to be divine, they made 'themselves the equivalent of gods – arbitrary, all-powerful beings beyond human morality – through the use of arbitrary violence'.[1] South Sudanese living in communities around the Bilnyang and connected rivers explicitly saw the arbitrary violence of government in god-like terms. The early awful, extreme violence of the *hakuma* and their guns resulted in contestations between the government and divine authorities not only over the power to kill, but whether such killing could happen with impunity. By the 1920s and 1930s, as the Anglo-Egyptian Sudan government established its administration, the cosmic contests over peace and violence were taking new forms. In this era, the government made many divine authorities sacred by incorporating these authorities and their peace-making powers into laws and legal institutions.

Part I starts with these older histories of violent peace and cosmic competitions as these histories are still remade and retold; they reach forward into contemporary political imaginaries. These histories inform what people see as politically possible, morally acceptable and cosmologically sensible. Popular histories can be disruptive of divisive and authoritarian power structures,[2] as well as entrenching them. Either way, these histories inform people's archives of moral knowledge.[3] Wendy James used the concepts of 'cultural archive' and 'repository of knowledge' to explain the reuse of meanings and histories among the Uduk in Sudan as they tried to find meaning amid armed conflict and extreme violence. The past is both consciously represented and also contained in a cultural deposit or 'archive' of unremembered events from distant

---

[1] David Graeber and Marshall Sahlins, *On Kings* (Chicago: HAU Books, 2017), page 81.

[2] Naomi Oppenheim, 'Popular History in the Black British Press: Edward Scobie's Tropic and Flamingo, 1960–64', *Immigrants & Minorities* 37:3 (2019): 136–162.

[3] Wendy James, *The Listening Ebony: Moral Knowledge, Religion and Power among the Uduk of Sudan* (Clarendon, 1988).

pasts that are visible in 'habitual ritual action' as well as in language.[4] There is flexibility in *la parole* but stability in *la langue*. This archive creates a basis for validation and 'constitutes the foundations of a moral world'.[5]

The first two chapters are largely based on histories told to me in the era after the 2005 Comprehensive Peace Agreement, as well as drawing on archival sources and relevant literature. In these chapters, I do not focus on how these accounts were being used after 2005, but the accounts of this oral, popular historical archive itself. At the same time, as much as they tell us about the nineteenth century, they also provide insights into the cultural archive and moral world in this post-2005 period. The repetitive focus on impunity, government violence and continued divine authority may be as much a reflection of cosmic politics in the 2000s and 2010s as it is of such politics in the 1800s. For example, many of my interviews about prophetic activity took place between 2013 and 2018. At this time (as later chapters show), people were again confronting *hakuma* displays of killing with impunity, and shifting political economies that left them cow-less and less capable of peace. The retelling of these histories tells us as much about priorities of South Sudanese in the 2010s, as it does about their priorities a century before. Yet, this makes these histories no less valuable. These chapters are crucial not only as they locate contemporary struggles in longer-term patterns of violence and resistance in South Sudan, but also because they highlight their contemporary, everyday prominence in the contemporary collective imagination.

When I was in South Sudan, I would often end the day interviewing informally in the marketplace while drinking tea. This section is largely based on what I describe as 'marketplace histories'. In the post-CPA era, rural markets could be found scattered across South Sudan. These small, rural markets would often have a few dozen shops constructed from some assortment of iron sheets, plastic sheets, poles, grass and bamboo. Some shops would sell small bags of tea, sugar, salt, sweets and other essentials. Other shops would serve sweet tea. In Juba, these tea shops would provide a range of coffees, teas and spices. In many rural markets, only black tea and piles of sugar were available. These tea shops were spaces where people gathered, sat for hours, and conducted their everyday analysis of what was happening around them. Therefore, marketplace histories are popular histories in a specific context. For example, the context was one of oral, not written, histories and it was a gendered space; women rarely drank in these spaces, even if those who made the tea were usually old women. Some of these histories were from local experts – people that I was guided to as they were locally seen as authorities on how things really had been. Yet, in these accounts, whenever possible, I

[4]   The idea of a 'cultural archive' draws on Foucault's work.
[5]   James, *The Listening Ebony*, page 6.

privilege marketplace histories as a way to notice popular understandings and common sources for moral validation. Marketplace histories are important as they help us see which histories were still living in common political discussions, and which political imaginaries in relation to peace were still prevalent.

Part I has two chapters. The first highlights the length of struggles against violent *hakuma* to contest the *hakuma*'s ability to kill with impunity. From the mid-nineteenth century, foreign traders and governments carried out seemingly arbitrary and deadly violence, and the extreme force of the gun made them appear to be able to do this with impunity. Divine authorities before them had been able to kill with impunity with the power of the curse, and now *governments* were killing with impunity through the power of the gun. In this way, the *government* was like a divinity. Yet, religious leaders played a key role in contesting the legitimacy and ability of government's claims to be able to kill with impunity. In Graeber's terms, they 'creatively refused'[6] cultures of the *hakuma* and remade cultures to resist and to make government accountable.

The second chapter is an account of how divine powers to make peace became entangled with the law during the Anglo-Egyptian Condominium governments. The nineteenth and early twentieth centuries' political and economic changes undermined local religious authorities' ability to make peace; they had relied on cattle for compensation and sacrifice, and cattle economies were changing fast. Peace-making had relied on framing conflict as feuding, with this allowing compensation to peacefully resolve the feud. The chapter discusses how the incorporation of compensation into law recoded conflict as a crime and an illegal act. Yet, it also entrenched the centrality of compensation in peace-making. At the same time, the making of compensation into a legal requirement subordinated divine authorities to the government, made the divine 'sacred' and reduced some of compensation's peace-making potential.

Together these two chapters provide an important account of the 'cultural archive' that shapes South Sudanese understandings of peace. Histories of the *hakuma*'s assertions of power, and subsequent remaking of cultures to refuse, have fashioned these archives; the archive is far from a collection of ahistoric memories and cultures. In addition, we see that the *hakuma*'s assertions of power took two dominant forms. The *hakuma*'s excessive violence displayed their ability to kill without accountability and so with impunity. At the same time, they undermined divine authorities by hedging them in with the law and making them sacred.

---

[6]   David Graeber, 'Culture as Creative Refusal', *Cambridge Anthropology* 31:2 (2013): 1–19.

CHAPTER 1

Priestly peace and the Divinity of the Gun: The Coming of Government in the Late Nineteenth and Early Twentieth Centuries

The coming of foreign traders, slavers and *hakuma* to the Bilnyang and connected rivers in the mid-nineteenth century brought new contestations to the cosmic polity. The form of the first contestations by the *hakuma* were contestations of spectacular, arbitrary violence and, in response, divine South Sudanese authorities attempted to contest the *hakuma*'s tacit claims of divinity and impunity. This chapter provides an account of how South Sudanese histories of the late nineteenth and early twentieth century portray governments' claims to be able to kill with impunity as equivalent to a claim to be divine. Histories near the Bilnyang Rivers also emphasise how local divine authorities challenged government impunity.

The late nineteenth and early twentieth centuries opened up Southern Sudan to large-scale foreign trade including in slaves and ivory. Equipped with guns, these new foreigners and *hakuma* could inflict lethal and devastating violence with apparent impunity. From the last years of the nineteenth century, the Anglo-Egyptian government came to control South Sudan and asserted their power through violent patrols and through the legal formalisation of their ability to kill with impunity. These new experiences of death and impunity brought new cosmological, moral and political uncertainties. It was easy to interpret foreign and government actions as claims to be god-like as they claimed the right to kill arbitrarily.

At the same time, people 'creatively refused' *hakuma*'s claims to be able to kill with impunity by remaking culture and asserting the power of divine leaders to hold the divine-like government to account. This chapter draws on the example of Nuer prophet Kolang Ket to illustrate how new forms of powers were negotiated and displayed that ultimately allowed peace to still be possible and that allowed the government's impunity and divinity to be challenged.

***

The late nineteenth and early twentieth centuries saw foreign governments and traders, and their Southern Sudanese colleagues, bring new experiences of gunpower to Southern Sudan. The latter had centuries of experience of international movement and political and economic engagement.[1] Yet, foreign traders and governments had been limited in their movement to Southern Sudan by the conundrum of the matted papyrus blocks of the Sudd that blocked the river routes south. The first foreign expeditions to break through the Sudd marshes took place in 1840–41 in the context of significant capital investment that was eager to profit from the growing demand in Egyptian and European metropoles for goods including ivory and slaves.[2]

By the 1850s, traders were establishing small trading centres (*zeribas* – literally 'enclosures') along waterways in Southern Sudan, and people found along the banks of the Nile were the first to encounter these foreign incursions.[3] These trading posts allowed foreign merchants to raid or negotiate for ivory and slaves. From the outset, these traders used excessive force to support their demands.[4] They relied on the power of the gun to capture slaves and ivory, or to bargain for local support for these ventures.

From the middle of the nineteenth century, the Bilnyang and surrounding river systems became central to *hakuma* activity in what is now South Sudan; these rivers were the *hakuma* access point to the whole of western Southern Sudan. By the mid-1850s, merchant ships from Khartoum had entered the Bahr el Ghazal River – the river to the west of the Bahr el Jebel section of the Nile – which started to open up *hakuma* access to the west. From this time, slavers started transactions and raids within the surrounding population.[5] By the 1860s, explorers and entrepreneurial traders were starting to look west and south-west for new sources of ivory and other goods.[6] *Zeribas* were established on the ironstone plateau that spreads out across south-western Southern Sudan and that quickly became known as the Bahr el Ghazal region (referencing the river which connected this region to the Nile and made exports possible).

---

[1]   Douglas Johnson, *South Sudan: A New History for a New Nation* (Ohio University Press, 2016).

[2]   Cherry Leonardi, *Dealing with Government in South Sudan: History of Chiefship, Community and State* (James Currey, 2013), page 18.

[3]   John W. Burton, 'When the North Winds Blow: A Note on Small Towns and Social Transformation in the Nilotic Sudan', *African Studies Review* 31:3 (1988): 49–60, pages 50–51.

[4]   Richard Gray, *A History of The Southern Sudan 1839–1889* (Oxford University Press, 1961), page 47.

[5]   Georg Schweinfurth, *The Heart of Africa: Three Years' Travels and Adventures in the Unexplored Regions of Central Africa, From 1868 to 1871*, Volume 1 (Harper, 1874), page 38.

[6]   Ibid., page 29.

In the 1860s, Meshra-el-Rek (Ar. 'landing place in the land of the Rek [i.e. Rek Dinka]'), or 'port Rek',[7] next to the Bilnyang River, became a regular landing point for operations into the Bahr el Ghazal region. Meshra-el-Rek was a landing point on a collection of small islands on a lake. This was the furthest point to the south into the Bahr el Ghazal region that could be navigated by water. The cluster of islands of Meshra-el-Rek were no more than four miles across and merchants created a small series of encampments of merchants, as well as *zeribas* including a large *zeriba* for cattle. Maps labelled it the south-westerly 'route to the interior'.[8]

For the latter half of the nineteenth century, Meshra-el-Rek became a crucial port for trade and foreign power in the south, and a key centre of the *hakuma*.[9] *Zeribas* were established across Bahr el Ghazal and down to the Congo watershed. Wau quickly became a significant *zeriba*. Yet, the goods and slaves collected at these multiple stations all had to be marched or carried to Meshra-el-Rek in order to be exported up the Nile. There were often dozens of merchants' boats docked at Meshra-el-Rek, delivering supplies for the *zeribas* or carrying back items to sell in Khartoum and abroad.[10]

Those communities living around and reliant on the Bilnyang Rivers were immediately aware of Meshra-el-Rek and the associated power of the *hakuma*. Their soldiers had hundreds of guns, as well as larger, less portable weapons.[11] Dinka communities to the west and south, between Meshra-el-Rek and other *zeribas*, saw supplies for the *zeribas*, and then slaves, cattle and other goods being marched through their land to access the port. Foreign descriptions of journeys made it clear that they passed through the grazing lands to the east of what became Gogrial.[12] These caravans of merchandise were carried and guarded by hundreds of men into Bahr el Ghazal and were a visible display of the gun-powered might of these merchants.

The lack of extensive, permanent dry land between the Bilnyang Rivers and Bahr el Jebel to the east meant that no *zeribas* were established to the east in what is now southern Unity State. However, the lack of *zeribas* among the Nuer (who lived to the east, on the far side of the Bilnyang and connected rivers) did not mean that they were shielded from the change brought

---

[7]   Ibid., page 35.
[8]   Ibid., page 37, map.
[9]   Romolo Gessi, *Seven Years in the Soudan* (Sampson Low, Marston & Company, 1892) cited in Burton, 'When the North Winds Blow', page 51.
[10] John Tinné, 'A Communication from Mr. Tinné Relative to the Dutch Ladies' Expedition from Khartùm up the River Bahr-el-Ghazal, Commencing 26th February, at a Point on the White Nile', *Proceedings of the Royal Geographical Society of London* 8:1 (1863–64): 12–18.
[11] Gessi, *Seven Years in the Soudan*, page 105.
[12] Ibid.

by foreign traders and *hakuma*. There were raids for ivory and slaves into the western Nuer, and in the Bilnyang River systems, they saw the *hakuma* close-up. Nuer would move their cattle into the grazing lands which hosted the sizeable Meshra-el-Rek port. While the swamps and river system are vast and can act as a barrier to movement, in the dry season the port would be less than a day's walk even from more permanent Nuer settlements and would have been known. Plus, neighbouring, Dinka-speaking communities, with whom they married and grazed together, all hosted *zeribas*. As discussed below, a few Nuer individuals even acquired guns, highlighting their contact with and knowledge of the *hakuma*. It is inconceivable that the *hakuma* in Meshra-el-Rek was not known by the Nuer, and such a claim ignores the significance of these grazing lands.[13]

The *hakuma* of Meshra-el-Rek was violent. Traders operating from Meshra-el-Rek became notorious for killing dozens of people.[14] With the power of the gun, they were able to kill large numbers without reprisals. They appeared to be able to kill with impunity; no-one had the power to hold them to account. For those living in the Bilnyang, the *government* clearly carried out extreme arbitrary violence.

People living around the Bilnyang Rivers did not only experience the brutality of force at Meshra-el-Rek, but also negotiated and purchased alliances. Traders realised that its security could be served by alliances with local authority figures. As Leonardi has highlighted, across Southern Sudan, the Southern Sudanese authorities did not only fight against but also often cooperated with these foreign forces.[15] The public authorities were often given support from traders, including gifts of guns, in exchange for their supply to *zeribas*.[16] In the diaries of an 1863 expedition to find the western affluent of the Nile, the following account was given of merchant-local relations:

> The origin and system of these merchants are different here from the White Nile [describing populations to the east of the Bahr-el-Jebel]. A man comes into a village, sets himself down, and begins by buying ivory and making friends with the negroes, promises to protect them if they will take the ivory to the ships in the Mishra [Meshra-el-Rek], and he either remains himself or leaves a vakeel [agent or representative]. He builds a house, surrounds it with

[13]   Johnson's *Nuer Prophets* focuses on the east of the Nile. His account of the history of Nuer prophets to the west plays down their awareness of and interaction with the *hakuma* in the 1800s.

[14]   'Itinerary of the Bahr el Ghazal River', in Count Gleichen (ed.), *The Anglo-Egyptian Sudan: A Compendium Prepared by Officers of the Sudan Government*, Volume 1 (London: Harrison and Sons for HMSO, 1905).

[15]   Leonardi, *Dealing with Government in South Sudan*, page 21.

[16]   Gray, *A History of the Southern Sudan*, page 56.

palisades, and, by degrees becoming master of the village, then proceeds to attack a neighbouring hostile village, and, having guns, of course they conquer. That village he attaches to the first, and so on till he had a good many villages, when he forces the negroes of the whole to furnish *doura* for his soldiers or fighting men, and they submit.[17]

For example, one foreign botanist staying at Meshra-el-Rek described a powerful local woman – 'Shol' (probably Achol) – that traders had befriended in order to prevent her threatening the Meshra-el-Rek and the water-route to this port.[18] Through cooperation with foreigners, she amassed large amounts of foreign jewellery as well as a herd of 30,000 head of cattle. Guns were also given as gifts of appreciation to cooperative local figures. In Gogrial, when chiefs were later appointed by the British, they were selected on the basis of either having divine power or having had previous experience with the slave traders and having acquired authority through gun ownership.[19]

While the force and behaviour of different foreigners was often indistinguishable for Southern Sudanese, there were significant armed conflicts between foreign *hakuma* themselves. In 1878, Gessi Pasha (then governor of the region in the Ottoman-Egyptian administration) violently fought slave dealers in Bahr el Ghazal. He aspired to establish (albeit through violence) a 'good and just government', 'to restore the confidence of natives in foreign authorities and to make trade legitimate'.[20] Seeing the illegitimacy and inhumanity in these foreign traders, he claimed to seek a new form of foreign rule. On Gessi's death in 1881, Frank Lupton became governor. Lupton had six companies of regular troops, but he also relied on the slaves of former slave dealers that were armed with double-barrelled guns.[21] The continuities of arms and military labour blurred together different factions of the *hakuma*.

The late nineteenth century's new displays of violence by the *hakuma* prompted ontological and cosmological puzzles about the nature of this new power, and the *hakuma*'s place in the cosmological hierarchies. They also bought new dilemmas about how to make peace. Could peace really be made with the *hakuma* when its power was so excessively and violently asymmetrical?

---

[17]   Ibid., 16.

[18]   Schweinfurth, *The Heart of Africa*, page 39.

[19]   Interview with key informant in Gogrial about chief's history, May 2022.

[20]   Frank Lupton and Malcolm Lupton, 'Mr. Frank Lupton's (Lupton Bey) Geographical Observations in the Bahr-el-Ghazal Region: With Introductory Remarks by Malcolm Lupton', *Proceedings of the Royal Geographical Society and Monthly Record of Geography* 6:5 (1884): 245–255.

[21]   Ibid., page 246.

As Graeber has described, authorities can 'make themselves the equivalent of gods – arbitrary, all-powerful beings beyond human morality – through the use of arbitrary violence'.[22] This equation of divinity and arbitrary violence resonated with Nuer and Dinka cosmologies. For example, Aiwel Longar is remembered as the first *bany e bith*. Accounts of the origins of his priestly authority involved Longar killing people with a fishing spear as they tried to cross the water to safety.[23] Idioms surrounding the Nuer prophets, as well as the Nuer and Dinka priests (*kuar muon* and *baany e biith* respectively), also point to their ability to curse people to death without punishment because of their divine authority. Therefore, the *governments*' repeated claims to be able to kill with impunity associated them with the morals and powers of the divine.

Patrols and impunity

British forces fought in the 1880s and 1890s to control Sudan, and an Anglo-Egyptian Condominium government to rule Sudan was formed in 1899. From the end of the nineteenth century, during this regime, the impunity of the government was formalised.[24] By 1901, Meshra-el-Rek, as well as Wau, Tonj and Shambe, had been occupied by Sudanese troops under British officers.[25] As Leonardi has discussed, the new towns under Condominium rule, mapped on top of the *zeribas*, blurred further differences between the old and new *hakuma*.[26] The Anglo-Egyptian government continued to invest in Meshra-el-Rek, including through telegraph wires and the building of a new access channel.[27]

In the subsequent decades of Anglo-Egyptian rule, there would be a more extensive commitment to systematically govern the Sudan. For those living around Meshra-el-Rek, the new *hakuma*, like the old, was dominantly visible through their raids of livestock, their killing of people and their displays of

---

[22]   Graeber and Sahlins, *On Kings*, page 81.

[23]   Godfrey Lienhardt, *Divinity and Experience: The Religion of the Dinka* (Clarendon, 1961), page 173.

[24]   Major Earl Winterton in United Kingdom, *Hansard Parliamentary Debates*, 5th Series, Volume 113 (1919), Columns 2362–2372; Captain William Ormsby-Gore in United Kingdom, *Hansard Parliamentary Debates*, 5th Series, Volume 121 (1919), Columns 746–752.

[25]   Robert O. Collins, *The Land Beyond the Rivers: The Southern Sudan, 1898–1918* (Yale University Press, 1971), page 81.

[26]   Leonardi, *Dealing with Government in South Sudan*.

[27]   Burton, 'When the North Winds Blow', page 54; Anglo-Egyptian Sudan, Meshra el Rek. 1:250000 series maps; Sheet 65-P. 1925 SAD.211/2.

violence.[28] 'Administration required the display of force by government and practical demonstrations of submission and obedience from subject peoples and their leaders'.[29] Across Southern Sudan, these displays of military might included violent patrols against civilians. They also included more symbolic violence, such as the bombing of the burial mound of the Nuer prophet Ngundeng in 1927.

Many of the displays of Anglo-Egyptian government were specifically against leaders who claimed authority from divine powers. The legacy of the anti-foreigner Mahidiyya in Sudan and the defeat of General Gordon and other European powers provided justification for government suspicion of religious authorities. The realisation of government power often became equated with the military defeat of a divine authority figure. For example, as Cormack's work highlights, it was not until the 1920s that the government established a permanent presence in Gogrial. Initially they were preoccupied by the defeat of the prophet of Ariathdit; they feared his rapidly acquired and widespread popularity.[30] Major Titherington had led the patrols against Ariathdit and became the region's first Condominium government administrator in 1922.[31] These patrols were armed and violent, relying on the power of the gun to challenge the power that built on claims about the invisible.

While busy suppressing divine authority figures, the government was itself becoming quasi divine. Its violence was arbitrary and, therefore, amounted to a claim to be all-powerful, beyond restraint and akin to a divinity.[32] For example, government patrols against whole villages and communities were often driven by collective punishment or government plans to move communities – reasons that did not justify such excessive violence in Nuer and Dinka moral worlds. Like divinities, they were claiming a legitimate ability to be able to 'step outside the confines of the human, and return to rain favour of destruction, with arbitrariness and impunity'.[33]

28 Douglas Johnson, *Empire and the Nuer: Sources on the Pacification of the Southern Sudan, 1898–1930* (Oxford University Press for the British Academy, 2016), page xxx.

29 Ibid., page xxxi.

30 Zoe Cormack, 'The Making and Remaking of Gogrial: Landscape, History and Memory in South Sudan' (PhD diss., Durham University, 2014); Martina Santschi, 'Encountering and "Capturing" Hakuma: Negotiating Statehood and Authority in Northern Bahr-El-Ghazal State, South Sudan' (PhD diss., University of Bern, 2013): 48–50.

31 Sudan Intelligence Report of April 1922 as discussed by Cormack: Cormack, *The Making and Remaking of Gogrial*, page 69.

32 Graeber and Sahlins, *On Kings*, page 81.

33 Graeber and Sahlins, *On Kings*, page 7.

The Anglo-Egyptian government also legally formalised claims to impunity. As early as 1899, the Sudan government entrenched in the Sudan Penal Code the government's impunity under the law. As the government relied on local officials, the expectation of government impunity demanded an alternative moral, legal and spiritual framework for these agents of government. Hutchinson highlights that this gave rise to the question of whether there were different spiritual consequences for Nuer when violence was carried out in the line of government duty.[34] This distinction was at the heart of the government rule as it allowed local chiefs to wield these quasi-divine government powers.

The example of Kolang Ket

Other divine authorities contested the *hakuma*'s implicit claims to be divine. They did this by challenging the government's power to kill with impunity. The rest of this chapter provides an example of how Kolang Ket challenged the divinity of government. Kolang Ket was one of the first Nuer prophets in the western Nuer and went on to be significant in this region. His own seizure can be seen as a cultural and cosmological development that, in Graeber's words, 'creatively refused' the assertions of the *hakuma*'s sovereignty. The history of Kolang's own death then contests the *hakuma*'s ability to kill with impunity and be god-like. At stake are divergent definitions of divinity:[35] the defining of what can be divine is intimately linked to assertions of power.

By the late nineteenth century, Kolang Ket, living to the east of the Bilnyang River, had become a victim of repetitive crises and had become an extremely poor man. He was the only living man in his family and he had two sisters – Nyanyuot and Nyaboura. Both of his sisters gave birth to sons, but shortly afterwards a smallpox outbreak killed both the sisters and the sons. The death of his sisters' sons left Kolang with a significant spiritual and moral obligation.[36] Despite new experiences of death and economic loss, existing posthumous social expectations were still being upheld. Kolang had the responsibility to provide a posthumous wife for these sons and Kolang married wives on their behalf. However, the bride-price requirements left Kolang with no cattle. The wives then gave birth to sons for whose care he was also responsibile,[37] thus leaving him a poor, struggling man.

---

[34]   Sharon Hutchinson, *Nuer Dilemmas: Coping with Money, War, and the State* (University of California Press, 1996), page 108.

[35]   This insight is thanks to Joseph Hellweg and his review of this book.

[36]   Discussed in Jedeit J. Riek and Naomi Pendle, *Speaking Truth to Power in South Sudan: Oral Histories of the Nuer Prophets* (Rift Valley Institute, 2018).

[37]   Interview with Paramount Chief Dingding Kuol Kolang Ket of the Jabany Section, Bentiu UN Protection of Civilians (POC) site, 16 July 2017, in Nuer.

Kolang Ket's poverty was the result of the new diseases and economies associated with the coming of foreigners (discussed further in Chapter 2), and the continuity of moral norms shaped in different political and economic times. This impacted Kolang's ability to resolve disputes peacefully; peace relied on cattle given in compensation and he had no cattle left. Kolang ended up in many fights and, during one fight, he killed two men. He did not have the cattle to meet the compensation demands of the families.[38] Therefore, he could expect them to seek revenge. In his poverty-induced vulnerability to revenge, Kolang Ket sought protection from Jiath Kor – a powerful figure among a neighbouring section of the Jagei Nuer, a section of the Nuer based around the area of greater Koch.[39]

Jiath Kor was an example of public authority and protection remade through the acquisition of a gun. Jiath did not have historic or divinely inspired authority. Instead, Jiath's power was cemented by his acquisition of a gun from one of the foreign traders. Living in one of the closest Nuer settlements to Meshra-el-Rek, it is likely that this gun was given to Jiath Kor by traders stationed there in exchange for Jiath's support in acquiring ivory or other goods, or for his promise of security. At the same time, Jiath was not only building his authority through the power of the gun, but was also drawing on older idioms of leadership. Through his offer of protection to characters like Kolang, Jiath invited comparison between his powers to protect using the gun and the physical and spiritual protection offered by the *kuaar muon* to those who had killed. Jiath's protection also directly challenged the necessity of compensation for safety after killing. He was able to offer protection that was not so intimately linked with histories of Nuer divine authority. The gun could offer physical protection while ignoring spiritual protection.

Kolang Ket, while living under the protection of Jiath, committed adultery with the wife of a powerful *kuaar muon*. These acts were not just an affront to this specific man, but showed a brave defiance of previously feared hierarchies of authority and codes of morality and purity. Such a daring act as committing adultery against a powerful *kuaar muon* was an affront to the priestly power itself, and conveyed a confidence acquired from being protected by the safety of Jiath's gun. Jiath's power through the gun had allowed Jiath to protect Kolang from paying compensation after killing when Kolang had no cattle to pay. This challenged the laws of compensation and the divine monopoly on protection. The question now arose of whether the power of Jiath's gun could also protect Kolang from the direct wrath of a *kuaar muon*.

In the end, Kolang decided the priest was more powerful than the gun, and he submitted to the power of the priest. While Kolang initially hid from

[38]   Ibid.
[39]   Ibid.

the *kuaar muon*, he eventually came to believe that protection by the gun would not have the power to protect him from the *kuaar muon*'s ability to kill. Therefore, even if the gun was being compared to the divine, the divine moral authority of the *kuaar muon* was still seen as more powerful and feared. In the context of this continued divine fear, Kolang Ket then begged forgiveness from the *kuaar muon* to the point of offering himself up to death.[40] In a theatrical act, he laid himself before the *kuaar muon* in the presence of Jiath Kor, and told the *kuaar muon* to kill him. It was a vivid recognition by Kolang of the *kuaar muon*'s continued power to kill with impunity.

The *kuaar muon* 'creatively refused' the *hakuma*'s new culture of government sovereignty; he asserted his own divine power by showing mercy. Showing mercy and favour is also indicative of being god-like.[41] In response to Kolang's theatrical act, the *kuaar muon* blessed him and his seizure by MAANI (a divine power) followed. This seizure made Kolang a '*guan kuoth*' ('owner of a divinity') which meant he had special abilities including the power for the divinity to speak through him. The *kuaar muon*'s favour creatively made space for a new divine authority figure who could be understood as continuous with his own power, but who would go on to have the power to challenge the *hakuma*'s impunity.

Kolang Ket was one of the first *guan kuthni* (pl; sing. *guaan kuoth*) in the western Nuer. The emergence of the *guan kuthni*, later becoming known as 'Nuer prophets', is the most known example of religious rupture at this time.[42] They are seized by a named divinity, and claim power over life and death. Seizures by divinities have long been part of cosmic polities among those living around the Bilnyang. In the late 1940s, British anthropologist Godfrey Lienhardt had recorded that there were a number of active, 'free divinities' among the Dinka of Gogrial including DENG, GARANG and MACARDIT.[43] These free divinities or 'sky divinities' (*kuoth nhial*), distinct from lower, earthly powers (*kuuth piny*) and from divinities that are bound to certain clans, made their presence known through illness and then through declaring their name and instructions through the words of this seized person.[44] Each of these free divinities had their own personalities and 'biographies'.[45] These free divinities were not seen as necessary competitors of the

[40]   Riek and Pendle, *Speaking Truth to Power in South Sudan.*
[41]   Graeber and Sahlins, *On Kings*, page 8.
[42]   Douglas Johnson, 'Prophecy and Mahdism in the Upper Nile: An Examination of Local Experiences of the Mahdiyya in Southern Sudan', *British Journal of Middle Eastern Studies* 20:1 (1993), page 47.
[43]   Lienhardt, *Divinity and Experience*, page 56.
[44]   Ibid., page 57.
[45]   Ibid., pages 81–95; Cormack, 'The Making and Remaking of Gogrial', page 246.

baany e biith but within the cosmological order in which the *baany e biith* held their priesthood. Demonstrative of this was the necessary involvement of the *baany e biith* in the initial recognition of the seizure of a person by a free divinity. 'Men of divinity' were from the clans of the *baany e biith* but with additional powers. They are seized by a divinity known by a special name.[46] Therefore, these powers relied on clan membership but also on divine recognition. Lienhardt described 'men of divinity' as uniting clan divinities and divinity itself. The most powerful 'men of divinity' were from the clans of the *baany e biith*,[47] indicating that these prophetic figures were situating their claims to authority within existing registers.

Seizures allow for the emergence of new cosmic powers and focus, and to this extent represent a rupture. At the same time, they are within the existing cosmologies and divine authority structures. Seizures make the appearance of new divinities an expectation, and the role of the *baany e biith* subsumes these figures into these existing structures. Ariathdit was the most famous Dinka prophet of the time and likely seized in the second decade of the twentieth century.[48] While based among the Malual Dinka near what is now Aweil, his influence is said to have extended as far east as Meshra-el-Rek and as far south as Tonj.[49] Their overlapping spheres of influence make it also certain that Ariathdit and Kolang Ket would have been aware of each other's divine powers. Dinka sought the intervention of Kolang Ket and later his daughter – the prophetess Nyuarac. Nuer in turn sought help from Dinka prophets.[50]

MAANI's seizure of Kolang Ket pre-dated that of Ariathdit by two or three decades. It took place when Kolang was fishing in the rivers near the Bilnyang. Divine power came to Kolang Ket from the river, just as divine authority had come to Longar in riverside encounters and just as the *hakuma* had come from the rivers. The power of the *hakuma* and the gun had also come through the rivers at Meshra-el-Rek. Therefore, the Nuer prophets' arrival did not equate to a discontinuity with previous notions of divine authority. Instead, the prophets were new authority figures who drew on previous religious idioms but who resembled new forms of authority to help preserve a previous moral order in times of incredible change and daily displays of the divinity of the gun.

The claims of MAANI and Kolang Ket to power were also intimately tied to the martial youth and the need to bring them under the authority of

---

[46] Lienhardt, *Divinity and Experience*, page 76.

[47] Ibid., page 74.

[48] Cormack, 'The Making and Remaking of Gogrial'; Lienhardt, *Divinity and Experience*, page 76.

[49] Cormack, 'The Making and Remaking of Gogrial'; Lienhardt, *Divinity and Experience*, pages 76–77;

[50] Lienhardt, *Divinity and Experience*, pages 74–75.

reconfiguring hierarchies. Shortly after being seized by MAANI, Kolang Ket demanded that the next cohort of youth not be initiated into a new age set until he returned from a journey. Initiation would give them new rights but also fighting responsibilities. When someone else initiated them in his absence, she was cursed to death by Kolang. This resulted in a recognition of his authority from the youth.[51]

It is hard to imagine that new forms of cosmic power and ontological uncertainties that came with the *hakuma* were not connected to the new prophetic seizures of people like Kolang Ket. This does not mean that prophets are inherently rebellious, but it is inconceivable that prophetic idioms were not at least partly shaped by experiences of the *hakuma*. They are best understood as acts of 'creative refusal' by carefully nuancing culture and cosmologies to allow the divine to contest the unrestrained power of the *hakuma*. Johnson has carefully argued that prophets emerged to the east of the Nile to form new moral communities after flood and famine induced migrations.[52] Flooding, famine and disease undoubtedly played their role. Yet, Johnson has been too eager to ignore the context of the coming of the *hakuma*. He was writing at a time when governments too often saw prophets as inherently anti-government, but hidden in this work is the assumption that governments do have some value and right to rule, and that Nuer prophets would have less moral value if they were opposed to government. It is not that Nuer prophets are inherently opposed to *hakuma*, but we also cannot ignore the seismic political and cosmological shifts that the *hakuma* was creating at the time the prophets emerged.

Challenging the *hakuma*'s power to kill with impunity

Kolang Ket's main challenge to the impunity of the *hakuma* came through his death. The example of revenge for the death of Nuer prophet Kolang Ket provides an early example of the contestation between a prophet and a government official over the government's ability to claim that they could kill with impunity. When the Anglo-Egyptian government first approached Kolang Ket in July 1923, relations were reported by the government as cordial.[53] However, in the 1920s, Dinka-Nuer raids and retaliations resulted in the death of Kolang Ket's son.[54] In obedience to government, Kolang had initially not

---

[51]   Riek and Pendle, *Speaking Truth to Power in South Sudan*.
[52]   Douglas Johnson, *Nuer Prophets: A History of Prophecy from the Upper Nile in the Nineteenth and Twentieth Centuries* (Clarendon Press, 1994).
[53]   Johnson, *Nuer Prophets*, page 261.
[54]   Ibid., pages 259–61.

retaliated – despite the local unpopularity of this stance.[55] Yet, after his son's death, he sought violent revenge. The government interpreted his retaliation as an act of defiance against the government itself and not just the Dinka. By using force without the government's permission, Kolang Ket had effectively challenged the government's claim to a monopoly on violence. For the government, this justified violent, punitive patrols against Nuer communities and the government arrest of Kolang Ket and his imprisonment in Malakal.

Kolang Ket was already an old man and local memory recounts that he fell gravely ill during this imprisonment. British officials in the Sudan government were said to have made the decision to send him home to die. The Nuer government official Caath Obang was given the task of escorting him home from the Nile port of Adok.[56] Caath was part of a vanguard of Nuer who were promoted into government leadership based on displays of government support. Johnson described how Caath had been subordinate to Chief Wuon Kuoth but was ambitious and gravitated to government.[57] In 1924 he was eventually deported from the Nuerlands for oppressive acts against his fellow Nuer.[58] Later, in 1929, he would briefly be appointed to the Dok chieftaincy further south. Yet, his lack of local support would quickly see his downfall. Caath Bang represented to the Nuer the imposition of the government.[59]

On reaching the western Nuer with Kolang Ket in June 1925, Caath killed Kolang Ket by burying him alive.[60] Popular memory upheld this account of Kolang Ket's death and was still widely told when I was interviewing in 2013:

> When Kolang Ket got sick, they brought him back from Malakal. When he reached Thoar [just inland from the Nile port of Adok], the soldier Caath Bang caught Kolang again. He caught him and killed him. He dug a grave while the man had not yet died and put him in alive. He ordered the people to put much soil on it.[61]

The burial of Kolang while still alive is common to most accounts of his death. Yet some accounts suggest that Caath's stance against Kolang was only to refuse to let him go home to die. Caath then buried him away from his

---

55   Ibid., page 261.
56   Ibid., page 265.
57   Ibid., page 265.
58   Percy Coriart, Western Nuer District Report, 1 February 1931, page 303.
59   Interview with youth, Adok (Ler County), 30 April 2013 (in Nuer).
60   Johnson, *Nuer Prophets*, page 265. Some accounts instead claim that Kolang Ket died from age or illness and that he was not buried alive but buried after this death in Adok.
61   Interview with youth, Adok (Ler County), 30 April 2013 (in Nuer).

home.[62] Either way, Caath was using his government authority to confront and subvert MAANI's power over life, death and burial. Caath directly challenged MAANI's power over death and claimed his power as a government official to kill with impunity and to have authority to decide burial. Still today, Kolang Ket's grave is a sizeable mound on the main road to Adok. Local residents say that they have not marked or tended the grave to show disapproval at the way Kolang died.

Soon after Kolang's death, MAANI directly challenged Caath's, and therefore the *hakuma*'s, ability to kill with impunity. In the 1990s, Johnson records that Caath's death in 1930 was attributed to MAANI.[63] The following is an account given to me in 2013 of MAANI's revenge:

> As he was buried, Kolang said to Caath, one day I will come back as an elephant. When the time came, in the morning there were clouds in the east that looked like a lone elephant coming. There was an elephant on the ground and a black cloud above. When the soldier saw, he told them not to go to it but that he himself would kill it. He went out shooting but no bullets came out. So, the elephant captured him and killed him.[64]

Others provide similar accounts.[65] Through the elephant's act of revenge, MAANI displayed his superior power over the government and the gun, and showed that the government too would be held accountable for its lethal killings. The government was not beyond spiritual consequences nor could it successfully claim impunity. The story continued to remind people that the power has limits, despite its brutal and lethal nature. The story tells us that, despite Kolang Ket's death at the hands of government, MAANI still retains the power to sanction those who kill, including government. Government reports record Caath Obang briefly becoming a chief of the northern Nyuong after Kolang Ket's death, suggesting that the killing was not immediate. Yet even the government records did recount an elephant killing Caath while out hunting.[66]

Conclusion

Importantly, from this chapter we see both that, from the outset, the *hakuma* was experienced as incredibly and brutally violent, and also that the *hakuma*'s behaviour as it entered the communities around the Bilnyang meant that people

---

62   Interview with son of Nyaruac Kolong, Koch, 3 May 2013 (in Nuer).
63   Johnson, *Nuer Prophets*, page 272.
64   Interview with youth, Adok, Ler County, 30 April 2013 (in Nuer).
65   Interview with son of Nyaruac Kolong, Koch, 3 May 2013 (in Nuer); Johnson, *Nuer Prophets*, page 272.
66   See Johnson, *Nuer Prophets*, page 272.

equated the *hakuma* with the divine. The *hakuma* interrupted peace not only because new political economies impacted institutions of peace-making, but also because the violence of the *hakuma* made peace with the *hakuma* itself more difficult. Histories told of the nineteenth and early twentieth century in the Bilnyang are histories of the first foreign *hakuma* using guns and asymmetrical military might to conduct arbitrary violence and brutal killings while claiming impunity. The port of Meshra-el-Rek and this access to the west of Southern Sudan made the Bilnyang central to the power of the *hakuma* in the Southern Sudan. This included both foreign traders and slavers using arbitrary violence in raids to capture resources. At the end of the nineteenth century, the Anglo-Egyptian government captured control of this area but still asserted power through predatory raids on villages and displays of their military might. They also legalised their impunity. Graeber argues that such arbitrary violence with impunity is a claim to be akin to a god. South Sudanese, who observed these early, violent *hakuma*, also compared them to the gods. Early divine authorities, like the *hakuma*, killed arbitrarily with impunity.

At the same time, the *hakuma*'s claims were not unchallenged. Cosmic powers were reconfigured and reasserted to challenge the *hakuma*'s claims of impunity. The story of Kolang Ket's seizure illustrates cosmic reconfigurations after the coming of the *hakuma*. In many ways, the emergence of the prophetic idiom can be seen as part of the re-creation of culture and cosmologies to creatively refuse assertions by the *hakuma* of its power to kill with impunity. Prophets emerged as a centralising authority, but an authority that was often symbolically subservient to the existing cosmic hierarchies of the *kuar muon and baany e biith*. The story of Kolang Ket's posthumous revenge against the government official that killed him also showed how divinities were contesting government claims to be able to kill with impunity. Yet, these divine contestations were far from necessarily non-violent and, in this case, involved a fatal elephant attack. For this book, it is important to recognise the late nineteenth and early twentieth century experiences of the potential violence of both the *hakuma* and divine authorities that contested the *hakuma*.

CHAPTER 2

Sacred Authority and Judicial Peace: Peace-making during the Anglo-Egyptian Condominium

When the Anglo-Egyptian Government of Sudan moved beyond violent occupation and tried to establish their administration, cosmic contestations took new forms. The *hakuma* no longer only asserted its authority through spectacular violence and impunity identical to that of divinities, but also by making sacred previous divine authorities and their powers to make peace. By the 1920s and 1930s, the *hakuma* was no longer dominated by foreign slavers and traders, or even violent patrols by the Anglo-Egyptian government; instead, the Anglo-Egyptian government had started to try to bring administrative order to the region. At the same time, these government officials still represented continuities with foreign-backed, gun-dominated power, spatially mapped on to previous geographies of power.[1]

The government from the 1920s tried to capture into law and legal institutions peace and the priestly peace-makers. 'To be "sacred", in contrast [to being divine], is to be set apart, hedged about by customs and taboos'.[2] The government now sought to not kill divine authorities, but to hedge them in through legal institutions and the customary law. As the ultimate maker and arbitrator of the law, the *hakuma* sought to rest above these hedged-in divine authorities. The *hakuma* displayed its power over the law both through its standardisation and through the *hakuma*'s insistence that judicial redress be sought and that feuds be solved through the courts. This allowed the cosmic politics to be concealed in claims of criminality and legal technicalities.

This chapter describes the making of the legal nature of peace in South Sudan during the first half of the twentieth century. It also links this to the limiting of the power of other, non-government divine authorities by making

---

[1]   Cherry Leonardi, *Dealing with Government in South Sudan: History of Chiefship, Community and State* (James Currey, 2013).

[2]   David Graeber and Marshall Sahlins, *On Kings* (HAU Books, 2017), page 8.

Figure 2. A chief, an elder and a court clerk sit at the front of a chiefs' court hearing in Gogrial East County, Warrap State, May 2010 (Naomi Ruth Pendle).

them sacred. Among the Nuer and Dinka, priests (*kuar muon* among the Nuer and *baany e biith* among the Dinka) relied on notions of feuding and 'pollution' to create systems in which purity and, therefore, peace could be possible. They also heavily relied on cattle for compensation and sacrifice. The wars, violence and diseases that came with foreign *hakuma* resulted in the depletion of cattle and new dilemmas in peace-making. When the Anglo-Egyptian Sudan Government sought to administer the communities around the Bilnyang and connected rivers, they demanded the non-government violence be seen not as a political conflict but as a crime against the state. The government had a new legal vision of conflict and peace.

Although the Sudan government projected an image of conflicts as criminal (and a legal violation) and not political, law is always a form of politics and can be used as an instrument of the ruling class and also as a form of ideological power.[3] By the 1920s, law had already long been a cornerstone of British strategies to govern their empire.[4] Massoud has highlighted that, in the Sudans, law has been used by successive governments as a way to maintain power.[5] 'As an agent of a state's long-term policy, the rule of law can be used to win the tacit consent of the governed in a way that posing a credible threat

---

[3]   Edward Palmer Thompson, *Whigs and Hunters: The Origin of the Back Act* (London: Breviary Stuff Publications, 2013 [1975]).

[4]   Mahmood Mamdani, *Citizen and Subject: Contemporary Africa and the Legacy of Late Colonialism* (Princeton University Press, 1996).

[5]   Mark Fathi Massoud, *Law's Fragile State: Colonial, Authoritarian, and Humanitarian Legacies in Sudan* (Cambridge University Press, 2013).

of force may not'.[6] At the same time, 'law is never just an instrument, a tool available to political elites to use as they wish. It has its own rules, actors, and practices, along with the need to maintain some semblance of justice if it is to appear legitimate'.[7] Massoud describes how, by creating courts, the government created a space where people could air grievances which allowed the regime to present itself as a moderate, legitimate authority.[8] At the same time, these spaces did provide opportunities for government power to be confronted and subverted.[9]

The Condominium era is remembered by those living near the Bilnyang as having captured into *hakuma*-backed law previous ideas of peace that revolved around compensation and justice for the deceased. This legal peace drew on cultural archives and resonated with existing ideas of peace. Yet, subtle changes in rituals and meanings shifted power over peace to the *hakuma* while entrenching its legal nature.

This chapter also draws out the cosmic politics at play through the example of Nuer prophet Nyaruac Kolang and Dinka Chief Giir Thiik; these examples illustrated how the *hakuma* hedged them in and made them sacred via their incorporation in legal institutions. When Nyaruac's family finally agreed to become a chiefly family, Nyaruac became blind. This is interpreted as a physical demonstration of her declining spiritual power because of the merging of both government and divine power. Giir Thiik's power appeared to increase with his merging of the power of the *bany e bith* with that of the government chief. Yet, stories of Giir Thiik's willingness to be beheaded by government echo the stories of the previous chapter when Kolang Ket was willing to be beheaded by a *kuaar muon*. However, in the account of Giir Thiik, ultimate submission is to government.

While demanding legal and non-violent peace among South Sudanese, the *hakuma* continued to inflict violence. Violent patrols were becoming less frequent, but the government still insisted on death sentences to stop conflict. *Baany e biith* continued to push back against such government powers to kill with impunity. However, the mid-twentieth century is remembered as a time of growing *hakuma* authority and their often successful attempts at limiting (if not destroying) the powers of the previously divine.

***

6   Ibid., page 48.
7   Sally Engle Merry, 'The Rule of Law and Authoritarian Rule: Legal Politics in Sudan', *Law and Social Inquiry* 41:2 (2016), page 468.
8   Massoud, *Law's Fragile State*, page 45.
9   Leonardi, *Dealing with Government in South Sudan.*

Killing and being killed in times of conflict prompts various moral and ontological uncertainties that need to be understood and resolved if peace is made. Spiritual pollution was a central key framing in the way that killing was understood. Among the Nuer, *nueer* was (and still often is) a potentially lethal pollution that arises after transgression of divinely sanctioned prohibitions, such as killing.[10] The anthropologist Sharon Hutchinson defines *nueer* as a pollution that distinguishes between flows of blood and food that are culturally defined as negative, death-ridden and anomalous from others deemed to be properly mediated, positive and life promoting.[11] Therefore, killing did not only have consequences for the deceased and their family, but it also left the killer polluted and in need of the restoration of purity.

After killing, killers among the Nuer and Dinka would seek the help of priests (*kuar muon* among the Nuer and *baany e biith* among the Dinka) to allow the restoration of a state of purity. This would bring the priests into the peace-making role, and would make public who had carried out the killing. This also placed the priest in a position to coordinate peace-making with the aggrieved family.

In the Bilnyang, in the nineteenth century, cattle were central to priest-led peace-making. Cattle were key both for compensation and for sacrifice. Cattle compensation was necessary among Nuer and Dinka as it allowed the acquisition of a wife for the deceased. Wives were married after the exchange of bride wealth and this bride wealth was made up of contributions from family and friends, as well as from the husband himself. If the man had died, his contribution to his new wife came from the cattle paid in compensation. Posthumous marriage was important as it provided children and a lineage for the deceased. A relative would biologically father children with the wife for the deceased, allowing the deceased's legal paternity to continue and allowing his name to be securely carried into posterity.[12] Failure to secure children for

---

[10]   Edward Evans-Pritchard, *Nuer Religion* (Oxford University Press, 1956): 293–294; Sharon Hutchinson, *Nuer Dilemmas: Coping with Money, War, and the State* (University of California Press, 1996), pages 106–107; Sharon Hutchinson, '"Dangerous to eat": Rethinking Pollution States among the Nuer of Sudan', *Africa: Journal of the International African Institute* 62:4 (1992): 490–504.

[11]   Hutchinson, *Nuer Dilemmas*, page 107; Hutchinson, '"Dangerous to Eat"'; Evans-Pritchard refers to *nueer* as 'a grave sin': Evans-Pritchard, *Nuer Religion*, page 129.

[12]   Francis Mading Deng, *Customary Law in the Modern World: The Crossfire of Sudan's War of Identities* (Routledge, 2010), page 131; Godfrey Lienhardt, *Divinity and Experience: The Religion of the Dinka* (Clarendon Press, 1961), page 25; Naomi Pendle, '"The Dead Are Just to Drink From": Recycling Ideas of Revenge among the Western Dinka, South Sudan'. *Africa* 88:1 (2018): 99–121.

the deceased risked moral and spiritual condemnation for his relatives, and their unwillingness to make peace with the killer. Conversely, securing a wife and children for the deceased gave the dead a continued social presence and continuity despite death.

Cattle sacrifice was then needed as part of the completion of compensation payments. As Evans-Pritchard and Hutchinson have documented, cattle were needed in this process due to their equivalence to people.[13] After the exchange of compensation, priests would perform rituals that included the sacrifice of an ox to end the feud. Feuding Dinka families would witness the sacrifice of a young ox (*muɔr adɔɔr* or 'ox of peace', or *muɔr de yuom* or 'ox of splitting': literally, 'ox of the bone') to bring an end to the feud.[14] Before the cow died, priests would speak to the cow about why they must die – cows cannot die for no reason.[15] They would also speak over the cow threats of curses if anyone broke the peace and reignited the feud.

The power of compensation and cattle sacrifice to resolve feuds and bring peace was challenged in various ways by the coming of foreign powers. Firstly, foreign powers and their guns radically changed the nature of conflict. As discussed in the previous chapter, foreign traders and governments created a network of supporters to allow them to operate in the region. This created new divisions between those working for government and those not. At the same time, these overlapped with pre-existing ideas of identities. People fought new wars with new types of weapons. They also fought with and against different groupings.

Secondly, the shifting distribution of cattle created a class that was too poor to make peace, as we see in the example of Kolang Ket in Chapter 1. The coming of foreign *hakuma* brought new livestock diseases, and changed cattle ownership and socio-economic classes which threatened to undermine the use of cattle compensation to make peace. The poverty brought by raids, but also by new disease outbreaks, exaggerated the inability of the poor to have enough cattle to pay compensation and to make peace.

For example, from the late 1880s, rinderpest spread quickly into Southern Sudan, killing vast numbers of cattle.[16] The 1888–89 drought forced cattle,

---

13   Edward Evans-Pritchard, 'The Sacrificial Role of Cattle among the Nuer', *Africa: Journal of the International African Institute* 23:3 (1953): 181–198; Hutchinson, *Nuer Dilemmas*.

14   Jok Madut Jok, 'The Political History of South Sudan', in Timothy McKulka (ed.), *A Shared Struggle: The People and Cultures of South Sudan* (Kingdom of Denmark/Government of South Sudan/UN, 2013): 85–144.

15   Interview with local government official in Gogrial East County, May 2022.

16   John A. Rowe and Kjell Hødnebø, 'Rinderpest in the Sudan 1888–1890: The Mystery of the Missing Panzootic', *Sudanic Africa* 5 (1994): 149–78.

as well as wild game, to congregate at fewer water sources, spreading the disease quicker.[17] In eastern Sudan, the devastation from rinderpest brought new myths and changing lifestyles.[18] Among the Nuer, people described to Evans-Pritchard that, as a result of rinderpest, they reduced their herd sizes. The period before rinderpest became known as 'the life of the cattle', indicating the significance of their loss.[19] South Sudanese were creative in introducing quarantine methods to keep cattle safe, yet cattle still died in large numbers.[20]

Periods of deadly human disease also resulted in greater demands on a family's cattle, preventing their use for peace-making compensation. After the death of male family members, especially those who did not have male children, there was an expectation that surviving family members would use their families' herd to marry a wife for the deceased in order to produce children in their name and, hence, their social continuity after death. In periods of epidemics, when deaths were high, this put a significant strain on cattle to be used for marriage, bringing further poverty to the family. Smallpox was prevalent in Southern Sudan at the time.[21] While there were long histories of smallpox in the Sudan, the lack of movement between the south and the trading hubs of the north meant that Southern populations had relatively little exposure and a lack of immunity.[22] Failed inoculation schemes used by slavers and traders were exacerbating its spread. When disease spread through a family and brought significant death, the living faced a large burden in having to use their cattle to marry for the deceased.

These new experiences of cattle-less poverty made it very difficult for the poorest people to make peace. When fights occurred, revenge became increasingly the only option to avoid killing having happened with impunity. Therefore, at the time of the Anglo-Egyptian Government establishing its authority in communities surrounding the Bilnyang and connected rivers, priests were grappling with dilemmas about how to make peace possible when cattle were in decline and peace relied on cows.

[17]   Douglas Johnson, 'The Great Famine in the Sudan', in Douglas Johnson and David Anderson (eds), *Ecology of Survival: Case Studies from Northeast African History* (Lester Crook Academic, 1988): 63–64.

[18]   B. A. Lewis, *The Murle – Red Chiefs and Black Commoners* (Oxford University Press, 1972), pages 85, 186.

[19]   Edward Evans-Pritchard, *The Nuer: A Description of the Modes of Livelihood and Political Institutions of a Nilotic People* (Clarendon Press, 1940), page 66.

[20]   Evans-Pritchard, *The Nuer*, page 66; Johnson, 'The Great Famine in the Sudan', pages 63–64.

[21]   Ahmed Bayoumi, 'The History and Traditional Treatment of Smallpox in the Sudan', *Journal of Eastern African Research and Development* 6:1 (1976): 1–10.

[22]   Ibid., page 7.

Making compensation the law

The Anglo-Egyptian Sudan government claimed sovereignty over the Sudan from the very end of the nineteenth century, but it was not until the 1920s that this government actively started to engage in the administration of the regions that surround the Bilnyang and connected rivers. Government only created a permanent presence at Gogrial during the defeat of Ariathdit.[23] By this stage, the Condominium was producing detailed maps of settlements on this higher, drier, ironstone plateau to the west of the Bilnyang,[24] but the Nuer-speaking areas to the east of the Bilnyang and connected rivers were not getting much government attention. In 1931, the governor was still calling it 'an administrative no-man's land'.[25]

Government priorities included the stopping of Nuer-Dinka fighting, intra-ethnic fighting, as well as tax collection.[26] The Condominium government's earliest demands were that the government had the right to settle all grievances and that self-help justice through raiding and revenge should end.[27] Conflict was now to be seen as not only an affront to the other party but to government itself. Conflict was redesignated by the government as criminal and not political, and therefore the response was to be legal hearings and law enforcement.

After local authorities conceded the *hakuma*'s excessive displays of violent power, government officials' vision of peace was increasingly judicial. In the early years, the District Commissioner acted as arbitrator and settled disputes. For example, in the mid-1920s, Nuer travelled south to the country headquarters in Rumbek to seek the District Commissioner's interventions to settle disputes. To make the District Commissioner's task more manageable, the government appointed chiefs and established courts. By the 1930s, the Sudan government shifted to a more explicit policy of indirect rule and the government formulated its famous Southern Policy in which it would govern 'self-contained' 'racial or tribal units'.[28] The government went on to entrench the chiefs and their courts as a key part of the 'tribal structures' through which

---

[23] Zoe Cormack, 'The Making and Remaking of Gogrial: Landscape, History and Memory in South Sudan' (PhD diss., Durham University, 2014).

[24] Ordinance Survey 1912, 'The Anglo-Egyptian Sudan'.

[25] Charles A. Willis with Arthur H. Alban, *The Upper Nile Province Handbook: A Report on Peoples and Government in the Southern Sudan*, edited by Douglas H. Johnson (Oxford University Press for the British Academy, 1995 [1931]), page 3.

[26] Paul Philip Howell, *Manual of Nuer Law* (Oxford University Press, 1954), page 9.

[27] Douglas Johnson, *Nuer Prophets: A History of Prophecy from the Upper Nile in the Nineteenth and Twentieth Centuries* (Clarendon Press, 1994), page 257.

[28] Civil Secretary H. A. MacMichael, Memorandum on Southern Policy, in Civil Secretary to Southern Governors, GB-0033-SAD.485/1/3-8, 25 January 1930.

it would govern. As elsewhere in the empire, the chiefs' courts were to become a key part of the central government's control over South Sudan.[29]

Governance by chiefs became part of the government's imaginings of a series of territorialised communities around which administrative boundaries could be drawn.[30] Occasional officials explicitly recognised that this would be a social change 'away from arcane lineage-based identity and towards 'modern' territorial-based identity'.[31] Governance would be organised around provinces, districts and, within them, a series of chiefdoms. The government divided the areas around the Bilnyang and connected rivers into different districts based on their perceptions of tribal units. Over time, names, boundaries and province membership changed. Court structures were arranged to overlap with these districts, and meetings and periodic courts were held between the districts.

Making the divine sacred

To make peace through courts and local meetings, the District Commissioners needed to appoint chiefs who both had authority and respected government.[32] Colonial governments have been accused of secularising authority by replacing divine authority figures with secular figures. However, around the Bilnyang and connected rivers, divine authorities, especially *baany e biith*, but also Nuer prophets, were appointed as chiefs.

In Gogrial, District Commissioner Titherington appointed chiefs among the Rek based on what he described as 'ancestral claims to respect'.[33] These ancestral claims were not discrete from the clans of the *baany e biith*. The government found that the dominant public authorities that upheld the normative order were spiritual authorities, such as the *baany e biith*. Therefore, despite their suspicions of the *baany e biith*, they could not be ignored.[34]

For instance, the government appointed Giir Thiik as chief of the Apuk Dinka; he went on to be a powerful chief for decades. In recent interviews about Giir Thiik's appointment, various reasons are given for his selection.[35]

[29] Mamdani, *Citizen and Subject*.
[30] Zoe Cormack, 'Borders are Galaxies: Interpreting Contestations over Local Administrative Boundaries in South Sudan', *Africa* 86:3 (2016): 504–527.
[31] Ibid., page 508.
[32] Cherry Leonardi, Leben Moro, Martina Santschi and Deborah Isser, *Local Justice in South Sudan* (London: Rift Valley Institute, 2010); Leonardi, *Dealing with Government in South Sudan*.
[33] G. W. Titherington, 'The Riak Dinka of Bahe El Ghazal Province', *Sudan Notes and Records* 10 (1927): 159–209', page 165.
[34] Cormack, 'The Making and Remaking of Gogrial', page 74.
[35] Interview with elder from Pathuon East (Gogrial East, Warrap State), Yiikador,

The District Commissioner was apparently impressed by a local welfare system that Giir Thiik had instigated. Giir Thiik led a *wun mieth* – a cattle camp of milk – that allowed people who had no milk to drink milk from his herd on the condition that they also contributed to the herd's care. At the same time, part of the reason for Giir Thiik's large herd was his divine authority and the power of his clan. Giir Thiik was from a clan of *baany e biith* and he held significant divine powers himself. He is still remembered as a *bany e bith* and not just a chief. The neighbouring chiefdoms also saw the appointment of *baany e biith* or close relatives of *baany e biith* as chiefs. The chiefs appointed under Giir Thiik were also all from 'bitter' (spiritually powerful) families with the exception of one sub-chief who had worked closely with and been armed by the slave traders.

The appointment of Giir Thiik as a government chief elevated his own power and that of his clan. The practice of the chiefdom being passed down within the family allowed the capture of this power within the clan, just as the divine powers of the *baany e biith* were a preserve of the clan. The chiefdom gave this clan the backing not only of divinity but also, now, the power of the gun and the force of the government.

In the western Nuer, in the 1920s, the first District Commissioner (Fergusson) recognised the prophets' authority.[36] Describing the Prophet of Teng, based in Ler, Fergusson said: 'His word is absolute law and it is indeed fortunate that we have been lucky enough to make a favourable impression on him'.[37] This recognition meant that many of the earliest chiefs in the western Nuer were prophets or others with divine sources of authority. Yet, as discussed in the previous chapter, Nuer opposition to government prompted suspicion and suppression of some prophets.

At the same time, for decades, the government ignored the most powerful prophetess in Western Nuer District. Following Kolang Ket's death in 1925, his daughter, Nyaruac Kolang, was seized by MAANI. As she was a woman, when the Condominium government sought pre-existing authority figures, they overlooked Nyaruac.[38] Johnson attributes her superior divine power to her ability to be separated from and ignored by the powers of government.[39]

For government chiefs, Nyaruac's detachment from the chiefs' court system was a problem. Those facing punishment from the chiefs' courts would run to Nyaruac for sanctuary and protection. The government chiefs feared Nyaruac

---

April 2012 (in Dinka); interview with grandson of Giir Thiik, Luonyaker (Gogrial East, Warrap State), May 2012 (in Dinka).

36 Ibid.
37 As quoted by Johnson, *Nuer Prophets*, page 260.
38 Johnson, *Nuer Prophets*.
39 Ibid.

and so did not pursue those accused into the sanctuary offered by Nyaruac. In the nineteenth century, the power of the gun had offered impunity and sanctuary from divine law (in the case of Kolang and Jiath); in the early twentieth century the power of the divinity was now offering impunity and sanctuary from government law and the gun.

The government chief in the area persistently insisted that Nyaruac and her family take the chieftaincy to end this effective impunity. Nyaruac rejected the offer of government power for a long time. She feared that if the powers of MAANI were merged with that of government, they would be too powerful to ever separate. Nyaruac finally allowed her prophetic family to be given the government chiefdom and her brother became chief.[40]

At the same time, the merging of the powers of the divine with the powers of the *hakuma* did threaten to reduce their power. This is partly as it reduced divine power to the sacred. In their *Divine Kings*, Graeber and Shahlins argue that reducing a divine authority figure (such as a king) to being 'sacred' restrains sovereign power in space by limiting his total power to being present in certain times and spaces.[41] As divine authorities become sacred, they become more limited in their ability to carry out arbitrary violence with impunity, reducing them from divine, sovereign actors to those who are merely sacred.

The Sudan government through indirect rule contained the divine authorities that it appointed within broader, government-initiated institutions that hedged in the divine through remade customs and taboos, as well as the rhythms of the legal system. As chiefs, the *baany e biith* and Nuer prophets had to implement the law as sanctioned by government. Ultimately, the *hakuma*, and not their own divine power to curse, backed up their rulings. So, they were subsumed within the legal systems, and their divine powers were clipped; any increase in power was dependent on their guns and the government.

South Sudanese in these communities saw this merging of government and divine powers in such terms. Among the Nuer, people understood that the eventual merging of divine and government powers in the family of Nyaruac limited her divine powers and, ultimately, reduced her powers overall. Soon after her brother became chief, Nyaruac became blind. The confluence of events meant that her blindness was widely understood as representative of her loss of power and knowledge to the logics of government rule.[42]

---

[40]   Naomi Pendle, 'Contesting the Militarization of the Places Where They Met: The Landscapes of the Western Nuer and Dinka (South Sudan)'. *Journal of Eastern African Studies* 11:1 (2017): 64–85.

[41]   Graeber and Sahlins, *On Kings*, page 4.

[42]   Interview with elder from Koch, Bentiu PoC, 2018.

Dinka also recognised the potential loss of power through proximity to government. Another story is still sometimes told about Giir Thiik's appointment as chief. The District Commissioner apparently asked if anyone among the Apuk was willing to be beheaded in exchange for their son being given the chiefdom. Giir Thiik apparently volunteered. His demonstrated bravery and respect of government prompted the government to appoint him chief instead of beheading him.[43] This account of Giir Thiik's appointment resembles but reconfigures the story of Kolang Ket's divine blessing as retold in the previous chapter. In the story of Kolang Ket, while Kolang had toyed with seeking protection and remaking the moral order through men empowered by the gun, he eventually submits to the *kuaar muon* and existing hierarchies of cosmic authority by offering himself to be beheaded by a *kuaar muon*. This results in the latter blessing Kolang and him being seized by the divinity MAANI. The people of the Apuk graze their cattle near the rivers of the Bilnyang and, over the four decades between Kolang's seizure and Giir Thiik's appointment as chief, they would have heard Kolang's story. In retelling this story of Giir Thiik's willingness to be beheaded, people have seen the resonance of submission to authority through the personal sacrifice of offering oneself to be beheaded. Yet, for Giir Thiik forty years later, his ultimate submission was to the power of the *hakuma* and not to the cosmic hierarchies of his priesthood. This difference is highlighted in the retelling of such a similar tale.

The appointment of *baany e biith* as chiefs restrained their powers to the space and procedures of the courts, making them sacred and less divine. For example, *baany e biith* who became chiefs did not usually themselves threaten curses to enforce truth-telling. Instead, the courts would often send parties to other *baany e biith* who were not chiefs in order for them to evoke truth-telling. For example, Giir Thiik would send parties to Muordit Dhel – a relative and a *bany e bith* – if people needed to swear oaths or participate in blood sacrifices. Plus, their demands and conditions of peace were increasingly subsumed within expectations of the customary law, and their power was reliant on government appointment.

Government also now provided the sanction behind the law. Historically, the *baany e biith* had not needed the power of the gun to enforce their rulings and uphold moral norms. They had direct powers to curse and other means of inflicting punishment. For example, one *bany e bith* in what is now Tonj North is remembered for his power over bees. Deng Ngor was the *bany e bith* of a cattle camp and even the bees in a hive in the cattle camp were said to obey his authority. Deng commanded the bees to stay peacefully with people and cattle in the camp. At the same time, he warned people that the bees would attack if anyone violated the rules and regulations of the camp. As people have since described, the bees were Deng's 'police'.[44]

Cattle compensation and sacred priests

In chiefs' courts, cattle compensation became legally entrenched as the dominant means by which cases were settled between feuding parties. Government officials did argue over whether violent crimes should still be solved through compensation. Yet, officials quickly recognised the significance of cattle for settling grievances. Major Titherington described the Dinka judicial system as founded on 'equality before the law, and the possession of cattle by all'.[45]

Later, officials with anthropological training highlighted the need among the Nuer for cattle so that 'the fundamental principle that a deceased person must be "married a wife" so that her children, begotten by some kinsman on his behalf, will bear his name, belong to his lineage, and may concern themselves with his interests in posterity'.[46] The exchange of cattle embedded in the law recognition of the spiritual demand for a posthumous wife. Government officials in the 1950s were explicit about this reasoning and recognised that blood wealth needed to be equivalent to bride wealth.[47] Therefore, the continuity of cattle compensation in the courts implicitly embedded recognition of the divine and divinely sanctioned norms into the chiefs' courts. Court-enforced cattle compensation both explicitly gave cattle to the *kuar muon* and the *baany e biith*, recognising their authority over blood,[48] and also upheld the cosmological logics that cattle were needed to make peace by preventing death. This, in itself, allowed these priests to construct a continuity in their monopoly over blood.

'The reason why the murder case is brought back to the *baany e biith* is because of the need to swear that the feud will not be reopened. Blood is never managed by the government or chief; it is only the *bany e bith* that manages'.[49]

At the same time, the role of the *kuar muon* and *baany e biith* in ending the feud increasingly became ceremonial and sacred, and not divine. When compensation was fully paid, these divine authority figures were not expected to question the chiefs' courts' expectation that full compensation would automatically end the feud. Although these figures threatened to curse those who

---

[44] Interview with male elder 1, Gogrial, May 2019, in Dinka.

[45] Titherington, 'The Riak Dinka', page 167.

[46] Howell, *Manual of Nuer Law*, page 41.

[47] Ibid., page 63.

[48] Letter from District Commissioner of Zeraf to Governor of Upper Nile Province, Zeraf District, 9 March 1940, SSNA 66.G.3.

[49] Interview with man in Gogrial, May 2018, in Dinka.

fought and reopened a feud, the government would also use punitive force against anyone fighting. While the *kuar muon* and *baany e biith* continued to have a visible, ceremonial role, their political power to contest the judicially established outcome faded. They became sacred and confined by ceremony, more than being divine.

As Hutchinson has highlighted among the Nuer, another significant problem was that both the government-backed courts and customary law also fixed the number of cattle paid for specific offences, thus standardising the number of cattle paid over time. This prevented flexibility in blood wealth that was historically needed to ensure that blood wealth was adequate for bride wealth to allow the marriage of a posthumous wife. The government also often demanded cattle from among the blood wealth, reducing that available for bride wealth.[50]

Expanding jurisdictions

An expression of the control of the law by the *hakuma* was the standardisation of the law and compensation payments. By the 1940s, standardisation of compensation payments became a big part of the government's intervention through the courts. While chiefs' courts made a lack of peace a breach of the law within chiefdoms, chiefs' meetings became a key method for government to assert peace between chiefdoms or 'tribes'. Government officials 'constituted meetings as opportunities for the elites of the local state, particularly chiefs, to question, debate, and at times challenge government policies'.[51] These meetings absorbed these judicial notions of governance and peace; they would often spend a considerable amount of time amending the details of common laws, as well as applying these laws to specifically problematic cases. Therefore, the government enforced a clear, judicial logic of peace.

The Sudan government's authority across much larger geographic areas than pre-Condominium authority figures did create new opportunities for peace-making. For instance, by the 1940s in the western Dinka and Nuer, the Sudan government had formalised various cross-ethnic border courts and annual chiefs' meetings.[52] Similar policies in Upper Nile allowed Nuer to

50   Pendle, '"The Dead are Just to Drink From"'.
51   Cherry Leonardi, 'Points of Order? Local Government Meetings as Negotiation Tables in South Sudanese History', *Journal of East African Studies* 9:4 (2015), page 665.
52   Douglas Johnson, 'Judicial Regulation and Administrative Control: Customary Law and the Nuer, 1898–1954', *The Journal of African History* 27:1 (1986): 59–78; Interview with man in his twenties, Greater Rumbek, May 2012 (in Dinka); Interview with Town Chief, Panyijar, May 2012 (in Nuer).

speak of their relationship with the Dinka as only an intermittent '*ter*' (feud) as opposed to a '*kor*' (war).[53]

In the 1930s and 1940s, a persistent puzzle for government officials was how to deal with cases between 'tribes'.[54] Government attempts to standardise compensation rates within a district often meant that they ended up varying with compensation rates of other districts.[55] Some District Commissioners were vocal about the realities that relations and compensation rates were often more similar with groups from other districts than within the districts.[56] So standardising rates within the district increased inter-district differences and complexities in building peace. At the same time, government officials tended not to blame government action but a lack of pre-government peaceful conflict resolution mechanisms for inter-ethnic divisions.[57]

The government perceived problems in different cattle compensation being used for different purposes. For example, letters were exchanged between District Commissioners in Upper Nile over a case in the 1930s of a Nuer killing a Dinka man and then running to his *kuaar muon*. At the time, the Nuer gave twenty cattle as blood money including one cow for the *kuaar muon* and one for the chief for collecting the compensation. The Dinka exchanged twenty cattle, but an additional cow was given to the *bany e bith* for collecting the compensation and an additional bull was slaughtered at the final peace ceremony. The decision was made to compensate according to the identity of the aggrieved.[58]

By the 1940s, the government was starting to standardise customary law across wider areas. This was to stop conflict and build peace. The governor of Upper Nile (B.A. Lewis) at the time hoped he could also use the harmonisation of the customary laws to make a Nuer-wide confederation and political identity, securing the Nuer a louder voice in Sudanese politics.[59] Speaking at a meeting of District Commissioners and chiefs in 1947, Lewis said: 'I told you two years ago at Fangak that it was necessary for the Nuer to work together and speak with one voice. Since then there has been much talk in

---

53   Douglas Johnson, *The Root Causes of Sudan's Civil Wars: Peace or Truce* (James Currey, 2003), page 171.
54   'Correlation of Customary Compensation Payments as between Different Tribal Divisions', SSNA UNP 66.G.3.
55   Report on Tribal Meeting Held At Fangak Between 27.8.41 and 3.9.41, SSNA UNP 66.G.3.
56   Letter from D. C. Western Nuer to Governor UNP, 12.3.42, S. S. Metemis, SSNA UNP 66.G.3.12.
57   'Correlation of Customary Compensation Payments'.
58   Letter from District Commissioner of Zeraf to Governor of Upper Nile Province, Zeraf District, 9 March 1940, SSNA 66.G.3.
59   Johnson, 'Judicial Regulation and Administrative Control', page 76.

Khartoum about starting one Council for the whole Sudan. The Nuer must be represented in any such Council'.[60]

Unifying the court system in the Nuerlands and creating a common Nuer customary law was seen as the efficient, affordable 'machinery' for forming this confederation.[61] District Commissioners did not agree on whether 'pockets of variant law' should be allowed to remain.[62] It was concluded that standardisation should not be enforced[63] but that there should be a standardisation of general principles.[64] Standardisation of Nuer customary law also provided opportunity for government review and change of the law based on its own ideas of equity[65], despite the ongoing rhetoric of preservation of tradition.

As with the Nuer laws of Fangak, Wathalel was presented as a static, bound body of law that hoped to conjure a new imaginary of a common Dinka moral and legal community, and to increase conflict resolution between groups. The laws reflected a common government sentiment at the time that each ethnic group should be subject to its own laws. One District Commissioner explained in 1946:

> The most important thing about any new warrant is that it should give legal recognition to the universal Dinka feeling that Dinka law, though liable to minor local variations, is essentially one and that as a corollary a Dinka judge's opinion is legally valid anywhere in Dinkaland and not only in his own court area.[66]

Dinka judges had the ability to sit on different courts in different Dinka districts due to the commonality of the law, emphasising the common legal standards and moral community of the Dinka. Yet, Wathalel was never 'simply a set of rules and sanctions, but a contextually defined process, involving flexibility, negotiation and reinterpretation of a dynamic body of knowledge'.[67]

Local memory attributes Wathalel to a specific incident of government pressure for conflict resolution. Elopement between the Dinka of Tonj and Dinka of Agar had prompted violent conflict. Variance in compensation between these groups prevented ease of judicial redress for elopement.

---

60 Nuer District Commissioners and Chiefs Meeting, July 1947, SAD.767/6/3.
61 Howell, 1943, SAD.68/4/1-36.
62 Ibid.
63 Memorandum of Nuer Laws and Customary Payments Discussed by Chiefs. SAD.767/2/31.
64 Howell, *Manual of Nuer Law*, page 1.
65 Memorandum of Nuer Laws and Customary Payments Discussed by Chiefs, SAD.767/2/31.
66 A Court Warrant, February 1946, SAD.767/8/45.
67 Leonardi et al., *Local Justice in South Sudan*, page 5.

Wathalel constructed a common code and levels of compensation between these groups. In the context of chiefs' meetings in the 1940s, the content of the common Dinka law was agreed in a dialogue between the government and the chiefs. The chiefs' courts continued to apply varied rates in practice, but their reference to Wathalel became a recognition of government and court authority over conflict.

In the Bilnyang, as other parts of South Sudan, social interactions had never been ethnically bounded. In the early 1940s, the governor of Upper Nile was still pushing for District Commissioners to standardise rates within their districts.[68] Elsewhere in Southern Sudan, the solution posited by the District Commissioners was often to standardise customary payments across an even wider area.[69] Yet, standardising Nuer-Dinka rates between Bahr el Ghazal and Upper Nile was not posited. Instead, District Commissioners in Bentiu and Gogrial agreed that the aggressor had to pay compensation at the rate current in the complainant's section. These different compensation rates between communities made these communities into different legal communities. As peace was increasing through legal channels and institutions, the lack of flexibility in compensation that would allow case-by-case legal unity made it harder for peace to be realised.

At the time, blood money among the Dinka was thirty cattle and among the Nuer, forty to fifty cattle.[70] This meant that, if a Dinka was killed, only thirty cattle were owed in compensation, and if a Nuer was killed, fifty cattle were owed. To 'stop Nuer from rating Dinka life cheaper than their own' the government also enforced a fine of ten or twenty cattle when a Dinka was killed by a Nuer.[71] This also ensured a significant financial benefit for the government. At other times, the government reduced compensation rates. For example, in Nuer areas, they claimed to have reduced it from forty to twenty head of cattle.[72]

[68]   Letter from C. G. Davies (Governor Upper Nile) to District Commissioner of Western Nuer, 13 April 1942, SNA 66.G.3.13.
[69]   Report on Tribal Meeting Held at Fangak between 27.8.41 and 3.9.41, SSNA UNP 66.G.3; 'Correlation of Customary Compensation Payments as between Different Tribal Divisions', SSNA UNP 66.G.3.
[70]   Letter from D. C. Western Nuer to Governor UNP, 12.3.42, S. S. Metemis, SSNA UNP 66.G.3.12.
[71]   Ibid.
[72]   'Correlation of Customary Compensation Payments as between Different Tribal Divisions', SSNA UNP 66.G.3.

The *Hakuma*'s impunity to kill

With the excuse of peace-making or maintaining law, the government continued to claim the right to kill with impunity. The *hakuma* was no longer to be imagined as a party in the conflict but was instead, through the courts, able to naturalise itself as beyond legal and moral sanction and capable of making this order. Individuals and tribal groups were forced to negotiate peace, but government violence was not a violation of peace and so not the focus of peace discussions.

The courts ordered compensation. Yet, sometimes this compensation was not enough. Cattle compensation was standardised. As Hutchinson has previously highlighted, this prevented flexibility in blood wealth that was historically needed to ensure that blood wealth was adequate for bride wealth to allow the marriage of a posthumous wife.[73] The government also often demanded cattle from among the blood wealth, reducing that available for bride wealth.[74] Therefore, a family, even if there was compensation, might still not be willing to split the bone and accept peace if the demands of their dead could not be met through marriage. Often, at best, compensation would only delay revenge to the next generation.[75]

At the same time, aggrieved families were now bound by threat of government force to accept compensation. The government issued violent, punitive measures against those who broke the blanket government peace. Those who engaged in violent conflict were also confronted with government violence. The government tried to criminalise those who inflicted conflict. At the same time, government actions were often interpreted not as those of a neutral force but as part of the cycles of revenge. The government was sometimes seen as taking sides in a feud. For example, Kolang Ket interpreted government actions as siding with the Dinka when they tried to stop raids from his area.[76] The government did not always succeed in establishing itself as a neutral actor.

Yet, government enforcement of peace via violence was not uncontested. When I was researching near Tonj, one famous example of early Condominium attempts to make peace was often recited. The story goes that some of the first British officials in the area set up a court in an area now known as Madol. It was a court in the grazing lands around the rivers and that met intermittently to solve cases between the Luac Dinka and the Haak Nuer. The first Luac

---

73 Hutchinson, *Nuer Dilemmas*; Pendle, '"The Dead are Just to Drink From"'.
74 Pendle, '"The Dead are Just to Drink From"'.
75 Sharon Hutchinson and Naomi Pendle, 'Violence, Legitimacy and Prophecy: Nuer Struggles with Uncertainty in South Sudan', *American Ethnologist* 42:3 (2015): 415–430.
76 Johnson, *Nuer prophets.*

Dinka found guilty in Madol had raided and killed a Haak Nuer man. His sentence was to be hanged from a tree in Madol. His home community objected.[77]

At the time, there was one tree in the area suitable to carry out a hanging. The night before the man was due to be hanged, the *bany e bith* is said to have cursed this tree. By the morning the tree had died and withered and a hanging there became impossible. The execution later took place in Wau.

Conclusion

By the 1920s and 1930s, the cosmic politics of peace was taking new, but not necessarily less violent, forms. As elsewhere in its empire, British colonial officials sought to use law as a tool of governance, and the law was imposed through violence or the threat of violence. Through the law, the *hakuma* claimed its authority to kill with impunity. Death sentences were introduced for those who reopened feuds or who engaged in conflict. The *hakuma*'s legal peace was a physically and lethally violent peace, but a violence that the *hakuma* tried to limit to only being implemented by itself. *Baany e biith* continued to contest government power to kill with impunity, even by killing trees where government hangings were going to take place. Yet, ultimately the government's militarised might allowed it to insist on legal peace – a 'peace' that permitted its own lethal violence but not the lethal violence of others.

Importantly these decades also cemented the primacy of law and the inclusion of compensation in the making of peace. Peace was still made when purity was restored through the exchange of cattle. Yet, purity now involved a form of legal compliance. To not accept peace was now an illegal act; conflict became a technical case for the law, and not a political negotiation between parties.

The implications for cosmic politics in the Bilnyang's communities was the hedging in of divine authorities by making them subordinate to the customary law and legal institutions. Divine authorities lost control over the boundaries and occurrence of war or peace, and instead became restricted by standardised law. The government demonstrated its control over the law both through the standardisation of the law, and also through its insistence on the accepting of compensation through legal institutions. The histories of Nyuaruac Kolang and Giiir Thiik both narrate a local understanding of the government weakening divine power not through direct violent opposition but through recognition and co-opting of this divine power. The *hakuma*, in Graeber's words, was making the divine 'sacred' by making divine authorities subject to the law.

---

[77]   Interview with Dinka elder, Makuac (Warrap State), 11 March 2013 (in Dinka) in Pendle, 'Contesting the Militarization of the Places Where they Met'.

PART II

Negotiating Peace

Regulating the Proliferation of Divine Power: Wars 1980s–2000s

Chapter 3 is a fast introduction to the wars of the 1960s and 1980s–2000s that were fought by Southern rebels against the Sudan government. The chapter provides a brief introduction to this time when the *hakuma* (the broad government/socio-political sphere, including foreign traders and slavers) went to war with itself, and describes the involvement in these wars by people around the Bilnyang. The chapter then moves on to explore the implications of the wars for the cosmic polity and answers this question largely by focusing on western Dinka. The 1960s and particularly the 1980s and 2000s saw new scales of physical violence and new patterns of violence with more people wielding lethal weapons. This has implications for the power and ability of divine authorities. Yet, the real story of this period is the continued attention and legitimacy of the divine authorities despite the divine claims of the *hakuma*. New free divinities and *baany e biith* creatively refused their irrelevance through the refashioning and reapplication of cultural and cosmological norms. At the same time, cosmic politics continued between these divine authorities, as well as with government.

The chapter starts by highlighting how, in these communities, *baany e biith* actively refused the Sudan government's developmentalist agenda, politically aligning with some of the frustrations that caused Anya-Nya rebellion against the Sudan government beginning in the 1960s, before which there were protests in the 1950s. The Sudan government was reluctant to admit that the Anya-Nya were active and that the war had come to Bahr el Ghazal (the northwestern third of Southern Sudan including to the west of Bilnyang) and they coded Anya-Nya violence as criminal to dismiss their claims of war. However, the rebels drew on moral norms around revenge to contest the government's ability to violently and lethally enforce the law with impunity. When peace was made in 1972, Anya-Nya forces were absorbed into government, and this placed people from the clans of the *baany e biith* in government in Wau. There was ambiguity over whether these authorities were still caught in cosmological hierarchies of the villages. Divinely seized authorities creatively remade rituals to assert the continued authority of *Nhialic* (the supreme creator God) over those officials in the town.

The 1980s–2000s provided an even larger conundrum in cosmic politics. The Sudan People's Liberation Army (SPLA) rebellion against the Sudan government from 1983 brought a proliferation of guns and the threat of their potential to kill with impunity. These guns democratised divine-like powers by giving so many people the power to kill and to implicitly claim impunity. However, existing divine authorities continued to contest impunity and the associated impossibilities of peace even as the war continued. These decades also saw new interpretative labour from the *hakuma* about the existence of pollution in government wars, and the connected relevance of the priesthoods. At the same time, norms around the priesthood were creatively remade to assert their continued relevance and centrality.

The chapter finishes with a reflection on the proliferation of new free divinities during these war years. This includes discussion of MABIORDIT and MAGOTDIT who provided new divine protection. Despite the vivid displays of the guns' powers, people sought out divine help and protection, creatively remaking understandings of the divine to better fit contemporary social groupings and militarised demands. At the same time, while MABIORDIT and MAGOTDIT asserted themselves as part of existing cosmic hierarchies, their inclusivity of those beyond the *bany e bith clans*, and their exclusive focus on the cattle camp, remade cultures to resemble the new political focus on the military power of the cattle camp. These free divinities had the potential to challenge the power of the *baany e biith*. The priests used an eclectic variety of strategies to co-opt and contest divine-like powers to absorb new free divinities into existing cosmic hierarchies.

A war of the *hakuma*

'They called the *baany e biith* to stop the railway construction'.[1]

As elsewhere in Africa, the post-Second-World-War era brought a shift in the emphasis of the colonial metropole in favour of development in the colonies.[2] The new energy of the Sudan government for economic and political development was also driven by the shift in London's policy to favour Sudan's rapid independence from British and Egyptian rule.[3] Yet, this development

---

[1]   Interview with chief, Luonyaker, Gogrial, May 2019, in Dinka.

[2]   This resonates with other colonial policies in the 1940s across Africa. Frederick Cooper, *Africa Since 1940: The Past of the Present* (Cambridge University Press, 2002); H. A. Morrice, 'The Development of Sudan Communications', *Sudan Notes and Records* 30:1 (1949): 1–38.

[3]   Douglas Johnson, *The Root Causes of Sudan's Civil Wars: Peace or Truce* (James Currey, 2003), page 25.

was not necessarily in support of the needs of most of the country. At independence in 1956, the new Sudan government was run by an elite empowered by previous decades of cotton production in the north, and without a need for populist support from the south or other peripheries.[4] The Sudan government did continue to pursue developmentalist projects, yet they continued a prime focus on development for the benefit of the riverine centre near the Sudanese capital, Khartoum. Government plans for construction of the Jonglei Canal are a clear example; through the canal's construction, the government in Khartoum planned to increase the Nile flow in northern Sudan by draining the swamps upon which millions of Southern Sudanese depended.[5]

The railway into Southern Sudan was an example of development spending in the south which was seen as primarily for the benefits of urban areas in the north, both by supplying northern cities with food and by increasing national exports. The aim of the railway was to start moving millet, groundnuts, oilseed, rice, timber, livestock and 'tropical produce' from Bahr el Ghazal north by train.[6] By 1958 the Khartoum government had secured foreign funding and started work to expand the railway system including the construction of a southern extension to Wau.[7] Railways, compared to roads and rivers, are a more centrally controlled transport infrastructure.[8]

The relevance for people in Gogrial of the railway to Wau was both their proximity to Wau and the question of whether the railway would run through Gogrial before reaching Wau. In the end, the railway to Wau was built through Aweil. Elders in Gogrial remember officials visiting in the 1950s to see if this was a preferable route for the railway.[9] They even remember them bringing sections of railway track to help their explorations. When discussing this with people in Gogrial in 2018 there were mixed feelings whether Gogrial would have benefited from the railway. Chiefs retold accounts of chiefs in Gogrial in the 1950s seeing the railway as a threat. They could have realised that the railways would facilitate a predatory exploitation of Southern resources for northern cities. Yet, specifically, the chiefs are remembered as fearing that the

---

4   Edward Thomas, *South Sudan: A Slow Liberation* (Zed Books, 2015), page 170.
5   Ibid.
6   International Bank for Reconstruction and Development, *Appraisal of the Development Program of the Sudan Railways*, World Bank Documents, pages 6, 19.
7   Ibid., page 16.
8   Peter Woodward, 'Review of *City of Steel and Fire – A Social History of Atbara, Sudan's Railway Town (1906–1984)* by Ahmad Alawad Sikainga', *Annales d'Éthiopie* 20 (2004): 281–283; Ahmad Alawad Sikainga, *City of Steel and Fire – A Social History of Atbara, Sudan's Railway Town (1906–1984)* (James Currey, 2002).
9   Interview with two elders in Gogrial, June 2018.

railways could bring social and moral rupture; they were unsure they wanted things of government so close to their homes.

Divine authority figures were part of the contestations against the northern government. To contest these plans, *baany e biith* were called to stop the railway construction. After the *baany e biith* made multiple sacrifices, the engineers moved the railway route away from Gogrial and to Aweil. The lack of railway in Gogrial cemented the chiefs' and *baany e biith*'s authority both by an apparent display of the latter's authority over government decisions, and by reducing the presence of government (through the lack of railway) in Gogrial.[10] The *baany e biith*'s protest against this government decision also demonstrated moral and spiritual backing for such resistance.

The push-back by South Sudanese against the Khartoum government did not only come from divine authority figures. Southern Sudanese who were part of the broad sphere of the *hakuma* itself in the end became the main opposition, and the *hakuma* itself divided. Southern complaints that were mounting against the Sudan government were often explicitly about a lack of representation and access to government power. Southern members of the *hakuma* protested against their own lack of representation and eventually violently rebelled. On the 18 August 1955, soldiers in the barracks in Torit (south Southern Sudan) had mutinied. Soldiers in other barracks across the south followed, and many hundreds of people were killed. The following eight years were a period of growing uncertainty and violence in Southern Sudan.[11] The new Sudan government regime of General Ibrahim Abboud from 1958 brought increased tensions between Southern Sudan's educated elite and the ruling powers in Khartoum.[12] In 1963, on the anniversary of the Torit Mutiny, an armed group formed, championing the liberation of Southern Sudan and called itself 'Anya-Nya'.

The Anya-Nya rebels were spatially centred in the Equatoria region, and the Sudan government was reluctant to admit that the Anya-Nya war included significant support in areas around the Bilnyang. Anti-government activity was often played down. For example, in 1952, during national strikes, the crew of the S.R.S. Tamai (then on District Service near Bentiu) and the workers building the Bentiu School participated in strikes.[13] The District Commissioner described the effect as minimal and limited to the staff of central government

---

[10]   Interview with man in Gogrial, June 2018, in Dinka.

[11]   Øystein Rolandsen, 'A False Start: Between War and Peace in the Southern Sudan, 1956–62', *The Journal of African History* 52:1 (2011): 105–123.

[12]   Øystein Rolandsen, 'Civil War Society? Political Processes, Social Groups and Conflict Intensity in the Southern Sudan, 1955–2005' (PhD diss., University of Oslo, 2010).

[13]   Letter to Commissioner of Labour (Khartoum) from M.Z. Amara for District

departments working in the district. For the District Commissioner, the strikes at this stage were not a problem for remote areas such as Ler or Bentiu. At the same time, to the west, there was enough concern for government officials to close schools across Gogrial and Tonj during 1952–53.[14]

For people in Gogrial, the common route into the *hakuma* blurred the line between the powers of the *hakuma* and the powers of the *baany e biith*, raising new cosmological questions. In the mid-twentieth century in Gogrial, the main route into the social sphere of *hakuma* was through a school education. Initially church-run schools offered an education to a select few Southern Sudanese. Missionaries first accessed Southern Sudan in the mid-nineteenth century, making use of access routes opened by merchants, and even trading in ivory to fund their missionary work.[15] The global Catholic Church leadership even became concerned about the entanglement of the missionaries and merchants.[16] Yet, this entanglement from the earliest days meant that many Southern Sudanese associated churches with the broad spheres of the *hakuma*. During the Condominium period, the churches were reliant on the Sudan government's permission to operate[17] and, in Gogrial in the 1920s, District Commissioner Major Titherington urged the Verona Fathers to open a mission in Kuajok to help pacify the area.[18] Cormack highlights that the Fathers had already been making plans for this move and had recognised Kuajok's significance as a meeting place of important clans.[19] At this time, churches became closely associated with education as the first schools in Southern Sudan were run by churches; from the mid-1920s, these were often funded by government. Only in the late 1940s did the government itself start to run schools in the south. Schools in Gogrial in the twenty-first century are still called '*pan abun*' – 'home of the priest'. This created an enduring association between the *hakuma*, the church and education.

Commissioner, Western Nuer District, Bentiu, 20 March 1952, SSNA UNP 37.B.10, page 14.

[14] Interview with Chief Morris Ngor Ater, Mayen Rual (Gogrial State), 31 July 2017.

[15] Roland Werner, William Anderson and Andrew Wheeler, *Day of Devastation, Day of Contentment: The History of the Sudanese Church across 2000 Years* (Paulines Publications Africa, 2000), pages 139–141.

[16] Ibid., page 139.

[17] Francis Mading Deng and M. W. Daly, *Bonds of Silk: Human Factor in the British Administration of the Sudan* (Michigan State University Press, 1990), page 174; William L. Cleveland and Martin Bunton, 'A History of the Modern Middle East', 4th edn (Westview Press, 2009), pages 105–106.

[18] Werner et al., *Day of Devastation*, page 224.

[19] Zoe Cormack, 'The Making and Remaking of Gogrial: Landscape, History and Memory in South Sudan' (PhD diss., Durham University, 2014), page 81.

The Verona Fathers in Kuajok started a school, but there was initially a lack of local popular demand and the children attending church schools were from further afield. They also gained some popularity with people and clans that lacked power: church and education offered an opportunity to challenge existing class structures in which they had been excluded. However, over time, District Commissioners put pressure on the chiefs to send children to school so that they could gain the education needed to be court clerks.[20] The Fathers promoted their education by sending salt home with their pupils during the school holidays, salt being expensive and hard to obtain at the time.[21] Those who were educated gained access both to baptism and to government employment.

School blurred the line between the divine authority of the *hakuma* and of other divinities. By the 1940s, many of those who went to school were from families of chiefs. As the spiritually empowered families of *baany e biith* overlayed with the families of the chiefs, many of those who were educated and became part of the *hakuma*, especially in Gogrial, were also connected to the powers of the *baany e biith*. This gave rise to questions of whether these government figures from the families of the *baany e biith* ultimately gained power from, and were accountable to, the *hakuma* or *Nhialic* (creator God). In Kuajok, the place of the mission and the school also blurred the *hakuma*–divinity line as the place was associated with three 'bitter' *bany e bith* clans.[22] Furthermore, church historians highlight how the Catholic missionaries of the early 1900s saw the Dinka religion as compatible with Christian faith. For example, Father Nebel, equated GARANG and ABUK (Dinka figures from creation) to the biblical Adam and Eve, and he discussed the similarities between DENG (a divinity that seizes prophets) and Jesus.[23] Yet, a significant theological shift was the promise of resurrection after death and immortality through that resurrection rather than through future generations.[24]

At the same time, there remained competition between the church and *baany e biith*. A Church historian, Nikkel, retells Father Nebel's experience with a *bany e bith* (probably Giir Thiik – discussed in Chapter 2) when he crossed the River Jur. The chief *bany e bith* forbade Father Nebel from shooting, asserting his superior power over this area. In turn, Father Nebel asserted that he had 'come to reveal the Word of God to everybody and to teach them to write' and that he had authority to shoot animals for meat on this land. Two

[20]   Mark R. Nikkel, *Dinka Christianity: The Origins and Development of Christianity among the Dinka of Sudan with Special Reference to the Songs of Dinka Christians* (Paulines Publications Africa, 2001), pages 176, 225.

[21]   Ibid., page 176.

[22]   Interview with man in Gogrial, July 2018, in Dinka.

[23]   Werner et al., *Day of Devastation*, page 226.

[24]   Ibid., page 227.

antelopes then appeared that he shot. The appearance of the antelope seemed to empirically demonstrate the Father's superior power. Yet, in the story, Father Nebel goes on to give the *bany e bith* the liver, to make a peaceful relationship.[25] Alternatively, local histories focus on a different competitive moment. People recount how missionaries and government wanted to arrest Giir Thiik. The government officials put him in a car to take him to prison in Wau. When Giir Thiik entered the car, the car would not move. When he was taken out of the car, the car would move again. Eventually they were said to have accepted his powers.[26] This directly parallels the story of the arrest of Nuer prophet Kolang Ket by the Sudan government in the 1920s. Kolang had been arrested by a local government official and was being taken to prison in Malakal via a boat from Adok Port. When Kolang was in the boat, the boat would no longer move.[27] At the same time, the government and church recognition of Giir Thiik's authority and his ability to preserve locally his status allowed him to work increasingly with the *hakuma* of the church and government. Giir Thiik was one of the first chiefs to send his own son to school in Kuajok. Later he even accepted a small school teaching basic literacy being built in his home area, adjacent to his own *luak* (cattle byre with circular mudded walls and a tall, thatched roof) and court tree.[28] Over time, graduates of these missionary schools entered government and gained jobs such as court clerks and chiefs. As Southern positions in government became more senior, these school graduates went on to acquire leadership positions in the government.

In the 1960s, the Sudan government hoped that the Anya-Nya were absent from Bahr el Ghazal, including the regions around the Bilnyang. Yet, they were not. Central to the Anya-Nya forces in Gogrial were those who had gone through, or were still attending, these schools and had become associated with the church, as well as their own family ties. Bernadino Mou Mou, a nephew of Chief Giir Thiik and born in Greater Gogrial, had been educated and became a prison warden and corporal in the Sudan government. In 1961 he defected and travelled to Congo to join the Anya-Nya forces. He had served with the Anya-Nya in early offensives in the Equatorias. By 1962, he was training recruits in Congo in order to return to Bahr el Ghazal (the north-western third of South Sudan that includes the communities to the west of the Bilnyang).[29] Training

25   Ibid., page 176.
26   Interview with man from Gogrial, Juba, March 2020.
27   Jedeit J. Riek and Naomi Pendle, *Speaking Truth to Power in South Sudan: Oral Histories of the Nuer Prophets* (Rift Valley Institute, 2018).
28   Nikkel, *Dinka Christianity*, page 177.
29   Ibid., pages 254–255.

was carried out in secret using sticks as guns.[30] By then, recruits to the Anya-Nya, including government officials and school students, were moving from Gogrial to Congo to receive weapons and training.[31] In late 1963, William Deng visited these recruits from Gogrial and the wider area of Bahr el Ghazal in camps in Congo.[32] In August 1963, Deng appointed Bernadino Mou Mou as Anya-Nya overall commander for Bahr el Ghazal. They travelled back to Bahr el Ghazal and in 1964 Mou Mou and his forces attacked Wau. They may have had as few as a hundred men and one rifle. The ambitious attempt failed and Mou Mou was captured.[33]

Despite the attack on Wau, the government wanted to deny the existence of the Anya-Nya war in the region. Therefore, the response of the government to the attack on Wau was a response of judicial redress and the criminalisation of the rebels. Bernadino and two others were hanged, five imprisoned for life and fifteen given other prison terms.[34] The government refused to accept that they were prisoners of war, contesting the notion that the Anya-Nya war had now come to Bahr el Ghazal. Despite their defeat, the attack on Wau demonstrated that the Anya-Nya could now operate in Bahr el Ghazal.

The punishment of these Anya-Nya rebels becomes a clear example of the use of law to violently insist on peace. Whether or not there is peace or war is often a highly contested question with significant political implications. Recently scholars have narrated how the normalisation of emergencies prevents authorities facing scrutiny and control, as well as how the emergency reshapes the 'normal' itself.[35] In these debates, the focus has been on the power to declare the exception; when the exception is declared governments justify acting without constraint. Instead, in these events in Wau, the government asserted its power by declaring and legally constructing a lack of exception. According to the government, this was not an exceptional time of war, but an ordinary time of peace. The violent imposition of criminal accountability asserted this. The classifying of the attack on Wau as a criminal act also justified the government being allowed to commit the violence of hanging and imprisonment with impunity.

[30] Cormack, 'The Making and Remaking of Gogrial'.
[31] Interview with Chief Morris, 31 July 2017, Mayen Rual, in Dinka.
[32] Øystein Rolandsen, 'The Making of the Anya-Nya Insurgency in the Southern Sudan 1961–64', *Journal of Eastern African Studies* 5:2 (2011), page 225.
[33] Ibid., page 225.
[34] *The Daily Telegraph*, 22 February 1964, as cited in Storrs McCall, 'Unpublished Manuscript on the History of the First Civil War in South Sudan (Anya-Nya)' (Sudan Open Archive, 1972), page 83.
[35] S. Dezalay, 'Wars on Law, Wars through Law?' *Journal of Law and Society* 47:S1 (2020).

The Anya-Nya resisted the government's framing of criminality. After Bernadino's arrest and execution, the Anya-Nya captain in Bahr el Ghazal formed a company called 'Guor Mou' ('Avenge Mou' in Dinka).[36] The Anya-Nya framed the violence of the government's hanging of Mou as morally repugnant. Within a very different moral framing, this put the government in a feud with the Anya-Nya and demanded a response of revenge. In June 1964, there were further attacks in Tonj, and Arab traders and civilians were repeatedly targeted. Plus, ambushes started around Gogrial. Even in the 1960s, ideas of revenge and blood feud were being used to mobilise support for wars of the *hakuma*, and rebel narratives of revenge were contesting the *hakuma*'s ability to sit outside of moral norms. By declaring the war an act of revenge against the *hakuma*, the Anya-Nya was also challenging the government's implicit claims of power to commit violence with impunity. If the war was a feud between the Anya-Nya and government, the government was not a party that stood outside of these normative regimes. Instead, the government was subject to consequences for their moral violations and these consequences would be violently enacted by the Anya-Nya.

Cormack has documented how, in this context of growing unrest in Bahr el Ghazal, a massacre occurred in October 1964 at Lol Nyiel near Gogrial.[37] Two days before the massacre, an Anya-Nya soldier had captured and killed a northern Sudanese trader in Gogrial. Cormack describes how the Anya-Nya commander, Valentino Akol Wol, then pinned a note to the body of the deceased northern Sudanese with the written words: 'Sentenced to death by Valentino Akol Wol, Anya-Nya Chief Justice'.[38] Pivoting the claims of the government in the hanging of Bernadino, these words asserted the claimed legal authority of the Anya-Nya and used this claim of legal legitimacy to justify arbitrary killing. In response, government police forces rounded up, tortured and burnt a hundred or more local people. This display of spectacular violence was an attempt to create a deterrent against support for the Anya-Nya.[39]

The west of the Bilnyang also experienced the Anya-Nya conflict. For example, in Ler, on 22 January 1965, an Anya-Nya force led by Paulino Arop (sent from Bahr el Ghazal) was sent to attack Ler. He worked with local residents around Ler, but they only had four guns between them. They did manage to overrun the government post, killing fifteen northern policemen and taking

---

36   Kuyok Abol Kuyok, *South Sudan: The Notable Firsts* (AuthorHouse UK, 2015), page 255.

37   Cormack, 'The Making and Remaking of Gogrial'.

38   Interview by Cormack with Bona Malwal: Cormack, 'The Making and Remaking of Gogrial', page 205.

39   Ibid., page 202.

four Southern police into the Anya-Nya.[40] They also captured twenty rifles, one machine gun and 3,000 rounds of ammunition – one of the largest loots from Anya-Nya raids. When the government attempted to reopen a post the following year, local support for the Anya-Nya meant that the government was violently repelled by them.

Peace and cosmological configurations

The 1970s brought peace between the Sudan government and the Anya-Nya rebels. A series of secret talks by the World Council of Churches (WCC) and the All-Africa Conference of Churches (AACC) with the Sudan government and Anya-Nya rebels made the possibility of talks tangible.[41] During the negotiations, church negotiators used breaks for prayer at strategic moments to calm tensions between parties.[42] Canon Burgess Carr (AACC) explicitly drew on Old Testament texts, common to Muslim and Christian faiths, to try to unite the parties.[43] In February 1972, the Addis Ababa Peace Agreement was signed. The peace agreement also committed to incorporating the Anya-Nya into the national army and government, and into its payroll. It provided a reward through future salaries for the service of these forces.

The incorporation of the Anya-Nya forces into the Government of Sudan also brought new cosmological questions. In response, divinely seized figures remade rituals to 'creatively refuse'[44] government claims to be the ultimate authority even in the towns. Anya-Nya forces in the region, many of whom had familial connections to *baany e biith*, now found themselves in government jobs in Wau as a result of the 1972 peace agreement. This brought ambiguity and contestation over whether these government officials from local *home* communities, and even in the *hakuma* space of the towns, were ultimately responsible to the Sudan government or still subject to the moral and cosmological hierarchies of home. In this context, various divine authorities asserted their power over these government officials. For example, in the mid-1970s, a divinely seized song composer came from rural Gogrial to Wau.

---

[40]   Ibid., page 3.
[41]   John Ashworth, 'Wunlit Peace Conference (1999)', in John Akec et al. (eds), *We Have Lived Too Long to Be Deceived: South Sudanese Discuss the Lessons of Historic Peace Agreements* (Rift Valley Institute, 2014): 33–36, page 34.
[42]   Douglas Johnson, 'Addis Ababa Agreement (1972)', in John Akec et al. (eds), *We Have Lived Too Long to Be Deceived: South Sudanese Discuss the Lessons of Historic Peace Agreements* (Rift Valley Institute, 2014): 8–10, page 9.
[43]   Cormack, 'The Making and Remaking of Gogrial', page 333.
[44]   This references Graeber's discussions: David Graeber, 'Culture as Creative Refusal', *Cambridge Anthropology* 31:2 (2013): 1–19.

He would often socially gather with the former Anya-Nya government officials from Gogrial. One night he dreamt of someone coming from the eastern part of Gogrial to Wau.[45] He described the man and the next day the man arrived. The composer called the government officials from the man's home area to come to him and sacrifice a goat. This ritual sacrifice by leaders or observers was not a normal part of the routine of song composition, but was a creative way for the composer to both demand compliance by government officials and the performance of a ritual associated with ritual practices of the villages, even though they were in the town. He remade culture to creatively refuse the exclusion of the cosmological order of the *home* in the town. Even though they were government officials, they came and complied with this divine instruction. In the cosmic politics, the government officials did not trump more 'bitter' divine authorities.

New intra-*hakuma* wars

The peace of the 1970s collapsed within a decade. During this time, the Sudan government was loaned large amounts of money to carry out large-scale mechanised agriculture. However, food exports fell during the 1970s alongside global declines in food production. Sudan's debt quickly escalated into the billions and there was little money to spare to support the nascent Southern government.[46] This meant that the new Southern Regional Government, created by the 1972 Addis Ababa Peace Agreement, was significantly underfunded. Along with this, there was an increased drive by the government to extract resources from the South to increase the Sudanese national income. For example, the 1970s brought the re-initiation of the Jonglei Canal project to drain the southern swamps in order to increase water flow downstream in northern Sudan and Egypt.[47]

In the 1970s, Chevron also discovered oil in Southern Sudan. The first oil sites were discovered just to the east of the Bilnyang Rivers, between these swamps and the Bahr el Jebel. The government was now eager to secure its control of the oil. In the early 1980s the Sudan government had already started arming militia groups to the north to raid south into the lands of the oilfields.[48]

---

[45] Interview with man who had this song written, May 2022, Luonyaker (South Sudan).

[46] Johnson, *The Root Causes of Sudan's Civil Wars*, pages 43–44.

[47] John Garang, 'Identifying, Selecting and Implementing Rural Development Strategies for Sudan' (PhD diss., Iowa State University, 1981).

[48] Georgette Gagnon and John Ryle, 'Report of an Investigation into Oil Development in Western Upper Nile' (Canadian Auto Workers Union; Steelworkers

From the perspective of the Anya-Nya, from the signing of the Addis Ababa Agreement there was resistance from some and especially those from Bahr el Ghazal and Upper Nile. For example, in 1972, an ex-Anya-Nya soldier encouraged chiefs in the western Nuer to not collect taxes in opposition to government and to intentionally violate the new peace deal. He was arrested on the 21 December 1972 and his rifle and ammunition were confiscated. He was taken to Malakal for investigation and trial.[49] Small cohorts of the rebels resisted integration into the army and fled to Ethiopia where the Ethiopian government allowed them to establish bases. Throughout the 1970s, Southern sympathy grew for the what became Anya-Nya II. For example, when Samuel Gai Tut, its leader, was arrested in Juba in 1982 for smuggling arms to the rebels in Ethiopia, Southern leaders working with the government, namely Barrister Ambrose Riny Thiik (from Gogrial) and Appeal Court Judge Justice Michael Makuei, secured his release.[50]

Kerubino Kuanyin Bol was born in Twic County (northern Gogrial) and fought with the Anya-Nya. After the Addis Ababa Peace Agreement, he was absorbed into the Sudan army and put in command of Battalion 105 in Bor (to the east of the Bahr el Jebel). On 16 May 1983, Kerubino led a mutiny of this battalion. At the time, John Garang, himself from Bor, was a senior general in the Sudan army, posted at its headquarters in Khartoum. He was sent by President Nimeiri to solve the problem of Kerubino's mutiny, but instead joined the revolt. After these defections, they fled to Ethiopia, were joined by others who were defecting and formed the Sudan People's Liberation Army (SPLA). This rebellion against the Sudan government continued until the signing of the Comprehensive Peace Agreement in 2005.

At the inception of the SPLA, support for this rebel army grew quickly among former Anya-Nya from Bahr el Ghazal and in Gogrial. For example, Salva Kiir (from Gogrial), having fought for the Anya-Nya, had become a major in the Sudan army, stationed in Malakal. Kiir defected to join the SPLA from its inception. Kiir encouraged former Anya-Nya, such as Bona Bang Dhel, to also defect. Bona recruited students and former Anya-Nya from Wau and Rumbek to rebel and travel to Ethiopia.[51] Popular support for the SPLA grew around the Bilnyang as the Sudan government backed militia raids into

Humanity Fund; Simons Foundation; United Church of Canada, Division of World Outreach; World Vision Canada, 2001), page 13.

[49]   Letter to Minister of Regional Administration, Juba, from Moese Chuol, Commissioner, Upper Nile Province, 4 January 1973. SSNA.UNP.SCR.36.B.3/3.

[50]   Kuyok, *South Sudan: The Notable Firsts*, page 415.

[51]   Dolku Media, 'Gen. Bona Bang Dhel on SPLA DAY', *YouTube* video, length 27:52, 1 June 2018. www.youtube.com/watch?v=uXENcSq3HpI&t=653s, at 10:53, accessed 20 December 2020.

Southern Sudan. Many early SPLA recruits narrate that they travelled to Ethiopia to get guns from the SPLA to defend their homelands.[52]

Garang's core justification for the SPLA's rebellion was not the demand for Southern autonomy but his complaint that development was behind throughout the peripheries of Sudan. The SPLA's manifesto evoked Marxist analysis and was heavily influenced by Dar es Salaam theorists and dependency theory.[53] This stance was more palatable to the Ethiopian government. The SPLA also received significant military support from the Eastern Bloc and from Libya in the context of the then-ongoing Cold War, and in later years from President Museveni in Uganda.[54] From its earliest days, the SPLA's power was intimately connected to its international, regional relationships, which brought with them military might and a degree of legitimacy. Therefore, it was never solely dependent on South Sudanese people for its legitimacy and claims to authority. This reshaped the relationship the SPLA had with Southern Sudanese and often allowed it to have a predatory relationship with the communities it controlled.

The SPLA inception alienated the Anya-Nya II forces. Although some of these forces joined the SPLA, many Anya-Nya II forces refused. In May 1984, at the encouragement of the Ethiopian regimes, Garang turned on the Anya-Nya II movement and killed their leader, Gai Tut,[55] which led to a lasting rupture and deep distrust between these different armed forces of the South. Paulino Matip took over from Gai Tut as the leader of the Anya-Nya II forces and returned to his homelands in Bentiu and Mayom (to the north and east of the Bilnyang Rivers) as a base for his alternative Southern armed rebellion against Khartoum. Initially Anya-Nya II remained hostile to the government in Khartoum. In 1984 the rebellion abducted and killed Chevron oil workers, stopping this initial phase of oil exploration in the area.[56]

Over the next two decades, battles took place across many regions of South Sudan and also in the Blue Nile and Nuba Mountains regions of northern Sudan. Lethal, armed violence took place in rural areas, as well as large, bloody campaigns for urban settlements. Some of the worst fighting was not directly between the SPLA and the Government of Sudan (GoS) but between

---

52   Cherry Leonardi, 'Paying "Buckets of Blood" for the Land: Moral Debates over Economy, War and State in Southern Sudan', *The Journal of Modern African Studies* 49:2 (2011): 215–240.

53   Thomas, *South Sudan*; Sudan People's Liberation Movement Manifesto, 1983, GB-0033-SAD.89/6/53-92.

54   John Young, *The Fate of Sudan: The Origins and Consequences of a Flawed Peace Process* (Zed Books, 2012), page 49.

55   Ibid., page 48.

56   Gagnon and Ryle, 'Report of an Investigation', page 16.

these divided, Southern armed forces. Anti-SPLA forces included Anya-Nya II but also other community defence forces who resisted the SPLA's governance of the South.

The fall of the Soviet Union resulted in significant southern divisions. By 1989, the SPLA had achieved impressive military victories over the Sudan government and controlled two-thirds of the South.[57] The fall of the Soviet Union and the linked fall of Mengistu Haile Mariam's Ethiopian regime in 1991 had dramatic repercussions for the SPLA. The new regime in Ethiopia expelled the SPLA from its terrories, which meant that it had to appeal to a new global configuration of powers to maintain its international support. The uncertainty and weakness of the SPLA at this time also created internal tensions. In 1991, Dr Riek Machar Teny rebelled against Garang. He justified the revolt based on accusations of Garang's dictatorial leadership, and Machar also highlighted that the SPLA under Garang had committed widespread human rights abuse and recruited large numbers of child soldiers especially from the Nuer. Riek's justification for rebellion played into the international post-Cold War concern with good governance and upholding basic standards of human rights and humanitarian law, and his rhetoric also made ethnic claims about the way that power was configured under the SPLA.[58] Army leaders on both sides sought to remake ethnic boundaries and divisions as ways to mobilise supporters to war.[59] In the mid-1990s, the Bilnyang was deeply impacted. Riek's father had lived in Ler, and Riek had been born there. In the mid-1990s, he mobilised support to carry out violent raids across the Bilnyang and connected rivers into SPLA-controlled Greater Gogrial and Tonj. This killed hundreds and remade the grazing land as a place of danger.[60]

At the same time, intra-Dinka and intra-Nuer wars were just as deadly. A year after Riek Machar's rebellion against Garang, Kerubino Kuanyin rebelled in Gogrial. In the late 1980s, Kerubino had been imprisoned by Garang. He was released in 1992, immediately mobilised anti-Garang forces and moved Nuer forces to Gogrial. He started campaigns of forced and voluntary recruitment across Twic and Gogrial, as well as displays of extreme violence. Between

[57]   Gérard Prunier and Rachel M. Gisselquist, 'The Sudan: A Successfully Failed State' in Robert Rotberg (ed.) *State Failure and State Weakness in a Time of Terror* (Brookings Institution, 2003).

[58]   Jok Madut Jok and Sharon Hutchinson, 'Sudan's Prolonged Second Civil War and the Militarization of Nuer and Dinka Ethnic Identities', *African Studies Review* 42:2 (1999): 125–145.

[59]   Ibid.

[60]   Naomi Pendle, 'Contesting the Militarization of the Places Where They Met: The Landscapes of the Western Nuer and Dinka (South Sudan)', *Journal of Eastern African Studies* 11:1 (2017): 64–85.

1995 and 1997, Kerubino led various raids on the populations of Gogrial that killed and abducted, looted cattle, and burnt crops. This gave rise to the 1998 Bahr el Ghazal famine.[61]

Alliances between Paulino Matip (Anya-Nya II leader) and Kerubino, and Kerubino's growing predation in Gogrial, prompted SPLA attacks into Unity State. From 1994 to 1997, the SPLA confrontation with Matip was enacted through tit-for-tat raids over the grazing lands of the Bilnyang Rivers.[62] This Nuer-Dinka fighting violated previous ethics of war, such as restraining from violence against women and children, and acted to militarise ethnicity.[63] For example, an attack in the *toc* resulted in the burning of twenty-five Dinka villages, killing of many people and the capture of thousands of cattle.[64] This also transformed the *toc* of the rivers of the Bilnyang from a place of meeting and abundance, to a violent no-man's land.[65] The unrestrained violence suggested the genesis of 'a war that does not end'.[66]

The Nuer civil wars in Unity State (to the east of the Bilnyang) were also incredibly deadly. In Mayom, Paulino Matip had significant forces, controlled key trading routes and had significant support from Khartoum.[67] His ability to protect Talisman Energy's oil concessions in Block 5a from the SPLA and to clear civilians from proximity to the oil fields gave the Sudan government a strong incentive to court him as an ally.[68] Machar had formally appointed Matip as governor of Liec State (approximately equivalent to contemporary Unity State) in 1994, but Matip already had control over the region. In 1998, when Machar attempted to remove him from the governorship, Matip's forces attacked Machar's forces in violent raids into southern Liec. Khartoum backed Matip, who was able to forcibly displace large swathes of the population from near the oil fields and from areas to the north. With support from Matip, the Sudan government was able to open the oil pipeline into the most northerly Southern Sudanese oilfields in 1999.[69]

61 Peter Adwok Nyaba, *The Disarmament of the Gel-Weng of Bahr El Ghazal and the Consolidation of the Nuer – Dinka Peace Agreement 1999* (Pax Christi for New Sudan Council of Churches, 2001).

62 Ibid., 129.

63 Ibid., 131.

64 Ibid., 131.

65 Pendle, 'Contesting the Militarization of the Places Where They Met'.

66 Peter Adwok Nyaba, *Politics of Liberation in South Sudan: An Insider's View* (Fountain Publishers, 1997), page 5.

67 Johnson, *Root Causes*.

68 Jok Madut Jok, *Sudan: Race, Religion and Violence* (Oneworld Publications, 2007).

69 Jok and Hutchinson, 'Sudan's Prolonged Second Civil War', page 130.

War as cosmological rupture

The intra-*hakuma* wars of the 1980s and 1990s brought a raft of potential social, moral and cosmological ruptures. This had the potential to challenge the power of the Nuer and Dinka priesthoods. Firstly, lethal force became more prolific. The 1980s brought the proliferation of guns in the communities near the Bilnyang. Young men travelled to Ethiopia to join the SPLA. Both the SPLA and GoS made use of proxy forces to support their own war efforts, which involved the warring parties arming young men who often were still living in their home communities. For example, the SPLA armed cattle herders from Gogrial and neighbouring SPLA control areas. These forces became known as the *titweng* (an armed cattle guard).[70]

In past decades, men had become like the gods through their acquisition of guns and their new powers to kill with impunity (Chapter 1). Now, many people were armed with guns and lethal power. A prominent concern was whether these new lethal powers were restrained and whether there could be accountability for killing with a gun. If the gun carried the potential to claim the divine-like character of killing with impunity, then the proliferation of gun ownership could be equated with the proliferation of the divine.

Secondly, a related question was a new ambiguity about purity. Hutchinson's research among the Nuer was seminal and vivid in its descriptions of the new dilemmas faced by Nuer in relation to purity after killing. She describes how, by the early 1980s, Nuer were actively debating notions of *nueer* pollution because of the brutality of the Anya-Nya wars.[71] In the east Nuer they were questioning whether *nueer* only came about if the slain and the slayer were previously known to each other. Hutchinson describes how, during wars of the 1980s and 1990s, Nuer to the west of the Nile started equating bullets with lightning – 'the deceased of both being thought to create a uniquely direct, spiritual linkage with divinity that could be cultivated through cattle sacrifice and, thereafter, effectively called upon in times of danger by surviving kin'.[72] In the intra-Nuer wars of Unity State, further dilemmas arose as a result of Matip's policy of forced recruitment in rural areas and from western Nuer students in schools in Khartoum. This meant that some of his fighters could end up fighting against their own brothers and kin. How pollution worked in such a context was unclear.

---

[70]   Naomi Pendle, '"They Are Now Community Police": Negotiating the Boundaries and Nature of the Government in South Sudan through the Identity of Militarised Cattle-Keepers', *International Journal of Minority and Group Rights* 22:3 (2015): 410–434.

[71]   Sharon Hutchinson, *Nuer Dilemmas: Coping with Money, War, and the State* (University of California Press, 1996), pages 106–108.

[72]   Hutchinson, *Nuer Dilemmas*, pages 107–108.

Parts of the *hakuma* sought to construct an ontological and moral distinction between two types of war – wars of the *hakuma* (*koor kume*) and wars of the home. This would allow wars of the *hakuma* to be governed by different moral logics and encourage a lack of restraint. In an interview with Hutchinson, Riek Machar (then Western Upper Nile zonal commander for the SPLA) said that he had tried to persuade people that deaths caused by violence during these wars should not be understood as causing pollution or spiritual consequences. Hutchinson describes how, in effect, the SPLA leadership was arguing that a *koor kume* (a government war) should take precedence over the interrelations of combatants and their social and spiritual ramifications.[73]

Thirdly, the gun brought new ambiguity over the power of the priests to bring peace and end feuds when these conflicts included the use of guns. The gun's spectacular power, including to kill, minimalised the displays of power by these priests. A central role of the priests was the remaking of purity and peace and, with such dramatic wars, it was unclear that this was still possible. Killing was on such a large scale, it was unclear if *nueer* could still be removed.

War as continuity and the maintenance of the priesthood

This period of rupture had consequences for the politics of the cosmos in the Bilnyang and challenged priestly authority. At the same time, stories of the *baany e biith* in the 1980s–2000s narrate continuity instead of rupture. What we do not see is a period where culture and claims of cosmic powers are static; the world was changing fast and divine power had to be responsive. Instead, we see the fast-paced creative remaking of culture and the reassertion of priestly authority. New norms were asserted as a way to creatively refuse claims of impunity of the *hakuma* and gun carriers. Ideas of the divine were reinterpreted to highlight the continued significance of the *baany e biith*. The histories, part of the cultural archive, are now still being told about the continued prominence of the *baany e biith* in this period. The stories described below are part of these campaigns to assert the continuity of cosmological hierarchies.

Firstly, *baany e biith* accepted to provide support to the SPLA. They were themselves challenging the division between the *hakuma* and other divine power so that they could simultaneously draw on multiple sources of power. While there was no formal link to the operations of the SPLA, military figures in the SPLA stationed in Gogrial did seek support and protection from the *baany e biith*.[74] For example, Sudan government offensives against the SPLA in Gogrial included aerial bombardment.[75] At this time, popular stories

---

[73] Ibid., page 108.
[74] Cormack, 'The Making and Remaking of Gogrial', page 255.
[75] Jok, *Sudan*.

in Luonayaker (contemporary Gogrial East County, Warrap State) retell of how SPLA leaders called together *baany e biith* to mess up the sky so that they would remain safe from aerial attack. Famously, one of the only bombs that fell in Luonyaker fell directly into a cooking pot, preventing the spread of shrapnel and any deaths.[76] Leaders of the SPLA were criticised for their ad hoc demands of *baany e biith*. They would ask for support but then not return to thank them or display reverence. Many years later one elder mused that maybe the SPLA's lack of thanks had meant that the *baany e biith* never restored the order of the sky. He pondered whether that was why Garang's helicopter crashed in 2005.[77]

Other histories perceive divine support as the cause of SPLA victories. In January 1997, a powerful *bany e bith* called Manyual Kuol Jok brought two bulls out from his herd – white and black – and tied them to his shrine peg. He then recited invocations over them over many days. People brought home-brewed alcoholic drinks and crowds gathered. As his invocations concluded, he told the bulls to face Warrap Town. At this time, Warrap Town was controlled by the Sudan government. Manyual declared that if Warrap Town belonged to the Sudan soldiers they would remain there, but if it was his they would leave by the end of the year. He then killed the bulls. In May 1997, the SPLA retook control of Warrap Town. The large SPLA offensives across Bahr el Ghazal at the time prevented the Sudanese soldiers from receiving support from Wau or Tonj, and Warrap became SPLA-controlled.[78]

Secondly, the *baany e biith* continued to demonstrate their power, even against the Sudan government. Others still testified to the *baany e biith*'s powers to provide protection. For example, in 1997, one well known *bany e bith* was hunting in the *lil* (grasslands) between what became Gogrial East and Gogrial West. Here there is only long grass and no trees to hide behind. Kerubino's forces appeared and started moving across the *lil* in a long line. The *bany e bith* was in their path. To defend himself, he picked up some of the dust on the ground. He threw some on the left and some on the right. The line of soldiers curved off to the left and the right, and the *bany e bith* was saved.[79] The point of these histories was not to simply assert causation but to establish the *baany e biith* as able to claim authority despite and even over the militarised might of the *hakuma*.

Thirdly, the *baany e biith* also sought to rein in the *hakuma*, including Southern rebels. The destruction and defiance of the military did challenge the

---

[76]   A common story of the 1990s told in Luonyaker marketplace and homes during fieldwork 2010–13.

[77]   Interview with man in Gogrial, May 2018, in Dinka.

[78]   Ibid.

[79]   Ibid.

powers of the *baany e biith*. Cormack documents Ajingdit (a very powerful *bany e bith*)'s failure to persuade Kerubino to stop his rebellion against the SPLA as an example of the limits of *baany e biith* power.[80] However, other histories of the period interpret Kerubino's defiance of the *baany e biith* as having lethal consequences. In 1998 Kerubino managed to seize control of Wau and, from this position of strength, sought to rejoin the SPLA. These events fell shortly after chiefs and *baany e biith* in Gogrial had come together to sacrifice bulls and ask *Nhialic* to change the heart of Kerubino so that he would return to the SPLA. Garang accepted Kerubino's return and organised for him to fly to Nairobi. At this point, before leaving Gogrial, a large gathering was organised by Pieng Deng Majok (SPLA commander) in Luonyaker, at Giir Thiik's *yik* (shrine), to bless Kerubino's departure and peace. During this meeting and the invocations over the animals that would be sacrificed, the *baany e biith* declared that if Kerubino were to rebel again he would never return home to them in Gogrial.[81]

Kerubino went on from there to Nairobi to meet Garang. He joined the SPLA. Garang gave Kerubino a headquarters role instead of as a significant commander in the field. Kerubino almost immediately rebelled again and joined the Khartoum-aligned South Sudan United Army led by Paulino Matip from Mayom. Shortly afterwards, Matip fell out with his deputy – Peter Gadet. During fighting in Mayom in 1999, Kerubino was killed. This has been interpreted by supporters of these priests as demonstrative of the power of the *baany e biith*'s curse including over the most powerful military actors. This highlighted the continued lack of impunity of the *hakuma*, even in times of war, and the continued power of the *baany e biith* to curse those, even army generals, who break a peace. The cosmic contestations continued, but the *hakuma* remained constrained by the divine.

Fourthly, *baany e biith* asserted their authority over the *titweng* and armed youth of their communities. Growing numbers of cattle camp youth were armed as they formed a vanguard of community defence, as well as acting as supporting militia for the SPLA.[82] While many young men still sought divine protection from external forces in battle, the new power of the gun was also challenging governance within the cattle camps, whose occupants were starting to reject the necessity of having a *bany e bith* as the leading public authority, instead opting for those with strength in cattle. Yet stories and *baany e biith* contested this. For example, there was a cattle camp of Gogrial in the 1980s that was in the *toc* adjacent to Mayom. This was an increasingly

---

80 Cormack, 'The Making and Remaking of Gogrial', page 255.
81 Interview with two village elders (including one relative of Giir Thiik), Luonyaker, December 2018.
82 Pendle, '"They Are Now Community Police"'.

precarious position as, in the early 1980s, it became the frontline between the SPLA- and Anya-Nya-II-controlled areas. The young men in the cattle camp were heavily armed by the SPLA and through community purchase of arms. At this time, it is said that a man came to the cattle camp. He was welcomed and given milk. In the evening, the man asked who the *bany e bith* of the camp was. The members of the camp replied that there was no *bany e bith* in charge and that they were happy to be led by a brave man known as Anguet. The guest disputed whether a cattle camp could be led by a brave person instead of a *bany e bith*. The man left. The next morning, the calves were led into the forest by the boys. The guest had transformed himself into a lion and started attacking the calves. On hearing the commotion, the young men of the cattle camp, including Anguet, ran to the scene. The lion waited, ran past the other young men and killed Anguet. At the death of Anguet, the others raised their spears to kill the lion. The lion returned to the form of a man. The visitor then ordered the camp to appoint a *bany e bith* as leader. There was a member of Pagong (a 'bitter' clan of the *baany e biith*) in the camp and he was appointed as the leader and *bany e bith* of the camp, based on his ancestral authority. During an interview in 2018, one middle-aged man paraphrased the visitor's words as follows:

> I want you to look for the *bany e bith* and to make him the one responsible and the leader of you because the *bany e bith* can find the footprint of the lion in front of the camp in the morning and pick the soil where the footprint is and throw it away so that the lion cannot come back to kill the cows and people. If the cattle diseases break out, then the *bany e bith* can take it away. If the people have fought in the camp, then the *bany e bith* can solve it and reconcile them.[83]

Fifthly, people creatively remade cultural norms in order to spatially expand the power of the *baany e biith* over new spaces far from home. For example, in the 1980s, as discussed above, many people were recruited by the SPLA in Wau and Gogrial, and then walked to the SPLA training camps in Ethiopia. Many died along the way of disease, starvation and drowning. When talking in 2018 in Luonyaker, one person recalled being in a group with another young man from the *bany e bith* clan of Pakuec (the clan of Chief Giir Thiik). The man had never acted as a *bany e bith* and he would not act as a *bany e bith* after the war. However, his membership of the clan connected him to the powers of the *baany e biith*. This group, as they journeyed to Ethiopia, had already lost many men during fighting with Anya-Nya II forces and as a result of disease. One day, someone in the group found the skin of a *gong* (hedgehog). The hedgehog is associated with many of the most bitter (i.e.

---

[83]   Interview with man in Gogrial, June 2018, in Dinka.

spiritually powerful and dangerous) clans of *baany e biith*.[84] The skin was given to the group's leader to use as a bowl. They found water and placed it in the skin and found a bull to slaughter. The leader sprinkled the water over the group. When the bull was killed, the femoral bone was removed and given to the man from Pakuac; the femoral bone was associated with this clan as well as other clans of the *baany e biith* such as Pa'hol. This man of Pakuac accepted the bone, dipped it in the water in the *gong* skin and sprinkled it over the people in the group to bless them and protect them. After this blessing, no-one else in their group died during the rest of their journey to the SPLA camps in Ethiopia. This man from Pakuac went on to be a senior military and political figure in the SPLA and did not continue practicing as a *bany e bith.*

Importantly, this is an example of the remaking of rituals in ways that allowed their continuity despite massive ruptures in space and circumstance. People creatively insisted that the war allowed the most bitter powers of the priesthood, at least temporarily, to be dispersed to others, making room for a larger priesthood in the absence of a *bany e bith*.[85] At the same time, as the man was from a *bany e bith* clan, this authority remained tightly connected to kinship and clan configurations of authority.

War's demands for new divinities

The brutal power of the gun and government offensives meant that people not only sought protection and power from the gun, but also other divine authorities. The wars of the 1980s–2000s gave people new experiences of invisible powers that *baany e biith* either had to compete with or include within their own cosmic orders. For example, those in Gogrial saw soldiers in the Sudan Armed Forces using *ran wal* (purchased medicine or magic) that they wore on their arms and that could stop bullets penetrating them. Specifically, the 1980s–2000s also saw the emergence of new free divinities in Gogrial.

In the 1990s came the emergence of new free divinities in Gogrial that were specifically associated with war and spatially associated with the cattle camps. This reflected the growing dangers and politics of the cattle camp, especially with the emergence of the SPLA-backed *titweng* (cattle guards) and the proliferation of guns. The divinities that came were specifically *jok tong* (divinities of war). This included MABIORDIT and MAGOTDIT.[86] Cormack traces

---

[84]   For more discussions of 'bitterness', see Eisei Kurimoto, 'An Ethnography of "Bitterness": Cucumber and Sacrifice Reconsidered', *Journal of Religion in Africa* 22:1 (1992): 47–65.

[85]   Interview with man in Gogrial, June 2018, in Dinka.

[86]   Interview with man in Gogrial, May 2018.

the emergence of MABIORDIT to Tonj in the late 1980s. Cormack notices that he came to the attention of the authorities when MABIORDIT requested the man it had possessed kill his eight-year-old son.[87] However, in Gogrial, MABIORDIT did not emerge until the late 2000s, after the Comprehensive Peace Agreement (CPA).

MABIORDIT and MAGOTDIT were renowned for making people immune to bullets. Powers that make bullets unable to harm are far from unique to MABIORDIT and MAGOTDIT, or even to South Sudan. In the Democratic Republic of the Congo (DRC), the famous Mai Mai rebel group won support from the population by demonstrating their legendary invulnerability to bullets. They would sprinkle a domestic animal or garment with blessed water – *maï* – before shooting it. When the object or animal was unharmed, their power was proved.[88] Immunity to bullets made their possessors notorious fighters as they were often fearless and lethal in battle. These free divinities appealed to young men as they offered protection in this context of armed conflicts,[89] and gave them power to confront the guns of governments, including the Sudan government.

Whether these *jok tong* were a continuation of cosmic systems, or a creative remaking of culture, was debated. In the late 1940s, British anthropologist Godfrey Lienhardt had recorded that there were a number of active, free divinities including DENG, GARANG and MACARDIT.[90] These free divinities made their presence known through illness and then through declaring their name and instructions through the words of this seized person.[91] Each of these free divinities had their own personalities and 'biographies'.[92] These free divinities were not exclusive for the *baany e biith* and Lienhardt sees their proliferation as undermining *beny e bith* authority.[93]

At the same time, MAGOTDIT and MABIORDIT did represent a creative remaking of warriors' relationships to the divine, and they challenged the exclusive nature of the priesthood. They were a 'creative refusal' (in Graeber's terms) both of the power of the *hakuma* and the power of the gun to kill, and of the *bany e bith* clans to exclusively provide protection. MABIORDIT did

[87] Cormack, 'The Making and Remaking of Gogrial', pages 247–249.
[88] Kasper Hoffmann, 'Myths Set in Motion: The Moral Economy of Mai Mai Governance', in Ana Arjona, Nelson Kasfir and Zachariah Mampilly (eds), *Rebel Governance in Civil War* (Cambridge University Press, 2015): 158–179, page 159.
[89] Ibid.
[90] Godfrey Lienhardt, *Divinity and Experience: The Religion of the Dinka* (Clarendon Press, 1961), page 56.
[91] Ibid., page 57.
[92] Ibid., 81–95; Cormack, 'The Making and Remaking of Gogrial', page 246.
[93] Lienhardt, *Divinity and Experience*, page 169.

not limit his seizure to the clans of the *baany e biith*. People could also call on MABIORDIT by sacrificing animals to him. This implied some agency to call on the divine through reverence and for protection, and this allowed his protection to be directly obtainable by a much larger number of people. As discussed above, the divine was democratised. The willingness of both MABIORDIT and MAGOTDIT to seize not only members of *bany e bith* clans challenged the monopoly *baany e biith* often claimed over close relations with the divine.

MAGOTDIT and MABIORDIT also reinforced the cosmic significance of the cattle camp as they were exclusively for those in the cattle camp. As discussed above, this was a period of the increased militarisation of the cattle camps and a growing focus on these cattle camp youth as a community defence.[94] The focus of the free divinities on the cattle camp also suggested a new social order and new prominent social divisions that mimicked militarised re-orderings of the time. Based on her research in the post-CPA period, Cormack highlights the emergence of MABIORDIT as a challenge to the authority of the *baany e biith*.

Baany e biith sought to manage this competition including through co-option. One *bany e bith* sought to co-opt and not contest MAGOTDIT by acquiring this free divinity. For example, the cattle camp and community of the Amuk decided to acquire MAGOTDIT. This was possible by sacrificing animals to a cow and calling MAGOTDIT into the animal and into the camp. Deng, a brave warrior and son of a *bany e bith*, was seized by MAGOTDIT. In Deng, the power of MAGOTDIT and powers associated with the *baany e biith* were powerfully combined. They also became hereditary and passed on to his son Ngor Mabior. As Deng had MAGOTDIT, on his father's death, the formal priesthood passed to his brother Wol. These two siblings became cooperative, although occasionally rivalrous, divine authorities.

In accounts since the 1980s, even if free divinities have challenged the exclusive power of *bany e bith* clans, *baany e biith* have still attempted to assert regulatory authority. They claim to have unique powers to recognise free divinities by making sacrifices and demanding that they declare their names. A *bany e bith* has the power to dedicate a cow to these free divinities through the sacrifice of a chicken or goat and through invocations over the cow. This interprets these new activities of free divinities as continuities of older cosmic and priestly hierarchies. Some *baany e biith* even themselves started to claim that they could offer protection from bullets.

---

[94]   Pendle, "'They Are Now Community Police'".

Conclusion

The wars of the 1960s and 1980s–2000s brought new contestations against the continuity of the power of the priests and their power to make peace. The proliferation of guns, the brutality of their power and the complexities of having Southern Sudanese in government who had close relations to the *baany e biith* all brought new conundrums about hierarchies of authority, the continuity of pollution as a consequence of killing, and the ability to curb and be protected from the power of the gun. For the *baany e biith* to maintain authority and relevance, rituals were remade to creatively refuse rupture in more orders and cosmological hierarchies. Histories of *bany e bith* defiance were also experienced and retold, forming a revised cultural archive that demonstrated the *baany e biith*'s continuity and not absence, despite war.

One of the main challenges to the power of the priests was not the direct threat of the guns of the *hakuma*, but the proliferation of new divine authorities. These new divine authorities also sought to provide protection against guns and government, but were not subsumed within the existing hierarchies of priestly power. In response to this cosmic politics, *baany e biith* did not simply push back, but some even co-opted and acquired these new divinities. They creatively remade theological ideas to allow the merging of powers and the continuity of their own authority. They often relied on their ability to carry out violence in order to claim power to make peace. The 1960s and 1990s–2000s saw the growth of the gun and, with it, the presence of government. Yet, this growth did not subsume other cosmic powers but saw the continuity of authority figures who drew on divine might. The cosmic polity had become more contested, but remade ideas of divine authority were central to contesting the power and impunity of the *hakuma*.

CHAPTER 4

'Local peace' and the Silencing of the Dead: The 1999 Wunlit Peace Meeting

The 1999 Wunlit Peace Meeting is repeatedly remembered as 'the most successful peace meeting in the history of the Sudans'.[1] Plus, it provides an archetypal example of the 'local turn' in peace-making whereby international actors champion 'local' forms of peace-making when national efforts are failing (see Introduction). Wunlit's fame has meant that it was both an agreement that sought to elevate the peace-making power of local leaders, and a model for the proliferation of local peace efforts across South Sudan over the following decades.[2] The Wunlit Peace Meeting did clearly reduce armed conflict between communities and achieve cooperation on a scale that was previously thought impossible. It was a remarkable achievement. At the same time, in reality, Wunlit also pushed against some of the existing logics of peace-making and re-crafted 'customs' in order to reshape political hierarchies, social identities and possibilities of peace. The peace was supported by powerful sections of the SPLA and was visibly backed by military might. Simultaneously, the language of the 'customary' helped naturalise and perform continuity despite significant changes to the logics of peace. Wunlit made priests sacred and not divine in the peace-making process (in Graeber's and Sahlins' terms) by hedging them inside remade customs. Wunlit also shifted the logics of peace away from a judicial peace towards one of negotiation, and this, in turn, entrenched

[1] John Ryle, Douglas Johnson, Alier Makuer Gol, Chirrilo Madut Anei, Elizabeth Nyibol Malou, James Gatkuoth Mut Gai, Jedeit Jal, Margan Riek, John Khalid Mamun, Machot Amuom Malou, Malek Henry Chuor, Mawal Marko Gatkuoth and Loes Lijnders, 'What Happened at Wunlit?: An oral history of the 1999 Wunlit Peace Conference', page 6, https://riftvalley.net/sites/default/files/publication-documents/RVI%202021.06.28%20What%20Happened%20at%20Wunlit__Pre-print.pdf, accessed September 2021.

[2] Mark Bradbury, John Ryle, Michael Medley, and Kwesi Sansculotte-Greenidge, *Local Peace Processes in Sudan: A Baseline Study* (London: Rift Valley Institute, 2006).

the divine-like power of the *hakuma*. In this way the peace of Wunlit can be seen as violent in that it amounted to a militarily enforced restructuring of cosmic politics and the norms of peace-making. At the same time, Wunlit's rejection of compensation, and an associated push against the demands of the dead, arguably did encourage more inclusive ideas of community that had the potential to bring a less violent peace if implemented.

The context for Wunlit

From late February 1999, the New Sudan Council of Churches (NSCC) gathered 1500 people in the village of Wunlit (Greater Tonj, to the south-west of the rivers connected to the Bilnyang) for a peace conference.[3] In the weeks before, with funding from international churches, a team of three hundred labourers had built one hundred and fifty *tukals* (grass, thatched huts) and a large meeting hall. A convoy brought supplies over a three-week road journey from Kenya.[4] Holes were also dug around the village as hiding places in case of an Antonov attack from the Sudan forces. Chiefs and church leaders were dominant at the event, but SPLA commanders, 'traditional spiritual leaders', women and international journalists also attended. This meeting brought together people from the communities around the Bilnyang and connected rivers. It was described by its organisers as a Nuer-Dinka peace conference for those on the west bank of the Nile, and included people from what became Warrap, Unity and Lakes states. The conference hoped to reconcile communities that had fought since the mid-1990s after the rebellion of Riek Machar from John Garang's leadership of the SPLA and their attempts to mobilise along ethnic lines.[5]

Michael Wal Duany, from eastern South Sudan, had been a political leader in the Anya-Nya, before going to the USA for education. He married Julia whose home area was to the east of Wunlit. Michael and Bill Lowrey (an American Presbyterian Church leader), with the backing of the Presbyterian Church in the USA, had attempted to reunite Riek Machar and John Garang

3   *Dinka-Nuer West Bank Peace and Reconciliation Conference* (New Sudan Council of Churches 1999), www.sudanarchive.net/?a=d&d=SLPD19990200-01, accessed 11 December 2022.

4   Chiefs of Dinka and Nuer Stir Crowds, Emotions and Perform Rituals – *Dinka-Nuer West Bank Peace and Reconciliation Conference* (NSCC, 1999) page 2,www.sudanarchive.net/?a=d&d=SLPD19990220-01&e=-------en-20--1--txt-txIN%7ctxTI%7ctxAU-----------, accessed 13 December 2022.

5   Jok Madut Jok and Sharon Hutchinson, 'Sudan's Prolonged Second Civil War and the Militarization of Nuer and Dinka Ethnic Identities', *African Studies Review* 42:2 (1999): 125–145.

through a personal mediation process. Yet, in the end, these protagonists had refused to meet. As an alternative route to peace, they instead decided to initiate a people-to-people process. The Nairobi-based New Sudan Council of Churches became the institutional channel for external funding. Initially, in June 1998, they brought a handful of chiefs together in the safe, distant location of Lokichogio (north-west Kenya). This was followed by a series of visits of chiefs across warring lines in order to build trust for the large Wunlit conference. Lowrey and his colleagues, such as John Ashworth, emphasised that the people-to-people approach of Wunlit was not just a meeting but a process of bringing people together.[6]

The Wunlit Peace Meeting was explicitly inspired by a global turn to the 'local' in the context of the failure of national-level peace-making attempts. In the Sudans, from the early 1990s, the warring parties had shown some appetite for peace. From 1993, the Government of Sudan accepted the role of IGADD (that transformed into IGAD in 1996) in the negotiations.[7] From 1993, President Moi of Kenya played a major role in the negotiations, partly to bolster his waning domestic legitimacy. The first significant achievement in the peace process was the 1994 Declaration of Principles that stipulated the right to Southern self-determination through a referendum and, as an alternative, secular democracy within a unified Sudan. However, for years, the Sudan government refused to sign these principles.[8]

Peace was not fast coming. For the Government of Sudan (GoS), growing Middle East tension around Israel meant that there was new international pressure to be visibly aligned to the new global poles. This strengthened Sudan's Islamic inclinations resulting in the northern declarations of the war as *jihad*. From 1995, the USA became increasingly active in supporting 'frontline' states that had an antagonistic relationship with Khartoum. The SPLA also aligned itself with these new global poles and it sought opportunities in Christian sympathies.[9] With the USA's support, the SPLA grew in strength on the battlefield, while the Sudan government became increasingly desperate to access the oil revenue from Southern oilfields.

---

6   John Ashworth, 'Wunlit Peace Conference (1999)', in John Akec et al. (eds), *We Have Lived Too Long to Be Deceived: South Sudanese Discuss the Lessons of Historic Peace Agreements* (Rift Valley Institute, 2014).

7   John Young, *The Fate of Sudan: The Origins and Consequences of a Flawed Peace Process* (Zed Books, 2012), pages 83–84.

8   Mathew Arnold and Matthew LeRiche, *South Sudan: From Revolution to Independence* (Hurst and Co., 2012), page 107.

9   Andrew Wheeler, 'Finding Meaning Amid the Chaos: Narratives of Significance in the Sudanese Church', in Niels Kastfelt (ed.), *Religion and African Civil Wars* (Palgrave Macmillan, 2005): 54–81, pages 56–57.

In this context, the Sudan government initiated the Khartoum Peace Agreement which was signed in April 1997 between the Government of Sudan (GoS) and non-SPLA Southern armed forces. For the SPLA, this cooperation between GoS and non-SPLA Southern forces was more akin to an assertion of war than a declaration of peace. Southern forces that signed with GoS included the remnant Anya-Nya II forces under Paulino Matip, Riek's forces and other Equatorian groups. By signing this agreement, these forces were brought together under the umbrella of the South Sudan Defence Force (SSDF), which the Sudan government then funded to fight the SPLA and clear the Southern oil fields.[10] Divisions between the Southern Sudanese *hakuma* continued to be extremely violent for soldiers and citizens. As the war in Southern Sudan was mainly being fought by divided Southern forces, peace appeared to need not only the involvement of GoS and the SPLA, but also the SSDF and other Southern armed groups. At this time, rival political elites, such as Garang and Riek, were even refusing to meet.

Wunlit as 'local' and 'traditional'

Globally, frustrations with elite peace processes had encouraged a local turn in peace-making.[11] The NSCC's initiation of the Wunlit process in the home-lands of key Southern elites and factions was seen as an opportunity to make peace from below. The reconciliation of Garang and Riek, just over a year after Wunlit, allowed this process to be hailed as a success for the ability of local peace to force elite reconciliation.

This Wunlit peace process was presented as a 'grassroots' movement, based on the instrumentalisation of 'traditional peacebuilding techniques',[12] and as an effort at the 'revitalization of the Nuer culture and systems of governance'.[13] Church leaders encouraged chiefs to reflect on how their ancestors had historically dealt with conflicts and restored peace.[14] While Lowrey

[10]   Douglas Johnson, *The Root Causes of Sudan's Civil Wars: Peace or Truce* (James Currey, 2003); Young, *The Fate of Sudan*, pages 56–57.

[11]   Roger Mac Ginty and Oliver P. Richmond, 'The Local Turn in Peace Building: A Critical Agenda for Peace', *Third World Quarterly* 34:5 (2013): 763–783.

[12]   New Sudan Council of Churches, *The Story of People-to-People Peacemaking in Southern Sudan* (NSCC, 2002), page 55.

[13]   William O. Lowrey, 'Passing the Peace ... People to People: The Role of Religion in an Indigenous Peace Process among the Nuer People of Sudan' (PhD diss., Union Institute Graduate School, 1995).

[14]   New Sudan Council of Churches, *The Story of People-to-People Peacemaking*, page 55.

explicitly recognised the wartime changes to the culture, the assumption was that a pre-existing culture could be re-discovered and asserted to bring peace.

As scholars have long discussed, there is no such thing as 'traditional society'.[15] If 'traditional' or 'customary' were understood as an 'ideal type' that was contrasted with change, the 'modern' and 'the state', it did not exist.[16] After all, 'custom' and 'tradition' were often 'invented' or constructed, including to support colonial or authoritarian regimes.[17] Yet, 'invention' was never simple and powerful authorities always had to enter into a process of messy contested co-production.[18] So 'custom' and 'tradition' both inform and are shaped by everyday practice. Following the arguments of Graeber, evoking a 'tradition' can also be an act of cultural refusal that contests authoritarian rule.

In reality, while Wunlit was presented as 'tradition', it changed the logics of peace-making and re-crafted 'customs' in order to reshape political hierarchies, social identities and possibilities of peace. The language of the 'customary' helped naturalise these changes. This chapter will discuss how Wunlit; performed tradition, increasing the authority of the church and made other priests sacred; made identity more inclusive by ignoring the dead; and removed the judicial logic of peace.

Peace as a performance of 'tradition'

Bill Lowrey, one of the instigators of Wunlit, had worked for ACROSS (Association of Christian Resource Organizations Serving Sudan) until 1993, before doing his PhD in the USA on traditional methods of conflict mediation,[19] based on his 1994 involvement in a peace meeting to end the

---

[15]   Georg Elwert and Thomas Bierschenk, 'Development Aid as Intervention in Dynamic Systems', *Sociologia Ruralis* 28:2/3 (1988): 99–112, page 99.

[16]   Comaroff and Comaroff, 'Chiefs, Capital, and the State'.

[17]   Terence Ranger, 'The Invention of Tradition in Colonial Africa', in Eric Hobsbawm and Terence Ranger (eds) *The Invention of Tradition* (Cambridge University Press, 1983): 211–262. For recent discussions, see: Kasper Hoffmann, Koen Vlassenroot and Emery Mudinga, *'Courses au pouvoir*: The Struggle Over Customary Capital in the Eastern Democratic Republic of Congo', *Journal of Eastern African Studies* 14:1 (2020): 125–144; Judith Verweijen and Vicky Van Bockhaven, 'Revisiting Colonial Legacies in Knowledge Production on Customary Authority in Central and East Africa', *Journal of Eastern African Studies* 14:1 (2020): 1–23.

[18]   Comaroff and Comaroff, 'Chiefs, Capital, and the State'; Cooper, 'Conflict and Connection'; Feierman, *Peasant Intellectuals*; Spear; 'Neo-traditionalism'; Stoler and Cooper, 'Between Metropole and Colony'.

[19]   William. O. Lowrey, 'A Flicker of Hope in Sudan', Sudan Open Archive, 1998.

Lou-Jikany Nuer fight in eastern Southern Sudan at the request of Riek Machar. Lowrey was explicit in his recognition of the religious centrality in Nuer life.[20] In Lowrey's doctoral thesis, he wrote: 'At the heart of Nuer life and society is their religion. The basic beliefs and practice of Nuer traditional religion are woven into the fabric of culture along with the dominant motif of Spirit, or *kuoth* (Evans Pritchard, *Nuer Religion* 315)'.[21] He went on to describe how many Nuer are also now followers of the Christian faith, and that their belief system can be understood as layers of belief constructed with the basic layer being traditional religion and culture. This both legitimised the church's role in peace and also encouraged Lowrey to include Nuer and Dinka religious figures in the peace negotiations.

Church leaders explicitly related Nuer and Dinka practice to Christian belief. For example, Lowrey described how a:

> calabash of water was brought with sesame seed floating in the water. The seed represent new life. The calabash was passed and each person spit ritually into the gourd bow. This symbolized the joining of life fluids with one another. In addition, the fine spray spittle represents the coolest part of the tongue that can be the root of conflict or contribute to healing and peace. We all came forward and washed our hands in the water. Then we took water in our cupped hands and threw water as a sprinkling over each other. We were being sprinkled clean from the past sins and conflict and enabled to start anew to build the peace. The second libation was similar the next day. But this time there was no spitting or passing the calabash. The oldest Dinka chief walked around the circle with a young woman carrying the calabash. As he came to each person, he dipped the water and sprinkled water on the feet of each of us. This signified the cooling down from the heat of conflict and the preparation of our feet for the work of peace.[22]

Lowry explicitly interpreted this with reference to Isaiah's description that 'how beautiful on the mountains are the feet of those who bring peace / good news'.[23]

The work of Lowrey and his colleagues, such as John Ashworth, was a classic expression of the early 1990s local turn in peace-building that was advocated by scholars such as Lederach. As Ashworth explains, in Southern Sudan the leaders at the local level had 'the greatest stake in the outcome of

---

[20]   Lowrey, 'Passing the Peace ... People to People', page 11.
[21]   Ibid., pages 11–12.
[22]   Chiefs of Dinka and Nuer Stir Crowds, Emotions and Perform Rituals – *Dinka-Nuer West Bank Peace and Reconciliation Conference* (NSCC, 1999), page 4, www.sudanarchive.net/?a=d&d=SLPD19990220-01&e=-------en-20--1--txt-txIN%7ctxTI%7ctxAU-----------, accessed 13 December 2022.
[23]   Lowrey, 'Passing the Peace ... People to People', pages 4–5.

a peace process as well as an intimate knowledge both of the community's suffering and its resources'.[24] According to Lederach, international churches (specifically the Catholic Church for Lederach) have a unique role to play as they operate at every level (from the local to international).[25] At the mid-level, the church's role is described as one of civil society.

Lowrey described how people at Wunlit needed to reinstate rituals and truth-telling to build trust and make peace. For Lowrey, peace required the revitalisation of the Nuer culture and system of government.[26] In his thesis, he explicitly mentions that a limitation of his approach is that culture has undergone massive change after invasions, colonialism, central government power and Christian missionary activity. 'There are consequences to the battering of the traditional'.[27] Therefore, there was an awareness from Lowrey that the 'tradition' of Wunlit was not something static in the past, but something being remade as an instrument of peace-making. Scholars have explored how tradition and the boundaries between 'traditional' and 'modern' have been co-constituted.[28] Recent scholarship has become more interested in how customary authority is reimagined, crafted and drawn upon within social orders.[29]

[24]   John Ashworth and Maura Ryan, '"One Nation from Every Tribe, Tongue, and People": The Church and Strategic Peacebuilding in South Sudan', *Journal of Catholic Social Thought* 10:1 (2013), page 52.

[25]   Ashworth and Ryan, '"One Nation from Every Tribe, Tongue and People"'.

[26]   Lowrey, 'Passing the Peace ... People to People', page 16.

[27]   Ibid., page 19.

[28]   Filip De Boeck, 'Postcolonialism, Power and Identity: Local and Global Perspectives from Zaire', in Richard Werbner and Terence Ranger (eds), *Postcolonial Identities in Africa* (Zed Books, 1996); Corinne A. Kratz, '"We've Always Done It Like This... Except for a Few Details": "Tradition" and "Innovation" in Okiek Ceremonies', *Comparative Studies in Society and History* 35:1 (1993): 30–65; Helene Maria Kyed and Lars Buur, 'Introduction: Traditional Authority and Democratization in Africa', in Lars Buur and Helene Maria Kyed (eds), *State Recognition and Democratization in Sub-Saharan Africa: A New Dawn for Traditional Authorities?* (Palgrave Macmillan, 2007): 1–30; Carola Lentz, *Ethnicity and the Making of History in Northern Ghana* (Edinburgh University Press, 2006); Rijk van Dijk and Emile van Rouveroy van Nieuwaal, 'Introduction: The Domestication of Chieftaincy in Africa: From the Imposed to the Imagined', in Emile van Rouveroy van Nieuwaal and Rijk van Dijk (eds), *African Chieftaincy in a New Socio-Political Landscape* (Lit Verlag, 1999): 1–20.

[29]   De Boeck, 'Postcolonialism'; Kratz, '"We Have Always Done It Like This"'; Kyed and Buur, 'Introduction'; Lentz, 'Ethnicity and the Making of History'; van Dijk and van Rouveroy van Nieuwaal, 'Introduction'; Justin Willis, 'Hukm:

At Wunlit authority, custom and ritual were remade. As we will see below, Wunlit marked a significant rupture in the logics of peace-making (for better and for worse). At the same time, for custom to carry authority it needs to convey a pretext of the continuity. The peace of Wunlit drew on symbols of peace from the *kuar muon* and *baany e biith,* including the ritual slaughter of the white bull. The repetitive reference to tradition meant that Wunlit performed the peace as if it was a continuity; the reference to tradition created a veil of permanence and helped to naturalise and make acceptable the changes instigated. The partly illusionary sense that this new 'creolisation' of authority was familiar, helped people and pre-existing authorities accept it.[30]

Increasing the authority of the church

In the 1990s, many Southern Sudanese churches were experiencing new support and authority. For example, to the east of the Nile in Bor (where the SPLA's first mutiny took place and that was home to much of the SPLA leadership) there was a massive growth in the Episcopal Church of Sudan (ECS).[31] For church historian Zink, a key moment in the history of the church in the 1990s was the isolation of Southern Sudanese church leaders from the international church hierarchy. In Bor, this resulted in the minimum requirement for conversion no longer being a school-based education, but instead the burning of *jak* (spirits).[32] Many Southern Sudanese had been converted in the Ethiopian refugee camps, and their closing in the early 1990s brought evangelists back to Southern Sudan and the sudden growth of the church.[33]

For some, the church brought new dilemmas. Hutchinson has highlighted how, among the Nuer, the church failed to provide spiritual and moral solutions to pollution.[34] In contrast, Zink attributes Christian conversations to the failure

---

The Creolization of Authority in Condominium Sudan', *The Journal of African History* 46:1 (2005): 29–50.

[30]   Willis uses these ideas to discuss Ali el Tom's authority in the Sudan: Willis, 'Hukm'.

[31]   Jesse A. Zink, *Christianity and Catastrophe in South Sudan* (Baylor Press, 2018); Mark Nikkel, *Dinka Christianity: The Origins and Development of Christianity among the Dinka of Sudan with Special Reference to the Songs of Dinka Christians* (Paulines Publications, 2001), page 242.

[32]   Ibid.

[33]   Christopher Tounsel, 'Khartoum Goliath: SPLM/SPLA Update and Martial Theology during the Second Sudanese Civil War', *Journal of Africana Religions* 4:2 (2016): 129–153.

[34]   Hutchinson, *Nuer Dilemmas: Coping with Money, War, and the State* (University of California Press, 1996), pages 323–334.

of other religious beliefs to respond to the newly catastrophic nature of war, suggesting that the church best redressed their wartime social predicament.[35] Christian aid organisations also brought much aid to Southern Sudan. Some of this aid was channelled through local churches,[36] building their authority.

The 1990s also brought new opportunities for church leaders to assert their role in national politics. Two massive events reshaped the SPLA at the end of the 1980s and the beginning of the 1990s: in 1989, General Omer al-Bashir took power in Sudan, with his party's stronger, more exclusively Islamic agenda; and in 1991 the Marxist regime in Ethiopia, which had supported the SPLA, fell. The SPLA needed new international backing and this could now include anti-Islamists in the USA. The SPLA-church relations warmed.[37] This shifting international politics forced the resolution of the 1980s dilemma about how churches in Southern Sudan should relate to the SPLA.[38] The early Marxist ideology and Soviet support for the SPLA had minimised SPLA sympathy for the church.[39] At the same time, despite the SPLA's formal Marxist affinities, the SPLA operated with affinity to the church and many commanders in the SPLA were loyal church attendees. The camps in Ethiopia in the 1980s included both a model tending towards Marxist fighting units and also churches that provided aid and education. These were particularly influential over the 12,000 boys who had trekked to Ethiopia, many of whom were educated in Christian schools in the Ethiopian camps and who were then baptised. Their own long journeys and the comparison with biblical narratives gave them a way to understand their struggles.

It was in the late 1980s context of growing SPLA demands on the church that tensions arose between SPLA leader John Garang and the ecumenical Sudan Council of Churches. Garang convened a meeting with Bishop Paride Taban (Catholic Church) and Bishop Nathaniel Garang (ECS Church), and the New Sudan Council of Churches was formed as a result in 1989. This new body agreed to follow SPLA politics and include 'New Sudan' in its name, but the NSCC was explicit that it did not want to be the spiritual wing of the SPLA.[40]

Later, church leaders would highlight that the church (as in 'a broadly ecumenical Christian church') 'was the only institution that remained on the ground with the people'.[41] This was explicitly contrasted with the absence of

35   Zink, *Christianity and Catastrophe*.
36   Hutchinson, *Nuer Dilemmas*, page 347.
37   Tounsel, 'Khartoum Goliath'.
38   Bradbury et al., *Local Peace Processes in Sudan*, page 37.
39   Wheeler, 'Finding Meaning Amid the Chaos', page 56.
40   Bradbury et al., *Local Peace Processes in Sudan*, page 37.
41   Ashworth and Ryan, '"One Nation from Every Tribe, Tongue, and People"', page 47.

the government, the UN and secular NGOs and in the apparent context of the erosion of the authority of local chiefs 'by young "comrades" with guns'.[42]

By the mid-1990s, tensions still remained between the church and the SPLM/A. The SPLM/A accused the NSCC of being controlled by the Sudan Council of Churches and, therefore, failing to mobilise support and be active in favour of the SPLA's proclaimed liberation struggle. The church was accused of blocking SPLA recruitment and harbouring deserters; it was accused of being divided along ethnic lines and failing to be able to reconcile. The church also publicised abuses carried out by the SPLA.[43] In turn, the church was frustrated that its role in the liberation struggle was not recognised and that its attempt to be neutral was not understood. The church also highlighted that church workers had been harassed and even killed for their faith. At the same time, the SPLM were grateful for the NSCC's role in international advocacy.

On 11 October 1996, it was finally decided that a dialogue should be held between the SPLM and the NSCC. This was carried out the following July in Kejiko (Yei County). This was part of the series of conferences and workshops held by the SPLM after 1994 as it sought to comply with international pressure to democratise the movement. The vision statements of the NSCC and SPLA were similar – although the NSCC's was to preserve the 'spiritual and moral welfares of the people' and the SPLA's was to 'wage a just war for liberation'. The statement 'Here We Stand United in Action for Peace' was a slogan used to draw the church and SPLM together. The dialogue recognised the 'desperate need to reconcile the different ethnic, political and military groupings in Sudan', and the church was encouraged to have a role in reconciliation.

This gave the church a broad, SPLA-backed mandate to engage in peacemaking. This could be justified along biblical lines. It also gave opportunities for the church to assert itself as capable of wielding peace-making authority long associated with divine authorities in Southern Sudan. By taking on the role of peace and reconciliation, churches could assert their role as akin to figures such as the *kuar muon* and *baany e biith*, and use this as an opportunity to not only rebuild relationships with the SPLA but also to establish authority among Southern Sudanese.

Rituals and making other priests sacred

As the NSCC became the visible broker of peace at Wunlit, the *kuar muon* and *baany e biith* power was reshaped through ritual. Many leaders at Wunlit were practicing Christians, but the everyday spiritual life of villages and cattle camps in the region was controlled by figures such as the *kuar muon*, the *baany*

---

[42]   Ibid., page 47.
[43]   Tounsel, 'Khartoum Goliath'.

e biith and the Nuer prophets.[44] Churches have been divided on their relationships with these divine authorities and some have challenged their legitimacy
and power. Yet, the NSCC invited to Wunlit a significant number of *kuar
muon* and *baany e biith*. Wunlit also recognised the symbolic value of cattle
sacrifice,[45] ignoring some churches who had prohibited such sacrifices. They
opened proceedings by slaughtering a white bull; 'bitter' *kuar muon* and *baany
e biith* were among the first to address the conference on its opening day.

In many ways, the conference appeared to recognise and restore the authority of *kuar muon* and *baany e biith*. As Deborah Yier Jany, in interviews for
a recent oral history report described, '[t]hough it was organised by the New
Sudan Council of Churches, the council acknowledged the importance of traditional spiritual leaders in the peace process'.[46] A common discourse was
that the previous decades of wars had withered the authority of these religious
leaders, and that their authority needed to be rebuilt. Bradbury, Ryle, Medley
and Sansculotte-Greenidge even suggest that the conference enhanced the
moral authority of the *baany e biith* and the *kuar muon*.[47]

Furthermore, Wunlit and its preparatory meetings included various animal
sacrifices, conducted by these Nuer and Dinka priests, and Lowrey vividly
records many of them.[48] For example:

> In Thiet with Dinka chiefs hosting Nuer Chiefs ... twice bulls were sacrificed,
> flipped on their backs, four men holding their legs, a knife slitting the throat,
> geyser of blood spirting from the aorta, and each of us stepping across the slain
> bull, proclaiming in action that the conflict of the past was being cut from us
> all and the peace was beginning.[49]

Oral histories collected by researchers at the Rift Valley Institute (RVI)
also provide detailed accounts of Nuer and Dinka priests sacrificing white
bulls at Wunlit.[50] As recorded by RVI researchers, Executive Chief Gabriel
Kuol Duoth described how

> [t]he white bull means that all the spiritual leaders were united ... The white
> bull was killed so as our hearts could be as white as the color of the white bull.

44   Ryle et al., What Happened at Wunlit? page 80.
45   Ibid.
46   Ibid., page 81.
47   Ibid., page 46.
48   Ibid., page 13.
49   Chiefs of Dinka and Nuer Stir Crowds, Emotions and Perform Rituals – *Dinka-
      Nuer West Bank Peace and Reconciliation Conference* (NSCC, 1999), page 4,
      www.sudanarchive.net/?a=d&d=SLPD19990220-01&e=-------en-20--1--txt-
      txIN%7ctxTI%7ctxAU-----------, accessed 13 December 2022.
50   Ryle et al., What Happened at Wunlit? pages 66–78.

The Dinka called it dhoor, meaning peace. They said let it make our hearts *dhoor*, or peaceful'.[51]

Chief Yoal Dabun Dhoar described the threat that 'whoever will do any-thing wrong will have his blood pour out like the blood of the white bull'.[52]

In Kane's nuanced and ritual-focused account of Wunlit, he argues that these rituals were used as a means of wielding power against the SPLA as they were able to draw on power claims by God.[53] Drawing on Bell's observations that rituals set up hierarchical schemes, he argues that the bovine rituals of Wunlit re-created groups of people and chiefs who had political power against military leaders. According to Kane, this challenged the ethnicised politics of the armed groups and created new pathways to peace.[54]

However, the rituals of Wunlit were not only challenging the unlimited power of the SPLA and other armed groups. They also played into the com-petition between church leaders and the priests of the *kuar muon* and *baany e biith*. In reality, in the end and over time, Wunlit limited the peace-making power of these Nuer and Dinka priests.

Firstly, the *kuar muon* and *baany e biith* were pushed towards being sacred and not divine. In their work on kingship, Graeber and Sahlins make an impor-tant distinction between the 'divine' and the 'sacred'. For them 'sacred king-ship' is a 'means of containing sovereign power in space'.[55] To be 'sacred' is to be set apart in a way that highlights the transcendent nature, but that also hedges you in with customs and taboos. In making a king sacred, the king is ultimately controlled. Wunlit was full of references to the importance of these priests, just as the chiefs' courts during the Anglo-Egyptian Condominium had given chiefs legal authority. At the same time, Wunlit expected specific tasks of them and restrained them through these 'customs'.[56] The *kuar muon* and *baany e biith* were given a scripted role in a process that was initiated and planned by church leaders.

Rituals were also remade by the Wunlit leaders in a way that indicated that the *kuar muon, baany e biith* and all others present had to accept peace. At the opening of Wunlit, a white bull was killed, apparently following the custom in Dinka and Nuer that the killing of a bull or ox makes peace.[57]

---

[51]   Ibid., page 69.

[52]   Ibid.

[53]   Ross Kane, 'Ritual Formation of Peaceful Publics: Sacrifice and Syncretism in South Sudan (1991–2005)', *Journal of Religion in Africa* 44 (2014): 386–410.

[54]   Ibid.

[55]   Graeber and Sahlins, *On Kings*, page 4.

[56]   Discussion with *bany e bith*, Gogrial, January 2013; discussion with *bany e bith*, Maper (Lakes State), July 2012.

[57]   Bradbury et al., *Local Peace Processes in Sudan*, page 13.

However, the animal was usually only killed at the end of peace meetings, or after the feud is settled in the court, to cement peace and threaten curses against anyone who restarts the conflict.[58] The killing of the bull at the opening and not closing of Wunlit forced participants to engage in a ritual that suggested that peace had been realised before discussions even took place. As one chief remarked, as the white bull had been slaughtered they had all agreed to peace and they might as well have left immediately (before discussions) and gone home. Nuer chief Isaac Magok said: 'Now we have slaughtered a bull and washed our hands in the same calabash. All these things are over by the law of Wunlit.'[59] The power of the chiefs to debate whether there should be peace had been ended by the demands of the meeting's agenda and rituals.

The silencing of the dead

Part of the new logics of peace at Wunlit was the silencing of the dead. Wunlit did not include any exchange of compensation. Some chiefs complained about the lack of compensation being exchanged,[60] and discussions recognised the need for a future legal space for exchange of compensation.[61] Yet, those who died in the wars that Wunlit would end would not be compensated with cattle. This dulling of the dead was also enacted through the ritual sacrifice of the white bull. Before and after Wunlit, prophets and Nuer and Dinka priests usually insisted on the exchange of compensation before the killing of the *muɔr adɔɔr* ('ox of peace').[62] Church and military leaders re-crafted the ritual to allow the sacrifice without compensation exchange. This was not unprecedented, but it gave force to the ignoring of the dead in times of extreme warfare.

As discussed in previous chapters, priests and prophets had actively sought to preserve the need for peace to satisfy the demands of the dead. They had entrenched the ability of cattle compensation to buy a posthumous wife for the dead. Through her children the dead could gain another chance of life and maintain their place in the family lineage. The demand of the dead for children kept the dead socially alive. Therefore, at Wunlit, the lack of compensation ignored the demands of the dead for children after death.

---

58   Interview during peace meeting in Warrap Town (Tonj North County, Warrap State), February 2022.
59   Julie Flint, 'Consolidating the Process' (unpublished, Christian Aid, 2001), page 25, quoted in Bradbury et al., *Local Peace Processes in Sudan*, page 47.
60   For example, Chief Gaijal Dor.
61   Chief Mabior Chuot, Wunlit Peace Meeting, 1999.
62   See Chapter 2 and later chapters.

While neglecting the dead was a cosmological shift, this shift could have been used to imagine a much larger community that was not bound by clans and the local dead, and that, therefore, made peace more likely. Ancestors socially tie people to small socio-political units. The silencing of the dead and the ability to make peace without satisfying their demands asserted a new logic of peace that was built on a more inclusive community. This broader political community would have resonated with Christian ideas of identity and biblical challenges against tribal divisions that were often highlighted by church leadership in Sudan.

However, the attempt at Wunlit to silence the dead, to create a more inclusive community, failed on two accounts. Firstly, the larger community performed at Wunlit was still exclusive and ethnic. Wunlit unnecessarily reinforced the idea that a Nuer-Dinka division was politically and militarily salient. This was apparent through the underlying assumption of Wunlit that inter-ethnic reconciliation was necessary. Lowrey's work and research focused on 'ethnic and inter-ethnic' conflicts. He saw these conflicts as a product of the Sudan government and SPLA making 'strategic use of divide and rule modalities that tend to multiply the number of smaller conflicts underway'.[63] After inter-Nuer fighting in late 1998, the Nuer chiefs were brought together to 'heal their intra-ethnic wounds' before being transported in shuttle flights by the NSCC to the Dinka-Nuer conference.[64] This fighting highlighted the fact that the conflict was not along ethnic lines.[65] There was no need to pursue this ethnic framing. Chiefs during speeches at Wunlit explicitly suggested that peace needed to be made between the SPLA and the people, not the Nuer and the Dinka. Chiefs also questioned why the Nuer were being treated as if socially and politically homogenous.[66] This reinforcing of Nuer and Dinka identities had implications for how future wars and peace were understood. Wunlit was a missed opportunity to use the rituals of peace to frame a more inclusive identity capable of entrenching peace.

Secondly, the silencing of the dead did not bring more inclusive identities, and left ambiguity about how to respond to the dead. As discussed in later chapters, the dead continued to have social significance. Wunlit failed to

---

[63]   Lowrey, 'Passing the Peace ... People to People', page 12.

[64]   Chiefs of Dinka and Nuer Stir Crowds, Emotions and Perform Rituals – *Dinka-Nuer West Bank Peace and Reconciliation Conference* (NSCC, 1999), www.sudanarchive.net/?a=d&d=SLPD19990220-01&e=-------en-20--1--txt-txIN%7ctxTI%7ctxAU-----------, accessed 13 December 2022.

[65]   Johnson, *The Root Causes.*

[66]   *Dinka-Nuer West Bank Peace and Reconciliation Conference* (NSCC, 1999) www.sudanarchive.net/?a=d&d=SLPD19990220-01&e=-------en-20--1--txt-txIN%7ctxTI%7ctxAU-----------, accessed 13 December 2022.

overturn cosmological and normative social habits that gave continued social power to the dead. Part of this struggle was because the silencing of the dead was also at odds with the elevating of the power of the chiefs. Some chiefs at Wunlit were eager to control the younger generation. There was discussion of the armed cattle guard (the *titweng*) and the chiefs' struggle to control this younger, armed generation. Years later, when people started to return from places of exile, chiefs were also challenged by the authority of the educated youth. The power of the chiefs rested in the preservation of the authority of elders which was connected to the continued social power of the dead. If people after death can still bring blessing and punishment, they must be treated justly until the end of their life.

The late 1990s were also a period of militarised power. Douglas has framed the existence of socially interventionist dead as a way for the 'living old to impose their authority on the living young'.[67] This is because, in most contexts, the living old are closer to death. However, in the late 1990s in the areas of the Bilnyang and connected rivers, the living, armed young were closer to death. They were mobilised in such vast numbers into such deadly wars that young men were constantly confronted by the proximity of their own mortality. Therefore, they also had an interest in keeping alive the social power of the dead to demand compensation.

The failure of Wunlit to silence the dead meant that the demands of the dead still existed. Hearts were not cooled and bitterness between those who had been feuding remained.[68] Many people who attended or were represented at Wunlit would seek revenge for violence in the 1990s over the decades to come. Wunlit, at best, was an agreement to pause revenge for a generation, so the sons of the slain would eventually carry out violence. After the 2005 CPA, and as conflict increased with changes in the political economy, peace would quickly give way to a relationship of feud. The children of the late 1990s were among those who conducted door-to-door ethnic killings in Juba in December 2013. They cited unsolved grievances from the 1990s to encourage young men to carry out this violence.[69]

The continued divinity of government

Through Wunlit, certain SPLA commanders were able to assert their authority to wield power to command or withhold peace. Garang refused to sanction

---

[67]   Mary Douglas, *Jacob's Tears: The Priestly Work of Reconciliation* (Oxford University Press, 2004), page 189.

[68]   Focus group discussion with chiefs and elders, Gogrial, May 2012; interviews with youth, Mayendit, August 2013.

[69]   Interview, pro-government armed man, Juba 2013, via telephone.

Wunlit. Its initiators directly approached Salva Kiir – the then regional commander. He decided to support the peace process and guarantee security for Wunlit despite Garang's reluctance. For Kiir, there were various possibilities and advantages to making peace with the western Nuer. The war between Riek and Matip in the western Nuer had made it politically necessary for Riek to seek support in the South, and Kiir's internal SPLA position would benefit from Riek being more aligned to Kiir than to Garang. The wars also meant that his supporters were desperate for refuge in the Dinkalands. This, in itself, became part of Garang's concern that Kiir was no longer submissive to his leadership, and this escalated into a heated meeting in Rumbek in 2004.

Kiir clearly asserted his power to make peace through Wunlit. Before Wunlit, Salva Kiir spent nearly two days meeting with the Presbyterian leaders of the process to work out security issues in the Dinkalands.[70] He also gave them soldiers to guard them day and night, ostensibly as a sign of their status and to prevent crowds. In the pre-Wunlit exchanges, Salva Kiir had guaranteed Nuer chiefs' security when they visited Bahr el Ghazal, and had also encouraged Dinka chiefs to go to Nuer areas.[71] Kiir explicitly reminded the chiefs that the peace process would fail without their reciprocal display of trust after Nuer chiefs had visited Bahr el Ghazal. Kiir sent them despite the complex security arrangements in the western Nuer and the fighting between Nuer forces that controlled the area.

In addition, in the opening speeches of Wunlit, Kiir made it clear that he would take punitive measures against Dinka who had raided Nuer cattle in order to prevent revenge. He was explicitly willing to use military force to enforce the peace. The government, not explicit divine authorities, was the force behind peace. At the Wunlit meeting, the SPLA was explicit that it should take the 'back seat' and allow the chiefs to talk.[72] However, commanders and governors of the SPLA gave speeches that opened the conference. While their presence might have been needed for security, it also created a peace-making space that was SPLA-controlled. The Wunlit conference was pro-peace, Kiir's SPLA was visibly in support of peace and it was unclear if there was any political space to oppose peace. Therefore, the Kiir-controlled part of the SPLA and its government effectively asserted their power to demand

---

[70]   Chiefs of Dinka and Nuer Stir Crowds, Emotions and Perform Rituals – *Dinka-Nuer West Bank Peace and Reconciliation Conference* (NSCC, 1999), page 6, www.sudanarchive.net/?a=d&d=SLPD19990220-01&e=-------en-20--1--txt-txIN%7ctxTI%7ctxAU-----------, accessed 13 December 2022.

[71]   Ibid., page 5.

[72]   Nhial Deng Nhial, Wunlit – Dinka-Nuer West Bank Peace and Reconciliation Conference (Wunlit: NSCC, 1999), page 8, www.sudanarchive.net/?a=d&d=SLPD19990200-01, accessed 11 December 2022.

peace (however arbitrarily) and therefore assert their divine-like nature (in Graeber's sense).

At the same time, government powers did potentially feel threatened as the NSCC grew in authority through its role in peace-making. In November 2000, the NSCC held a meeting called 'Strategic Linkages' in Wulu and then, in June 2001, a further meeting in Kisumu (Kenya). The SPLM refused to endorse this meeting, possibly as they felt challenged when the church's mandate to bring peace and reconciliation now appeared to be empowering people and the church.[73] The message of the Kisumu gathering was to support the war with GoS but to criticise the division between Riek Machar and John Garang. The two doctors reconciled soon afterwards and it was claimed that 'the Kisumu conference was a major factor'.[74]

In such an account, through the church, people and chiefs gained power to push back against the logics of government and wars of elites.

Peace as a product of mediation and not law

Wunlit was based on the assumption that peace would be made through mediation and conciliation. This ignored previous models of peace-making based on law and, therefore, Wunlit renegotiated the logics and meanings of peace, and the power in peace including the relations between rulers and the ruled.

The substantive meeting discussions at Wunlit highlighted the chiefs' willingness to return to legal order. People explicitly compared the conference to Fangak conferences. The Fangak conferences had been convened every five years by the government from the 1940s until President Nimeiri abolished the Native Administration in 1973.[75] The Wunlit meeting also concluded with reinstating the chiefs' role in the judiciary and renewing the regular review of the customary law. The resolutions of Wunlit included the promise to reinstate Nuer-Dinka border courts. However, this never took place.

Wunlit opened the door for international donor funding in Southern Sudan for NGO-led people-to-people peace-building programmes and local peace conferences. Within seven years of the Wunlit meeting, another fifty NGO-backed local peace meetings had been held, and an uncounted number have happened since.[76] Wunlit is still often referenced in discussions about how to build peace. These processes relied on donor funding to cover the significant

---

[73]   Ashworth and Ryan, "'One Nation from Every Tribe, Tongue and People'", page 57.
[74]   Ibid.
[75]   Bradbury et al., *Local Peace Processes in Sudan*, page 39.
[76]   Ibid., page 18.

Figure 3. The army looks on to provide security while people participate in a UN-funded, local authority-organised 'local' peace meeting, Lakes State, May 2012 (Naomi Ruth Pendle).

Figure 4. Soldiers look on as people discuss in groups the details of the peace meeting's resolution, Lakes State, May 2012 (Naomi Ruth Pendle).

expenses of moving people around Southern Sudan.[77] As donor funding cycles were short, the focus often became the short-term conference instead of the longer-term process of bringing people together. Agreements repeatedly focused on a negotiated, signed agreement and presented peace meetings as a one-off-event, and not a long-term pattern.

[77]   Judith McCallum, 'Wunlit Conference (1999)', in John Akec et al. (eds), We Have Lived Too Long to Be Deceived: South Sudanese Discuss the Lessons of Historic Peace Agreements (Rift Valley Institute, 2014): 29–30, page 29.

CHAPTER 5

The 2005 Comprehensive Peace Agreement

On the 9 January 2005, peace apparently started in Southern Sudan. The 241-page Comprehensive Peace Agreement (CPA) was signed in Naivasha (Kenya) by the Sudanese President Oma Bashir and SPLA leader John Garang. The agreement was an aggregate of various agreements signed over the previous years, starting with the signing of the Machakos Protocol in 2002. The CPA ended the war between these parties, created an oil-rich Government of Southern Sudan dominated by the SPLA, and committed to a referendum on Southern seccession after nationwide elections.

The CPA was an archetypal example of an internationally backed neoliberal peace agreement.[1] Since the 1990s, internationally backed, national peace agreements have gone beyond demanding a cessation of hostilities and have repeatedly linked economic and politically liberal conditions to stability.[2] If the end of the Cold War was an 'end of history', the ideological battle had been won in favour of political and economic liberalism.[3] Peace could be used to imagine, perform and create this liberal order. Some claim this liberalism was itself necessary for peace, while other scholars were already highlighting how these liberal reforms could be deeply violent and inequitable.[4]

This chapter considers the CPA from the perspective of people in the communities around the Bilnyang and connected rivers. For people living in the communities of the Bilnyang and connected rivers, the CPA was experienced as an increase in violence and armed conflict. Having experienced a period of relative decline in conflict after the Wunlit Peace Agreement, the CPA brought

---

[1]   John Young, *The Fate of Sudan: The Origins and Consequences of a Flawed Peace Process* (Zed Books, 2012).

[2]   Mark Duffield, *Global Governance and the New Wars: The Merging of Development and Security* (Zed Books, 2014).

[3]   Francis Fukuyama, *The End of History and the Last Man* (Hamish Hamilton, 1992).

[4]   Duffield, *Global Governance and the New Wars*.

a new period of armed violence. This chapter introduces the CPA, its imagined reconstitution of the political order and the performative nature of this
peace. In later chapters, I go on to explore how armed conflict increased after
the CPA.

The unsettlement of the CPA came from the shifts it envisaged and the
uncertainty about their realisation. The CPA demanded two massive shifts for
the people of Southern Sudan: firstly, it demanded a shift from war to peace;
secondly, it asserted constitutional reforms in that it remade relationships of
power. The CPA was not just a cessation of hostilities, but a package of politically and economically liberal constitutional reform. In this way, the CPA
remade the relationship between different parts of the *hakuma* and between
Southern Sudanese people and the *hakuma*. The chapter starts by outlining the
changes imagined and projected by the CPA.

To make a new political order, it is necessary for those making it to step
outside of it, and for them to be seen as legitimate in doing this. Graeber and
Sahlins argue that 'in order to become the constitutive principle of society, a
sovereign has to stand outside it ... the various "exploits" or acts of transgression by which a king marks his break with ordinary morality are normally
seen to make him not immoral, but a creature beyond morality'.[5] The CPA
was a massive rupture and remaking of the political order; the parties to the
agreement, as well as the process itself, had to establish their legitimacy to
do this. The chapter progresses to discuss how the parties to the agreement
set themselves apart as legitimate to reconstitute the political order. Political
leaders and diplomats drew on national and international cultural archives
of peace and state making. Cultural archives include norms that are habitual
and unremembered, alongside histories that are retold, that can be a basis for
validation and 'constitutes the foundations of a moral world'.[6] Firstly, they
performed rituals that affirmed their own and the peace agreement's social
distinction from Southern Sudanese people. The peace agreement took on an
ethereal quality. Secondly, the legal document of the peace agreement, made
it directly inaccessible and incomprehensible to most Southern Sudanese. A
lack of sense can be the very expression of authority as accepting it involves
accepting that there is someone wiser than you.[7] The lack of sense was not
just a result of the contradictions in the ideas of 'popular sovereignty',[8] but
also because the CPA was recorded in a non-sensical form for most Southern

[5]   David Graeber and Marshall Sahlins, *On Kings* (HAU Books, 2017), page 74.
[6]   Wendy James, *The Listening Ebony: Moral Knowledge, Religion and Power among the Uduk of Sudan* (Clarendon, 1988), page 6.
[7]   Graeber and Sahlins, *On Kings*, page 463.
[8]   Ibid.

Sudanese. Thirdly, the parties set themselves apart by declaring their own impunity for the arbitrary violence they had committed.

The CPA was also an expression of the god-like nature of the SPLA and new Southern Sudan government as it arbitrarily reined 'favour' to the extent that it demanded peace and the suspension of war. When governments and states rain favour, or destruction, or when they demand war or peace, with arbitrariness and impunity, they are setting themselves 'outside the confines of the human' and acting as if they were gods.[9] For many in Southern Sudan, the peace of the CPA ended very recent experiences of killing and lethal violence. It pivoted the *hakuma*'s demands, often framed in moral language, from that of war to that of peace. While Southern Sudanese welcomed peace, it was often not clear if the moral and spiritual dilemmas that had driven them to war had been settled. The cosmic polity was not clearly stabilised. The CPA's vision of post-conflict 'purity' was acceptance of the CPA-created Government of Southern Sudan, but for many Southern Sudanese this did not satisfy the wartime pollution they felt.

The chapter ends by reflecting on the ways that the CPA reformed power and peace-making. The CPA reasserted the *hakuma*'s power over peace, and also modelled this arbitrary, asserted, not judicial, peace. It also created a new Southern Sudanese elite enriched with petro-dollars. Their investment of these dollars in cattle had implications for the cattle-based peace-making systems around the Bilnyang. Changes to land, labour, resource and property rights also newly incentivised politico-economic elites to try to forge static, bounded territorial communities including through the making of unending wars and the impossibilities of peace.

Background to the CPA

The negotiations that concluded with the signing of the CPA on 1 January 2005 had their roots in the early 1990s negotiation of a Declaration of Principles, and years of preceding negotiations. Then, in 2001, US President George Bush appointed John Danforth as Special Envoy for Peace to take a lead on the USA's involvement in Sudan.[10] After 11 September 2001 (a few days after Danforth's appointment), the USA's notion that its security was linked to common interests of countries around the world was reinforced.[11] This was especially the case in Sudan. In this new, post 9/11 context, the US government

---

9   Graeber and Sahlins, *On Kings*.

10   Sally Healy, 'Peacemaking in the Midst of War: An Assessment of IGAD's Contribution to Regional Security', Crisis States Working Papers Series 2, no. 59 (LSE, 2009).

11   For a discussion of post-Cold War commonality, see Zoe Marriage, *Formal*

increasingly cooperated with the Sudan security services, alleviating some of Government of Sudan (GoS)'s concern about US favouring of the SPLA.[12] The USA had a new inclination to demand peace in Sudan, and it demonstrated its power over the Sudans by demanding peace.

At the heart of the CPA was an elite deal between SPLA leader, John Garang, and the President of Sudan, Omar el-Bashir, that created an oil-rich Southern government. Part III of the Power Sharing Agreement (May 2004) stated that 'there shall be a Government of Southern Sudan (GOSS), as per the border of the 1/1/56'.[13] The CPA promised a referendum of Southern Sudan's independence, allowing GOSS to be understood not simply as a regional government but as a state government in waiting. The CPA then gave the SPLM/SPLA dominance in the new Southern Sudan government. According to the Agreement, prior to the elections, the SPLM was given 70 per cent of the representation of the new legislature and executive, while 15 per cent went to Sudan's ruling National Congress Party (NCP) and the other 15 per cent to other Southern parties. The promise of elections in the CPA was a veil of commitment on paper to political liberalism, but the entrenching of the dominance of the SPLM/A created a de facto one-party system.

Scholarly criticism of the CPA has focused on it being an agreement between politico-military elites.[14] 'These deals often focus on elite power and resource-sharing arrangements, while ignoring the communal and societal dynamics that fed the war and leave embers in its wake'.[15]

Rupturing and reconstituting Southern Sudan

Firstly, peace itself was a rupture and a reconstituting of political order. Southern Sudanese had fought wars for over two decades. The mediators of the CPA distilled 'the complexities of Sudan's wars down to what they supposed was its essence: a conflict between the north (represented by the

---

Peace and Informal War: Security and Development in Congo (Routledge, 2013), pages 15–17.

[12] Douglas Johnson, 'New Sudan or South Sudan? The Multiple Meanings of Self-Determination in Sudan's Comprehensive Peace Agreement', *Civil Wars* 15:2 (2013), page 147.

[13] For discussion of the deal that made this possible, see Arnold Matthew and Matthew LeRiche, *South Sudan: From Revolution to Independence* (Hurst and Co., 2012), page 109.

[14] Jok Madut Jok, 'Lessons in Failure: Peacebuilding in Sudan/South Sudan'. In: T. McNamee and M. Muyangwa (eds), *The State of Peacebuilding in Africa* (Palgrave Macmillan, 2021).

[15] Ibid., page 364.

Government of Sudan and the ruling National Congress Party (NCP)) and the south (represented by the Sudan People's Liberation Movement and Army (SPLM/A))'.[16] The CPA saw the war in statist terms; it was a war between the state of Sudan and the 'state *in potentia*' of Southern Sudan.[17] The CPA was shaped to respond to these understandings of the war. The South was given the opportunity to vote on a leader of Sudan and then vote on Southern independence, seemingly overcoming the need for war.

For many Southern Sudanese, justifications for mobilisations to war involved a much more complex web of moral imperatives. The 1980s and 1990s had involved significant challenges to moral and cosmological systems (as discussed in Chapter 4). The CPA had provided no resolution to the divisions and confusion over pollution that had been brought by decades of war, nor any explanation to why wartime relationships of vengeance should suddenly become peaceful. This was particularly acute for those who had fought the SPLA itself.

The CPA suddenly remade it so that those who opposed the SPLA were not only enemies of the SPLA but also enemies of peace. The government could now delegitimise as war-making and criminal those who contested its legitimacy. The SPLA could use this internationally backed peace of the CPA to legitimise its sovereign claims and violently suppress opposition.[18] The post-CPA period was littered with government disarmament campaigns, often supported by international actors.[19] Southern Sudanese often experienced these campaigns as violent.

16   Alex de Waal, 'Sudan', in Alpaslan Özerdem and Roger Mac Ginty (eds), *Comparing Peace Processes* (Routledge, 2019): 303–318, page 304.
17   Joshua Craze, 'Unclear Lines: State and Non-State Actors in Abyei', in Christopher Vaughan, Mareike Schomerus and Lotje De Vries (eds), *The Borderlands of South Sudan: Authority and Identity in Contemporary and Historical Perspectives* (Palgrave Macmillan, 2013): 45–66, page 64.
18   This parallels dynamics in Sri Lanka. See Suthaharan Nadarajah, '"Conflict-Sensitive" Aid and Making Liberal Peace', in Mark Duffield and Vernon Hewitt (eds), *Empire, Development & Colonialism: The Past in the Present* (James Currey, 2009): 59–73.
19   Matthew B. Arnold and Chris Alden, '"This Gun is our Food": Disarming the White Army Militias of South Sudan', *Conflict, Security & Development* 7:3 (2007): 361–385. Jairo Munive, 'Disarmament, Demobilisation and Reintegration in South Sudan: The Limits of Conventional Peace and Security Templates', DIIS Report 2013:07 (Danish Institute for International Studies, 2013), www.econstor.eu/handle/10419/97057, accessed 17 July 2022; John Young, 'Sudan People's Liberation Army Disarmament in Jonglei and its Implications', Institute for Security Studies Papers no. 137 (2007), https://journals.co.za/doi/abs/10.10520/EJC48795, accessed 17 July 2022.

Secondly, the content of the deal and the agreement projected further rupture and unsettlement. The unsettlement of the CPA was because of the radical rupture and dissonance with reality, and the reconstitution that it projected. Bell, Pospíšil and others working together at the University of Edinburgh have highlighted how many neo-liberal peace agreements do not create political settlement and instead often intentionally create political unsettlement through the issues they fail to resolve in their written content.[20] This unsettlement can either be understood as difficult decisions being punted a few years into the future in order to try to build peace, or an intentional construction of a turbulent political system in which authoritarian elites are able to gain more power. This form of political unsettlement was visible in the CPA: both the right for self-determination in SPLA-controlled areas of the Nuba Mountains and Blue Nile[21] and the status of Abyei[22] were left unsettled.

At the same time, the rupture of the CPA was not only based on what its content failed to resolve. Instead, its unsettlement was based on the significant unrealised imaginary that it projected, leaving uncertainty about the extent to which this imaginary could be realised. Part of the imagined political reconstitution in the CPA was its projection of an imaginary of SPLA military control in Southern Sudan. Large numbers of Southern forces had fought against the SPLA for two decades, and at the signing of the CPA the SPLA did not clearly control the majority of territory in Southern Sudan. The CPA was very optimistic in assuming that they would accept joining the SPLA or the Sudan army. This was apparent in communities around the Bilnyang. One of the largest anti-SPLA Southern groups, namely the South Sudan Defence Force (SSDF) under the leadership of Paulino Matip, was based in Mayom. The CPA imaginary placed Mayom under SPLA control although this area had never been controlled by SPLA forces. Therefore, the CPA assumed it could reconstitute the divisions between the factions of the *hakuma*.

John Garang died in a helicopter crash in July 2005. His deputy – Salva Kiir – replaced him as SPLA/M leader and, therefore, President of Southern Sudan. Salva Kiir's Presidency helped solve some of the difficulties between the CPA's imaginary and the realities of military control. Kiir was a more palatable political friend for SSDF leader Paulino Matip, and Kiir was able

---

[20]   Christine Bell and Jan Pospisil, 'Navigating Inclusion in Transitions from Conflict: The Formalised Political *Un*settlement'. *Journal of International Development* 29:5 (2017): 576–593.

[21]   Johnson, 'New Sudan or South Sudan?'.

[22]   Luka Biong Deng Kuol, 'Political Violence and the Emergence of the Dispute over Abyei, Sudan, 1950–1983', *Journal of Eastern African Studies* 8:4 (2014): 573–589.

to bring Matip's forces into the SPLA through monetary reward.[23] Yet, the terms of the CPA still left key questions undecided. In this way, it was an example of political *un*settlement.[24] For example, Abyei was a contested, oil-rich region near the new Sudan-Southern Sudan border. In the CPA there were ambiguous provisions in the CPA to determine the future of Abyei.[25]

Standing outside the order – rituals, impunity and a written performance of power

As the parties rewrote the political order in the CPA, they needed to legitimately stand outside of this order to gain authority to be the sovereign that could reconstitute society.[26] The negotiations and signing of the CPA performed rituals that entrenched SPLA and Sudan government dominance and supranatural power. The CPA and the years of preceding negotiations were an opportunity for the SPLA/M to perform like a state for the international community and also for Southern Sudanese. As a rebel movement, the SPLA had already drawn on symbolic models associated with the state.[27] 'Stateness' had been part of their repertoire in claiming authority, with administrative structures, taxes and permits that mimicked state behaviour.[28] The CPA brought another opportunity for re-creating performances of statehood and new configurations of state power. Plus, the CPA also claimed the SPLA as 'set apart' and morally distinct from its people through the assertion that it could remake the political order. The CPA set the SPLA apart in various ways.

Firstly, the CPA negotiations made a 'divine' space in that it made a space that, in practice, could only be accessed by those who wielded the power to kill with impunity. The negotiations were held in large, foreign hotels, in spaces beyond the reach or familiarity of most Southern Sudanese. Being held in a lake-side resort in Naivasha, the talks were physically isolated even from

23   Alex de Waal, 'When Kleptocracy Becomes Insolvent: Brute Causes of the Civil War in South Sudan', *African Affairs* 113:452 (2014): 347–369.
24   For discussion of unsettlement, see: Jan Pospíšil, *Peace in Political Unsettlement: Beyond Solving Conflict* (Palgrave Macmillan, 2019); Bell and Pospisil, 'Navigating Inclusion in Transitions from Conflict'.
25   de Waal, 'Sudan', page 312.
26   Graeber and Sahlins, *On Kings*, page 74.
27   Ana Arjona, Nelson Kasfir and Zachariah Mampilly (eds), *Rebel Governance in Civil War* (Cambridge University Press, 2015).
28   Hansen, Thomas B. and Finn Stepputat. 'Introduction. States of Imagination', in Thomas B. Hansen and Finn Stepputat (eds), *States of Imagination: Ethnographic Explorations of the Postcolonial State* (Duke University Press, 2001): 1–40.

everyday life in Kenya, and were even further from Southern Sudan. The hotel complex was guarded by security staff and access limited. Only the parties and mediators were allowed in this space, and these parties had spent the last two decades effectively asserting their divine power to kill with impunity. Therefore, the space could be seen as divine in that it excluded those who did not have such powers.

At the same time, the CPA negotiations themselves projected a civil vision of the state with an absence of military apparatus or costumes. Although many people at the talks had significant military experience and were there because of their military power, at the negotiations they dressed in business suits and were far from a parade of military might. Being hosted in another country and far from the battlefield also made this fitting. The SPLA/M performed in line with this neo-liberal vision of the state, with politics and the army separated.

The SPLA was set apart from Southern Sudanese people by the latter's exclusion from the talks. Southern Sudanese spectators and participants were kept at a distance from the negotiations. They were physically excluded from the talks, but also from any events or participation in festivities surrounding the talks. Civil society and church groups who tried to attend, even when they had international funding to travel, were physically barred from proximity to the negotiations. A demonstration of support and cooperative relationship with the Southern Sudanese public was not part of these talks. This did not just exclude Southern Sudanese input into the constitution-like document of the CPA. It also meant that Southern Sudanese people were not part of the ritualised performance of the new Southern Sudan. These rituals helped reinforce notions of an exclusive class and a politically excluded public.

People in Southern Sudan heard about the CPA over the radio and through the commanders on the ground. The circulation of print media was limited and almost all the communities around the Bilnyang and connected rivers did not have access to a phone network at the time. When the CPA was implemented back in Southern Sudan, it reabsorbed a militarised understanding of state power. After the signing of the CPA, Garang toured Southern Sudan (and parts of Sudan). At the local level, rivalrous commanders also met and toured together, giving public addresses and demanding cooperation. These tours are still vividly remembered. Annually, on the 9 January from 2005 until the referendum, people celebrated CPA day as a national holiday. On these days, people would gather in the state and county capitals for parades, speeches and dances. Soldiers paraded, mounted guns were on display, and government officials addressed gathered crowds.

Secondly, the long, written document of the CPA was also part of this performance and set it out-of-reach of most Southern Sudanese. The specialist lawyers employed by the CPA mediators worked on a detailed text, implying that the problem's solution could be formulated in writing.[29] With the common use of legal documents in peace agreements, scholars have noted the benefit of formal legalised public agreements to increase the reputational risk associated with breaching the peace.[30] However, for many Southern Sudanese, this also acted to set the *hakuma* apart from public knowledge and accountability. Few Southern Sudanese have the legal literacy to read and comprehend such a text. Whether or not those rulers could read it, they linked themselves to the text and set themselves apart by associating themselves with this superior, detached knowledge.

The written nature of the CPA also linked the SPLA into long histories of government power associated with written texts. Since the coming of government in the late nineteenth century, their power had included their production and circulation of vast amounts of written text. Yet, the lack of schools in Southern Sudan had limited citizens' literacy. Literacy had radically changed during the 1990s, including many Southern Sudanese accessing education in refugee camps.[31] However, in Gogrial, Ler and nearby areas, illiteracy was still exceptionally high. Written texts were still associated with government and the epistemic access of government-like figures.

Thirdly, government impunity was a key part of setting the signatories outside of the rules of the political order. The CPA proclaimed the legitimacy of the warring parties' assertions of being able to commit violence with impunity and, therefore, having divine-like sovereignty. The CPA contained no provision for GoS and the SPLA to be held accountable for their wartime behaviour. During the wars of the 1980s and 1990s, GoS and the SPLA had both carried out extreme violations of local and international normative codes of conduct in war, including in communities around the Bilnyang. The Sudanese government had bombed villages of civilians, forced brothers to fight against brothers, and killed children or recruited them into their armies, as well as causing widespread starvation. Violence had often been arbitrary, spectacular and devastating.[32] Therefore, both the SPLA and GoS had a shared interest in entrenching notions of government impunity and this was confirmed at the outset of the negotiations in Machakos in 2002. The impunity granted at the

---

29   de Waal, 'Sudan', page 312.
30   Kenneth W. Abbott, Robert O. Keohane and Andrew Moravcsik, 'The Concept of Legalisation', *International Organisation* 54 (2000): 401–419; Christine Bell, 'Peace Agreements: Their Nature and Legal Status', *American Journal of International Law* 100 (2000): 373–412.
31   Abraham Diing Akoi and Naomi Pendle, '"I Kept My Gun": Remaking and Reproducing Social Distinctions during Return in South Sudan', *Journal of Refugee Studies* 33:4 (2020): 791–812.
32   de Waal, 'When Kleptocracy Becomes Insolvent'.

CPA affirmed the ability of those in the *hakuma* 'to step outside of the confines of the human'.[33] By acting beyond the moral order, and by the CPA's claims that they could do this with impunity, they could be seen as beyond the moral order. They were its makers, but acted beyond it themselves.

The reality of changing power and peace

Around the Bilnyang, the CPA shifted peace-making in two ways – firstly through promoting a model of peace based on negotiation and not judicial norms, and secondly through the subsequent massive shifts in the cattle economy.

Judicial peace

For those living near the Bilnyang and connected river systems this impunity also further normalised a lack of judicial peace. As discussed in the previous chapter, the Wunlit Peace Agreement had already started to challenge the judicial nature of peace-making, and the lack of the application of consequences for those who kill. The CPA was presented as a rupture between times of war and a time of peace. Therefore, actors did not have to be punished and there was no continuity of judicial norms. Peace was agreed between political actors. Even more than this, the CPA's long document claimed to have a legal authority and to create a whole new legal order. While such a claim was far-fetched in reality, it did again claim that peace could cut across previous predictable, judicial practices; and it left no social space for the dead. As the CPA ignored most living people in Southern Sudan, it also ignored the dead. As discussed in previous chapters, in the Bilnyang, a lack of impunity was partly asserted by peace and compensation addressing the demands of the dead. The CPA left the hearts of people in Southern Sudan still hot and hurting.[34] They had struggled to survive, had suffered injury and had grieved multiple deaths and had been unable ot provide for the dead. Therefore, there was a further sense of unsettlement and need for justice.

A new cattle class

In reality, the most significant change brought by the CPA to experiences of power around the Bilnyang was the creation of a new cattle class. The CPA made the government oil-rich, and also promoted the liberal vision of private ownership. Pinaud argues that this made a new 'aristocracy' of oil-rich elites in Southern Sudan as those in government and its military were able to acquire vast amounts of this oil wealth for personal use.[35] For the first time an elite,

---

[33]   Graeber and Sahlins, *On Kings*, page 7.

[34]   Interviews and focus groups in Gogrial in 2012; interviews in Panyijar in 2012; interviews and conversations in Mayendit in 2013.

[35]   Clemence Pinaud, 'South Sudan: Civil War, Predation and the Making of a

governing class also had significant, personal interests in resources of labour, land, oil and timber. Craze has argued: 'It cannot be emphasized enough that the enrichment of a dominant class of elite military leaders was also the result of the immiseration and displacement of Southern Sudanese civilians, and the hollowing out of many forms of communitarian organization'.[36]

The new Juba-based elite from communities around the Bilnyang invested much of their new petro-wealth in large herds of cattle that they purchased. In communities around the Bilnyang, cattle ownership was a way to convert their economic power into local, political power: cattle have long given political authority.[37] Through their herds and the ability to gift cattle, this new elite could make themselves powerful in local marriage arrangements and in local political contests. These herds followed existing grazing patterns and moved through annual migratory routes alongside family herds. Yet, they increased the cattle in the *toc* and the land needed for grazing. Kiir himself and his commanders from Gogrial used their oil money to buy thousands of cattle that were, at that time, kept in the grazing lands of Gogrial. Having brought Matip into government, his herds and those of his commanders were also kept to the east and north of the Bilnyang in Unity State.

These large, individually owned herds sat alongside and challenged previous norms of cattle ownership in which herds were owned by the family and across the generations. It was a revolution in control of property. In contrast to family cattle camps, these camps were guarded by individually selected *titweng* (armed cattle guards) known for their abilities and for their loyalty to the owner. They were paid for their service and were armed by their employer. They were private defence forces that could be bought with money. They broke away from the clan-based structure of cattle camps and shifted the governance of cattle to a more individualised, marketised system. Youth's power because of military might was elevated and without the necessary restraint of chiefs. This is discussed further in later chapters.

As cattle were key for peace-making, via compensation and ritual sacrifice, changes in cattle ownership brought new questions about peace. Through cattle, elites also gained new powers to make peace and avoid spiritual consequences of slaying as their large herds meant that compensation could easily be paid and peace easily demanded. Chiefs have argued that compensation from large herds becomes meaningless as its payment carries no pain for the

Military Aristocracy', *African Affairs* 113:451 (2014): 192–211.

36   Joshua Craze, Jérôme Tubiana and Claudio Gramizzi, 'A State of Disunity: Conflict Dynamics in Unity State, South Sudan, 2013–15' HSBA Working Paper 42 (Small Arms Survey, 2016).

37   Godfrey Lienhardt, *Divinity and Experience: The Religion of the Dinka* (Clarendon Press, 1961); Sharon Hutchinson, *Nuer Dilemmas: Coping with Money, War, and the State* (University of California Press, 1996).

slayer,[38] who can still meet the legal demands. It was not that elites themselves implemented violence, but it allowed them to expect aggressive behaviour of their herding youth to defend or expand their herds. Because of their excess cattle ownership, compensation was almost costless and elites or those from large camps effectively gained impunity.

At the same time, the purchase of cattle kept this part of the elites' wealth within familiar registers of authority. Therefore, as much as purchased cattle were used by elites to assert authority, these cattle also brought them within the moral, legal and spiritual demands associated with cattle. Chiefs and divine authorities used elites' visible cattle ownership to insist that they supported their families and upheld obligations to pay compensation that arose in the chiefs' courts. Through their care of the elites' cattle, local leaders had a small hook to insist that even the highest government elites were still subject to the moral boundaries of their home communities.

A new demand for unending wars

The economically liberal regime of the CPA also brought changes to land, labour, resource and property rights that incentivised politico-economic elites to try to forge static, bounded territorial communities including through the making of unending wars and the impossibilities of peace.[39] Land is a major point in which authorities and citizens engage, and therefore land regimes have been important in constituting the political order.[40] Condominium structures in Southern Sudan had long before tried to create rural districts that were comprised of homogenous ethnic or section groups that formed around imaginaries of shared kinship. As elsewhere in Africa, this often overwrote 'pre-existing cultural diversity with new, officially imposed ethnic labels'.[41] Over time, states have hardened their recognition of ethnic identities.[42]

---

[38]   Naomi Pendle, '"The Dead are Just to Drink From": Recycling Ideas of Revenge among the Western Dinka, South Sudan', *Africa* 88:1 (2018): 99–121.

[39]   David K. Deng, '"Land Belongs to the Community": Demystifying the "Global Land Grab" in Southern Sudan', LDPI Working Paper no. 4 (Land Deal Politics Initiative, 2011); Cherry Leonardi, Leben Moro, Martina Santschi and Deborah Isser, *Local Justice in South Sudan* (Rift Valley Institute, 2010); Nassem Bagayoko, 'Introduction: Hybrid Security Governance in Africa', *IDS Bulletin* 43:4 (2012): 1–13.

[40]   Catherine Boone, 'Land Regimes and the Structure of Politics: Patterns of Land-related Conflict', *Africa* 83:1 (2013): 188–203.

[41]   Catherine Boone, 'Sons of the Soil Conflict in Africa: Institutional Determinants of Ethnic Conflict Over Land', *World Development* 96 (2017): 276–293, page 278.

[42]   Sara Berry, *No Condition is Permanent: The Social Dynamics of Agrarian*

As the Southern Sudan government established itself in accordance with the CPA, in 2009 the Land Act was published. Land, according to the Act, included public, community and private land. The definition of community was vague, with communities being constructed around ideas of ethnicity, residence or interest. Globally, privatisation and the transferability of title was the 'gold standard' of good, liberal land reform for actors like the World Bank.[43] Yet, by the 2000s, neo-traditional African leaders, often in response to the inequities of privatisation, were advocating for communal rights.[44] But communal land rights leave ambiguities over what kind of community has rights, how these rights should be enforced and what histories are salient.[45] The CPA and subsequent land laws involved a formal recognition of neo-customary land tenure that evoke these Condominium-created ideas of territorial identity and sectional land ownership. At the same time, the meaning of these neo-customary rights changed and became more ambiguous as they were overlayed with new ideas about exclusive ownership. Sectional identities were entrenched as government recognised and enforced political statuses through land regimes. These neo-customary land tenure regimes did not reflect but did instead 'produce and sustain ethnicity',[46] and made salient the state-recognised groupings.[47] These regimes empowered local communities, via state-backed communal leaders, whose authority is rooted in kinship and ancestral custom. At the same time, the neo-customary was not the only land regime, with provisions in the land reforms for more government and private ownership. In practice, the new land regimes created new ambiguities over who had customary rights and what land tenure regimes applied.

In practice, the ambiguities over land empowered the state and local governments. While there were provisions for elections, in almost all of Southern Sudan throughout the post-CPA era, county commissioners and state governors were directly appointed by the national leadership. They were military as well as political figures. With land rights being ambiguous, it was this local military leadership who determined who had rights and who was recognised. The roles of state governor and county commissioner were powerful and crucial as the commissioner and governor de facto had the power to oversee which communities could claim which land.

Change in Sub-Saharan Africa (University of Wisconsin Press, 1993).
43 Catherine Boone, 'Property and Constitutional Order: Land Tenure Reform and the Future of the African State', *African Affairs* 106:425 (2007): 557–586.
44 Ibid.
45 Ibid., page 571.
46 Catherine Boone, *Property and Political Order in Africa: Land Rights and the Structure of Politics* (Cambridge University Press, 2014), page 93.
47 Boone, 'Sons of the Soil Conflict in Africa', page 281.

These contestations were not just about access to wealth. Property relations over land and natural resources, as well as labour, produce relationships
between individuals, communities and states.[48] Boone argues that rural property
regimes constitute the political order in that they 'create relationships of political dependency and authority, define lines of social cooperation and cleavage,
and segment territory into political jurisdictions'.[49] Communities feared governor appointments that could deprive them of access to land and resources, as
well as this being indicative of their broader alienation from the state.

Neo-customary land claims also helped the remaking of the security arena.
A large dynamic of the post-CPA context was the remaking of military power
and, over the coming two decades, the withering of the power of the SPLA.
The post-CPA Juba government increasingly built security forces that were
loyal to the regime, as opposed to being an independent army. Salva Kiir supported members of his cadre to recruit new forces including forces recruited
from specific geographic areas. Forces such as the Mathiang Anyoor are discussed in later chapters, such as Chapter 11. Neo-customary land regimes created large constituencies of beneficiaries to mobilise for political support.[50]
These constituencies, and their armed youth, could be used for support at the
centre and in rural contestations.

Therefore, the Southern Sudanese leadership were claiming land and loyal
military labour through shared sectional identities. Violence has always been
a way to forge identities, and this has been demonstrated by the divisive wars
of the 1990s and 2000s. Encouraging violations of norms of war and restraint
was a way for leaders to encourage unending wars and deep divisions between
communities, not only creating identities, but making them more bounded,
static and long-lasting. This is discussed further in subsequent chapters.

Conclusion

For many Southern Sudanese the CPA was a violent peace as physical violence and armed conflict did not end with the CPA, but instead the CPA often
reconfigured and increased violence. Global, scholarly discussions about the
problems with comprehensive peace agreements have often focused on the
content of the agreement – the legal wording of the documents signed, or
the elite deals that are behind these written texts.[51] There is a need for a more

---

48   Boone, *Property and Political Order in Africa*; Boone, 'Property and Constitu-
      tional Order'.
49   Boone, *Property and Political Order in Africa*, page 3.
50   Boone, 'Sons of the Soil Conflict in Africa', page 281.
51   Mushtaq H. Khan, 'Political Settlements and the Analysis of Institutions', *Afri-
      can Affairs* 117:469 (2018): 636–655; Virginia Page Fortna, *Does Peacekeeping*

holistic account of peace agreements that includes the international rituals in their making and the hierarchical power this entrenches. For those living in areas close to the Bilnyang and connected rivers, the CPA had an ethereal quality, being formed in distant places and empowering people who were at a significant social distance.[52] It was negotiated in lavish, unimaginable hotels, spatially set apart and discrete from Southern Sudanese, and it bestowed on Southern Sudanese leadership international recognition and legitimacy. Moreover, the CPA was made up of a long legal text that was incomprehensible to most people in these communities (and to most non-lawyers wherever they were in the world).

At the same time, the socio-political and spatial distance of the CPA from the people of Southern Sudan, including those near the Bilnyang, did not mean that it was inconsequential. Instead, this distance allowed it to have a divine-like spatial qualities and power, and to convey the authority needed to reconstitute the political order. The political order that was imagined by the CPA was far from the contemporary reality in Southern Sudan, and this created ambiguity and unsettlement over what of this imagined order would and could actually be realised.

The chapter highlights the CPA as another way that the *hakuma* displayed itself as quasi divine. The *hakuma* could seemingly arbitrarily demand peace, as it had demanded war. The wording of the CPA also re-entrenched the *hakuma*'s impunity for the large-scale death and destruction that its wars of the 1980s and 1990s had caused. The CPA also entrenched an elite government class that changed the cattle economies around the Bilnyang. With a system of peace reliant on cattle, this had implications for peace-making.

Finally, the CPA remade government-citizen relations through the remaking of regimes of cattle and land rights. Changing cattle economies complicated the abilities of cattle compensation to make peace. Changing land rights produced new ambiguities and fears, with new incentives for the wealthy to create unending wars to make bounded and static identity groups. This produced incentives for some governing elites to discourage and interrupt intra-Southern Sudanese peace.[53] The following chapters explore the implications of this in communities around the Bilnyang and connected rivers.

Work? Shaping Belligerents' Choices after Civil War (Princeton University Press, 2008); Jan Pospíšil, *Peace in Political Unsettlement: Beyond Solving Conflict* (Palgrave Macmillan, 2019).

52   Discussions in Gogrial in 2010 and 2011; discussions in Mayendit and Ler in 2013.

53   Joshua Craze, *The Politics of Numbers: On Security Sector Reform in South Sudan, 2005–2020* (LSE, 2021), www.lse.ac.uk/africa/assets/Documents/Politics-of-Numbers-Joshua-Craze.pdf, accessed 6 December 2020.

CHAPTER 6

The Proliferation of Conflict in Gogrial, post-2005

Since 2005, Warrap State has had an autochthonous *hakuma* in that people born in Warrap State, and with families in Warrap State, have held powerful positions in the local, state and national governments. As Salva Kiir became president and other people from the region gained power in politics and business, the highest positions of state were held by sons of their own soil. Even though people in Warrap State often welcomed this, it brought new ambiguities as ruling elites tried to assert their power and distinction in the homelands of their families. Through the state they were claiming god-like powers and impunity. At the same time, liberal economics and land reform meant that resources, including labour and land, could be accessed through autochthonous claims that asserted their 'sameness' with home communities. The new autochthonous *hakuma* demanded land and labour by identifying as members of these communities, while simultaneously struggling to assert their distinction to give them the authority to do this.

This chapter explores how armed conflict proliferated in Warrap State after the CPA, and acts to introduce the context that allows discussion of peace-making in the region in Chapters 9 and 10, and links this to this new complexity over understandings of the *hakuma* itself. One way that ruling authorities claimed legitimacy to control killing, while still being members of the community, was by demanding new patterns of violence during conflict. These patterns of violence evoked and remade custom to manufacture unending wars and peaceless feuds. Some (but not all) elites used their intricate knowledge of local cosmologies to re-craft these norms to incite violence and create these longer-term dispositions to conflict. For example, by advocating for the killing of women and children, previous normative prohibitions of such killings could be cited to demand further revenge and the impossibility of peace. Revenge was remade as a moral necessity as judicial justice was made unavailable. Some elite politicians contested these subtle creations of unending wars.

In Pinaud's 2021 book, she describes how 'violent ethnicised wealth accumulation was one of the engines of extreme ethnic group entitlement'.[1] The intra-Dinka wars in Warrap State, and the complexity of intra-Dinka relations discussed in the following chapters, pushes against Pinaud's claims of ethnic homogenisation.

***

In 2005, as a result of the signing of the CPA and the death of John Garang in a helicopter crash, Salva Kiir, from Akon in Gogrial West (Warrap State), became leader of the SPLA and President of Southern Sudan. While Kiir's government over time has included a broad range of leaders from different places and political backgrounds, his premiership has included significant power for other government figures from Warrap State. As discussed in the previous chapter, the CPA created a bunch of complex ambiguities for the Southern Sudanese across the country about the nature of political authority, citizenship and the new state itself. While the CPA document itself was full of ambiguities and unsettlement, what primarily mattered to Southern Sudanese was not the clauses of a written constitutional document, but the realities of how these ambiguities and uncertainties, as well as the written certainties, were being contested and reshaped in politics that manifested locally. Uncertainties in the real implications of the CPA took a particularly acute form in Warrap State, especially after the national leadership fell to Warrap's sons. Salva Kiir was born in 1951 in Akon (Gogrial West), and was educated in Akon, Kuacjok and Wau. During Kiir's 1960s service in the Anya-Nya, he had been part of the Bahr-el-Ghazal command. In the SPLA, from 1995, he had overall command in Bahr el Ghazal. Many of those from Warrap State who grew in power in Kiir's government have similar histories. From 2005, Warrap State (to the west of the rivers of the Bilnyang) had one of its own 'sons' as the head of the emerging Southern Sudanese state. This autochthonous *hakuma* was a new experience for people in Warrap State and inevitably brought uncertainty.

'Autochthony' or 'sons of the soil' are ideas of belonging and rights that have become widespread in discourses worldwide as politics seeks to include and exclude in the context of globalised political economies.[2] Such ideas are based on an essentialist ideology of culture and identity that imitate colonial

---

[1]   Clémence Pinaud, *War and Genocide in South Sudan* (Cornell University Press, 2021), page 3.

[2]   Birgit Meyer and Peter Geschiere (eds), *Globalization and Identity: Dialectics of Flow and Closure* (Wiley-Blackwell, 1999).

discourses about 'primitive people'.[3] At the same time, these ideas have become important in claims over land, especially in the wake of liberal reforms.

Over the following, post-2005 years of 'peace' and an autochthonous national leadership from Warrap State, brutal and often arbitrary armed conflict continued in Warrap State. In Greater Gogrial (south of Twic and north of Greater Tonj, in Warrap State) alone, by 2018, senior chiefs calculated that intra-Gogrial conflict had directly killed 4,028 people.[4] This excluded indirect deaths through increased hunger or lack of access to health facilities. For example, for years, people from Gogrial East County did not feel safe to access the Médecins Sans Frontières (MSF) health facility in Gogrial West County because of their fears of having to sleep there, effectively denying them access to adequate healthcare. In other Southern Sudan conflicts, excess mortality from causes such as ill health has been double the number directly killed by conflict.[5]

Warrap State has seen extractive, violent political economies and *hakuma* for over a century. As this book narrates, histories of the region from the mid-nineteenth century included violent raids by ivory and slave merchants, and violent patrols by British and then Sudanese officials in the Sudan government. At the same time, the emergence of an autochthonous *hakuma* meant that people in Warrap faced new uncertainties about implications for the power of the *hakuma* and its contestations with other divine powers.

In commentaries on national politics, de Waal has argued that violence in South Sudan can best be understood through the South Sudanese kleptocratic political market. He argues that this system is characterised by violence as 'contending elites use violence as a means of bargaining'.[6] Leaders lay claim to resources through rebellion and conflict. They demonstrate their strength through extreme violence, and this establishes their bargaining position with the president and government leadership that allows them to demand resources including positions of power.

Some commentary in Gogrial resonates with these explanations and suggests that violence is also used as a means to bargain for power at state level. In South Sudan, in practice, the president directly appoints state governors.

---

3   Adam Kuper, 'The Return of the Native', *Current Anthropology* 44:3 (2003): 389–402.
4   Deputy Governor, opening speech at Ajiep Conference, 25 April 2018.
5   Francesco Checchi, Adrienne Testa, Abdihamid Warsame, Le Quach and Rachel Burns, 'Estimates of Crisis-attributable Mortality in South Sudan, December 2013–April 2018' (London School of Hygiene and Tropical Medicine, 2018), www.lshtm.ac.uk/south-sudan-full-report, accessed 7 December 2020.
6   Alex de Waal, 'When Kleptocracy Becomes Insolvent: Brute Causes of the Civil War in South Sudan', *African Affairs* 113:452 (2014): 347–369, page 349.

Even at state level, elites who are not given power are said to use violence in order to demonstrate to the president that they must be taken seriously and included in the bargaining for power in the state. Violence also acts to undermine the current leader's ability to control his state and prove that he could access the government's claimed authority to kill with impunity. As one chief proclaimed at a peace meeting with governors present,

> Are you guys [the *hakuma*] done now? Have you finished with the civilian killing? A little while ago, it was the position of governorship that made you kill us. It happens that whenever a person wants the post of governorship, he starts thinking up what will make the incumbent leader fall – to discredit him as inferior leader. He politically carries out atrocities.[7]

However, focusing on intra-elite competition too easily misses the important role of shifting political economies, including about land and labour, and how violence and conflict are often part of the wider complexities of having an autochthonous *hakuma* in a context where the *hakuma* has long been associated with being god-like. The combination of the CPA and this autochthonous leadership increased conflict in various ways: firstly, the CPA changed the political economies of land and labour, re-entrenching resource acquisition through claims of autochthony; secondly, the *hakuma* suddenly had epistemic insights that previous *hakuma* in Warrap State had lacked, allowing them to more explicitly grapple with cosmic politics; thirdly, as leaders were from these communities, it increased their need to establish their distinction as governing forces, and control over and impunity for violence was a way to do this.

Land and labour

As described at the end of Chapter 5, the CPA and subsequent laws changed rights over land and labour, cementing neo-customary access to these resources through community membership. For members of the *hakuma* to mobilise rights to land and labour for themselves they both needed communities to be increasingly bounded and static, and also for them to themselves be clear members of these communities.

By 2005, the social autochthony of those in the *hakuma* was not necessarily a given. Leaders of SPLA born in Warrap State had gained their leadership experience at a spatial and social distance from their home communities. They built their power through service in national armies or rebel armies that often involved them fighting wars and commanding forces far from their homelands. Some also received education in schools, universities and military academies around Sudan and the world. The lack of schools that could offer a higher

---

[7]   Chief, speech during Ajiep Kuach Peace Conference, 20 April 2018.

level of education in Warrap State throughout most of the twentieth century meant that distance from rural or home areas was a necessary pre-condition of higher levels of school education and thus access to the *hakuma*. From the 1980s and the start of the SPLA, many leaders from Warrap State fought or commanded in the state and surrounding areas. Yet, they still were often perceived as much as part of the *hakuma* as the home communities.

Douglas has argued that, when governments of nations rely on centralising authority, this involves confronting powerful autonomous lineages and their claims over land. Governments have attacked cults of the dead to undermine the lineage system.[8] However, in South Sudan in the post-CPA and Land Act context, members of the *hakuma* in their home areas have made claims over land by asserting lineages, using cattle to establish authority, and keeping alive the ancestors who allow such claims. Therefore, from 2005, these *hakuma* leaders needed to reassert their membership of these communities to access land and labour. In their home areas, Southern Sudanese in the *hakuma* have competed with each other over land through autochthonous claims. In Warrap State, a few *hakuma* gazetted large farms through claims of autochthony. Yet, for most in Warrap State, both in the *hakuma* and not in the *hakuma*, claims over livestock grazing rights have been more politically prominent.

The Land Act's ideas of discrete ownership and discrete boundaries around land contested previous ideas of land ownership and usage,[9] and many people in the *hakuma* from Warrap State invested their new government- and oil-produced wealth in cattle that they kept in the grazing lands of Warrap State. Therefore, they needed to establish their rights to graze, often through claims of autochthony. New notions of exclusive land rights created uncertainties about whether certain communities had the right to exclude others from the grazing land, despite the lack of precedent for such exclusion. In Greater Gogrial, for example, access for those in Gogrial West County to one of the largest *toc* (grazing) areas involved them moving through Gogrial East County. This allowed those in Gogrial East to claim exclusive rights to the *toc* and attempt to control or prevent access. People were explicit that state borders and new land rights had brought conflict. 'We had been living in harmony all those years, without borders'.[10] Fluidity of movement and a lack of borders had not only been important for annual grazing but also for safety.

Furthermore, after the CPA, the state boundaries across Southern Sudan were re-arranged and divided. Around the time of the 2005 CPA, the country

8   Mary Douglas, *Jacob's Tears: The Priestly Work of Reconciliation* (Oxford University Press: 2004).
9   Zoe Cormack, 'Borders are Galaxies: Interpreting Contestations over Local Administrative Boundaries in South Sudan', *Africa* 86:3 (2016), 504–527.
10   Elder and retired military leader, 20 April 2018, Ajiep.

was re-divided into ten states and multiple counties within each of these states. The east of the Bilnyang and connected rivers fell into Unity State and the west fell into Warrap State. Former districts were sub-divided into counties. For example, in the counties around the Bilnyang, Gogrial West County was separated from Gogrial East County (Warrap State), and Koch, Leer and Mayendit counties were separated (Unity State). Through notions of communal land tenure, administrative boundaries could also be claimed as demarcating land rights. Therefore, the politics of administration quickly became entangled with the politics of land.

In addition to the entrenched salience of autochthony, the ambiguity of the CPA and Land Act also made military might more salient. The ambiguous nature of the CPA and Land Act, such as what constituted a 'community', made these legal changes unclear, and left space for these uncertainties to primarily be resolved through military might. Scholarship has highlighted that many of these struggles were between those who claimed rights through autochthony and those who claimed rights through national citizenship and the new territorial identity of Southern Sudan. National legislation was ambiguous, and this ambiguity provided an opportunity for those in the *hakuma* to exploit and grab land.[11] Instead, in Warrap State, competing autochthonous claims have often resulted in armed conflict as the different parties assert their claims.

People in the *hakuma* also demanded labour. This labour was partly for private enterprises such as their farms and for care of their large herds. It also became increasingly clear that power in Juba would be best secured through armed forces that were loyal to individual commanders and not governed through the SPLA structures. On taking the leadership of the SPLM/A, Kiir had to tackle the reality that the SPLA hierarchies had been shaped by Garang through the 1980s and 1990s to support the security of Garang's leadership. Garang had developed a loyal cadre of educated, militarily astute leaders who now dominated the higher echelons of the SPLM/A. These 'Garang boys' had supported Kiir's leadership selection. Their choice was encouraged by the need for a quick appointment at a time when the CPA looked fragile. Kiir's long-term leadership required him to reshape the power within the SPLA and challenge the assumption that the 'Garang boys' would remain 'king-makers'. In the short-term, this was achieved through the overnight absorption of the South Sudan Defence Force (SSDF) into the SPLA in the 2006 Juba Declaration. However, this left Kiir reliant on the support of its leader, Paulino Matip. Therefore, for Kiir and other leaders in the *hakuma*, there was an appetite to develop a new cadre of strong, loyal, military forces.

---

[11]   Cherry Leonardi, Leben Moro, Martina Santschi and Deborah Isser, *Local Justice in South Sudan* (Rift Valley Institute, 2010).

From 2012, commanders from Bahr el Ghazal started recruiting, sometimes forcefully, forces from their home communities.[12] Chiefs sometimes resisted attempts to recruit the most able *titweng* (armed cattle guards), but home communities repeatedly proved a good source of more obedient militarised labour.[13] Government figures have often drawn on ideas of autochthony, and have claimed common interest with other 'sons of the soil', in order to make demands over this militarised labour.

A knowledgeable *hakuma*

Secondly, as sons of the soil, and having commanded in Bahr el Ghazal during the 1980s and 1990s, the *hakuma* had a newly intimate knowledge and interest in local dynamics. They understood the intricacies of local politics and claims over authority and power; they also understood the implications of reshaping rituals and divine references. Part of the historic strategies for Southern Sudan to resist the *hakuma* has been the latter's distance from and ignorance about the workings of the home. This was no longer the case. Government generals were explicit about this knowledge and the power that it gave them. For example, in April 2018, General Dau Atorjong (commander of the 3rd Division at the time) asserted at a peace meeting:

> Everything in this community is known by the politicians. Even us who were in the bush know everywhere here in Gogrial. We did set up houses here. We know who is who here. We know who is wise and who is not.[14]

People of Warrap State were acutely aware of this new distinction between a government of autochthonous leaders and a government that was not. As one chief described, 'now the government is not different from the rest. We no longer separate leaders from civilians at the moment'.[15]

---

[12]   Luka Biong Deng Kuol, 'Dinka Youth in Civil War: Between Cattle, Community and Government', in 'Informal Armies: Community Defence Groups in South Sudan's Civil War' (Saferworld, 2017); Nicki Kindersley and Joseph Diing Majok, *Monetized Livelihoods and Militarized Labour in South Sudan's Borderlands* (Rift Valley Institute, 2019); Naomi Pendle, '"They Are Now Community Police": Negotiating the Boundaries and Nature of the Government in South Sudan through the Identity of Militarised Cattle-Keepers', *International Journal of Minority and Group Rights* 22:3 (2015): 410–434.

[13]   Ibid.

[14]   General Dau, 20 April 2018.

[15]   Interview with Chief A, Ajiep Kuach (Gogrial), 20 April 2018.

The distinction of the *hakuma*

Thirdly, the new *hakuma* also needed to struggle to construct their distinctiveness in their home communities to support their claims of power and impunity. As Sahlins has repeatedly argued, native kings have to struggle to 'assume the identity and sovereignty of exalted kings from elsewhere' to show their distinction from those they rule.[16] Without such distinction, these 'kings' cannot claim to be different from those they govern, and therefore have no authority to rule over them. More than this, the histories of *hakuma* in these areas, as this book narrates, has meant that the *hakuma* is seen as god-like in that previous *hakuma* have repeatedly claimed the ability to kill with impunity. Making oneself distinct and foreign is not easy, and it is even harder when claims over labour and land demand sameness, not distinction. To achieve claims over land and labour, the *hakuma* needed to be able to make seemingly arbitrary requests beyond local expectations while also gaining voluntary support from people of their homes based on their own autochthony and 'sameness'. Members of the *hakuma*'s engagement with local norms and claims of autochthony threatened to entangle them with registers of accountability. Members of the *hakuma* used various economic and social resources to establish their distinction and authority.[17] A key way autochthonous *hakuma* have sought to do this is through their assertion of control over peace and war, and the patterns of violence that are acceptable in war, even when they were at a spatial distance in Juba. The rest of the chapter focuses on conflicts in Gogrial to provide an example of how these contestations and ambiguities caused deadly violent conflict, and how ideas of a quasi-divine *hakuma* were embedded in these contestations.

Conflicts in Gogrial: 2005–2018

Since 2005, there have been repeated episodes of extreme intra-Gogrial conflict. The conflict has often been framed as a conflict between the Apuk Dinka of Gogrial East County and the Aguok Dinka of Gogrial West County – new counties that were formed around the time of the CPA. In more recent years, the Kuac Dinka of Gogrial West County were also accused of playing an active role in support of others from their county. These conflicts have been

---

[16]   David Graeber and Marshall Sahlins, *On Kings* (HAU Books, 2017), page 5.

[17]   Jon Abbink and Tijo Salverda, *The Anthropology of Elites: Power, Culture, and the Complexities of Distinction* (Palgrave Macmillan, 2013); Chris Shore and Stephen Nugent, *Elite Cultures: Anthropological Perspectives* (Routledge, 2002).

heavily armed; in the 2018 disarmament, over five thousand guns were collected by the army.[18]

Like many conflicts in South Sudan, to the outsider and on the surface, these conflicts have often been dismissed as 'communal fighting', almost suggesting that people had a natural propensity to violence. However, these assumptions contrast sharply with local diagnoses of the conflicts. In Gogrial, the repetitive accusation is that these conflicts in Gogrial are started by those in urban centres, and those with military and political connections.[19] Supplies of ammunition for these conflicts have repeatedly been transported to Gogrial by government vehicles. One chief explained at a 2018 peace conference, while contrasting contemporary wars with those of the past:

> Today this war with Aguok, it has its root from urban areas ... We, the elders today, are pointing the finger at the educated leaders who are the ones killing our children. This kind of division is brought by the circulation of written messages and letters around the communities.[20]

On Facebook, one youth leader wrote: 'We the youth are being fooled into war by the people who sleep in the lodges and hotels, their children learning in a clean environment. They even sleep as far as Nairobi but making us to die of their frictions.'[21] A South Sudan Member of Parliament for neighbouring Twic also described how politics in the state's centre was being fought out violently in Gogrial:

> We don't fight in Juba. We don't fight in Kuajok. We are staying together. But, you fight in your own areas. Why do you stay in Juba in peace with people from all the communities in Gogrial, yet you insist on fighting yourself here [in Gogrial]?[22]

People in Gogrial have been grieved by the lack of consequences for those who incite the fighting. It is 'fuelled by the politicians but the funny thing is that their children are schooling and none of them attend any battle. So, others' children are left orphans while their children have parents'.[23]

---

[18] Legislator, speech during Ajiep conference, 21 April 2018.
[19] Interview with Chief A, Ajiep Kuach (Gogrial), 20 April 2018; Interview with Chief C, Ajiep Kuach (Gogrial), 20 April 2018.
[20] Interview with Chief B, Ajiep Kuach (Gogrial), 20 April 2018.
[21] Youth leader, Ajiep Peace Conference, 20 April 2018.
[22] MP for Twic in the South Sudan National Assembly, opening speech Ajiep Peace Conference, 21 April 2018.
[23] Chief C, Ajiep Peace Conference, 20 April 2018.

Land

Cormack's research in Gogrial has highlighted how conflicts over local boundaries are rooted in the existence of different border paradigms and attempts to resolve them – often violently.[24] Governments have repeatedly mapped administrative units onto Dinka territorial sections, but these linear borders did not correlate with existing understandings of land. Over the last hundred years, however, there has been a gradual intermeshing of the ideas of government with these indigenous logics of territory, which has often caused tensions.[25]

To continue to contest rights over land, in Greater Gogrial, the dead were kept alive. People from Gogrial continued to visit the eastern parts of the *toc* to carry out ritual sacrifices to the dead who had been buried there decades before. At times it was so dangerous that only a few heavily armed young men would do this. However, it was through these ancestors that people claimed a connection to the soil and the rights over the land. The connection to the ancestors allowed local elders to assert control over the land. This was not always in contestation against the elites. Elites also sought to draw on these familial claims to lands for private herds and farms.

People also evoked and creatively remade notions of clan-based powers. A woman at a peace meeting described how, '[t]here is a bird called Agumut, which comes and sits on the peak of a house. It says this farm was for the forefathers of my clan. The person living there must relocate or face the danger of a curse'.[26] Again, the continued power of ancestral claims and associated divine powers over land were evoked to counter other notions of property ownership.

However, this woman drew no distinction between claims based on the cultural archive and the powers of the *hakuma* to claim land. During the 1980s and 1990s, the SPLA occupied various villages in Gogrial. Many soldiers who were stationed there died. For the woman, this gave the SPLA and the *hakuma* the ability to claim this land as their ancestral land.[27] Government claims over land were reinterpreted not as arising from peace agreements written in Kenya and laws written in Juba but instead, they were recaptured as consistent with property rights that gave social power to the dead.[28]

---

[24] Cormack, 'Borders are Galaxies'.

[25] Cormack, 'Borders are Galaxies'.

[26] Woman leader from Kuac, speech Ajiep Peace Conference, 21 April 2018.

[27] Ibid.

[28] Cherry Leonardi, 'Paying "Buckets of Blood" for the Land: Moral Debates over Economy, War and State in Southern Sudan', *The Journal of Modern African Studies* 49:2 (2011): 215–240.

Normative boundaries in conflict and burial

Another way that autochthonous members of the *hakuma* have claimed to be both distinct and members is to assert their power over war and peace by remaking moral norms and patterns of violence in intra-Gogrial conflict. Juba-based politicians have solicited new patterns of violence that have incited larger-scale conflict. Government elites have often tried to remake norms of revenge in order to encourage conflict. If there was a grievance, leaders 'used it to lure people into a hot fight'.[29] Some senior Juba-based politicians have encouraged the killing of women and children knowing that this will cause a feud that will be particularly hard to settle.[30] While men could be given a second chance at life through a posthumous marriage, women could not gain such a second chance through marriage and so their death could not be compensated in the same way, and their families' hearts could not easily be cooled. These repertoires of violence had previously been used in Gogrial by the *hakuma* and against enemies in government wars. By encouraging new patterns of violence by the local armed youth, politicians were reconfiguring moral and cosmological norms, and boundaries with the *hakuma*.

'Today is very different because people fight as if there won't be peace in future and the war is also fuelled by the unknown source. That is why we are accusing the government in this fight between Apuk and Aguok'.[31] As conflicts 'originated in urban lands' and are entangled with politics, they are harder to solve.[32] These new patterns of violence fostered an unending war. They also helped the autochthonous elite set themselves apart through conjuring displays of extreme violence.

This remaking of revenge and an endless war relied on keeping alive the social significance of the dead. Revenge was necessary as the dead had to be appeased by seeking justice for their deaths. As discussed in the previous chapter, the CPA document itself ignored the dead who had been killed by the government and gave the government immunity. However, in the realities of politics and conflict in the communities in Greater Gogrial, politicians were still inciting the importance of the dead in order to build exclusive communities. It was not that these politicians created these norms and cosmological understandings from nothing. Their intricate knowledge of local cosmologies and their politics allowed them to re-craft these norms to incite violence and create these longer-term dispositions to conflict.

[29] Elder and retired military leader, 20 April 2018, Ajiep.
[30] Naomi Pendle, 'Competing Authorities and Norms of Restraint: Governing Community-embedded Armed Groups in South Sudan, *International Interactions* 47:5 (2021): 873–897.
[31] Interview with Chief A, Ajiep Kuach (Gogrial), 20 April 2018.
[32] Interview with Chief C, Ajiep Kuach (Gogrial), 20 April 2018.

At the same time, chiefs used the dead to contest the violence of government. For example, the three children of a chief from Gogrial East were violently killed in 2017 – a son in class seven, and three-year-old and five-year-old daughters. The children's mother was from the opposing side in the conflict. After their deaths, the chief refused to bury their bodies as he wanted government officials to see what was happening. He pointed to tyre tracks near their bodies to suggest government figures had been involved. Only NGOs and government officials have cars in Gogrial.

In not burying his children, the chief intentionally evoked horror through the dead. It was not that these children were socially silenced. When I asked the chief if his son would have a posthumous wife, he said that he would when his age-mates married. Girls are not compensated after death with husbands. Yet, not burying their bodies was a horrifying normative violation that the chief could use to symbolise and memorialise the other horrifying violations of the conflict.

Conclusion

If the post-CPA period was meant to be a period of peace, in Warrap State, it was a period of violent peace as it brought new ambiguities and new forms of armed and deadly conflict. Warrap State's experience of this period was uniquely shaped by it being the homeland of South Sudan's president and a powerful cadre of Warrap-born government and military leaders who became increasingly powerful during Salva Kiir's premiership. Therefore, for the first time, at a local, state and national level, people in Warrap State experienced an autochthonous *hakuma* – a *hakuma* that was made up of brothers and sons of the community. An autochthonous *hakuma* brought various and contradictory dilemmas, especially in the context of the CPA's reshaping of the political economy. The CPA's liberal vision resulted in the Land Act and the remaking of the meaning and value of land. Militaries with private loyalties also became central to state power. Both of these resulted in members of the *hakuma* drawing on and reasserting themselves as autochthonous – as part of and one with their communities – in order to make claims over labour and land. At the same time, to be recognised as *hakuma*, they needed to assert supernatural power and impunity; they needed to assert their distinction from the communities they wanted to govern over. In this context of ambiguities and contradictory contestations, the autochthonous *hakuma* often asserted their power by creatively re-narrating the cultural archive (which they knew) and creatively reshaping culture. They used cultural norms to make conflicts to claim new forms of violence and to describe conflicts as unending in ways that allowed them to mobilise labour and secure claims over land.

CHAPTER 7

The Proliferation of Peace in Gogrial, 2005–2020

After the 2005 CPA, there has not only been a proliferation of conflict in Warrap State, including in Gogrial, but also a proliferation of peace meetings. There were at least eight of these between 2005 and 2018. These peace meetings were organised by local governments, church leaders, NGOs or the UN, and were attended by people from local and national government, chiefs, other local leaders, sometimes youth, and often the international sponsor. The many peace meetings did provide opportunities for people to 'vomit truth', speak about issues (even if prohibited by the *hakuma*) and to mock certain elites. One woman compared the government to a farting man. However, they did not challenge the *hakuma*'s claims to impunity nor reverse the dynamics that drove conflict.

The meetings and agreements entrenched the power of the *hakuma* and limited change. The *hakuma*'s god-like power was enhanced through asserting the government's impunity for spectacular, arbitrary violence, by establishing a negotiated, non-judicial model of peace. When governments rain with arbitrariness and impunity, they are setting 'outside the confines of the human' and are acting as if they were god.[1] Peace meetings have repeatedly legitimised the *hakuma*'s authority to do this. Therefore, the peace meetings become entangled in the cosmic politics, as a tool of the *hakuma*.

The frequency and multiplicity of peace became an assertion of its arbitrary nature, and also another expression of the divine nature of the *hakuma*. As it could demand peace at will, peace was just a peace of the *hakuma*, self-enforced, and based on its current interests in peace. At the same time, despite their frequency, they were not routine. Peace was temporary, and politically dependent on the will of the political *hakuma* of the moment. Peace meetings became short-lived. People knew that, as they agreed to peace and new post-peace political and security arrangements, they would likely be overturned within a year or two.

---

[1] David Graeber and Marshall Sahlins, *On Kings* (HAU Books, 2017).

Peace meetings did sometimes support judicial solutions, but courts over-turned previous understandings of compensation and justice. For example, at the court at Pan Acier (present day Gogrial East), legal rulings about responsibility for compensation remade the social unit responsible for com-pensation and entrenched a larger-sized social unit as appropriate to wage war. This holding of this large group accountable for compensation payments also removed responsibility for compensation from members of the *hakuma* and those who incited violence. The way compensation was exchanged also detracted from its use to quieten the social demands of the dead.

As the *hakuma* continues to be akin to the divine, divine authorities have been key contesters seeking to set limits to the power of the *hakuma*. MABIORDIT became a significant divinity in these cosmic contestations. Through peace meetings, the *hakuma* sought to assert their legitimacy to end MABIORDIT's violence. Supporters and possessors of the divine authority MABIORDIT were criminalised for their violence, while the government's violence was asserted as beyond accountability.

***

I would often hitch a lift with an NGO vehicle and that is how I first travelled to Kuajok – the Warrap State capital. It was 2010 and I joined half a dozen others on the side-facing benches at the back of an NGO Land Cruiser. We twisted our bodies to try to face frontwards so the ride was more comfort-able. The air conditioning in the Land Cruiser had broken long before, so we slid open the windows to catch some breeze despite the flying dust. It was the dry season and so, to access Kuajok, we could drive through the parched grasslands and the emptied, sandy riverbed of the River Jur. At the time there was no bridge over the river at Kuajok. This was the first time I had crossed the *lil*. As we drove, a local NGO worker described to me the significance of the dried grass landscape in the centre of Greater Gogrial. The *lil* is an area of high grass, where water remains longer into the dry season than on the higher, drier, tree-covered land nearby.[2] It is a place for grazing until the grass fully dries out and the cattle move on to the *toc* for the height of the dry season. Ajiep is a large village on the edge of a *lil* and near the River Jur. When Gogrial was divided into Gogrial East and Gogrial West Counties, at the time of the signing of the CPA, the *lil* was close to the un-demarcated boundary between these two counties. Much fighting has taken place in and around

---

[2]   The *lil* is changing. More and more trees are starting to grow in this landscape that is being reshaped by cattle and environmental changes. However, that is a discussion for another book.

Ajiep. They say that so many have been killed in the area that if you walk through the grass, human bones can be seen scattered around.

As Ajiep has hosted fighting, it has often also hosted peace meetings. In 2018 a peace meeting was held to try to end the latest escalation of conflict. During the meeting, one woman stood up and compared the government-citizen relationship at peace meetings to the relationship between an abusive husband and his wife. She said,

> The situation in our homes is that your husband can beat you up and claim that you do not know how to do things. Your sister, neighbour or friend will come to you to give you hope .... With all this support you will go back to prepare the meal for your husband despite the bruises on your face. In the evening, he will take his food and will be given water to bath. We women again accept to sleep with him in the same bed despite all that he has done. My sisters, is that not the same as this peace?[3]

In the decade and a half since the CPA, there has not only been a proliferation of intra-Gogrial conflict, but also a proliferation of peace meetings. It would be easy to be optimistic and assume that these peace conferences were expressions of local agency pushing back against interests of the *hakuma* and claims of impunity. However, these multiple local peace meetings are not a simple inverse to the political dynamics that drive conflict. Instead, they are best understood as continuous with conflict and part of the entrenching of power that makes it hard to contest supranatural claims of the *hakuma*.

As this woman at the 2018 peace conference highlights, peace, like conflict, has been part of the structures of violence that have forced citizens into abusive relationships with *hakuma* over time (just as many women suffer forced, abusive relationships with their husbands that are tacitly supported by the courts' and the law's resistance to divorce). Rituals and words of comfort, as for an abused wife, serve to assert violent hierarchies and not contest them. This chapter highlights how peace meetings did provide an opportunity to 'vomit truth' even against the government. Yet, this did not bring change and, if anything, entrenched structures of violence by appeasing dissent through listening to complaints. Instead, in many ways, peace meetings were crafted to assert the power of the *hakuma* including through regulating divine authorities such as MABIORDIT, by asserting the government's impunity for spectacular, arbitrary violence, by establishing a negotiated, non-judicial model of peace and by quietening the dead. This has provided the government a further opportunity to overcome the ambiguous tension, outlined in the previous chapter, of both being autochthonous rulers and legitimate holders of power

---

3   Woman leader from Kuac, speech Ajiep Peace Conference, 21 April 2018.

to kill with impunity. At the same time, the government is not homogenous in its response, understandings or interests.

This chapter first outlines the peace agreements held and the opportunities for speaking truth to power. Then it discusses peace meetings as assertions of *hakuma* power including by regulating MABIORDIT, asserting their impunity to commit violence, promoting a non-judicial peace and quietening the dead.

The peace conferences

Between 2005 and 2018, government officials and, occasionally NGOs or the UN, organised at least eight peace conferences in Greater Gogrial, primarily to address the intra-Gogrial conflict. There have been other peace meetings involving people from Gogrial but to address other conflicts such as conflicts with neighbouring communities beyond Gogrial. Some of these peace conferences did bring temporary moments of reduced hostilities. The most successful conference at Kal Kuel in 2008 stopped hostilities for eight years.

Peace meetings and special courts on intra-Gogrial conflicts between 2005 and 2018:

2005 – Kuanyal Peace Meeting

2005 – Mayen Rual Peace Conference

2006 – Panacier Court

2008 – Kal Kuel Peace Meeting

2012 – Tiek Thou Peace Meeting

2017 – Abuokdit Peace Meeting

2018 – Ajiep Peace Conference

2018 – Kuajok Peace Meeting

2018 – Wau Peace Meeting

This chapter initially describes some of three key peace meetings, before describing their cumulative impact on peace and power.

2005 – Mayen Rual Peace Conference

In the 1990s, the Mayen Rual market was one of two large commercial centres in SPLA-controlled areas in the whole of the Bahr el Ghazal region. During the years of conflict between GoS and the SPLA, Mayen Rual's market was constructed where there was previously forest to operate as a key alternative to inaccessible, older urban centres such as Wau.[4] The local chief

---

[4]   Anai Mangong Anai, 'Warrap State Peace and Reconciliation Conference – Mayen

at the time – Chief Morris Ngor – employed various strategies to build Mayen Rual up as a regional trading centre and, in so doing, build his own authority. He presented Mayen Rual as a safe, rule-governed, inclusive market which allowed it to successfully compete with the rival market of Pankot in neighbouring Tonj. He also actively encouraged equity before the chiefs' courts, with all living in Mayen Rual able to use the chiefs' courts irrespective of their home area or chieftaincy. This resembled the rule of law in urban centres in Southern Sudan and allowed an eclectic range of traders and people to operate safely in Mayen Rual.[5]

People from across Greater Gogrial also came to see Mayen Rual as a safe space. After Kerubino Kuanyin Bol's 1992 escape from prison, he came to Gogrial in 1993 to recruit forces against Garang and the SPLA. He reached the northern edge of the River Jur at Pan Acier (further north in the *lil*).[6] By 1994 he had received arms from the Sudanese Armed Forces (SAF) and based himself in Gogrial Town. Kerubino's forces were brutal and predatory, raiding rural areas for food and to force young men to join their militia. For safety, many people in the north-west of the River Jur fled south and Mayen Rual proved a useful refuge.

One of the first post-CPA peace meetings in Gogrial was held 27– 31 May 2005 in Mayen Rual Town (Gogrial East County). This peace conference was organised just three months after the intra-Gogrial conflict erupted, but seventy people had already been killed.[7] PACT (an NGO) helped facilitate the meeting. Over four hundred people attended from the counties of Greater Gogrial and Greater Tonj. There was also a high-level government presence including Salva Kiir (then still deputy to Garang), Ambrose Riiny Thiik (then Chief Justice for Southern Sudan) and Pieng Deng Kuol (then commander in Bahr el Ghazal and later Southern Sudan police chief).

The holding of the meeting in Mayen Rual emphasised its role in reasserting post-CPA authority and order. The CPA's ending of the SPLA-GoS war created uncertainty both for the future of Mayen Rual as a political and economic hub (as Wau suddenly became accessible), and also of the rights and obligations of those who lived there both over land in Mayen Rual and as citizens in the new Southern Sudan. There were new disagreements about whether those living in

Rual', PACT, Report of Warrap State Peace and Reconciliation Conference, Mayen Rual, Southern Sudan, 17 June 2005.

5   Chirrilo Madut Anei and Naomi Pendle, *Wartime Trade and the Reshaping of Power in South Sudan: Learning from the Market of Mayen-Rual* (Rift Valley Institute, 2018).

6   Zoe Cormack, 'The Making and Remaking of Gogrial: Landscape, History and Memory in South Sudan' (PhD diss., Durham University, 2014), page 214.

7   Anai, 'Warrap State Peace and Reconciliation Conference – Mayen Rual'.

Mayen Rual had tax obligations to the chief there or to other chiefs in areas where they had previously lived. Some even started to claim that Mayen Rual should be seen as a town and not a *payam* as it did not belong to one section.[8] For authorities in Mayen Rual, as across Southern Sudan, the CPA brought uncertainty and questions over whether this amounted to a period of rupture or return to pre-war arrangements. While Mayen Rual's own uncertainties were symptomatic of wider questions, the meeting was called to tackle the broader question of conflict across Greater Gogrial.

Before the meeting at Mayen Rual, a meeting had been held at Kuanyal. However, chiefs from one side of the conflict refused to go as 'the artilleries taken to that meeting were used to kill Paan–Machar Mawien [the clan of Machar Mawien].[9] They were explicit that militarised rulers had used violence to kill and were now using the same violence – and the same physical guns – to assert peace. They saw this as intolerable. In many ways the presence of the same guns was demonstrative of the *hakuma*'s power to rain favour or destruction, peace or war, at their will.

The dominant item on the agenda of the 2005 Mayen Rual Conference was a discussion of the details of recent fighting in the newly formed Warrap State. Much of this was around who had taken which cattle, where they were now hidden or where they had been slaughtered, and who was responsible for this violence. People counted out various numbers of lost goats, sheep and cattle.

Salva Kiir himself opened the conference. His family and community in north-west Greater Gogrial had not yet been involved in the conflict, but historic allegiances meant that it was foreseeable that surrounding communities would be drawn into the fight.[10] At the meeting, Kiir opened by stating that 'we come here to cry for the dead who died after peace [the CPA] was signed'. Kiir himself highlighted that it was all an issue of governance and a 'lack of proper management'. He asserted that 'people have to accept law and order'. He presented peace as demonstrative of compliance with the authority and order of the new Government of South Sudan.

2008 – Kal Kuel (Tonj) Peace Conference

The next significant peace meeting happened in 2008 after the 2006–07 escalation of fighting. In the 2006–07 dry season, the chiefs from Gogrial East prohibited cattle herders from Gogrial West from entering the *toc* ahead of

---

8   Executive Chief of Tonj North County, ibid., page 21. *Payams* are administrative units that are below and smaller than the county and above the *boma* (the lowest-level administrative division).

9   Sub-chief from Konggoor, Tonj North County, Anai, 'Warrap State Peace and Reconciliation Conference – Mayen Rual', page 11.

10   Anai, 'Warrap State Peace and Reconciliation Conference – Mayen Rual'.

the herds of Gogrial East. The Gogrial East chiefs justified this based on tensions between the two communities and fear of fighting. Those in Gogrial West interpreted it as demonstrative of those in Gogrial East believing that they had a new right to limit access to the *toc*.[11] This resulted in significant armed conflict. A 2007 special court (discussed below) held in Pan Acier only increased anger and hot hearts. Fighting increased until the eventual burning of Lietnhom – the Gogrial East County capital.

In 2008, President Salva Kiir called and attended a peace meeting in Kal Kuel (Tonj) that finally suspended hostilities. Victor Atem Atem (then Commissioner of Gogrial East) and Wol Deng Aleu (then Commissioner of Gogrial West) played an active role in bringing the chiefs together. This was accompanied by a group of the Juba-based elite touring Gogrial with the slogan '*akec akec*' – 'enough is enough'. The *hakuma*'s unified insistence on peace meant that peace was realised for the following eight years. Peace was at the command of the *hakuma*.

2018 – Ajiep Peace Conference

In December 2013, at a national level, the South Sudan government went to war with a new armed opposition. In 2015, they signed a peace agreement (as discussed in more depth in Chapter 11). In response to this peace agreement, President Salva Kiir re-divided the states of South Sudan and created twenty-eight states from the previous ten states. After the re-division of the states, conflict quickly grew in Greater Gogrial.[12] In April 2016, a peace meeting was held at Abuok Dit in Gogrial and resolutions were agreed among those attending. A small-scale disarmament took place following this meeting, with a couple of hundred guns handed in. However, many opted not to attend and opposed this attempt at peace. Fighting quickly escalated and people accused the meeting of causing tension.

In July 2017, President Kiir declared a state of emergency in Gogrial and deployed troops to carry out disarmament. This was the fourth disarmament campaign in Gogrial since 2005, and soldiers were accused of raping local girls as well as using violence to acquire guns. In September, a new state governor was appointed. He was accused of ordering violent arrests and summary executions against those accused of leading the implementation of the violence. Disarmament and summary executions were both spectacular displays of the power of the *hakuma* to enforce their demand for peace. They felt unable to demand peace without the threat of deadly consequences. In early

---

11   Focus group with women, Lietnhom, May 2012.
12   Alex de Waal and Naomi Pendle, 'South Sudan: Decentralization and the Logic of the Political Marketplace', in Luka Biong and Sarah Logan (eds), *The Struggle for South Sudan* (I.B. Tauris, 2019).

April 2018, the summary execution of three men in Gogrial East County who were against peace, including popular youth leader Agoth Macholdit, was particularly surprising and provocative for people in this country. With burning hearts, people have repeatedly burnt this governor's private home in revenge.

This governor also initiated a series of peace meetings, including in Ajiep (on the Gogrial East-Gogrial West border) in April 2018, in Kuajok (Gogrial State Capital) in August 2018, and in Wau in November 2018. These included chiefs and *baany e biith*, and sometimes had United Nations Mission in South Sudan (UNMISS) or NGO support. Civil society organisations such as Community Empowerment for Progress Organization (CEPO) and Justice Africa have been active in encouraging a more inclusive attendance at these talks.

From 21 to 23 April 2018, hundreds attended a conference in Ajiep including chiefs, the state governors of Gogrial, Twic and Tonj States (the area covering the former Warrap State), as well as other politicians including the South Sudan Vice President James Wani Igga, senior army figures from Divisions 5 and 3, NGOs and UNMISS. This was the governor's first major peace conference and attempted to assert through dialogue his power over peace. James Wani had been sent to represent the president, and Kiir's support for the governor was important in asserting his demand for peace. At the same time, some people refused to attend, including those from his home area.

Vomiting against elites of the *hakuma*

The narratives spoken at the peace meetings were not completely controlled by the *hakuma* and repeatedly criticised the role of the *hakuma* and members of the government in the conflict. For example, an army general in 2018 explicitly warned against discussing land at the peace conference. Yet, chiefs did not hesitate to specifically blame members of the government for conflict and to discuss prohibited topics, such as land. Some argued for the need to 'vomit it out'. This vomiting of grievances was not to incite tensions, but so that hot hearts and grievances could be exposed and, therefore, solved. One legislator argued: 'You have said that nobody should mention the border issue and that anybody who does mention it will be considered to be inciting violence. It is not true. It is what is unsaid that divides people.'[13]

Conference attendees also used comical images to mock those who tried to restrain discourse at the meetings. For example, one woman in 2018 in Ajiep told the following story:

---

[13]   Legislator, speech during Ajiep Peace Conference, 21 April 2018.

A woman left her child with a man while she went to collect firewood. The man was so engaged with the child that when the woman returned, the man jumped up in fear. As he jumped, he let out a loud fart. Feeling ashamed, the man beat the woman in the head. The woman did not complain, but concerned neighbours took the case to the chief ... Because of the man's violence, the chief and whole village came to know that the man had farted loudly.[14]

The woman used this story to highlight that the *hakuma*'s violence had also made visible their faults and costly pursuits of their own interest. The *hakuma* was a farting man. She warned that people in the *hakuma* who tried to hide their faults through violently supressing criticism would only increase their visibility.

Criticism of the *hakuma* also often highlighted the class difference between the Juba-based members of the *hakuma* and those living in Greater Gogrial. As one chief asserted, 'let those who buy you guns come to fight themselves'.[15]

A repeated accusation in the peace discussions was that some elites from Juba – and often those who were not attending the meetings – were inciting violence and buying guns, while keeping themselves and their children at a safe distance from the conflict.[16] This visible class divide, which was manifest in who could and who could not stay safe and avoid the violence, was a repetitive, accusatory observation.

Specific Juba-elites were accused of distributing guns and of preventing their allies and relatives being arrested. As one chief said, '[t]oday, our government distributes guns like salt'.[17] Many weapons that were collected during periods of disarmament were quickly returned to local markets as soldiers got hungry and wanted to exchange weapons for money. Those speaking were usually careful to limit their accusations to unnamed but specific elites, as opposed to condemning all political leaders.

Peace meetings did provide a public forum to contest government power and legitimacy. However, this acted more to quieten dissent than to bring change. Discussions about law have highlighted how colonial and authoritarian rulers have created a semblance of listening to their citizens through law courts, which has actually helped them cement their unaccountable authority.[18] In many ways, for the government, these peace meetings had a similar function.

---

[14] Woman leader from Kuac, speech Ajiep Peace Conference, 21 April 2018.
[15] Chief from Gogrial East, speech at Ajiep Peace Conference, 20 April 2018.
[16] Interviews and discussions with people in Warrap State, 2017–2019.
[17] Chief, Ajiep Peace Conference, 20 April 2020.
[18] Mark Fathi Massoud, *Law's Fragile State: Colonial, Authoritarian, and Humanitarian Legacies in Sudan* (Cambridge University Press, 2013).

Peace as asserting the authority of the *hakuma*

The peace meetings were repeatedly organised and sanctioned by senior government figures, and often had a significant presence of army personnel and their weaponry. While the chiefs numerically dominated and were repeatedly the signatories of the agreements, it was also clear that these meetings were initiated by commissioners, governors and government in Juba, and enforced with their militarised power. Peace meetings relied on the will of the *hakuma*, and the *hakuma* was free to demand peace. The visible displays of weapons and soldiers at meetings demonstrated the government's brute strength. These displays could easily be equated with Condominium displays of power that were used to demand peace in Greater Gogrial nearly a century before. Peace meetings were repeatedly used as a forum by commissioners, governors and commanders to demand compliance to new orders. For example, at the 2018 Ajiep Peace Conference, the governor communicated the prohibition of meetings of more than five people in order to discourage opportunities to mobilise. His display of military firepower reminded people that he had lethal power to enforce this ruling.

Peace meetings were also a chance for the *hakuma* to remind people of their potential for arbitrary violence. For example, by the time of the 2018 Ajiep Peace Conference, the UN was criticising the governor for summary executions. The governor made it clear that future executions were still possible. He justified the previous executions based on the young men refusing to give themselves up for arrest. The senior army figure present also described how, decades before in a neighbouring state, he had had two people beheaded, and their heads buried, to discourage others from fighting. He recognised that, if the world had seen the army behaving like this, they would have said they were animals.[19] Yet, in many ways, they were not asserting their likeness to animals, but to gods, as they could carry out this violence with impunity.

The presence of the army was also used to test compliance. Chiefs were repeatedly ordered to feed the army from their communities.[20] This brought further hunger to families already struggling to find enough food. In Ajiep in 2018, the governor and commander asserted that the army would remain present in Gogrial for a long period. The governor illustrated this by telling soldiers to start finding fields to cultivate for food, implying that they would be there for at least six months until the harvest.[21]

Peace meetings were also a chance for the government to not only display militarised might, but to assert their epistemic powers both through their

---

[19]   General Dau, 20 April 2018.
[20]   Ibid.
[21]   Governor's speech at Ajiep Peace Conference.

knowledge of their home area as well as their knowledge of writing and the ways of the *hakuma*. While discussions at the peace meetings were openly critical of government, government officials and NGO workers (broadly associated with the sphere of the *hakuma*) wrote the minutes and terms of the peace. Written documents were associated with *hakuma* and most of the chiefs and others attending could not write or read. This allowed the government to re-craft and perform their preferred consensus through these written documents. The *hakuma* claimed power by its rulings being incomprehensible and by them demonstrating that they were cleverer.

Through peace meetings, the government also asserted its authority by trying to regulate MABIORDIT, asserting the government's impunity to commit violence, promoting a non-judicial peace and quietening the dead.

Regulating MABIORDIT

Cormack has carefully described the histories of MABIORDIT and their role in providing spiritual protection and mitigating spiritual consequences, including during fighting with guns.[22] As noted in Chapter 6, MABIORDIT emerged in Tonj in the 1980s but only really became prevalent in Gogrial in the 2000s, during these periods of conflict in Warrap State. In the 2005 Mayen Rual Peace Conference, MABIORDIT appears to still mainly be associated with Greater Tonj. Yet, patterns of conflict were also prompting groups from Greater Gogrial and groups from Greater Tonj to fight together. In Cormack's research in 2012, MABIORDIT was described as widespread. However, by 2018, there were only a handful of men thought to be possessed by MABIORDIT in Gogrial.

Some individuals possessed by MABIORDIT directly challenged the *hakuma*. Youth leader Thiik's seizure by MABIORDIT protected him during battles. He could not be killed by bullets, even of the *hakuma*. He was particularly feared in battle because of this inability to be easily killed. He was surrounded by supporters including military leaders, and this allowed him to demand war and peace against the wishes of the *hakuma*. Not only were they potentially more physically powerful than the state government, MABIORDIT also meant that this power was directly connected to divine cosmologies that, by their very nature, challenged the government's superior divinity.

The *hakuma* has repeatedly used peace meetings in Gogrial to regulate MABIORDIT and to grant the government power to kill with impunity. For example, one of the resolutions at the 2005 Mayen Jur conference read:

[22]   Cormack, 'The Making and Remaking of Gogrial'.

All persons reported to have been infested by a war kunyjuur by the name 'MABIORDIT' and who live or have come to those conflict areas to direct and fuel the wars, are to be arrested forthwith, and the Commanders of the Peace Keeping Forces are here directed to use force against resistance from such kunyjuurs. This use of force can include killing should the kunyjuur use force to resist arrest.[23]

At the peace meetings, government and chiefs' discourse used language to delegitimise MABIORDIT. *Kunyjuur*, more commonly written as *kujur*, itself presented MABIORDIT in foreign, derogatory terms. *Kujur* was a colloquial Arabic word used by governments, including the Anglo-Egyptian government, to lump together a variety of divine authorities.[24] Chiefs also questioned the contemporary relevance of MABIORDIT. They argued that it was not a customary power and, therefore, not part of the Dinka cosmological hierarchies. At most it was conceded as of temporary use during the SPLA-GoS wars. As one man asserted at the Mayen Rual Conference in 2005:

> There was nothing called MABIORDIT in the past. The SPLA might have called or allowed MABIORDIT to assist the Movement in their wars with the Nuers, the Government and the Murahelein. They have overdone their mandate. They disarmed the chiefs and the authorities.[25]

MABIORDIT was presented as equivalent to the guns of the 1990s that had been distributed to the youth of Gogrial to act as a home guard for the SPLA. In the 1990s, the young men from Gogrial provided an important local defence allowing SPLA soldiers to be a safety station in the area and in proximity to key sites such as the Unity State oilfields and cities such as Wau. Yet, now the claim was that these guns were undermining chiefly and government authority by distributing to large numbers of youth powers to kill. At the same time, for the young men, their guns and MABIORDIT offered protection.

The government's attempted regulation of MABIORDIT was violent. In 2018, the executions of youth associated with MABIORDIT were an explicit attempt to regulate MABIORDIT. However, the government's failure to capture Thiik ended up only affirming his powers. The government had captured and executed some of his close supporters. Thiik had even been previously arrested himself and imprisoned at the military barracks in Wunyiik. Yet, he escaped. For some this affirmed his divine authority. For others, his support from parts of the *hakuma*. As one chief explained, '[w]hat has lengthened this war up to now

---

23   Mayen Rual Peace Conference 2005, page 32.

24   Douglas Johnson, 'C.A. Willis and the "Cult of Deng": A Falsification of the Ethnographic Record', *History in Africa* 12 (1985), 131–150.

25   Man of Lou-Ariik, Tonj North County, Mayen Rual Peace Conference 2005, page 26.

is that we are governing ourselves. If your cousin is arrested and imprisoned, and if you are working in the police, then you release him illegally'.[26]

Those of the *hakuma* did try to disarm the armed home guard and did try to suppress MABIORDIT, yet the tension between these young men and the *hakuma* was not consistent. Many in the *hakuma* elite also armed and encouraged these young men. Crucially, MABIORDIT provided the young men with their own political space and independent source of authority.

Making government impunity and criminals

Peace meetings were used by the *hakuma* to explicitly criminalise those who supported MABIORDIT and other violence not sanctioned by government. This ignored the reality that many young men had been mobilised to arms by members of the *hakuma*, instead seeking to punish only those who implemented the violence. The lack of accountability for government violence and its seemingly arbitrary nature was affirmed in peace meetings and used to assert the *hakuma*'s divine-like authority. For example, in 2018 in Gogrial East County, a soldier in the county for disarmament, had apparently raped a 14-year-old girl. The chief organised the detention of the soldier and proposed to try the soldier in the chiefs' court to cool the situation. However, the army commander then came and released him. This was discussed at the Ajiep Peace Conference but the army general did not commit to any accountability.

Judicial or political models of peace

Most afternoons in Greater Gogrial, as the heat starts to wane, chiefs' courts gather under the largest trees. Much of the chiefs' daily labours and exercise of authority is through these courts. When chiefs were ordered to gather at the 2018 Ajiep Peace Conference, they were quick to highlight the histories of a judicial model of peace in Gogrial.

> When we were children, whenever something needed resolution, they said this would be solved under the court of Buk Alok. If not, it would be solved in the court of Giir Thiik. If not, it would be solved in the Court of Angui. If not, the court of Ngot Maperdit. So, for you Manut Ngot, we want this to be ended right here in Ajiep today. Ajiep is place of law. During the colonial time; the Jur-Luel war, in Abiem, was solved right here in Ajiep.[27]

This chief explicitly referenced the law, the chiefs' courts, of chiefs like Giir Thiik (discussed in Chapter 3) and histories of law-making peace. As previous

---

26   Chief, Ajiep Peace Conference, 20 April 2020.
27   Elder from Kuac, Ajiep, 20 April 2018.

chapters have discussed, on both sides of the Bilnyang River system, contestations and collaborations over peace since the early twentieth century between *hakuma*, chiefs and divine authorities had entrenched a law-based, compensation-based model of peace. Peace had become fundamentally judicial. The version of this judicial model included compensation exchange preceding the final acts of peace-making. This judicial model of peace required a powerful leadership – whether *hakuma* or prophet – that could enforce judgements and uphold sanctions. This model of peace embodied a direct relationship between the governed and the governing. The power of this judicial model of peace was in its ability to reduce conflicts to judicial affairs.

Wunlit had challenged the judicial model of peace. Other economic shifts were also challenging the this. For example, elites with large herds could give compensation without hurting, and escalating bride-prices meant that blood wealth was often not enough to secure a good wife for the dead.[28]

Peace meetings were used as a chance to lament the judicial model of peace. The accumulative nature of peace meetings and the details of their resolutions resulted in a political model of peace.[29]

Lamenting judicial peace

Repeatedly, discussions in the peace meetings in Gogrial since 2005 referenced the need for justice and a law-governed peace. This was sometimes through instigating future courts to hear future cases, and at other times installing courts to retrospectively hold people accountable for the recent violence.

At Mayen Rual, President Kiir was very explicit that the peace made should form a continuity and not a rupture with historic practices. He referenced how chiefs' meetings had long histories in Gogrial and Tonj. As discussed in Chapter 3, these chiefs' meetings, historically, often acted as courts and offered a judicial model of peace. Kiir also explicitly said that peace should not bring amnesty as this was not the model of peace used in Gogrial. 'In many peace treaties there is general amnesty granted but with our peace there is nothing of the kind'.[30]

---

[28] Naomi Pendle, '"The Dead Are Just to Drink From": Recycling Ideas of Revenge among the Western Dinka, South Sudan'. *Africa* 88:1 (2018): 99–121.

[29] For an interesting related discussion, see Baczko's discussion of political and judicial modes of governance in Afghanistan: Adam Baczko, 'Legal Rule and Tribal Politics: The US Army and the Taliban in Afghanistan (2001–13)', in Christian Lund and Michael Eilenberg (eds), *Rule and Rupture: State Formation Through the Production of Property and Citizenship* (Wiley, 2017): 213–234; Pendle, '"The Dead are Just to Drink From"'.

[30] Speech by Salva Kiir, Mayen Rual Peace Conference 2005, page 4.

As above, chiefs highlighted the benefits of judicial peace. One chief's speech referred to Abyei as having been peaceful since the 1940s because all grievances and claims were taken through the law.[31] Some politicians requested special courts and the empowerment of chiefs to hold trials 'as in the days of the SPLA'.[32]

Law of the government

In Mayen Rual in 2005, governing SPLM/A leaders who attended the meeting presented the solution in terms of the reinstating of judicial redress of grievances. Peace was understood as requiring a return to the rule of law and peace was discussed in judicial terms. There was a lack of consensus on which judicial model of peace would be used. For example, at the 2005 Mayen Rual meeting, a *bany e bith* at the meeting explicitly argued that the government itself should be made to compensate cattle lost.[33] In contrast, the government attempted to introduce a judicial model of peace that would limit *hakuma* accountability and help to construct their impunity for war and death.

Some *hakuma* used peace as an opportunity to assert a radically new vision of 'judicial' and, through this, to build their authority. The 2005 creation of the Government of Southern Sudan prompted a flurry of legislative drafting that described a hierarchy of legal and statutory authorities from the court of appeal and high courts to the chiefs' courts.[34] Statutory courts were incredibly limited in the staffing, skill and resources, and initiatives focused on Juba.[35] Plus, they would create significant ambiguity and legal uncertainty in Southern Sudan as they contested nearly a century of chiefs' courts' *de facto* supremacy in adjudicating law. Leaders in the new Southern Sudan judiciary needed to establish their authority and relevance by having cases and grievances to solve. The intra-Gogrial conflict provided this opportunity. At the 2005 Mayen Rual meeting, Daniel Awet (senior SPLA commander and politician) claimed that hundreds of Southern lawyers would now return to work in South Sudan.[36] Chief Justice Ambrose also presented the cause of the conflict as being the lack of judges in the 'New Sudan' – only thirty at the time.[37]

---

[31] Chief, opening speech Ajiep Peace Conference, 21 April 2018.

[32] MP for Twic in the South Sudan National Assembly, opening speech Ajiep Peace Conference, 21 April 2018.

[33] Speech by spear master, Mayen Rual Peace Conference 2005, page 21.

[34] Cherry Leonardi, Leben Moro, Martina Santschi and Deborah Isser, *Local Justice in South Sudan* (Rift Valley Institute, 2010).

[35] Nicki Kindersley, 'Rule of Whose Law? The Geography of Authority in Juba, South Sudan', *The Journal of Modern African Studies* 57:1 (2019): 61–83.

[36] Speech by Daniel Awet, Mayen Rual Peace Conference 2005, page 5.

[37] Speech by Chief Justice Ambrose, Mayen Rual Peace Conference 2005, page 6.

In 2006, the government installed a court in the village of Pan Acier to resolve the conflict. The final, written resolutions of the Mayen Rual Conference formed two committees that were headed by SPLA commanders and were to be directly accountable to the SPLA 3rd Front Command, and ultimately the SPLA hierarchies. These committees were given powers to arrest, punish and seize property. They were given powers to seize the cattle of chiefs who participated in attacks. Soldiers needed to apply such force were to be fed by collecting a hundred cattle from each of the six counties.

For the court hearing, which lasted from 2006 until 2007, the government brought in trained, English-speaking lawyers and applied statutory law. Marking a rupture from common practice, chiefs and other local leaders were only involved as witnesses. The court case also took place in English, preventing most people and leaders in Gogrial from understanding proceedings. The court was a mysterious, foreign, incomprehensible imposition that, in effect, asserted the community's ignorance of the ways of government, while also asserting the power of the latter to intervene in community affairs. The government's remaking of itself as foreign, to the extent it could understand and weld foreign laws, set it apart and helped justify its power.

The Pan Acier Court did uphold the judicial norms that compensation was to be paid in order for justice to be done and the law to be enforced. However, it also ruptured and created new ambiguities about who was responsible for the payment of compensation. The chiefs had, previously, consistently demanded blood wealth from the clan of the killer. Even in cases with multiple communities and chiefdoms involved, the blood wealth could be expected from the clan itself and not a wider community defined by administrative boundaries. The continuity of this norm of the chiefs' courts even in peace meetings helped transform the problems of conflict to a judicial matter.

The Mayen Rual resolutions themselves had stated:

> All Chiefs of sections involved in the looting of cattle of other sections are to be detained under open arrest by the respective Committees while their cows are seized and kept in the dairy by the Committees so that their respective subjects who looted the cattle are to bring those cows to the Committee for return to the owners. Failure after 30 days of the seizure of their cows, the Committees can compensate the looted cows with those cows of the Chiefs. Cows of the identified accused are also to be seized and handed over after 30 days in compensation for the cows they looted.[38]

Governments had occasionally demanded cattle payments from the whole chiefdom. This was done in order to force the chief to enforce the compensation payment from the family of the killer. As the chief had the power to

---

[38]   Mayen Rual Peace Conference 2005, page 32.

collect cattle, the threat of taking cattle from the chief was used by governments to force the chiefs to collect the compensation cattle. At Pan Acier, the judges asserted that the Apuk Dinka were collectively responsible for paying the compensation. This reasserted the legal significance of the Apuk Dinka identity – an identity constructed from the territories of the historic Giir Thiik chiefdom which were now the territories of Gogrial East, and not a clan identity. They justified this by saying that it was difficult to ascertain which individuals were responsible for which deaths.

This blanket obligation forced contributions from clans and sections of the Apuk who had not been involved in the fighting. They had not been mobilised to war. Yet now the court was enforcing their inclusion in an Apuk-size social unit of their making, with shared obligations for compensation. As compensation is linked to obligations for revenge, this also contributed to making the Apuk a social unit with a mutual obligation to revenge for each other. Elite *hakuma* had the potential to benefit from larger social units. This increased the land over which they could claim authority as sons of the soil, as well as the young men from whom they could demand militarised labour.

This broad responsibility for compensation further distanced the payment of compensation from those in the *hakuma* who had mobilised violence. They now shared the obligation with the poorest in the community as if they were an equal member of the Apuk and equally responsible for the violence. Since the Condominium era, Southern Sudanese who had joined the *hakuma* had been subject to the laws of the chiefs' courts. While this could be an opportunity to hold the government to account, it was also an opportunity for them to avoid accountability. In this case in Pan Acier, the government elite effectively used this norm to claim impunity for mobilising people to war and killing.[39] Therefore, through the judicial model at Pan Acier, the elite gained an impunity to kill through their membership of the community.

In anger at the Pan Acier ruling, chiefs from Gogrial East pushed back against the government. They did collectively pay the demanded compensation, but they paid it with poor quality cattle. This was a clear statement of their disapproval of the ruling. At the same time, as the cattle were given to compensate those killed, it was interpreted by those from Gogrial West as an insult to the dead. In response, the governor doubled the quantity of cows to be handed over by the chiefs of Gogrial East.[40] The SPLA were also charged with delivering the cattle. Yet, some cattle went missing during the SPLA's delivery. Chiefs from Gogrial East walked out of the court and violent conflict

---

[39]   Tinega Ong'ondi and Simon Simonse, 'Conflict in the Greater Gogrial: Report of the Fact Finding Mission to Assess the Possibility of a Church led Mediation Process' (Unpublished, 2008), page 8.

[40]   Interview with politician, Luonyaker, August 2012.

resumed before the case had even ended.[41] Furthermore, the court case took more than half a year. The length of the Pan Acier case prevented people from Gogrial West from gaining access to the *toc* in the dry months of 2007–08, further increasing hostilities. Within a few weeks, the conflict had attained an unprecedented level of violence. By early April 2008, within a month of the court's decision, more than 1,500 houses had been burnt, more than 15,500 people had been internally displaced and local government headquarters and NGO compounds had been destroyed.[42]

A negotiated peace

Ultimately, it was the proliferation of peace agreements that shifted peace to being political and not judicial, and made space for the *hakuma* to arbitrarily demand peace (or war). Each peace agreement was framed as a rupture; they claimed to end conflict and bring peace. Peace was new and, therefore, could be presented as needing new moral and social frameworks and new political hierarchies. However, what this meant in reality was that every peace was agreed with the anticipation that its terms would be short-lived because another peace agreement would soon be made which could overturn what was previously agreed. While peace agreements were frequent, they were not regular. They happened at the behest, or at least with the consent, of the *hakuma*. The *hakuma* chose when to make peace and when to revise rules and hierarchies through peace. The arbitrary nature of peace concentrated more power in the hands of the *hakuma*. Arbitrary peace-making, like arbitrary power generally,[43] was a way to strengthen the government.

> There shouldn't be many peace talks. It should be one ... what happened again after the peace talk in Abuokdie. That we finally made peace there and sacrifices were made for peace. Why have we left this behind until people were again shot dead in their sleep?[44]

Peace agreements' constant claims of rupture resulted in a logic of authority based on negotiation and not the consistency of the rule of law. So, while the individual peace meetings created a continuity and certainty that past agreements would not be enforced and, therefore, were partly fictious, overall they did create a rupture with previous logics of governance that had privileged the rule of law and a judicial model of peace. What the *hakuma* did was no longer bound by norms of peace, and could arbitrarily demand peace.

---

[41]   Leaders of Alek North Payam, group discussion, Lietnhom, May 2012.
[42]   Interview with politician, Luonyaker, August 2012.
[43]   Rebecca Tapscott, *Arbitrary States* (Oxford University Press, 2021).
[44]   Chief, speech at Ajiep Peace Conference, 20 April 2018.

Quietening the dead

As previously discussed, the post-CPA *autochthonous hakuma* in Gogrial had reasons to both cite the importance of the dead while also not being bound by them. Claims over land and demands for armed labour often drew on ideas of kinship and entangled commitments to deceased kin. At the same time, government authority wanted to push against these restraints especially when it stopped them shaping peace and war.

In recognition of the faults of the Pan Acier case, the Kal Kuel peace agreement signed at the end of 2008 forewent compensation;[45] the parties agreed to 'forsake all claims to losses of lives, stolen and looted cattle and property destroyed'.[46] Cattle were not claimed, even when they were visible in the other group's herd.[47] Chiefs were also empowered by the Kal Kuel peace agreement.

As with Wunlit, Kal Kuel in practice asserted that peace did not demand the exchange of compensation. Yet, with this came the problem of the moral and spiritual demands of the dead. Without the exchange of compensation, either the demands of the dead could now be ignored or the obligations to fund a posthumous wife now fell to the family. The family not only lost their relative but had to find bride wealth. Their hearts were not cooled, and revenge was often still demanded.

As political leaders in the *hakuma* had eaten together in Addis in 2014 (see the opening description in the Introduction to this book), chiefs also ate together in the 2018 Ajiep meeting and this was seen as an affront to the dead. These chiefs had not reconciled and the dead from both sides had not been appeased. Many still upheld that this carried dangers of pollution. One chief vocally complained that by eating together they were disregarding the dead. A woman echoed this complaint during the formal proceedings: 'Now we eating together yet we have really killed ourselves'.[48]

The assertion to forget the dead was often visible in other parts of these peace meetings and agreements. For example, most discussion at the 2005 Mayen Rual conference was silent on the question of how to respond to the deaths of people. At two moments during the conference, two different totals of dead were stated – one at seventy and one at just over a hundred and twenty.[49] However, there was no discussion around these posited figures. This was in contrast to longer discussions over cattle.

---

[45] Leaders of Alek North Payam, group discussion, Lietnhom, May 2012.
[46] Kal Kuel Covenant, 2008.
[47] Leaders of Alek North Payam, group discussion, Lietnhom, May 2012.
[48] Legislator, speech Ajiep Peace Conference, 21 April 2018.
[49] Meeting facilitator.

Even the governor's summary executions in 2018 were interpreted as an affront to the dead. Because Thiik had MABIORDIT and was such a fearsome fighter, his family had been intentionally targeted by people from Gogrial West in the 2016–17 conflict. All his close family, with the exception of one brother, had been killed. He spoke explicitly about his spiritual and moral obligation to still seek revenge. As peace would not bring justice or compensation for the dead, he violently sought resolution through revenge.

Conclusion

The proliferation of peace agreements in Greater Gogrial since 2005 has not proliferated peace and occurred alongside a rise in violence. The *hakuma* has demonstrated its god-like power by demanding peace including via displays of physical or potential violence. These demands for peace are also violent to the extent that they are arbitrary; they have broken with previous norms of peace and entrenched notions of peace that are negotiated, and not judicial, and are, therefore, at the behest of the *hakuma*. In this cosmic politics of the *hakuma*, divine authorities have continued to play a significant role in providing protection and challenging the *hakuma*'s ability to kill with impunity. For example, MABIORDIT is a divine power that protects its holders from bullets and, therefore, from the government's power to kill itself. Peace agreements have repeatedly been used by the *hakuma* to try to delegitimise MABIORDIT and to legitimise lethal violence with impunity against those seized by MABIORDIT. In this way, these peace meetings have become entangled in the cosmic politics of the region, and enact a vision of peace that is deeply and deadly violent.

CHAPTER 8

For Peace or Payment? The *Baany e Biith* and the Logics of Peace-making in Gogrial, 2005–2020

People in Gogrial resisted the authority of their *hakuma* in various ways, from comedy to theological doctrine.[1] This chapter focuses on how *baany e biith* after 2005 wrestled with new challenges to maintain their authority and their control over peace despite new national configurations of power. The chapter opens by considering how the proliferation of peace meetings further pushed the power of the *baany e biith* to being sacred and not divine, in that it was hedged in by custom and did not include actual power to decide.

De Waal has argued that, by this period, politics in South Sudan was marketised and monetised in that people traded political loyalty for money and demanded a share of the political market through rent-seeking rebellions. De Waal discusses this in relation to elite politics, but *baany e biith* in Gogrial also had new exposure to and opportunities to receive money in exchange for blessings, curses, loyalties and making peace. Senior politicians from Warrap State would seek to buy curses or blessings of powerful *baany e biith* with cash and expensive material items (such as cars). This has brought matters of money into the politics of the cosmos.

At the same time, people in Gogrial have not simply accepted these logics of power but have pushed back against the monetisation of politics and have contested the ability of money to secure legitimate power. Money and its exchange have different meanings in different contexts.[2] In Gogrial, people have creatively refused monetised politics by remaking culture, and evoking and enforcing the limits of money in relation to divine authority. They

---

[1]   Naomi Pendle, 'Commanders, Classrooms, Cows and Churches: Accountability and the Construction of a South Sudanese Elite', in Wale Adebanwi and Roger Orock (eds), *Elites and the Politics of Accountability in Africa* (University of Michigan Press 2021).

[2]   Marshall Sahlins, *Culture and Practical Reason* (University of Chicago Press, 1976).

have done this through contesting the power and legitimacy of those *baany e biith* who receive reciprocal payments for their services, and suggesting that the purity of the priesthood has to be maintained through distance from reciprocal exchange.

A significant part of the *baany e biith*'s power, and means for them to uphold peace, has been the power to kill with impunity through cursing. *Baany e biith* have often threatened such killing against anyone who broke the peace in order to uphold peace. Yet, recently, certain *baany e biith* have been accused of accepting money to kill through their curse. They have been negatively named – *baany e biith nak koc* – 'spear masters who kill people'. Many in Gogrial argue that these *baany e biith* now have polluted blood and that this, in turn, will prevent their own children's survival. Ideas of pollution that *baany e biith* have used in the past to enforce peace and warn of the dangers of post-peace killing, have now been creatively reshaped to high-light how *baany e biith* are themselves hedged in by pollution when they are motivated by money to kill.

***

On Sunday mornings when I was in the village in 2011, I would usually walk the twenty minutes to sit on the cut-branch benches that made up the rows of the church beneath the tree. A man would beat a drum rhythmically for hours to call people to church, and by mid-morning the choir would also join the music-making. There was never a priest at the church, but always a local, polygamous Catechist dressed in his white gown. Another regular attender at the church was a tall man, always dressed in striking red, who would sit on one of the frontmost benches. He was one of the most powerful *baany e biith* in the area. He clearly saw no contradictions between his continued priest-hood, its cosmologies and his church attendance, and his ease in bridging such potential contradicts appeared to exude authority and confidence. *Baany e biith* remained part of everyday life in Gogrial. One evening when we tried to count the number of *beny e bith* in the *payam* where we were staying, that had a population of about 15,000, we could name a dozen *baany e biith* with varying different functions.

At the same time, as discussed in the previous chapter, the post-CPA period did bring new cosmological complexities, including new divine-like powers from the *hakuma* and new manifestations of MABIORDIT, and this brought dilemmas for *baany e biith*. The priestly role of the *baany e biith* in peace and purity was particularly challenged. After Wunlit, the role of the *baany e biith* appeared to be, potentially, only ceremonial and sacred, and not divine. They had to maintain the relevance of the institution of the *bany e bith* itself.

The post-CPA *autochthonous hakuma* also brought new dynamics to *bany e bith* contestations for power. This was partly as some *baany e biith* in Gogrial were now brothers and close relatives of some of the highest members of the *hakuma* in Kuajok and in Juba. It was unclear and contested how these connections to the militarily powerful would influence the hierarchies of power among *baany e biith*. While *baany e biith* claimed to build authority through spiritual powers that were discrete from militarised might, it was ambiguous whether close connections to military and monetary power would necessarily be immaterial.

The *baany e biith* preserved their priestly authority both through interpretations of events that uphold the priesthood. *Baany e biith* have interpreted rivalry with other cosmic powers, including the *hakuma*, not as external rivalries but as rivalries between different *baany e biith*,[3] reserving the power of the institution. Plus, they have creatively remade culture to assert their authority over money and a monetised *hakuma*. De Waal has claimed that, by the post-CPA era, politics in Southern Sudan had become marketised in that political loyalties had been commodified and could be traded for money.[4] Politics became about monetary profits and political alliances were realigned at the speed of a marketplace transaction. De Waal, citing Nyaba, traces this monetarised politics of the SPLA to the 1980s when food rations were sold with impunity.[5] After the CPA, increasing *hakuma* leaders funded *bany e bith* loyalties and interventions. It was as if the money of the *hakuma* could also buy divine favour.

However, many people and *baany e biith* in Greater Gogrial have pushed back against the purchase of divine power. Monetary exchanges always have a variety of values and symbolic meanings.[6] Depending on how money is understood, its exchange can entrench kinship or hierarchy as much as

---

[3]   As Mawson illustrated in the 1980s, while these priests are prolific, it is only a few *baany e biith* who rise to significant authority through rivalry: Andrew Mawson, 'The Triumph of Life: Political Dispute and Religious Ceremonial Among the Agar Dinka of the Southern Sudan' (PhD diss., Darwin College, 1989); Godfrey Lienhardt, *Divinity and Experience: The Religion of the Dinka* (Clarendon Press, 1961).

[4]   Alex de Waal, 'When Kleptocracy Becomes Insolvent: Brute Causes of the Civil War in South Sudan', *African Affairs* 113:452 (2014): 347–369.

[5]   Peter Adwok Nyaba, *The Politics of Liberation in South Sudan: An Insider's View* (Fountain Publishers, 1997), page 55.

[6]   Jonathan Parry and Maurice Bloch, *Money and the Morality of Exchange* (Cambridge University Press, 1989); Marshall Sahlins, *Culture and Practical Reason* (University of Chicago Press, 1976).

market-style relations.[7] Graeber argues that there are various different moral logics that govern gifts and exchange, including of money. Exchange is based on equivalence and an expectation of reciprocity. There are also incidences when gifts are not reciprocal and instead are connected to social hierarchies and orders.[8] In Gogrial, moral discourses have tried to limit the ability of money to be exchanged for divine favour, and instead interpret its legitimate exchange as a sign of reverence and recognition of cosmic hierarchies.

Baany e biith and the proliferation of local peace meetings

For over a decade after the CPA, conflict and peace proliferated in Gogrial, as discussed in the previous chapters. Chiefs were active in contesting government power throughout this period, both by refusing to attend the chiefs' meetings and by giving critical speeches when they did attend. Yet, peace meetings amounted to ways for government to carefully re-craft peace-making norms and rituals, and to demand authority over peace and war, life and death.

A handful of *baany e biith* were consistently invited to the peace meetings in Gogrial. They were often given the chance to speak and to sacrifice a white bull. The government's invitation of the *baany e biith* and their performance of symbolic acts included the *baany e biith* in those authorities recognised by government.

However, their inclusion can be seen as continuous with previous patterns in which their authority was dulled. Like at Wunlit, their role seemed scripted by the government. Their time to talk and sacrifice was dictated, and their sacrifice was prescribed. Their power over peace was again hedged in as sacred and symbolic, and was not allowed the discretion of being divine. As earlier noted, '[t]o be "sacred", in contrast [to being divine], is to be set apart, hedged about by customs and taboos'.[9] The sacred roles of the *baany e biith* at peace meetings paused their decision-making power.

Historically the *baany e biith*'s role in peace had partly been to make it meaningful by threatening deadly curses if peace was broken. They had divine power to enforce peace. Now it was often the government that threatened violence if peace was violated. As one chief explained, 'anyone who restarts the conflict will now be killed by government'.[10] The lethal threat of the curse of the *baany e biith* was not needed.

Furthermore, the quietening of the dead and the lack of compensation in the new logics of peace-making made peace morally ambiguous. Therefore,

---

[7]   David Graeber, 'On the Moral Grounds of Economic Relations: A Maussian Approach' (Open Anthropology Cooperative Press, 2010).

[8]   Ibid.

[9]   David Graeber and Marshall Sahlins, *On Kings* (HAU Books, 2017), page 8.

[10]   Chief from Twic, Ajiep Peace Conference, 20 April 2020.

it was morally and spiritually unclear if *baany e biith* should be sanctioning such peace. Those *baany e biith* who did participate in these peace meetings made themselves vulnerable to moral critique. The moral ambiguity of peace meant that many *baany e biith* were not involved in these peace meetings; they were either not invited or they refused to attend. Those who did attend were accused of being paid by the government to attend.[11] They were seen as a group of *baany e biith* who were relying on proximity to the *hakuma* to remake their authority, and that this would bring access to wealth and power.

Proximities to the *hakuma*

The new autochthonous Southern Sudan government leadership brought a new relationship for the *baany e biith* to the cosmic politics of Gogrial. As chiefs of Gogrial had often been from clans of *baany e biith* and associated with their power, when the government forced chiefs to send children to school, they sent the sons of the *baany e biith*. Many educated sons went on to fight in the Anya-Nya forces and the SPLA, and now were part of the *hakuma*, claiming the divine-like power of the state over Southern Sudan. Many of the *hakuma* from Warrap were also relationally connected to powerful *baany e biith*. Some figures who entered the government offices in Juba remained mindful of their long knowledge of the potential powers of the *baany e biith*. As the new Southern government brought new rivalries in the South, politicians called on *baany e biith* to bless them to gain or keep positions of power. Politicians gave *baany e biith* money and gifts in advance, and then further gifts and money when power was retained. They sometimes flew them to Juba and elaborately hosted them there.[12]

In many ways, the ability of this new elite class to draw on the power of the *baany e biith* built on the inclusive, not exclusive, nature of the institution. Writing in the 1950s, Lienhardt wrote:

> The masters of the fishing-spear do represent an inclusiveness in the Dinka political system, in that anyone who succeeds in attaching himself to one of them makes himself sure of help through prayers and invocations. Individual strangers, therefore, may seek out masters of the fishing-spear if they want protection, and 'praise their heads' with gifts and songs.[13]

People in Gogrial still describe more powerful *bany e bith* experiences as coming from those who are far away, as if the social distance creates power.

---

[11]   Interview, Gogrial East, 2018.
[12]   Interview with man in Gogrial, June 2018, in Dinka.
[13]   Lienhardt, *Divinity and Experience*; Hutchinson, *Nuer Dilemmas: Coping with Money, War, and the State* (University of California Press, 1996), page 211.

Therefore, even if 'strangers', and even when government elites created themselves as an elite class of strangers, the powers of the *baany e biith* were still accessible to the elites.

In interviews in Gogrial East after the CPA, people described how the *bany e bith* clan of Paghol had become particularly associated with powers to secure jobs for government officials. They had historically had powers to help with protecting and finding cattle. Cattle are wealth. Government jobs are now also associated with wealth. So, the *bany e bith* powers had been remade to assert power in this new political economy. This reshaping of their limits of power overlapped with many people from Paghol having government jobs in Kuajok (the capital of Warrap State) and in Juba. This creative remaking of culture could be seen as subsuming the powers of the *baany e biith* to the powers of mammon. At the same time, it was also a creative refusal of a secular interpretation of a monetised political world.

Maintaining the purity of the priesthood

The growing power of government and certain *bany e bith* clans associated with government prompted rivalry from other *baany e biith*. Debates have raged over the boundaries of the purity of the priesthood and their ability to retain their power while proximate to government.[14] There have been growing efforts to recast the *baany e biith* as more exclusive, not necessarily to one clan but to the logics of governance of the home communities instead of the *hakuma*.

Between government figures, political loyalties were apparently bought for cash among political elites.[15] Some politicians also tried to buy the loyalties and powers of *baany e biith* for money or material reward. This threatened to blur the moral and ontological distinction between the power of the gun and the power of the spirit. Yet, the meaning and morality of exchange have been contested to question the boundaries of buying divine favour.

Firstly, people and competing *baany e biith* in Gogrial have criticised *baany e biith* who are too close to government for breaking traditional norms and distinctions. It is not as if there was a static past without history, yet the history of the last hundred years had provided opportunities for *baany e biith* to question the benefits of proximity to government and especially the towns. *Bitter baany e biith* were associated with rural areas even if, occasionally, power was blurred with the chiefs.

---

14   Interview with chief, Gogrial State, 2019, on the phone; interview with elder from Gogrial, Juba, 2018; discussions with key informants from Gogrial, 2018 and 2019.

15   de Waal, 'When Kleptocracy Becomes Insolvent'.

Secondly, they are criticised for losing their vision of being supporters of the welfare of the community. The claim is that, historically, *baany e biith* served the welfare of a wide community, and were a priesthood for the public. This vision of authority was about public welfare in that the *baany e biith* was able to petition the divine for the welfare of a broad, public group and was accessible to the whole community. *Baany e biith* who have become too close to the elite class of the *hakuma* have been accused of using their powers to bless individuals alone.[16] This is visibly demonstrable when they predominantly work in the home for individuals' private interests. Post-CPA, access to adequate health and education has often been the preserve of the political elite. The welfare brought by the *baany e biith* also becomes the preserve of the same elite. One elder in Luonyaker asserted:

> *Baany e biith* now should leave the government alone and go back home to their villages to help them. The reason I am telling the *baany e biith* to go away from the government affairs is that what they do cannot benefit the whole nation there. There is no good thing that comes out from it; only bad things. Nowadays there are some *baany e biith* who do come to Juba and go to the home of these big people and tell them I am a *bany e bith* and I will do this and that to you. What they will do to them does not benefit the nation as a whole. What I know is that the *baany e biith* can help the people including those with diseases and during drought. They can bring reconciliation. There is nothing that has brought them in the government. They should go back to the villages.

This was also a clear criticism of government. They, like the *baany e biith,* were prioritising their own interests.

Thirdly, critics have highlighted the moral ambiguity of money and profit by a *bany e bith*. The argument is that a pure *bany e bith* should not receive payment for his work, although a gift of adoration and thanks is acceptable. This criticism has been levelled against a wide range of *baany e biith* who now seem to demand payment for services. Welfare that used to be publicly available through the *baany e biith* now appears to be subject to the logics of the market.

However, paying for a *bany e bith* diminishes the power communicated by exchange. Gifts previously were given in awe and gratitude for the *bany e bith*'s authority. They were a recognition of authority and did not bind the *bany e bith* to any act in exchange. Payment for services limits the power of the *bany e bith* and renders him no longer free to opt out as cash payment is accompanied by an expected return to blessing. It is a contractual exchange.

Despite this, paying for *bany e bith* services is now so common it is almost expected. In 2018, while research was ongoing, a colleague texted me to

16   Interview with male elder, Gogrial, May 2019.

say that he would have to take another day off work to find his cow. He had already searched nearby *luak*s (cattle byre with circular mudded walls and tall, thatched roofs) and neighbours' gardens. Now he was going to go to a *bany e bith* to finally solve the conundrum. This *bany e bith* charged a goat for locating the cow. The payment would be upfront.

In February 2019, a *bany e bith* from Mayen Jur described it as follows:

> Years ago, we were the peace-maker, but now some of us are working to get profit for our children. This is because of this economic crisis and corruption. It has really increased now. If it was there before, it was even small. Some charge up to 3,000 SSP.[17]

At the same time, *baany e biith* have long become individually wealthy through the use of their powers. In the past, *bany e bith* wealth (like that of most people) was, historically, predominantly in the form of cattle. Descriptions of moral conduct of *baany e biith* include their keeping cattle given as gratitude for spiritual assistance separate from their families' own, private herds. Keeping these cattle together was thought to be spiritually dangerous. However, this danger was not described as emanating from the wealth or a sense of corruption itself. Instead, the fear was that cattle given when their histories and provenance was unknown, meant that the cattle could have been stolen and themselves unclean because of the way they were acquired. If they were then used for marriage, it was believed that the children would die.[18] Therefore, the separation of the cattle was to protect the family herd of the *baany e biith* and not to prevent the misuse of the gifted cattle. At the same time, *baany e biith* often became rich as their daughters attracted much competition for marriage and large amounts of bride wealth.

Despite this history of wealth, those critical of contemporary *baany e biith* who are close to government, money and those who make profits, have been criticised. As one elder said, 'There are now some *baany e biith* who have put their hearts into their food'.[19]

Killing and profit beyond moral boundaries

Accusations that some *baany e biith* are now impure are also often accompanied by accusations that they no longer adhere to moral boundaries. One interviewee gave the example of how, in 2012, two thieves killed an old medical professional within Tharkueng on the road to Gogrial Town. He owned a small pharmacy that sold a few medicines to the surrounding villages.

[17] Approximately USD $20 in a country where the majority live on under $2 per day.
[18] Interview with man in Gogrial, June 2018.
[19] Interview with man in Gogrial, May 2018.

Therefore, the thieves knew that he had some money and they killed him as they stole this money. Yet, after the man's death, the thieves started to fear the spiritual repercussions of their deed. So, they approached a *bany e bith* to ask for protection and to wash their bodies free of the man's spirit. The *bany e bith* agreed to help them but said that they should bring him a share of the loot for his power to work fully. He told the thieves to deposit his share in a certain mahogany tree. The thieves did not return and did not share their loot. Without this financial incentive, the *bany e bith* lost his appetite to hide the crimes of these two men. He explained later that the old man's spirit had come to him at night to tell him to tell people who had killed him. The *bany e bith* went to the relatives of the slain who then went to the police. The two thieves were arrested and fined. While this case became public, it appears that financial incentive would have encouraged the thieves' identity to remain the *bany e bith*'s secret.

This moral degradation is even more acute when *baany e biith* are accused of killing without restraint. This association with thieves is also said to diminish the *baany e biith*'s power over peace. Part of their role in peace is to encourage truth-telling. Their own deceit prevents their power to do this.

As early chapters in this book discussed, the power to kill with impunity through cursing is at the heart of the *baany e biith*'s authority. It is this power over life and death that gives them authority to demand war but also to demand and enforce peace. As the white bull is being prepared to be slaughtered to bring peace, the *bany e bith* usually utters that harm, often unto death, will meet anyone who reopens the feud. If people do again act with aggression and then die, this is easily interpreted as an act of the *baany e biith*'s power to curse with impunity. Therefore, the power to kill in itself creates and does not diminish the *baany e biith*'s power over peace.

A story is known in Gogrial of a recent example from Lakes State. To the east of Rumbek, a famous 'bitter' *bany e bith* made peace between two warring sections and threatened to curse to death whoever violated the peace. The peace was almost immediately violated. The *bany e bith*'s son was among those who violated the peace; his son quickly fell ill and died. People questioned whether the *bany e bith* should have killed his own son, but the act highlighted his impartial enforcement of peace.

After the CPA, people in Gogrial have accused some *baany e biith* of accepting money in exchange for cursing someone to death. These *baany e biith* have been nicknamed *baany e biith nak koc* – 'the spear masters who kill people'. The *baany e biith nak koc* are contrasted with the *baany e biith* who seek to reconcile and so have 'cold hearts' – *liir puoth* – and are 'without dirt in their hearts' – *acin puoth acuol.*

The acceptance of money to kill makes the power to kill subordinate to the logics of the market and money. This subordination undermines the distinct nature of the authority of the divine and undermines claims that they can offer an alternative moral economy. It is as if their powers have become used as an arbitrary weapon and are no longer bounded by the moral expectations of Dinka cosmologies and moral orders. Therefore, these killings become frightening displays of arbitrary power, and not acts of necessary justice contained by law.

'Raan aci thong kek weng tok'[20] – 'A man is not equivalent to only one cow'. An additional problem is that killing for money deflates the value of the dead. Some *baany e biith* are accused of being willing to curse to death for the price of only one cow. These exchanges are discussed as if the *bany e bith* is being paid for an assassination. In these discussions, people referenced that compensation for the dead is set at at least thirty-one cows that once had the ability to restore life through having an equivalence to bride wealth. Then the cattle could restore life through the posthumous wife's children. Yet, demanding only one cow to slay a man implies that a man's life has become worth so little and that there is no intention to seek life after death. The moral ambiguity of accepting money to kill is evidenced by accusations that *baany e biith nak koc* hide evidence of killed animals or invocations that evidence their acts. They are accused of carrying them out at night. People claimed to have witnessed their invocations over an animal that result in the immediate death of the named person.

Resistance from the dead and reinventing pollution

The continuity of moral norms, despite their rejection by *baany e biith nak koc*, provides a means for people to push back against this marketised and militarised vision of spiritual power. In reassuring themselves about the limits of the power of this morally abhorrent behaviour, elders discuss how these *baany e biith* will not be granted impunity by the divine. Instead, they anticipate punishment through pollution. People talk of the blood of the *baany e biith nak koc*'s children being cursed to the extent that none of their children will survive. As one elder said: 'These *baany e biith* do not have children that will survive as the blood of those they kill will come back to kill their children'.[21]

Drawing from cultural archives about killing and pollution, elders have been able to argue that the dangers of pollution of the blood from the slain are deadly and can extend through generations.[22] Elders who oppose these *baany e biith* reason that even if the pollution does not immediately kill the *baany e biith* it will kill their children and their deaths will prevent their powers being

---

[20]   Interview with Apuk elder in Juba, December 2018.

[21]   Interview with man in Gogrial, July 2018.

[22]   Interview with group of elders in Gogrial, July 2018.

inherited. Therefore, in accepting money to kill, the *baany e biith* lose their link to hereditary authority.[23] This does not only kill children as individuals but also suggests that the future power of the *baany e biith* will be shattered.

At the same time, this discourse remakes and asserts moral limits to the powers of the *baany e biith* in ways that could be said to differ from the cultural archive. The founding *bany e bith*, Longar, had killed with impunity when he stabbed people as they entered the river (see Chapter 1). These *baany e biith* who were controlled with money could no longer kill with impunity, distinguishing them from Longar and also divine claims.

In response to the *baany e biith nak koc*, the curse of the *bany e bith* is being remade by their opponents and through moral discourse as something which can potentially bring pollution to the *bany e bith* himself. At the same time, this is being limited to when the curse is being used as equivalent to a gun, in that it is being used for hire and for personal, not public, benefit. Therefore, ultimately, for a *bany e bith* to expect payment (as opposed to gifts) ends the divine power of this *bany e bith*.

This interpretation allows these *baany e biith* to be restrained by insisting on the spiritual consequences of their actions. To the extent that they are associated with *hakuma* and their attempted power to kill with impunity, this reinterpretation of pollution can also be seen as an insistence on the spiritual accountability of government.

As discussed in the previous chapter, the proliferation of peace meetings in Gogrial has protected the elite class from accountability for violence and predation. In these reinterpretations, those who oppose the *baany e biith* who are too close to government and too willing to kill, have reinterpreted pollution to allow spiritual accountability.

---

[23]   Interview with man in Gogrial, May 2018.

CHAPTER 9

Cosmological Crisis and Continuing Conflict in Unity State, 2005–2013

For people, and especially young men, living to the east of the Bilnyang and connected rivers, the post-CPA period was a period of ongoing fear of deadly violence. This short chapter provides a political and economic introduction to the post-CPA conflicts between Warrap and Unity States, and within Unity State – the region to the west of the Bilnyang and connected rivers. It opens by discussing the ongoing armed conflicts between the peoples of Unity and Warrap states in the post-CPA era. These conflicts were a continuity of the politics of the 1980s and 1990s. At the same time, some members of the *hakuma* resisted the re-establishment of border courts, creating a permanent relationship of feud between these states. The chapter then highlights the internal, intra-*hakuma* rivalries over this oil-rich state, and traces their shifting configurations after 2005. These internal Nuer wars created an endless state of feud and insecurity.

The chapter also introduces local understandings that linked spiritual impurity to the ongoing conflicts in Unity State. Parts of the *hakuma* had claimed a lack of pollution as a result of wars of the *hakuma*. However, in contrast, some people living locally claimed that the wars and patterns of violence of the 1980s and 1990s had brought intolerable levels of spiritual pollution. This forced the absence of significant Nuer prophets, such as MAANI, and this resulted in the continuation of suffering. While framing it in spiritual terms, this explanation highlighted the continuity between the ongoing armed conflict and the wars of the previous 1980s and 1990s. It saw the solution in divine authorities who could both oversee compensation exchange and remake a situation of purity through rituals.

***

It was December 2012. With a little persuasion and financial promise, I managed to borrow a small Toyota pick-up truck to make a journey to the *toc*. This *toc* was the one that was fed by the River Jur, and waters that flowed north from the Bilnyang. I usually travelled by motorbike but a friend's recent accident had made me more risk-adverse. At that point in my research, I was primarily concerned with observing the large chiefs' courts that met on the western edge of the *toc* in Greater Gogrial in the dry season. This highest chiefs' court of the county formally sat in the headquarters in Lietnhom. However, during these dry-season months, the paramount chief followed the cattle and moved his court to Thiek Thou – a small settlement on an island of higher land closer to the grazing lands and cattle camps. As so many of his cases involved an exchange of cattle, the proximity of the court to the cattle made justice swifter and more tangible. As some peace had been established after the 2008 Kal Kuel Peace Meeting, this chief would also sometimes sit with chiefs from Gogrial West in the *toc* when cases arose between parties from Gogrial East and Gogrial West. This allowed a re-creation of a judicial peace at least for cases that had freshly arisen.

If you journey from Lietnhom to Thiek Thou in the dry season, your path crosses a network of dried riverbeds that confront you with thick layers of golden, parched sand. The sand is a rich colour, baked and warm from days and days of pounding by an unobscured sun. For cars, the riverbed is almost impassable, for the tyres of cars only slide into the sands and struggle to gain traction. I had previously listened to local drivers discuss the tactics of passing through the sand without getting stuck. Some thought you should go fast and hard, others that you should start slow and not accelerate, hoping to skim and glide over the sands. The drivers' theories varied widely but were all justified with a plethora of examples. That day, we made it through the first riverbed of the Jur. Yet, another twenty minutes drive further on, at a smaller riverbed, our car was almost immediately stuck. The sand covered the wheel hubs and the route was clearly impassable. The sand seemed to have a new malevolent character and held fast my car. There were no homesteads or villages in sight – nor even a tree for shade. My friend and I had no hope of shifting the vehicle.

As we waited and attempted to shuffle a little sand to preserve some hope of progress, a group of *titweng* (armed cattle keepers) appeared on the horizon. They were moving on foot from a visit to the local government county commissioner in Lietnhom back to their cattle camp near Thiek Thou. The previous month had seen large raids into the cattle camps from Mayom (Unity State) and the *titweng* continued a regular communication with the local government to ensure a coordinated security effort.

At that time, the county was littered with rumours of an imminent attack from Mayom by Peter Gadet's rebel forces. In 2011, Peter Gadet took leadership of the South Sudan Liberation Army and declared his rebellion against the SPLA government in Juba. In May 2011, there was fighting between the SPLA and Gadet's forces in Mankien (Mayom County). As the rebels were pushed out of the settlement, the SPLA followed and burnt seven villages.[1] Peter Gadet had once been aligned to Matip but gained a reputation for regularly changing allegiances. At the time of this rebellion, Peter Gadet was based in Mayom, on the north-eastern edge of the *toc*. Therefore, the *toc* again became a frontline between opposing areas of armed group control, as it had been in the 1980s and 1990s. As one Dinka chief described in 2012, 'It is now still as bad as the Anya-nya-2 times. There is no peace between us. They loot and kill us. We loot and kill them'.

When the *titweng* saw our car stuck in the sands, our need was quite obvious and they offered to help in exchange for a lift to Thiek Thou. The six of them simply picked up our car and lifted it out of the riverbed. They were happy with the reward of a lift on the back of our truck. I was happy with the promise of a strong work force to rescue us if we got stuck again.

When we arrived in Thiek Thou, the chiefs' court was a dominant feature at the heart of the settlement. Dozens of litigants had already crowded under the shade of a large tree and sat on the floor in a dozen, semi-circular rows. In front of the semi-circle, five chiefs sat in front of a table. To their left, the paramount chief sat in a larger chair strung with dried goatskin. A pick-up truck mounted with a gun was parked at the edge of the shade of the tree. The paramount chief had travelled up to the court in Thiek Thou from his house in Lietnhom for the day in this truck. He was commuting daily to the court. While the pick-up was parked next to the court in an imposing fashion, this militarised security was described by the paramount chief as a way to protect himself in case of raiding as opposed to explicitly interfering with the workings of the court. None of the soldiers appeared to be engaged with the cases being discussed and seemed more interested in watching the cattle. Yet, the gun remained a material display of the government's might that backed up the power of the paramount chief.

Later that day, the youths that had lifted my car out of the sand reappeared in Thiek Thou. We talked again. They mentioned that an NGO-funded peace workshop would be held the following week in Lietnhom. They invited me to attend. I was not sure if they had the power to invite me, but that week I sought permission from the commissioner and the NGO. In this post-CPA era of apparent peace, most international donor funding focused on development and state-building. One NGO, coordinating a consortium on a development project, had sought to prioritise peace-making in order that intra-Gogrial conflict did not interrupt their programming. They were hosting a series of workshops with chiefs, women leaders and youth to discuss peace. The

---

[1]   International Crisis Group, *South Sudan: Compounding Instability in Unity State* (International Crisis Group, 2011), page 13.

commissioner at the time had a good relationship with the NGO and forced the chiefs to attend. Large meals were also an incentive.

I sat through the days of meetings, listening to different discussions about war and peace between people in Greater Gogrial. The youth were the last group to attend the workshop. Both *titweng* and educated youth participated. The *titweng* were always told to go first for lunch as they needed to build up their strength to defend the *toc*.

On the second day, as we sat under the tree, with a flipchart and further conversation, the commissioner's pick-up truck rushed to the edge of the meeting. There were urgent fears of insecurity in the *toc;* the *titweng* were needed immediately. The *titweng* left the meeting and piled into this truck to rush to the *toc*. Others sped off in the same direction on foot. Despite this being the era of the peace of the CPA, and despite local peace meetings about intra-Gogrial peace, war was still anticipated and being fought.

The largest raid by Peter Gadet's forces ended up coming a little while later in May 2012. The day of Peter Gadet's raid had seemed like any other when we woke in the NGO compound further west, and away from the *toc*. Yet, as I walked to the market, things were different. People moved quickly. Shops were not opened, but men sat outside in small, huddled groups. More public transport cars than normal were at the roundabout in the market. They were loading fast with people and quickly moving away. They were moving not to Wau but towards Lietnhom in the north-east. Gadet's forces had killed over a hundred people and taken thousands of cattle during a dawn raid.[2] *Titweng* in Gogrial brutally fought back. Now women carried bundles of food and clothes with them, not knowing of their loved ones' circumstances but wanting to be prepared to help them. Young men with guns were given the first seats on the vehicles so they could speed to help the defence.

Tensions in the *toc* escalated not simply because of momentary political divisions, but also over claims of authority over land. In more peaceful times, many ancestors had been buried there. Even in the most militarised moments after the CPA, young, armed men still took risks to visit and make sacrifices on the gravesites of ancestors buried here. These visits also became closely connected with asserting ownership over the lands in the *toc*. As one young man explained:

> Our grandparents lived in the *toc*. That is where they are buried. That was really our land. We need power to reclaim our land again so our cattle are well fed and so our children are well fed. So, a few of us go back with our guns. We went last year to sacrifice a cow to my grandfather.[3]

2   Discussion with Gogrial East County Commissioner, May 2012, Lietnhom; discussion with UNMISS civil affairs officer, June 2012, Kuajok.

3   Interview, Yiik Ador (Warrap State), December 2011.

A lack of judicial peace

After the CPA, the lack of judicial peace between Warrap and Unity States entrenched a relationship of feud across the *toc*. During the 1980s and 1990s, the *toc* had become a 'no-man's land' and a place where chiefs' courts could not meet and where judicial peace was not possible.[4] The Wunlit Peace Conference had tried to make peace across the *toc;* the conference discussions and its agreements clearly saw joint Nuer-Dinka border courts as possible. Historically, there had been such courts.[5] However, the nationwide peace of the CPA brought new potentially for a deep peace through judicial redress and the subsequent reconciliation through spiritual cleansing and divine sanction against reopening a feud. If the CPA really was about peace, a major indicator of peace would be the reinstating of border courts.

As discussed in Chapter 6, the logics of the CPA did not make peace in South Sudan. The CPA remade political economies that required South Sudanese in the *hakuma* to have easily mobilisable labour including military labour. Such labour was more easily conjured if communities remained divided along political lines. A lack of judicial peace, and a permanent relationship of feud, was a means to do this. In this context, judicial peace was resisted by those in Juba. When I asked chiefs why border courts were not re-created after Wunlit and the CPA, chiefs spoke of the lack of permission from Juba.[6]

The lack of chiefs' courts between Unity State and Warrap State, the western Nuer and Dinka, constructed a post-CPA state of feud between these two regions. If times of apparent peace could not even solve the feud, the state of feud now seemed permanent. During the 1980s and 1990s, numerous acts of violence had been committed between these two communities. Legal and moral violations continued. With the prohibition of the courts across this borderland, people had no option to choose a judicial peace. Plus, a judicial peace, through compensation, was usually followed by a spiritual reconciliation process. The lack of chiefs' courts also meant a lack of reconciliation. This lack of justice and redress of grievances, and the lack of reconciliation, left people across the Unity-Warrap borders in a state of feud.[7] The need for justice through violence was entrenched.[8]

---

4   Naomi Pendle, 'Contesting the Militarization of the Places Where They Met: The Landscapes of the Western Nuer and Dinka (South Sudan)', *Journal of Eastern African Studies* 11:1 (2017): 64–85.

5   Naomi Pendle, '"The Dead Are Just to Drink From": Recycling Ideas of Revenge among the Western Dinka, South Sudan'. *Africa* 88:1 (2018): 99–121.

6   Interviews in Warrap and Unity States, 2012–13.

7   Pendle, '"The Dead are Just to Drink From"'.

8   Ibid.

A rivalrous *hakuma*

The post-CPA era saw people from Greater Gogrial rise to the highest positions of power in government. Rivalries remained but there was a submission to President Kiir's national premiership. In contrast, in Unity State, explicit, politically charged rival factions of the *hakuma* continued to shape life. For many in Unity State, explicit political antagonism was as acute within Unity State as it was with Warrap State.

During the 1990s and 2000s, Paulino Matip dealt in cattle and sorghum to amass a significant wealth and establish his elite role. Through tactical marriages, he also cemented control over Mayom County.[9] In 2005, President Kiir appointed Taban Deng as Governor of Unity State. Previously, Nguen Monytuil (from Mayom) had been the Khartoum-appointed governor. For Kiir, Taban's governorship limited the rival powers of both Riek Machar and Paulino Matip.[10] He deployed the same strategies as previous governments of governing Unity State by dividing the Nuer.[11]

For many in Unity State, his appointment felt like an external imposition and an indicator of Kiir's dominance over the states. In 2008, a rally by Kiir in Bentiu was disrupted by chants of 'Take Taban'.[12] The South Sudan Transitional Constitution required that 2 per cent of the oil revenue would go to the state. Yet, even officials in the state government did not know the amount of the transfers, preventing any easy accountability.[13] Popular opinion quickly perceived Taban Deng as corrupt and having either personally captured this oil wealth or sent it all back to Juba.

Frustrated with Taban Deng, in 2008, Paulino Matip allied with former enemy Riek Machar to support Nguen Monytuil's appointment tp the SPLM chairmanship in Unity State. He was elected as in April 2008. Then, the 2010 elections, as committed to in the CPA, brought a significant test of the relationship between South Sudanese, the state government and the Juba government. Taban was eager to remove Monytuil from the chairmanship in case it implied his candidature for the governor in the 2010 elections. First, Monytuil was appointed as Minister of Health in Juba. Then, in his absence from Unity State, Taban Deng reconfigured the state SPLM leadership.[14]

9   Joshua Craze, Jérôme Tubiana and Claudio Gramizzi, 'A State of Disunity: Conflict Dynamics in Unity State, South Sudan, 2013–15',HSBA Working Paper 42 (Small Arms Survey, 2016), page 19.

10   Craze et al., 'State of Disunity', page 28.

11   Ibid.

12   International Crisis Group, *South Sudan*, page 4.

13   Ibid., pages 4–5.

14   Craze et al., 'State of Disunity', page 29.

Despite the *hakuma*'s continued military might, they still had anxieties and limits. In practice, as much as the *hakuma* have claimed divine-like powers, their power as individuals has usually relied on their physical presence and this limits them. A repeated tactic by the Juba government to limit rivalrous claims over the states has been to bring the rival to Juba. Their physical distance from their base of authority has withered their power.

Rivalries over the 2010 election continued. The SPLM's Unity State Liberation Council initially selected Monytuil as the candidate for Unity State governor, but the process was then brought to Juba and the party's political bureau selected Taban Deng to the anger of many in Unity State.[15] In response, those opposing Taban Deng backed Angelina Nyakwech Teny (Riek Machar's wife) as an independent candidate for the governorship of Unity State.

During the 2010 election, commissioners and other government officials harassed and intimidated voters and polling staff.[16] According to Carter Centre observers, 'the elections in Unity State suffered from large-scale intimidation, violence, flaws in administration, and indications of manipulation'.[17] The state radio station announced the victory of Taban Deng before the National Election Commission had declared the result. Angelina rejected the result. When the resulted were announced, protestors immediately clashed with SPLA forces, with three people killed and many injured.[18]

In 2010, following his re-election, Taban Deng carried out another forced disarmament campaign in Unity State. For many people this was experienced as an attack on them by the government and the violent imposition of a predatory governor. For example, in April and May 2011, the SPLA carried out a violent disarmament campaign in Mayom, burning villages and preventing humanitarian access in an area that had recently opposed Taban Deng in the elections.[19]

Prophet Gatdeang (of Mut Turoah Nyaweach) was a significant prophetic figure in Mayom at the time. Gatdeang's cattle camp was among those being disarmed, and forces opened fire in their attempts to force the surrender of weapons. One of Gatdeang's sons was injured. Eight bullets were said to have

---

15   Ibid.
16   The Carter Center, *Observing Sudan's 2010 National Elections* (The Carter Center, 2010), page 45.
17   Ibid., page 167.
18   Ibid.
19   Joshua Craze, 'Unclear Lines: State and Non-State Actors in Abyei', in Christopher Vaughan, Mareike Schomerus and Lotje De Vries (eds), *The Borderlands of South Sudan: Authority and Identity in Contemporary and Historical Perspectives* (Palgrave Macmillan, 2013): 45–66.

penetrated the prophet's garment, and the soldiers left him for dead, but the prophet was not hurt.[20]

In response to the elections or to this affront to divine authority, various commanders explicitly rebelled against Taban Deng and the Juba government. This included Matthew Puljang, the nephew of Gatdeang and former supporter of Paulino Matip. These new rebelling forces found support from characters such as Bapiny Monytuil who had opposed the SPLA before the CPA and had refused to follow Matip into the SPLA at the Juba Declaration. Taban Deng was troubled by the array of possible new alliances including the possibility of new forces being integrated into the SPLA. He attacked Paulino Matip's home in Bentiu while also continuing with disarmament in Mayom.[21] Fighting continued in Mayom over the next two years. In was in this context, in March 2011, that Peter Gadet defected from the SPLA and based his rebellion at Mayom. From here he could oppose Taban Deng. He could also raid cattle from the *toc* of Gogrial, both to fund his movement and insult the central government's ability to provide security in their own homelands.

Reconciliation

During the period over the 2011 referendum and independence, there were new political attempts to reconfigure alliances. Machar sought to build a pan-Greater Upper Nile constituency to give him a support base through which to claim leadership. To do this, Machar needed reconciliation with the Dinka Bor community and in Unity State. In relation to the Dinka Bor, in 2012, Machar publicly apologised to the Dinka Bor community, seeking a reconciled relationship. Many in Bor had blamed Machar for the 1991 Bor massacre that killed thousands of Dinka in south-east Jonglei (Garang's home area) after the defection of Machar from Garang's SPLA in 1991.[22] Having contributed many men to the SPLA from its inception, the Dinka Bor are a powerful constituency in the SPLA/M and in Greater Upper Nile. While some in Bor were sceptical of Machar's apology, Garang's widow accepted the apology. Reconciliation efforts also started in Unity State. In late 2010, Taban Deng, Machar and Monytuil came together in a reconciliation conference.[23] In 2012, Machar tried to convene a reconciliation conference on the Unity, Warrap and Lakes border, in the border region of Madol. In August 2012, Paulino Matip died. By the end of 2012 and a few months after Matip's death,

20   Craze et al., 'State of Disunity', page 34.
21   Ibid.
22   Discussion with young men from Bor, 2011, Juba.
23   Craze et al., 'A State of Disunity', page 31.

Machar was actively organising to hold one of the first national reconciliation conferences in Mayom. Plans were nurtured through that year, with budgets for such efforts apparently approved by the Council of Ministers in late 2012.[24] However, Machar's focus on politically important constituencies prompted President Kiir to fear his motivations and end these attempts.

MAANI's absence

The protracted nature of the conflict, and Wunlit and the CPA's failure to end violence, brought cosmological conundrums. Firstly, this continued violence needed to be understood. Secondly, if conflict and unsettlement were the new social order, there was a need to understand if there was still space for purity and peace.

During the war years, some people in the *hakuma* had claimed that wars of the *hakuma* did not produce spiritual pollution. This was part of a broader claim of *hakuma* impunity. As Hutchinson has documented, Riek Machar had tried to persuade people that deaths cause by violence during these wars should not be understood as causing pollution or spiritual consequences. Hutchinson describes how, in effect, the SPLA leadership was arguing that a *koor kume* (a government war) had no spiritual ramifications and did not cause pollution.[25]

The *hakuma*'s claim of a lack of pollution from wartime killing was contested. One popular explanation for the post-2005 continuity of war and insecurity was the spiritual impurity. The explanation suggested that war had brought such intolerable levels of spiritual pollution (*nueer*) as people from the community committed acts of violence that violated normal moral boundaries including killing brothers, children and women.[26] This was moral impurity that either was too large for priests to solve or that had not been solvable because of priests' distance from the battlefield. The pollution was so extreme that it pervaded whole clans and communities.

Many people in Koch, including elders from the family of Kolang Ket, have suggested that this pervading spiritual contamination was forcing MAANI's absence and the possibility of peace and purity. Nuer prophets often excluded from their *luak* individuals who were polluted. Their own divinities cannot tolerate the pollution brought by this moral impurity, and they only allow people to spend time close to them and in their *luak* when compensation has

---

24   Speech by Angelina Teng, at IGAD-organised peace symposium in Addis Ababa (Ethiopia), 22 June 2013.
25   Sharon Hutchinson, *Nuer Dilemmas: Coping with Money, War, and the State* (University of California Press, 1996), page 108.
26   Interview with male elders and young men, Mayendit and Ler, August 2013; interviews with chiefs in Koch, April 2018.

been paid and rituals of reconciliation completed. Therefore, divine authorities are set apart from pollution. In this interpretation of the ongoing, post-CPA violence, MAANI was excluded from coming to rescue people because of the pollution rife across the land. MAANI could not dwell in such a space of pollution. One solution would be to seek judicial peace through cattle compensation and rituals that could restore purity.[27] This explanation clearly linked ongoing armed conflict to the preceding decades of war, and highlighted the need for justice that would allow purity.

Conclusion

For people in Unity State, armed conflict continued after the CPA both within Unity State and against forces and communities in Warrap and Lakes State. The ambiguities of the CPA left contestation and confusion over who should have the power of the *hakuma* in Unity State. For people living there, it meant that this era was still intermittently a time of mobilisation, attacks and offensives. People watched closely the fluctuating alliances within the *hakuma*, navigating how to stay safe despite this violence. Again, the peace of the CPA was violent.

At the same time, what was clear was that the post-2005 armed conflict was not discrete from the divisions of the 1980s and 1990s, nor from the reconfiguring of these contestations through the CPA. There was continuity and not rupture. One way that this was expressed was to describe the continuity of cosmic norms and cosmic politics during this period. A noticeable feature in Koch County was the absence of a prophet of MAANI – the divinity who was dominant from the 1920s–1970s through the prophets Kolang Ket and Nyaruac Kolang. The absence of MAANI in a time of such need explained the lack of peace and possibilities of purity. 'Nilotic societies normally treat God as a force profoundly distant and removed from the human world'.[28] Yet, by seizing prophets, divinities could be present to support people. MAANI's abandoning of his people during a time of such hardship required explanation. A dominant explanation was that the community was now too polluted, from the previous decades of war, to allow MAANI to come. MAANI demanded a higher level of moral and spiritual purity. Peace would not be found through remaking political alliances, but through the remaking of moral purity. In the cosmic contests, the fights of the gods of the *hakuma* were beneath this cosmic demand for a space where the divinity could dwell. Peace was violent as the cosmic polities had not been remade as peaceful and pure.

[27]   Interviews with chiefs in Koch, April 2018.
[28]   David Graeber and Marshall Sahlins, *On Kings* (HAU Books, 2017), page 89.

CHAPTER 10

Prophetic Proliferations: Making Peace in Unity State, 2005–2013

If the lack of peace was due to moral impurity, peace-making authority could be established through the power to purify. The post-Comprehensive Peace Agreement (CPA) period saw a proliferation of Nuer prophets in Unity State who offered purity and peace. These prophets remade cultural archives, evoking memories that connected priests to prophets, but also introducing a priestly role for the prophets. This creative remaking of the cultural archive was a creative refusal against the *hakuma* project that claim spiritual pollution was no longer a concern. As the *hakuma* was akin to the divine in that it claimed impunity for their own arbitrary violence, prophets asserted their own divine authority as a way to push back against the *hakuma*. It was divine authorities who demonstrated the main confidence and ability to try to restrain the *hakuma*, and they gained popular support, especially among the armed youth, for their willingness to confront *hakuma* power.

This chapter discusses other prophets but focuses on Nyachol – a new Nuer prophetess of MAANI. The chapter describes her seizure by MAANI, her struggles to gain recognition, her popularity with the youth of Mayendit and Ler Counties (Unity State), and her growing resistance to the *hakuma* of the day including through creatively remaking culture to refuse the logics of the *hakuma* and the persistence of the feud. Her rejection of the *hakuma* was selective; she did not oppose the *hakuma* in itself but its arbitrary violence. As discussed in Chapter 12, she still used the government-shaped customary law, and she also supported formal schooling and some politicians, such as the leader of the SPLA-IO and certain commissioners. At the same time, she was herself violent in seemingly arbitrary ways. She sanctioned armed resistance to the *hakuma*.

Nyachol's authority to make peace and bring purity was central to her building of authority among the youth and over the chiefs. As Hutchinson and I have previously highlighted, her vision of peace against the neighbouring

Dinka communities was 'hot' and demanded violent revenge.[1] Yet, her vision of a 'cool' peace among the Nuer was just as important. She re-created a priestly power for the prophets in order to re-establish the spiritual consequences of armed conflict and provide quasi-judicial punitive measures through reasserting the realities of *nueer* (spiritual pollution), including after killing. She could detect *nueer* on people and warned of its deadly consequences. She then offered to provide solutions to these deadly dilemmas including through judicial accountability for killing. Nyachol also actively sought to make the *government* subject to *nueer* and, therefore, capable of being limited and purified by divine authorities. Nyachol insisted that Nuer government officials still faced *nueer* after killing even if the killing was part of their government duty; the *hakuma* was not beyond moral laws, nor was it immune from the consequences of arbitrary violence. She asserted that all actions of the *hakuma* by Nuer officials still fell within these moral spheres and limits.

* * *

It was early 2013. The night before we had stayed in the iron-sheet-surrounded commissioner's compound in Mayendit (an administrative headquarters in Unity State). We had slept in tents in front of the soldiers' *tukals*. Behind were a couple of small latrines that doubled as showers. At the entrance to the compound sat various broken-down cars to supply parts to the remaining moving vehicles. Among them sat one Land Cruiser now covered in bullet holes. This Land Cruiser had not yet been harvested for its parts as its ownership remained politically contested. The Land Cruiser had belonged to the commissioner of Rumbek North (Lakes State). There had been tensions between Rumbek North and Mayendit Countries over the boundaries of their counties and over episodes of lethal cattle raiding. In 2012, UNMISS had decided to try to organise peace talks between the two commissioners. However, UNMISS apparently had failed to warn the Mayendit County Commissioner of their efforts and so escorted the Rumbek North Commissioner to Mayendit without an invitation from their host. Their unexpected appearance was immediately tense.

After initial hesitation, the Mayendit Commissioner invited the Rumbek North Commissioner into his office to talk. The bodyguards of the two commissioners remained outside. They were both nervous at their proximity; they and their brothers had recently been involved in violent conflict against each

---

[1]   Sharon Hutchinson and Naomi Pendle, 'Violence, Legitimacy, and Prophecy: Nuer Struggles with Uncertainty in South Sudan', *American Ethnologist* 42:3 (2015): 415–30.

other. There had been no attempt at judicial peace or reconciliation; a feud remained between them and both sides were intensely aware that the other had an obligation to revenge against them.[2] As the commissioners spoke inside, fighting started outside between the bodyguards. As would happen in 2016 in the Presidential Palace in Juba, the heavily armed nature of the bodyguards meant that fatalities were fast and dramatic. The Rumbek North Commissioner himself ran out to help and was nearly shot. He was only able to return safely to Rumbek North in the escorted car of the Mayendit Commissioner. A year later, the Rumbek North Commissioner was still demanding his Land Cruiser back. The Mayendit Commissioner neither refused nor delivered it. In early 2013, the Land Cruiser sat there as a quiet witness to the continued violence of life in the post-CPA South Sudan.

Having spent one night on the Mayendit Commissioner's compound, that next morning we headed north along the red murram road that traced a thin line over the swamps.[3] After another hour's driving, we finally turned off the murram road at the small market across the road from the MiirNyal football pitch and a broken-down lorry. The road then travelled to the left, passing the *payam*'s grass-fenced compound and circles of *tukals*. Vague tyre marks showed a route on into the village, past thin rows of trees that barely concealed the sweeping grasslands beyond. An older man gave us directions and pointed further on to beyond the edge of the village and into those grasslands of the *toc* of the Bilnyang where the cows were feasting. In the dry months, from October until April, the swampy lands in this western part of Mayendit dry out until the ground is black, baked, hard clay. The earth cracks as it dries, etching across the ground elaborate, endless patterns. Our car increasingly struggled as we passed over the sun-dried swamp bed. Littered with tufts of grass, the wheels repeatedly got stuck between these small obstacles and needed the engine's strength to move over them.

As the bumping car chugged to less than the speed of a walk, three boys caught up with the pace of the bouncing vehicle. Their hands were a sticky orange from the palm fruits they were cutting up with spearheads. They continued to chew as they approached us. The palm fruits are their morning feast and a staple diet for many children in the long, dry, hungry season. They did not introduce themselves explicitly as envoys of the prophetess but came to us with a clear message. They promised to lead us to near the prophetess's *luak*. They made it clear that the car could not come near the *luak* and that when they instructed us, we must leave the car and get out to walk. We agreed.

2   Conversations in Mayendit County and Rumbek North County, April 2013.
3   Jan Bachmann, Naomi Pendle and Leben Moro, 'The Longue Durée of Short-lived Infrastructure – Roads and State Authority in South Sudan', *Geoforum* 133 (2022).

The positioning of Nyachol's *luak* was an explicit act of resistance to the violence of the *hakuma*. The *luak* sat conspicuously on the western edge of the permanent settlements of Mayendit County (and the eastern edge of the Bilnyang and connected rivers and swamps). This village (Thor) had been raided and burnt during a 2010 raid by youths from Greater Tonj, across the *toc* of these rivers. They had killed children and women, re-creating Thor as a dangerous place to live and prompting total displacement from the village. The youth that carried out these attacks were not formally part of the Southern Sudan government, but they were understood by people in Mayendit as *hakuma* in a broad sense.[4] In the 1980s and 1990s, the cattle keeping youth of Warrap State had been absorbed into the sphere of the *hakuma* through their use as local defence forces.[5] While their subordination to the *hakuma* was contested,[6] they were often still seen as part of the sphere of the *hakuma*. Plus, as senior government members were from the region, people in Mayendit assumed that the attack came with the consent of people in the *hakuma*.

At the same time, people in Mayendit (Unity State) were not only fearful of the *hakuma* in Warrap State; they also increasingly feared their own *hakuma*. At a national level, the leaders of Warrap and Unity State were at peace and ruling together in Juba. Local government officials in Unity State were appointed by the governor who was appointed by the national president. Therefore, local government officials primarily kept their job through the will of the Juba leadership and not the community. The commissioner of the time had returned cattle to Warrap State after a raid by the Mayendit youth, and people in Mayendit feared this was indicative of him not supporting their needs and security.

After the attack in 2010, no one remained living in Thor. Despite local government promises that it was safe, no-one returned until 2012. When Nyachol built her *luak* in Thor, she was one of the first to return. By positioning her *luak* on the edge of Thor, Nyachol claimed she was contesting the construction of Thor as a place of danger by the *hakuma*. She wanted to re-create it as a place of safety and a place that was made safe by the power of her divinity known

---

[4]   Interviews in Dablual and Mirmir, 2013.

[5]   Luka Biong Deng Kuol, 'Dinka Youth in Civil War: Between Cattle, Community and Government', in Victoria Brereton (ed.), 'Informal Armies: Community Defence Groups in South Sudan's Civil War' (Saferworld, 2017); Nicki Kindersley and Joseph Diing Majok, *Monetized Livelihoods and Militarized Labour in South Sudan's Borderlands* (Rift Valley Institute, 2019); Naomi Pendle, '"They Are Now Community Police": Negotiating the Boundaries and Nature of the Government in South Sudan through the Identity of Militarised Cattle-Keepers'. *International Journal of Minority and Group Rights* 22:3 (2015): 410–434.

[6]   Pendle, '"They Are Now Community Police"'.

as MAANI. Nyachol described how she had first been seized by MAANI after the government's attack on Thor. This timing also demonstrated to people that MAANI's coming to Nyachol was to allow her to push back against the violence of the *hakuma*.[7]

As instructed by our young escorts, we parked our large, white 4x4 vehicle a hundred metres away from Nyachol's *luak*. The car was parked adjacent to a pile of other objects that appeared to be the disallowed possessions of other visitors to the prophetess. There were at least a dozen AK47s among items in the pile, as well as an assortment of clothes laid out on top of the spiky ends of the grass tufts. This was the invisible but explicit boundary of the space of the prophetess. Guns, cars and many clothes were excluded. She was creating a spatial boundary that omitted certain material objects and constructed a new materiality in proximity to her. She later described to me how manufactured clothes, items of technology and constructions of large roads were for her closely associated with the *hakuma* that she contested. She was creating a material space around herself in which these material goods were excluded. Nyachol was creatively remaking culture to refuse materially the political vision of the *hakuma*. Within this constructed boundary of the *luak*, Nyachol was enacting a political vision that excluded the *hakuma*. The objects littered at a distance from her *luak* were symbolic of the broader powers of *hakuma* that were experienced by many in Mayendit for a century as predatory, violent and inherently uncertain. She offered a different political vision and a re-creation of an imagined, more certain time that could politically and materially exclude the *hakuma*. Nyachol was asserting that it was MAANI who could not tolerate these material objects of the *hakuma*. While this had not historically been part of the prophetic idiom, she was remaking culture as a way to politically contest the politics of the *hakuma*.

Nuer prophets seized by divinities in the post-CPA era, like the *baany e biith*, were wrestling with their relationship to money, marketised politics and the new Juba elite. Politicians recognised the power of Nuer prophets, either because they shared their cosmological assumptions or because they saw the large numbers of armed youth that the prophets were capable of mobilising.[8] Senior Nuer and Dinka politicians invited these prophets to Juba to champion their private interests, and they were often showered with monetary or expensive gifts. For example, a prophet in Panyijar had been given a Land Cruiser by President Kiir. The prophet had no money or skill to maintain it, so within a couple of weeks it became abandoned on the commissioner's compound in Panyijar. Yet, the gift had been accepted. In contrast, Nyachol strictly separated herself from the money and power of the government. Nyachol was

7   Interviews in Dablual and Mirmir, 2013.
8   Interview with the Commissioner of Mayendit County, March 2013, Mayendit.

never offered a Land Cruiser but she did refuse to ride in a government Land Cruiser when offered by the commissioner.

At the same time, there were apparent contradictions in Nyachol's boundaries with the *hakuma*. She claimed authority based on continuity with the power of Kolang Ket. Her construction of isolation contrasted with memories of him. Kolang Ket's authority had been intimately associated with his superior knowledge of the government through his travels to the north. Initially, before direct government violence against him, he also interacted peacefully with government. Nyaruac also ended up combining her powers with those of *hakuma* by accepting the government chiefdom, as discussed in Chapter 2. There was clearly not a necessary opposition between the *hakuma* and the prophets.[9]

Nyachol's rejection of government was also contingent and not consistent. She praised Riek Machar, and mobilised support for him when he led the armed opposition. In later conversations, I asked the prophetess for permission to run a literacy programme in Thor. I had been teaching in the western Dinka, and formal education had become a default response to the situation. She agreed immediately and rebuked my surprise. She explained, 'Thor used to have a school. It had a school before. It is not for me to stop the school. It will help rebuild Thor'. Schools and formal education were much newer than the *hakuma* in the western Nuer, but they were still associated with the sphere of the *hakuma*. She selectively interpreted history to allow her to accept them. In addition, she enforced the customary law and encouraged use of the chiefs' courts. This was despite their association with *hakuma*.[10]

Evoking the cultural archive

In order to push-back against the *hakuma*, Nyachol relied on asserting her divinity. It was only with the divine power of MAANI that Nyachol would resist the *hakuma*. As the *hakuma* was god-like, divine power allowed her to be part of the cosmic politics and push back. To assert this divine authority, Nyachol evoked various cultural archives.

At the time of her seizure, Nyachol had initially become very ill. She had even attended a local clinic and had been warned that her sickness was going to leave her infertile. She was already married with children. The clinic could not heal the sickness and she became increasingly immobile, infirm and

---

9   Douglas Johnson, *Nuer Prophets: A History of Prophecy from the Upper Nile in the Nineteenth and Twentieth Centuries* (Clarendon Press, 1994).

10   Naomi Pendle, 'Politics, Prophets and Armed Mobilizations: Competition and Continuity over Registers of Authority in South Sudan's Conflicts', *Journal of Eastern African Studies* 14:1 (2020): 43–62.

seemingly mad. It was only then that people started to recognise MAANI in her. They sacrificed a bull to MAANI and the illness waned. People started to accept that she had been seized by MAANI. This equation of illness with seizure draws on long cultural archives of the seizures of previous prophets.

Nyachol drew on and remade other expressions of religious orthodoxy in the cultural archive to claim authority. Early on after Nyachol's claimed seizure by MAANI, she travelled from Mayendit to the *luak* of the late Kolang Ket and Nyaruac Kolang in Limpout (Koch County) to sacrifice multiple bulls at the *luak* of the former prophets of MAANI. While Nyaruac had died forty years earlier, her family continued to assert their authority as regulators of prophetic activity in these lands between the Nile and the Bilnyang River system. However, the family of Kolang Ket and Nyaruac Kolang refused to accept that Nyachol had been seized by MAANI and doubted her authority. They were especially sceptical as she only had a link by marriage to the clan of Kolang and Nyaruac. This family are still waiting for MAANI to seize another member of their family.

After Nyachol's rejection by the family of Kolang Ket, she returned to Mayendit and to her home village of Thor. While she drew on claims of custom and continuity with Nyaruac, she was forced to challenge the assumption that divinities belonged to certain clans. In many ways, her seizure by MAANI, despite not being from Kolang's clan, re-crafted a more inclusive or democratic vision of the divinity in that it was not limited to clan history. Instead, Nyachol championed a much wider vision of a Nuer identity, an identity that echoed a growing political resistance to the government of the day.

A proliferation of prophets

The seizure of Nyachol was one of many prophetic seizures in Unity State in the post-CPA period that evoked cultural archives to establish divine power. People were increasingly drawing on claims of divine authority to give them the power to contest the supranatural claims of the *hakuma*. The post-CPA dangers, impurities and violence meant that these divine authorities quickly gained popular appeal by offering safety, purity and resistance. The flurry of ecstatic divine activity surrounding new seizures provided opportunities to rage against violence and injustice, through songs, invocations and physical violence. Prophets quickly won popular support among the armed youth who were facing the brunt of the *hakuma*'s predatory violence.

For example, in 2008 in Panyijar (southern Unity State), David, the son of a former prophet who had died in 1997, was seized by the same divinity as his father. David had previously worked for an international NGO, but then took on the full-time role of a prophet. People went to David to ask for advice, healing and strength for raids,[11] as well as keeping their cattle together with his herd when they feared insecurity.[12] He rapidly mobilised a significant group of youths. This prophet was both courted and criminalised by different government officials.

Going into Nyachol's *luak*

These new prophetic seizures and ecstatic activities often highlighted the anxieties of the new Southern Sudan government officials, especially at a local level. The prophets were not legible in that they were subject to random, unpredictable displays of divine power and possession. Plus, they were also militarily powerful as they often had the support of large numbers of armed youths. They challenged local government authority as they were repeatedly willing to challenge *hakuma* impunity.

In their anxiety about the prophetic proliferation, local governments responded in different ways. The commissioner at the start of 2013 asserted that he was an educated Christian man and could not believe the claims of Nyachol. He contested her power, and sought to demonstrate militarily the superior power of the government. However, first, it sought to negotiate with her. Only a week before my first visit, the government commissioner had demanded that a group of senior chiefs visit Nyachol to negotiate with her.[13] She had made it clear that she would only meet them after displays of their submission to her authority. She insisted on them taking their clothes off; they did not refuse. She insisted that they bring her gifts of bulls. When some that were brought were too small, she rejected them. Caught between the demands of the commissioner and Nyachol, the chiefs complied and brought larger bulls. At the same time, they felt humiliated.[14]

The chiefs' visit had warned me of her opposition to the *hakuma* and the likelihood of nakedness. On that first visit, at the boundary to the space of her *luak*, I was instructed to leave my flip-flops. We then walked to a tree where we waited for the prophetess's permission to meet her. When permission was granted, we would leave our other clothes beneath that tree. It was already the heat of the day and the strong sun had quickly heated the black earth. Walking shoeless the fifty metres to the tree itself felt like a test of endurance and itself an ordeal of submission to the prophetess.

---

[11]   Interview with an elder in Panyijar, July 2012; interview with prophet in Panyijar, July 2012.

[12]   Interview with cattle camp leader in Panyijar, June 2012.

[13]   Interview with the Commissioner of Mayendit County, 2013.

[14]   Ibid.; interview with chief who had visited Nyachol, Mayendit County, 2013; discussion with Nyachol, Mayendit County, 2013.

We were ushered to a grass mat beneath two small trees that offered a little shade. We waited there for a few hours, growing in our speculations about what was to happen. We had been warned that a significant legal case about clan feud had been brought to the prophetess that morning and that she was still busy arbitrating between the parties. No certainty was given that she would agree to meet us. We would only be considered when it was our turn.

As we waited, the space seemed quiet and almost empty. A few women prepared sorghum and a couple of men stood nearby talking, yet there was not much movement in the landscape or near the large *luak*. We felt quite alone and I imagined the *luak* was as other *luaks* I had visited – a large empty space with the host in one corner of this thatched roofed atrium. It did not seem that any other visitors were likely to be there in significant number.

I was asked to undress.[15] As I had been warned, I had borrowed some boxer shorts from a colleague and worn extra layers. I was grateful that I had. My travelling companion ended up in just boxer shorts. I took off my skirt but remained in boxers and bra. The requests to remove clothing were not universal. When asked why our clothes were to be removed, the prophetess answered that they were signs of *hakuma* so she did not want them on her compound. As one elder explained, this was to demonstrate that 'you didn't know the *hakuma*'.[16] Their removal was a ritual submission and the performance of a large political vision. The lack of clothes also had the advantage of making it impossible to conceal weapons.

Nyachol's husband then came to talk to us. He was dressed in a replica Arsenal football kit. The outfit was so worn, the football club could hardly be identified. I had seen similar football outfits on sale in the Ler market. The traders had brought them from northern Sudan in large 'Khartoum' lorries – lorries mechanically altered in Khartoum to give them the strength to trek along the roads of Sudan.

A tall, older man then led us to the *luak*. Without shoes on, the sun-heated sand burnt my feet and it was hard to focus on anything but the pain. I was relieved to be brought in front of the shade of a small neem tree on the far side of the clearing from the *luak*. The man lined us up and sprinkled water from a gourd over us. Then he led us towards the *luak* and paused at the large pile of cattle dung ashes (*pou*) beneath a woven grass platform. He took a little dust

---

[15]   There was no indication that Nyachol or those with her knew of the pictures taken by Evans-Pritchard among the Nuer. Many of his photos of the Nuer at the time include a lack of clothes and have been heavily criticised for these dehumanising portrayals. Her asking me to undress was not, but could have been, a comical reversal of power relations through my state of undress. I was grateful that she prohibited cameras.

[16]   Interview with elder, Miirnyal Market (Mayendit County), April 2013 (in Nuer).

and smeared it on each of us. A few girls sat adjacent to this ash pile. Evans-Pritchard pondered whether the importance of cattle dung ash (as opposed to wood ash) was because of *pou*'s association with the cattle.[17] It was the same ash that was later smeared on the sacrificial bull.

As my feet burnt beneath me, as soon as I was allowed, I rushed to the *luak* eager to get inside away from the burning sun. I often interviewed people inside their *luaks*. They were a routine place of meeting in the villages, where people would gather to negotiate and decide family matters. Their tall, coned roofs made them incredibly cool compared to the blazing heat outside. They were built to contain many dozens of cattle. So, in the daytime, when the cattle were out grazing, they contained ample space for small groups of people to gather.

As I stepped inside, my eyes slowly became accustomed to the darkness. At my feet and stretching out in front of me to every edge of the *luak*'s floor, was a densely packed sea of seated bodies. Like us, the young men that filled the *luak* had taken most of their clothes off. These young men were the audience. Scattered at the sides and the back were also a few dozen girls and older women. To the right of the small door, elders were sitting. They were the elders of families who had come to Nyachol for legal settlement of their feud. They were more eclectic in age and sat with less ease. Yet, they pushed themselves further back to make space for me to sit in front of them. To the left of the door, Nyachol sat with her back to the wall, facing the young men. Her eight disciples sat to her left, creating a line along the wall.

Nyachol was dressed in just a grass skirt with a leopard skin hung over her small, fragile-looking frame. Our entrance into the *luak* appeared to go unnoticed as she did not look up. She was focused on a small pipe in her hands and was trying to stuff the tobacco into it and then light it from a small fire to her left. In wearing a grass skirt and leopard skin, she invoked references to the *kuaar muon* (priestly) authority. Nyaruac was remembered as wearing grass skirts. Nyachol visibly performed in her clothing both the claim that her authority rested on the continuity, not rupture, of religious idioms, as well as the prophetic re-crafting and capturing of these priestly powers.

I glimpsed back at the young men, who all seemed to be looking at us. I tried to count the rows and the columns. I estimated that about eighty were there. I was too afraid to really turn and stare and count. One of the young men introduced a chant and the rest of the crowd burst into a sung response. Nyachol still did not flinch. They sang of war with the Dinka and called the Nuer men to war.

---

[17] Edward Evans-Pritchard, *Nuer Religion* (Oxford University Press, 1956), page 262.

Eventually Nyachol and I talked as this audience behind us went quiet and listened. We would talk repeatedly over the next few months. Over time, she demanded less that I undress. She always asked me to take something off as a symbolic expression of my intention. All cameras and phones were left far away, as were the cars or motorbikes.

Making peace with me

As we talked, she explained that her initial reluctance to talk to me was because I was an outsider. As a white person, I was a foreigner. I must have come from *hakuma*. Yet, MAANI moved her enough to let us talk. I told her that a minor prophet in Ganyliel had named me Nyaluak. She named me 'Made by God'. She said, 'Your father is Riek Machar'. Her political alliances were not concealed. Despite her rejection of *hakuma*, she accepted him. Even though I was *hakuma*, like Riek, she could also reconcile our meeting by associating me with Riek. She said she was perplexed by her affinity to me, but she was glad that we were at peace. She called me to sit in front of her, and my translator ushered me forward. She placed around my wrist a brass bracelet. They forged this by melting down the shells from bullets. I had bought similar bracelets made by the blacksmiths on the edge of Rumbek town.

As discussed, when families were feuding, after peace was agreed and compensation paid, the new relationship of peace would be confirmed through the sacrifice of a bull. This was carried out by a *kuaar muon*, but also now by the prophets. Nyachol decided that she needed to make peace with me. If I represented a part of government, I could be mistaken for being in a feud with her. A bull would be sacrificed to restore our relationship and make peace.

The *luak* emptied to the area outside her *luak*. As I followed everyone outside, my feet quickly began to burn from its heat. Someone took pity on me and I was given a goat's skin to sit on. I had not brought water and felt close to fainting. The first bull that was sacrificed was to reconcile the feuding families that had come to her *luak* before us. The second bull was to reconcile Nyachol and me. Each time Nyachol led the final invocations over the bull, and other elders carried out the act of killing the bull. Many times, after visits, I would carry home (tied to the back of the motorbike) parts from a slaughtered bull. They were gifts of peace from Nyachol.

Remaking culture to refuse the feud

A key shift that was taking place was the prophetic merging with the role of the priesthood, and a growing emphasis on purity as the prophets tried to reinstate a moral, law-governed community. The Nuer civil wars of the 1990s and 2000s had not only brought excessive physical destruction, but also unprecedented spiritual and moral confusion. Brothers had fought on opposing sides and could not be certain that they had not slain their own kin. Commanders also often encouraged the slaying of women, children and the elderly. These large battles of government became entangled with local rivalries and became interpreted as feuds. The CPA and Juba Declaration had brought claims of political peace in Unity State and elsewhere. Yet, these intricate but deadly dilemmas were not addressed. As *hakuma* wars were entangled with local politics and cosmologies, the expectation of justice was either through compensation and judicial peace or through revenge. As the CPA was signed, chiefs from across Unity State listed hundreds of unsolved cases of killing that were now leading to cycles of revenge. The government formed a large chiefs' court with chiefs from across the state to try to solve some of these cases and prevent violent, self-help justice. Yet, many feuds remained open. These courts had no power to end the feud.

For young men in Unity State at the time, these widespread feuds and voids of judicial redress had created a perpetual state of uncertainty and violence. They were expected to seek justice for their deceased kin, as well as find cattle (often through raiding) to satisfy the demands for a posthumous wife. At the same time, as almost all clans had slayers among them, any young man was vulnerable to attacks of revenge. Their personal culpability was immaterial in making them an appropriate target to cool the hearts of the family of the slain.

As they offered a solution to feuds and impurity, Nuer prophets like Nyachol quickly gained large followings among the armed youth. At the height of her popularity, hundreds gathered to her *luak* on a daily basis. By late 2012 and early 2013, she was mobilising large, armed groups of over a thousand young men for raids against the Dinka.[18]

At the same time, the popular appeal of Nyachol for the youth also came through her promise of a judicial, 'cool' peace among the Nuer. She promised to re-establish the spiritual consequences of war and provide quasi-judicial punitive measures through reasserting the realities of pollution, and especially *nueer*, after killing. She then offered to provide solutions to these deadly dilemmas including through judicial accountability for killing. As previously discussed, the scale of killing in the Western Nuer in the 1990s left Nuer confused about the continued relevance of *nueer* and whether anyone had the spiritual authority to bring redress and healing.[19]

MAANI gave Nyachol the ability to recognise if someone was contaminated with *nueer*. In an unresolved feud where the facts were disputed, she was able to point out the slayers. The chiefs' courts had limited ability to investigate cases and, especially when guns were used, sometimes the killer

---

[18]   NGO Security Working Group Meeting, Minutes, 20 February 2013.
[19]   Sharon Hutchinson, *Nuer Dilemmas: Coping with Money, War, and the State* (University of California Press, 1996), page 107.

was unknown to all. Nyachol's knowledge of *nueer* allowed her to settle cases and end feuds. Chiefs' courts also started referring people to Nyachol to help establish the facts of the case.[20]

Nyachol was also demanding local, senior *kuar muon* to demonstrate their submission to her or risk losing their powers. She was asserting herself as the giver and taker of the powers to redress *nueer*. For example, on one visit to Nyachol in 2013, I found a local, respected *kuaar muon* in her *luak*. Just behind him sat two large, finely decorated bulls. The bulls were a gift to Nyachol and a material sign of the *kuaar muon*'s submission to her. However, she spent much of her time with him rebuking him for his tardy display of submission. When talking to this *kuaar muon* I never worked out whether his submission to her was from fear of MAANI or fear of the large numbers of armed youth that supported Nyachol. Nyachol did not only offer healing from *nueer* but enforced recognition of its dangers. She insisted that people needed to be free from *nueer* before they could even approach her for protection and advice including protection from bullets in battle.[21]

Nyachol's logic of intra-Nuer peace upheld socio-legal norms that linked peace and the exchange to cattle compensation. Since the early twentieth century, this exchange of cattle had been embedded in the government-backed customary laws of the chiefs' courts. Nyachol's upholding of the customary law in many ways was akin to the historic patterns of governments who had sought to govern through the customary law. Yet, Nyachol sought to re-create the very nature of customary institutions by demanding that the customary laws be reintegrated with divine authority. Nyachol presented herself as the restorer and custodian of a Nuer-wide moral community that rebuilt a notion of a Nuer 'customary' past that is backed by divine and not government power. She is not only pushing back against the militarised power of government, but also the power of government as it has sought to capture and secularise the customary laws.[22]

For the community's armed young men, Nyachol offered a radical departure from the chaotic, dangerous socio-political order presented to them by governments at the time through violence and negotiated peace. However, Nyachol did not gain unanimous support. Many who were formally educated rejected the epistemologies of the prophets as 'customary' and outdated. In 2012 and 2013, the local church's teaching explicitly condemned association and belief in Nyachol and other Nuer prophets. Among the older married men

---

20 Pendle, 'Politics, Prophets and Armed Mobilizations'.
21 Evans-Pritchard, *Nuer Religion*, pages 293–294; Hutchinson, *Nuer Dilemmas*, pages 106–107.
22 Pendle, 'Politics, Prophets and Armed Mobilizations'.

in the community there was an active debate that contrasted the powers of Nyachol with the powers of government.

Part of Nyachol's vision of peace was also metaphorically 'hot'.[23] Through divine activity, including seizures, songs and invocations over animals for sacrifice, people had social space to rage against the violence, pain and betrayal in their lives. She also embraced the pervading, militarised sub-culture of the post-CPA Southern Sudan and helped her supporters build a strong, armed, militarised defence against government forces.[24] Nyachol did not participate in battles and raids herself but her *luak* became the place to gather, to plan and prepare for coordinated offensives. She was directly associated with the strategic decisions made before an offensive, including its timing and location.[25] She would also guide combatants in relation to the moral boundaries that they should uphold in conflict.

The CPA had brought no justice against forces of the *hakuma* nor against specific political figures who had caused devastation to Mayendit and to other areas to the east of the Bilnyang. Instead, the CPA had elevated them to some of the highest positions of power in the current government hierarchies. Their elevation was an affront to the demands of the dead and also to the hot hearts of the living. In recognising the normative value of revenge against *hakuma*, Nyachol challenged the impunity of government to carry out violence and showed a willingness to limit government legitimacy and power through violence. Nyachol's vision of the *hakuma* blurred this identity with a Dinka identity. Partly because many of those forces who had attacked her home villages had come from the home state of the leadership of the national government and had the guns during a period of government disarmament in Unity State, these categories of enmity were merged together. By the end of 2012, she was calling for a just war against the *hakuma* and Dinka, as if the two were synonymous.

Part of Nyachol's appeal was her remaking of prophetic powers to protect her followers from bullets. Before cattle raids, young men could go to her for blessing. She also blessed tobacco that could be scattered over armed fighters as they entered battle. This was meant to make them impenetrable to bullets. In this way, the seizure of Nyachol by MAANI repeated the appeal of the seizure of young men by MABIORDIT to the west of the Bilnyang.

23   Sharon Hutchinson and Naomi Pendle, 'Violence, Legitimacy, and Prophecy: Nuer Struggles with Uncertainty in South Sudan', *American Ethnologist* 42:3 (2015): 415–430.

24   Ibid.

25   Interviews with Nyachol's supporters, in Nuer, and with Dinka in villages attacked by Nyachol's supporters, February 2013, in Dinka.

Nyachol and the art of making government accountable

Nyachol also attempted to make the *hakuma* accountable through the application of Nuer customary law. For example, in July 2013, I had heard that Nyachol had suddenly moved to another *luak* near Ler. She had dreamt of a Dinka raid from the west and so hoped to move to a safer place deeper inside Nuer settlements. I wondered how her perceived need to flee was challenging her assertions of control over the landscape.

When my research assistant (Gatluak) and I started our journey to visit her, we were deep into the wet season months. The flood plains were coated in deep water that had overflowed from the Nile and the Bilynang River System. Locally built dykes were dotted across the landscape as a means to control the flooding and also to provide walkable routes between settlements. We walked along in single file, jumping over the holes in the dyke where the muddied pile had deteriorated. The water flowed through, unthreatened by human attempts to contain it.

On our arrival, some of Nyachol's youth came out to greet us. We were welcomed. Yet, they had come out to meet us to warn Gatluak that he should not come any closer to the *luak*. He was 'polluted' and, therefore, could not come close to Nyachol without deadly consequences. Gatluak's paternal cousin had killed a man near Bentiu a few days before. Gatluak's cousin was a policeman and had been sent by his commanding officer with other policemen to arrest a man. When the man saw the policemen approaching, he hid inside his mud-walled *tukal*. From there, he fired a gun out of the hut towards them. He failed to hit any of the policemen. Gatluak's cousin returned fire in the direction of the *tukal*. He could not see the man but the shots inflicted a fatal injury. Nyachol sent a message to Gatluak that he and his family could not approach her *luak* until compensation had been paid through the chiefs' courts and until a sacrifice had been made to end the *nueer*. The messenger made it clear to Gatluak that Nyachol had nothing personal against him, but that MAANI could not tolerate this pollution and impurity, and that she wanted Gatluak to be safe until his family had met their obligations under the customary law.

By demanding compensation from Gatluak's family, Nyachol was making it clear that his cousin's act, even when an act of the government (as it was done when he was on duty and obeying commands as a policeman), was still bound by the Nuer customary law and the cosmic dangers of *nueer*. For Nyachol, the cousin's membership of government was immaterial. She was erasing the distinction between government and non-government, and demanding equal expectations of Nuer, whether they were acting on behalf of the government or not. Nyachol bound government employees to the same legal obligations as private individuals and entrenched the same spiritual consequences. As a Nuer prophet, Nyachol was able to challenge government distinctness and impunity by reasserting the power of divinity behind the law. At the time, Gatluak's cousin and his family were challenging in the chief's courts in Bentiu the necessity for the family to pay compensation. They were arguing that, as he was a policeman following orders, he did not need to pay. However, Gatluak did not hesitate to obey Nyachol's instructions that day.

A new government commissioner

It was August 2013. As usual, I walked to the market in the early morning to sit inside one of the tea huts and drink a strong morning coffee. That morning the tea huts were fuller and conversation was more animated. The evening before, the commissioner had literally been chased out of Mayendit County by the youth. Many young men, including close followers of Nyachol, had finally had enough of the commissioner's disclosure of their movements and planned raids to the Tonj East Commissioner. They hoped for a commissioner to help their internal security and not to side with the perceived enemy. The previous evening they had gone to the county headquarters and demanded that the commissioner leave. At gunpoint they had physically chased him the length of the night's walk from the county headquarters to the northern border of the county. The commissioner had been a personal friend of the then Governor Taban Deng and had his support. Yet this friendship offered him no protection in this moment of local anger.

Nyachol supported the armed removal of the commissioner. She also supported raids against those in Tonj East. Her vision of peace was a vision that included violence against parts of the *hakuma* that she perceived as in violation of moral and spiritual norms. The commissioner rejected her authority and she rejected his vision of a *hakuma* that promoted peace through intra-government talks across Nuer-Dinka lines.

A few weeks later a new, locally popular, commissioner was appointed. Despite the impossibility of accessing his county by car at that time of the year, he opted to walk from Bentiu to his county to take on his new posting immediately. I was staying in Rubkuany, one of the most northerly villages in Mayendit. It would be here that he was officially welcomed into the county. The market streets were lined with people celebrating the coming of the new commissioner. He had been a commander in the area in the 1990s and was trusted for his experience in security provision and for his willingness to prioritise local security. The evening after his arrival he welcomed me to join him for dinner. It was dark but we found our way to his makeshift camp on the edge of the village. He sat on a white plastic chair at the end of a long table. His supporters sat around feasting on a bull that had been slaughtered earlier that day. People came up in an almost constant flow to greet him and congratulate him. We talked a little as he had spent some time since the CPA learning English in Uganda, and he was eager to practise. He encouraged me to drink soda and to eat the feast. The next morning, at dawn, they would walk to visit Nyachol. I was invited to join them. He had prioritised seeing Nyachol before he even completed the journey to the county headquarters.

The next morning, I was quickly reminded that, unlike me, the new commissioner had decades of experience of marching through the sticky, muddy soils of the clay flood plains. His soldiers also seemed well-practised in the art. I was not a soldier and quickly fell to the back of the large movement of people and soldiers towards Nyachol. Every soldier who overtook me smiled with a knowing but welcoming smile of greeting.

By the time I reached Nyachol's *luak*, the commissioner was already inside with her and deep in conversation. Outside, the commissioner's soldiers were celebrating with the youth that followed Nyachol. The drum was beating. Four large bulls were tethered to posts in the midst of the crowd. They were gifts to Nyachol from the new commissioner. Nyachol had already pledged to sacrifice one of her bulls to MAANI to bless the commissioner's appointment. The new era of local government promised a different relationship with Nyachol, yet it did not lessen Nyachol's attempts to re-create *nueer* or to remake the dangers of *nueer* even for government officials.

Conclusion

As the god-like power of the *hakuma* continued despite the 2005 peace, divine authorities emerged to contest both the divine, arbitrary power of the *hakuma* and the prevalence of impurity that was bringing seemingly unending feuds. This chapter has focused on Nyachol's seizure by MAANI in 2010 as an example of the proliferation of prophetic seizures in the post-CPA era. Nyachol evokes cultural archives to assert her divine authority and to allow her to use this authority as a strategy to confront the *hakuma*. At the same time, she creatively remade cultural archives to allow her to refuse some *hakuma* assertions, and especially the lack of pollution. Like some divine authorities to the west, she offered protection from bullets. She could also detect and resolve pollution, allowing a way to end the feud and bring peace. This gave prophetic figures a newly priestly role.

In Unity State, to the east of the Bilnyang and connected rivers, as elsewhere in Southern Sudan, the post-CPA era was a period where the youth faced demands to kill and the constant threat of being killed. Feuds were ongoing from the 1980s and 1990s, and new feuds were emerging. The youth were targets and killed in these intra-Nuer feuds. In this complex spiritual context, the possibility of peace was intimately connected with the possibility of purity and of reconciliation post-judicial peace. The youth supported these new Nuer prophets not only as they offered battlefield blessings and protection from bullets, but also as they had the power to resolve feuds through detection of *nueer* and the power to curse. The Nuer prophets, unlike the *hakuma* of the day, offered the possibility of peace without violent conflict through the ending of feuds.

Nyachol had a clear political vision and she reshaped culture as a way to refuse the politics and moral logics of the *hakuma*. She refused material items associated with the *hakuma*. At the same time, her rejection of the *hakuma* was morally contingent, allowing her to accept parts of the *hakuma* who did not contest her moral and spiritual authority. Ultimately it was not the *hakuma* that she rejected. Instead, it was *hakuma*'s assertions to be able to kill and act with immunity, beyond moral boundaries, that she violently contested.

Nyachol's peace was still a violent peace. Her remaking of purity relied on her power to threaten a lethal curse. People confessed to killing, and feared reopening the feud, because MAANI threatened death. Entangled with this power to curse was also her command over many lethal guns. She sanctioned and blessed various deadly, armed raids. They were made in the name of justice, but they were physically violent and resulted in dozens of deaths. Her peace through the gun and the curse was hot and violent.

PART III

The Logics of Peace and the Shape of War

CHAPTER 11

A War for the Dead and Wars Made by Peace

The wars did not stop. This chapter both introduces the wars in South Sudan since 2013, and then discusses the repeated international response of comprehensive peace negotiations and agreements. The wars from 2013 have often been narrated in terms of political contestations for control of the government's power and wealth.[1] Through the wars, political configurations in the *hakuma* (the broad government/socio-political sphere, including foreign traders and slavers) were re-arranged and Salva Kiir cemented his control over the security arena. There were further displays of a supranatural power to be able to wage war and peace with impunity. At the same time, these political contestations were taking place in a cosmic polity.

For many South Sudanese, the wars only really made sense if understood in terms of the moral demands for revenge and the lack of purity after the wartime pollution of the 1980s, 1990s and 2000s. The moral contestations over the previous decades in rural Southern Sudan were carried by wartime recruits. The concept of revenge had been transformed over the previous decades through armed conflict and peace, as well as contestations to restrain the divinity of the *hakuma*, as discussed in previous chapters. For the pro-government forces, demands for revenge based on histories dating back twenty years allowed armed conflict to be seen as a moral imperative. Among the nascent armed opposition, the moral imperative to mobilise was framed around demands for revenge after killings in Juba in 2013.[2] Military leaders, chiefs and the youth continued to claim that people had an obligation to carry out revenge, including for events a century before. For communities

---

1   Alex de Waal, 'When Kleptocracy Becomes Insolvent: Brute Causes of the Civil War in South Sudan', *African Affairs* 113:452 (2014): 347–369.
2   Naomi R. Pendle, 'The "Nuer of Dinka Money" and the Demands of the Dead: Contesting the Moral Limits of Monetised Politics in South Sudan', *Conflict, Security and Development* 20:5 (2020): 587–605.

and combatants on either side of the armed conflict, the logics of revenge were central to the meaning of the violence and its legitimacy.

In previous decades, as discussed in earlier chapters, divine authorities had creatively remade norms of revenge and pollution to contest and resist claims of *hakuma* impunity and to reassert a system in which peace and purity were possible. This also reasserted that *hakuma* wars were subject to moral restraint and spiritual consequences. However, some post-2013 *hakuma* mobilisations manipulated these popular moral ideas in order to demand unrestrained violence. As patterns of violence disrupted historic norms of restraint, the fear among many communities in South Sudan is that recent violence has created an unending war.

Despite the centrality of revenge to the meaning of war, the international community quickly forged ahead with trying to broker peace and a new comprehensive agreement between the leaders of the warring parties. The first meetings started in Addis Ababa before the SPLA-IO had even met together and formalised as a group. The 2015 ARCSS only saw an escalation of conflict in South Sudan. The 2018 revitalised agreement did result in an explicit cessation of hostilities between the government and SPLA-IO, and they did eventually come back together to form a transitional government in Juba. Yet, the logics of the agreement did not fit with the logics of the war as a war of revenge. The peace agreement still left an absence of justice for the dead, and a latent moral demand for future vengeance. Therefore, with the lack of purity, whether there was war or peace was ambiguous. The actual details of the 2018 agreement also created a situation of even further conflict between parts of the *hakuma*. In this context, spiritual unease could easily be used to justify war.

***

The only car left in Tonj Town (Warrap State) that Sunday afternoon still planning to travel south-west to Rumbek town (Lakes State) was the car of an MP in the Lakes State Parliament. It was only a few months before that I had visited Prophetess Nyachol with the new commissioner, and now I was travelling to England for Christmas. That afternoon in Tonj, all the other commercial cars, where you could pay a fee for a seat, had already left to avoid the risk of still being on the road at night. The size and opulent interior of the MP's car testified to the personal monetary benefits of being an MP in South Sudan. On that Sunday afternoon, the MP's wife and four of his children were squashed together in the back of the car, but the MP himself was absent. A young driver with a good grasp of English sat in the front. As the MP's income was erratic, reliant on an unpredictable bureaucracy and his personal relations with higher ranks in Juba, on that day the driver had no money for fuel. I was given the prized front seat in the car in exchange for my financing of the fuel for the journey. I was eager to get to Rumbek as fast as possible.

The journey to Rumbek started peacefully; the children in the back were just eager to test my attempts to speak Dinka. The road from Tonj to Rumbek has a history that dated back to the Anglo-Egyptian Condominium government in the first half of the twentieth century. Between the towns, it is dominated by its passage through the notorious forest called *Ror Cuɔl Akol* (literally 'The Forest of Sun and Darkness'). The name refers to the fact that, if walking, and you enter the forest (*ror*) at sunrise (*akol*) you will not leave it until the sun has set (*cuɔl*).

Halfway to Rumbek, while still in the *Ror Cuɔl Akol*, our car bumped over something hard and audibly gained a puncture. I insisted that we stop. The driver refused. When we were still in Tonj and aware that other cars had left earlier, I had asked the driver about the safety of the journey. Despite his previous assurances, he now claimed it was too dangerous in the forest to stop. Armed thieves and raiders were known to often hide in the forest to escape accountability, and also to ambush people passing through the forest. The driver's fear of the potential of armed men kept him driving. We made it the last couple of miles to a village, safely changed the tyre and continued with ease the rest of the way to Rumbek. Yet, even in that mundane decision on a normal afternoon journey, fear of physical or even lethal violence was a background consideration in this post-CPA South Sudan.

When I reached Juba, I had planned to spend time with friends that I had met while researching in Gogrial, Mayendit and the communities surrounding the Bilnyang. Some of my closest friends in Gogrial had travelled from Kakuma Refugee Camp (in Kenya) to South Sudan, to their family homes in Gogrial a few years after the CPA. I had met them in the villages of their families' homes. They spoke brilliant English which overcame my insufficient Dinka, and we worked together as teachers in a local school. In 2010, the South Sudan government started to reopen universities in the south that had been in the north during the decades of war. Having won places, my friends had moved to Juba to go to university. When I met people from Mayendit, they also introduced me to their networks in Juba. These included people studying, working in NGOs and working in the black-market Forex industry.

The night I arrived in Rumbek was the 15 December 2013. When I was back in the range of a phone mast, I texted a friend in Juba to say that I had safely arrived in Rumbek and would continue my journey to Juba in the next day or two. I had first met this friend in Mayendit when I started researching there in 2012. In response to my text, my friend called me. He announced: 'The war has started'.[3]

---

3   Phone conversation, South Sudanese NGO worker in Juba via phone from

That evening, soldiers of the Presidential Guard in Juba had fought each other in a small barracks near the University of Juba. Political tensions in Juba were high at the time as the SPLM/A was meeting to decide its presidential candidate for the planned 2015 elections. Earlier in 2013, President Kiir had dismissed from government a host of senior figures including Riek Machar and some of those historically loyal to Garang. At the time of their dismissal, tensions were high but no shots were fired. Instead, those who had been dismissed had formed a loose political coalition to challenge Kiir's leadership of the SPLM and government.

On the night of the 15 December, my friend immediately, accurately, interpreted this gun battle between a few dozen soldiers in one barracks as the start of a national civil war. He was not alone in perceiving its national significance. By the following morning, the SPLA in Juba had split, and fighting instantaneously remade the urban political and economic centre of Juba into an active battlefield. The division in the SPLA was largely along the lines of those who had fought for the SPLA in the 1990s and those who had fought for other armed groups, often against the SPLA, such as former members of the South Sudan Defence Force.[4] Juba had hosted armed conflict in the battles of the 1980s and 1990s, but, since the CPA, had been remade into a booming capital city of international development workers and oil wealth. Until December 2013, while armed conflict might have been commanded from Juba, it had taken place at a spatial distance. On the morning of 16 December, the army fractured and started battling for weapons stores across the town. The capital city erupted as the epicentre of the new civil war.

While the army fought itself, young men in soldiers' uniforms targeted thousands of people in their homes.[5] Civilians were among those apprehended and killed in this violence during door-to-door searches.[6] Tens of thousands of people ran to United Nations bases to seek safety. These bases, and their new use as Protection of Civilians sites, provided a new, urban, international, militarised sanctuary and enactment of nascent protection ideas.

Over the following few days, as violence escalated in Juba, I remained with South Sudanese and international NGO friends in Rumbek. There were friends from Lakes State, but also Nuer speakers from Unity State. As we

---

Rumbek, late evening, Sunday 15 December 2013.

[4]   Douglas Johnson, 'Briefing: The Crisis in South Sudan', *African Affairs* 113:451 (2014): 300–309.

[5]   African Union Commission of Inquiry on South Sudan, *Final Report of the African Union Commission of Inquiry on South Sudan* (The Commission of Inquiry on South Sudan, 2014).

[6]   Skye Wheeler, 'South Sudan's New War: Abuses by Government and Opposition Forces' (Human Rights Watch, 2014).

watched the violence unfolding from a distance, my intuition was to repeatedly call friends in Juba to see if they were okay and to try to work out if I should be worried about the conflict spreading to Rumbek.[7] My calls found these friends, who had been born near the Bilnyang and connected rivers, in a variety of different places in Juba. Most were hiding in homes and in hotels with friends. Some vanished from contact for a few days and later confirmed that they had fled to the UN bases for safety. Those friends who I had met in Mayendit, Ler and Koch feared that the political histories of their home areas would prompt government soldiers to classify them as rebels. Riek Machar, whose family was from Ler, was already establishing himself as the leader of the opposition. Many people from the east of the Bilnyang were killed in those December 2013 door-to-door searches that targeted Nuer speakers. Other friends who answered were moving around the town in army vehicles. Areas to the west of the Bilnyang and connected rivers had been key recruiting grounds for the pro-government militia forces that leaders in government from Gogrial and Tonj were trying to incorporate within the national army. People had joined the army to gain sponsorship for their education, to appease their uncles' demands or because they perceived army service as a prerequisite for future authority. Their own family histories that were shaped in armed conflict around the Bilnyang since the 1990s, also gave many a deep fear of Nuer-led rebellions.

By Christmas Day, just ten days later, armed conflict had spread to the three states of Greater Upper Nile (the north-eastern third of South Sudan) and engulfed four of South Sudan's major cities (namely Juba, Bentiu, Bor and Malakal). In Bentiu, James Koang, who commanded the SPLA's 4th Division, defected from the Juba government and took the majority of his division with him. He justified this as an act of revenge for family members being killed by the government in their homes in Juba.[8] James was an exception to the SPLA-SSDF split as he had been loyal to the SPLA in the 1990s and 2000s, but now rebelled against them. The initial focus of battles in Bentiu between the government and the emerging armed opposition was control of Bentiu and then the oilfields in the region. He quietly escorted Dinka soldiers in his ranks to safety away from Bentiu. Then he declared his opposition and with his remaining defecting 4th Division, captured Bentiu town. The 4th Division was numerically dominated by locally recruited youths from Unity State who defected with him.

Over the following months, the initial armed opposition formally coalesced around the name of the Sudan People's Liberation Army – In Opposition

---

7   Rumbek Town itself never saw significant conflict between the government and
      a formal armed opposition group.
8   Interview, Nairobi, February 2014.

(SPLA-IO).[9] Shaped by alliances that repeatedly fragmented, the wars would continue over most of the following decade, with new theatres opening up. They resulted in millions being displaced and hundreds of thousands being killed or dying as an indirect result of the violence.[10]

A war to reorder

There is a continued disagreement over how to understand the wars that erupted from 2013. Diplomats, aid workers and journalists have often narrated the conflict in ethnic terms, with the war being a war of the Nuer and Dinka, and more recently a war of the Equatorians versus the Dinka. Pinaud offers a more nuanced account of ethnicity's role in the wars by linking ethnicity to class.[11] She argues that ethnically exclusive and predatory wealth accumulation was key in fostering ethnic group entitlement and an ideology or ethnic supremacy. She claims that this led to genocidal violence in 2013 that triggered the following decade of war. However, others have contested whether ethnicity really is the dividing line between wartime alliances. Johnson and Craze's detailed work on the histories of alliances highlighted how the divisions between warring factions were often divisions between former SPLA and former anti-SPLA forces. The wartime divisions of the post-2013 period mirrored those of the 1990s.[12]

De Waal's 2014 description of a South Sudanese kleptocratic elite quickly gained saliency among diplomats and humanitarian donors as the alternative narrative to understand the wars in South Sudan. According to de Waal, South Sudan is governed by a political marketplace in which power is demanded through armed rebellion and loyalties are bought with money. Armed rebellions are a way to seek a place at the peace-making table and rent in this

---

[9]   The SPLA-IO formalised its name and hierarchy after a meeting in April 2014 in Pagak on the Ethiopia-South Sudan border. Even at this time many of the commanders in the armed opposition were not sure about the 'SPLA-IO' title. This was especially the case among those who had fought with the South Sudan Defence Force (SSDF) against the SPLA in the 1990s. Riek Machar dominated the process of name selection.

[10]   Francesco Checci, Adrienne Testa, Abdihamid Warsame, Le Quach and Rachel Burn, 'Estimates of Crisis-attributable Mortality in South Sudan, December 2013–April 2018' (London School of Hygiene and Tropical Medicine, 2018), www.lshtm.ac.uk/south-sudan-full-report, accessed 7 December 2020.

[11]   Clémence Pinaud, *War and Genocide in South Sudan* (Cornell University Press, 2021).

[12]   Johnson, 'Briefing: The Crisis in South Sudan'; Joshua Craze, '"And Everything Became War": Warrap State Since the Signing of the R-ARCSS', HSBA Briefing Paper (Small Arms Survey, 2022).

market.[13] Having been removed from government in mid-2013, Machar and others rebel to show that they need to be bought back, through money, into the government. The decade of wars after 2013 are wars in which rebellions repeatedly ignite and in which alliances of politico-military leaders frequently change, suggesting loyalties are as fluid as marketplace transactions. The years of war following December 2013 did cement the political and military power of Salva Kiir and his cadre. If there is a political marketplace among South Sudan's leadership, it was not that Salva Kiir did not 'have the required skills',[14] but rather that he was a master of the art.

Works by Craze, Kindersley and Majok, Thomas, Nyaba and Uchalla have instead highlighted the structures of the political economy over decades that have given rise to the forms of government that caused these wars.[15] The post-CPA period saw the marketisation and monetarisation of society, with increasing inequities in South Sudan. The war was 'rooted in long-established patterns of authoritarian, violent, and extractive governance of the pre-colonial, colonial and post-colonial periods, which concentrated economic and political power at the centre'.[16] Pinaud described the emergence of a 'military aristocracy'[17] and D'Agoôt the 'gun class', partly as a result of the wealth and power given to elites by 2005 CPA.[18]

[13] de Waal, 'When Kleptocracy Becomes Insolvent'.
[14] Ibid., page 347.
[15] Nicki Kindersley and Diing Majok, *Breaking Out of the Borderlands: Understanding Migrant Pathways from Northern Bahr el-Ghazal, South Sudan* (Rift Valley Institute, 2021), https://riftvalley.net/publication/breaking-out-borderlands-understanding-migrant-pathways-northern-bahr-el-ghazal-south, accessed 5 December 2020; Jovensia Uchalla, *Trading Grains in South Sudan: Stories of Opportunities, Shocks and Changing Tastes* (Rift Valley Institute, 2020), https://riftvalley.net/publication/trading-grains-south-sudan-stories-opportunities-shocks-and-changing-tastes, accessed 6 December 2020; Peter Nyaba, *The Politics of Liberation in South Sudan: An Insider's View* (Fountain Publishers, 1996); Edward Thomas, *South Sudan: A Slow Liberation* (Zed Books, 2015); Joshua Craze, 'Displaced and Immiserated: The Shilluk of Upper Nile in South Sudan's Civil War, 2014–2019' (Small Arms Survey, 2019), www.smallarmssurveysudan.org/fileadmin/docs/reports/HSBA-Report-South-Sudan-Shilluk.pdf, accessed 5 April 2020; Joshua Craze, *The Politics of Numbers: On Security Sector Reform in South Sudan, 2005–2020* (LSE, 2021), www.lse.ac.uk/africa/assets/Documents/Politics-of-Numbers-Joshua-Craze.pdf, accessed 6 December 2020.
[16] Øystein Rolandsen and Nicki Kindersley, *South Sudan: A Political Economy Analysis* (Norwegian Institute of International Affairs, 2017), page 4.
[17] Clemence Pinaud, 'South Sudan: Civil War, Predation and the Making of a Military Aristocracy', *African Affairs* 113:451 (2014): 192–211.
[18] Majak D'Agoôt, 'Taming the Dominant Gun Class in South Sudan' (2018),

A key result of the wars since 2013 has been Salva Kiir's and his cadre's remaking of the military arena of South Sudan to cement his control over government. The years from 2013 saw the demise of the SPLA and the rise of an armed forced with a more direct loyalty to Salva Kiir. As scholars have highlighted, globally it is no longer the case that state pursue a monopoly over the use of force, and private armed groups, often termed militias or vigilantes, are often key to regime security itself.[19] In the neo-liberal global shift towards privatisation, the security of the government itself is privatised. In the context of South Sudan, the potential fluidity of the security arena has allowed Salva Kiir to oversee the rise of military forces more directly loyal to him and to move away from an SPLA that had been shaped by Garang.

In the 1980s–2000s, Kiir, like others, had contested parts of Garang's leadership. Part of Kiir's ability to counter and sustain his position despite Garang's power was the recruitment of the supportive *titweng* and *gelweng* (armed cattle guards) in different parts of Greater Bahr el Ghazal. These were proxy SPLA forces defending against Sudan Armed Forces attacks, but they also swelled the number of forces that Kiir could command, giving him a stronger bargaining tool within the SPLA itself. The benefit of directly loyal forces was also apparent after the 2006 Juba Declaration when Paulino Matip allowed Kiir to benefit from the loyalty of his forces and provide his regime with a military backstop. On Garang's death in 2005, Kiir had inherited a patchwork of alliances shaped by Garang that dominated the SPLA, and Matip's forces allowed Kiir to counter this. Then, from 2012, recruitment started in Bahr el Ghazal for a force from the region that would be more directly loyal to Salva Kiir. Since 2012, this has included Mathiang Anyoor, the Presidential Guard (Tiger Battalion) and forces of the National Security Service.[20]

One way to understand the wars since 2013 is not as a battle between the armed opposition and government, but instead a violent remaking of the whole security arena. In 2012, the SPLA had refused to allow Salva Kiir to absorb the Mathiang Anyoor in to the national army. A decade later, the majority of the

---

https://africacenter.org/spotlight/taming-the-dominant-gun-class-in-south-sudan, accessed 10 December 2017.

[19] Rebecca Tapscott, 'Vigilantes and the State: Understanding Violence through a Security Assemblages Approach'. *Perspectives on Politics* (2021): 1–16; Lynette Ong, '"Thugs-for-Hire": Subcontracting of State Coercion and State Capacity in China'. *Perspectives on Politics* 16:3 (2018): 680–695; Sana Jaffrey, 'In the State's Stead? Vigilantism and Policing of Religious Offence in Indonesia', in Thomas Power and Eve Warburton (eds), *Democracy in Indonesia: From Stagnation to Regression?* (ISEAS – Yusof Ishak Institute, 2020): 303–325.

[20] Alan Boswell, 'Insecure Power and Violence: The Rise and Fall of Paul Malong and the Mathiang Anyoor', Briefing Paper (Small Arms Survey, 2019).

SPLA was weak, unpaid, fractured and frustrated. Instead, a small number of battalions that were like the Mathiang Anyoor, in that they had a more direct loyalty to Salva Kiir and his cadre, make up the real armed forces. Moments of war when seen as apparent chaos can mask the reality that it is a moment of re-ordering and establishing new clarity about hierarchies.[21] For South Sudanese, these forces still implicitly claim to be the same as the gods, as previous governments, in that they rain favour and destruction. At the same time, the way they are recruited often blurs the line between the home and the *hakuma*.

A war for the dead

At the same time, for many engaged in these wars, they were not simply about a battle for control of the security arena. A striking feature of December 2013 and early 2014, was the speed with which armed conflict spread across Juba and then South Sudan. Rapid communications, including through mobile phone networks, allowed eyewitnesses of the violence in Juba to report instantly their interpretations of what they had seen to their home communities hundreds of miles away. People in the capital city were entangled, through families, networks of belonging and government, with people in the most distant, rural areas of South Sudan.

South Sudanese interpreted the physical, lethal violence in Juba as intimately linked to historical conflicts as continuities of their ongoing experiences of lethal violence and government claims of impunity. They interpreted news of events in Juba in relation to histories of armed conflict, ongoing lethal violence and contested logics of peace, and within dynamic moral, spiritual and legal frameworks of legitimate response that had been re-crafted in recent processes of peace. This prompted an almost spontaneous mobilisation of warring forces.

A perpetual puzzle in explaining conflicts that have clear benefits to certain elites is understanding why soldiers or armed men are mobilised to fight when their political and economic interests seem to be so diverse from these politico-economic elites.[22] The elite class of the *hakuma* in South Sudan in 2013 had a significant economic disparity with South Sudanese from their home areas, and yet elite rivalries still prompted the mobilisation of vast forces. The mobilisation of armed men is particularly hard to understand as the costs of fighting were so high, including high risks of a brutal, burial-less, battlefield death. For some soldiers who have fought in recent years, the realities of predatory forced recruitment make this an irrelevant question; they fought

[21]   Stephen Lubkemann, *Culture in Chaos: An Anthropology of the Social Condition in War* (Chicago University Press, 2008).

[22]   David Keen, *Complex Emergencies* (Polity Press, 2007).

as they were violently recruited and had no option to do otherwise. Yet, many young men opted to fight in the South Sudan's 2013–18 wars.

Political and economic inequalities and grievances do help us understand why people agree to fight.[23] At the same time, those who have implemented violence in these ways have repeatedly explained their mobilisation as motivated by revenge. Analysis that focuses on the political economy usually sees religious and moral narratives as a by-product of these more fundamental, political economy dynamics. For those from the Bilynang River System (as well as elsewhere, whatever side they were fighting on), revenge and fighting to appease the demands of the dead have been a dominant part of the rallying cry to war for both those fighting for government and those fighting for the armed opposition. Conflict as revenge can conceal underlying dynamics, but to ignore the dominance of this discourse also ignores the importance of the normative and cosmological order in mobilising people to war.

Narratives of revenge can clearly be instrumentalised by political elites to mobilise South Sudanese to fight. However, at the same time, interviews with armed men about revenge repeatedly incited duties of revenge that are embedded in moral and cosmological systems. The years before had seen divine authorities actively draw on cultural archives to reassert the spiritual consequences of killing, and conflict was now seen in such terms. If we dismiss revenge as only an instrumental mobilisation, we miss the deep, invasive remaking of normative and cosmological systems by governments and divine authorities over time. We also miss how people can push back against the *hakuma* through enacting revenge against the *government*, challenging elite assumptions of their own impunity.

Revenge should be understood as part of a historically contingent moral norm embedded in other beliefs and cosmological assertions, and potentially part of the creative remaking of the cultural archive as an act of refusal. While such 'norms' are never 'natural' in that they do not occur irrespective of history, they have the greatest social power when they are 'naturalised' and operate at an unreflective level.[24] These norms are often naturalised through evoking the cultural archive. Normative orders are sometimes explicitly revised, and public authorities can attempt to intentionally manipulate them to their advantage. Yet, there is explicit resistance, as well as the conservative nature of social norms.

---

[23]   Peter Adwok Nyaba, 'The Fundamental Problems of South Sudan: How to Sustain Peace and Conditions of Socioeconomic Development', *The Zambakari Advisory: Special Issue* (2019): 20–24.

[24]   Pierre Bourdieu, *Distinction: A Social Critique of the Judgement of Taste* (Routledge, 1984).

In his research on the Mai Mai rebel group in DRC, Hoffman has described how 'the mythico-religious values and beliefs were reprocessed into political values', having 'powerful politico-epistemological effects on how rebels organized themselves and related to civilians through rebel governance'.[25] For 2013, we can again see this reprocessing of ideas of compensation and revenge. Revenge is never an explanation of conflict in itself, nor is it indicative of a Hobbesian propensity to violence in the absence of the state.[26] As previously discussed, Stewart and Strathern have demonstrated how concepts of feuding and revenge are transformed through dialectic interaction with political circumstances. 'We are dealing with old ideas recycled through new political circumstances and themselves changing rapidly as a result, often becoming heightened rather than disappearing'.[27] For Stewart and Strathern, '[i]t is, in effect, the result of the existence of state structures and the mutual impingement of local and national processes that feuding systems cannot realise their own larger cyclicities of violence and peace-making'.[28]

In December 2013, South Sudanese recourse to revenge was a product of people's understanding of death, life, war, peace and revenge itself, which was embedded in cosmologies and struggles for authority, and which had been contested and worked out (and was still being worked out) over the previous century and through the post-CPA years. As explained in previous chapters, the post-CPA era and peace agreements during this time had cemented the repeated lack of compensation for deaths in violent conflict. The *hakuma* had stopped, or not reinstated, judicial peace, effectively creating a legally entrenched ethnic division. Prophets and priests had contested these shifts. There was an eagerness to reinstate the moral and cosmological community that did not allow anyone to kill with impunity (with the exception of the divine) and that did not ignore the demand of the dead for justice. However, the *hakuma* had impacted the logics of peace and many now see a 'hot' peace of violence as the only option.

---

25   Kasper Hoffmann, 'Myths Set in Motion: The Moral Economy of Mai Mai Governance', in Ana Arjona, Nelson Kasfir and Zachariah Mampilly (eds), *Rebel Governance in Civil War* (Cambridge University Press, 2015), page 160.

26   Katy Migiro, 'Aid Groups Raise Fears of Escalating Violence in South Sudan' (*Reuters*, 21 May 2015); Mary Kaldor, 'In Defence of New Wars', *Stability: International Journal of Security and Development* 2:1 (2013): 1–16; Paul Richards, 'To Fight or to Farm? Agrarian Dimensions of the Mano River Conflicts (Liberia and Sierra Leone)', *African Affairs* 104:417 (2005), page 3.

27   Pamela J. Stewart and Andrew. J. Strathern, *Violence: Theory and Ethnography* (Continuum, 2002), page 12.

28   Ibid., page 13.

In terms of the armed opposition, the rallying call to mobilisation was explicitly a call to revenge. Those who took up arms against the government in December 2013 rallied around the quickly spread claim that 20,000 Nuer had been killed by government forces in Juba.[29] The actual number is still unclear.

The demand for revenge for Nuer dead also re-created a moral community of the Nuer.[30] Ethnicities are always historically contingent and change over time.[31] In attempts to remake their constituencies, political leaders often seek to shape identities.[32] At the same time, leaders cannot fully control the way that identities are shaped.[33] Not only may others in society and with power try to shape identities, but identities are also restrained by pervading social habits that are only slowly reshaped over time.[34] Identities can sit beneath 'consciousness and choice'.[35] They can also be subject to sudden rupture in times of war.[36] The formation of identities and polities, including ethnicities, can be driven by the way violence is organised.[37]

The framing of the post-December 2013 conflict as a 'war of revenge' against the killing of Nuer remade the Nuer into a kinship-like community in which Nuer had kinship-like obligations to each other.[38] This moral logic of treating fellow Nuer as kinsmen was not a new concept and it had been naturalised during Wunlit and the post-CPA period (as discussed in Chapter 8). The implication of this new vision of the Nuer community was that military labour was not commodified but instead subject to the moral expectations of kinship.

---

[29]   Pendle, 'The "Nuer of Dinka Money"'.

[30]   Ibid.

[31]   John Lonsdale, 'Moral & Political Argument in Kenya', in Bruce Berman, Will Kymlicka and Dickson Eyoh (eds), *Ethnicity & Democracy in Africa* (James Currey, 2004): 73–95.

[32]   Alex de Waal, *Somalia's Disassembled State: Clan Formation and the Political Marketplace* (World Peace Foundation, 2019), abstract.

[33]   Koen Vlassenroot, 'Citizenship, Identity Formation & Conflict in South Kivu: The Case of the Banyamulenge', *Review of African Political Economy* 29:93–94 (2007): 499–516.

[34]   Pierre Bourdieu, 'The Social Space and the Genesis of Groups', *Theory and Society* 14:6 (1985): 723–744.

[35]   Pierre Bourdieu, 'Rethinking the State: Genesis and Structure of the Bureaucratic Field', *Sociological Theory* 12:1 (1994), page 15. As highlighted in Toby Dodge, '"Bourdieu goes to Baghdad": Explaining Hybrid Political Identities in Iraq', *Journal of Historical Sociology* 31:1 (2018): 25–38.

[36]   Adam Baczko, Giles Dorronsoro and Arthur Quesnay, *Civil War in Syria: Mobilization and Competing Social Orders* (Cambridge University Press, 2017).

[37]   de Waal, *Somalia's Disassembled State*.

[38]   Pendle, 'The "Nuer of Dinka Money"'.

It was not simply that politico-military leaders used cultural archives to incite violence in the moment, but that cultural archives had been politically reshaped over decades. In many ways, the mobilisation of the armed opposition in late 2013 and early 2014 was a bottom-up process driven by popular demand for an anti-government response, and not controlled by the leadership in that moment. At the same time, the popular demand for an anti-government war was shaped by pre-existing norms, moral expectations and the cultural archive that had been politically influenced over the previous decades. The popular call to arms against the government was not just to defend the Nuer from government force, but also to revenge for the acts carried out in Juba in December 2013.[39] The nascent opposition leadership did not construct notions of revenge in that moment, but people's demand for revenge was the product of the slow evolution of norms of revenge during the 1980s, 1990s and into the post-2005 peace. The previous decades had remade norms of revenge and made it possible to imagine the post-December 2013 conflict as a 'war of revenge'.[40]

For the armed opposition, the rapid mobilisation of anti-government forces in the army and communities created the movement and mobilised armed labour. Yet, it had disadvantages for Machar's vision of opposition. He had been eager to mobilise an opposition that was broader than the Nuer and the building of a pan-Nuer identity around revenge was undermining his attempt to build a cross-ethnic constituency of support.

The wars in the communities around the Bilnyang and connected rivers

The wars in December 2013 started in Juba and not in the Bilnyang, yet people from Bilnyang were significant in the numbers that perpetuated and experienced violence, and among those who commanded it. Perceptions of peace, the social power of the dead and the need for revenge are not normative ideas that are decided in a moment but are naturalised social habits that have social force over decades. Those social norms that had been remade at 'home' near the Bilnyang and in other similar rural areas, now shaped the normative contestations and violent wars in Juba.

The wars to the west of the Bilnyang

Young men from Gogrial and Tonj who implemented violence in Juba in December 2013 had a complex range of reasons to fight, but revenge was part

---

[39]   John Young, *Isolation and Endurance: Riek Machar and the SPLM-IO in 2016–17* (Small Arms Survey, 2017).

[40]   Naomi Pendle, '"The Dead are Just to Drink From"': Recycling Ideas of Revenge among the Western Dinka, South Sudan', *Africa* 88:1 (2018): 99–121.

of these reasons. It is reasonable to assume that the moral contestations of Gogrial still had resonance among the young men who formed the Mathiang Anyoor. Those recruited into the Mathiang Anyoor itself had recently fought against those from Mayendit, Koch and Mayom, including in the 2012 conflict with Peter Gadet. These young men had childhood memories and family histories of large-scale losses in the *toc* during the 1990s. In these histories, at this juncture, the Nuer had broken the earth. Commanders and Kiir explicitly frame the conflict in Nuer-Dinka terms.

Fighting between the armed opposition and the government never took place in the areas immediately to the west of the Bilnyang and connected rivers, but the war created ongoing demands for militarised labour, as well as economic hardship and new contestations over public authority. In the post-CPA period, commanders in Bahr el Ghazal conducted significant, sometimes forced, recruitment in Warrap State. This recruitment was initially for a force that became the Mathiang Anyoor, and commanders justified it in terms of Bahr el Ghazal needing a border defence against northern Sudan.[41] In 2012, these forces fought significant battles against the Sudan Armed Forces. In Greater Gogrial, this recruitment was already causing concerns and push-back against the government. Yet concerns escalated as these recruits were taken to Juba and then other parts of South Sudan to fight for the government. Many of these young soldiers would not return or be heard of again.

The wars to the east of the Bilnyang

Initially, fighting between the government and defecting SPLA in Unity State was focused on Bentiu and the oilfields. In the first months of 2014, there was still a hopeful naivety that the wars might remain in Bentiu and not move south. Thousands of people fled from Bentiu to Mayendit and Ler.[42] The local government actively registered them as internally displaced persons (IDPs) imagining that this would remain a place of safety.

In the end, the counties of Koch, Mayendit and Ler became some of the deadliest places in South Sudan in the wars that followed from 2013.[43] Government-backed forces repeatedly carried out offensives that violated humanitarian norms, killing civilians, burning homes and displacing tens of thousands.[44] As they had in the 1990s and 2000s, people from these counties

---

[41]   Boswell, 'Insecure Power and Violence'.

[42]   Conversation with SSRC officer in Mayendit, 26 December 2020.

[43]   Checci et al., 'Estimates of Crisis-attributable Mortality in South Sudan'.

[44]   Skye Wheeler and Samer Muscati, '"They Burned It All": Destruction of Villages, Killings, and Sexual Violence in Unity State South Sudan' (Human Rights Watch, 2015).

fought on all sides of the civil war and families were again divided between warring sides.

These rural areas had historic sympathies and relations with the armed opposition and the leadership of Riek Machar. The armed cattle guard also started to support the soldiers who had rebelled against the government. The emerging SPLA-IO tried to co-opt the cattle guard and gave them the name 'gojam', a term that vaguely references an Arabic word for army division. The gojam started using army-like ranks, yet they remained attached to their communities and local public authorities, as opposed to the army command.[45]

After the government retook Bentiu, and as areas to the south became opposition strongholds, government forces attacked from Bentiu into Koch, Mayendit and Ler. Large attacks occurred annually over the following years, and these areas saw extreme violations of humanitarian norms as children were killed, people raped and property burnt.[46] Thousands were directly killed, tens of thousands were displaced, and tens of thousands died of hunger-related illnesses and vulnerabilities.[47] Over time, the government captured control of more areas and mobilised local fighting forces. UN reports document how the violence was inescapable, brutal and often seemingly arbitrary.[48] The hakuma was raining destruction with impunity.

When James Koang defected in December 2013, the then governor (Monytuil) fled to Mayom. With Taban Deng joining the armed opposition with Riek Machar, the divisions in the politics of Unity State pushed Monytuil and others from Mayom towards Kiir.[49] In the early years of the conflict the South Sudan Liberation Army in Mayom acted as a pro-government militia who gained financially from Kiir's support. Yet, even commanders from Mayom were not unified in favour of the government. As pro-government forces in Mayom were organising to defend Bentiu and the Unity State oilfields, another senior commander from Mayom – Peter Gadet – had already rebelled against the government with his soldiers in Bor. He later commanded the SPLA-IO forces in Unity State.

Even brothers ended up fighting on different sides of the war. For example, until 2022, the government offensives into Koch, Ler and Mayendit never

45   Naomi Pendle, 'Competing Authorities and Norms of Restraint: Governing Community-Embedded Armed Groups in South Sudan', *International Interactions* 47:5 (2021), 873–897.
46   Wheeler and Muscati, '"They Burned It All"'.
47   Checchi et al., 'Estimates of Crisis-attributable Mortality in South Sudan'.
48   Wheeler and Muscati, '"They Burned It All"'.
49   Joshua Craze, Jérôme Tubiana and Claudio Gramizzi, 'A State of Disunity: Conflict Dynamics in Unity State, South Sudan, 2013–15', HSBA Working Paper 42 (Small Arms Survey, 2016).

achieved total control of these areas but they did allow the government to seize pockets of control in urban centres. When the government had captured Ler, they installed a pro-government commissioner to govern what was effectively an SPLA barracks in the town of Ler. The government commissioner of Ler was the brother of one of the most senior commanders in the SPLA-IO. In 2016, when Taban Deng claimed leadership of the SPLA-IO and was recognised as Vice President by President Kiir, further fragmentation took place. Those from Mayom, who had long rivalries with Taban, became more cautious about alliances with government. Opposition-controlled areas also divided.

For those living in Unity State, the years after December 2013 were another enactment of the god-like nature of the *hakuma* for South Sudanese through their experience of arbitrary violence. The wars involved brutal, deadly violence implemented by all parties in the conflict, and inflicted on soldiers and civilians. The *hakuma* in a broad sense continued to rein destruction and war, and people lost lives, homes and livelihoods.

An unending war

The way the war was fought evoked logics that made it unending. Combatants on either side implemented and experienced extreme levels of lethal force and some people were even subjected to extra-lethal killings.[50] It was not just the speed and scale of lethal violence that was shocking, but also the patterns of violence that were employed. Homes were burnt, children were killed, and thousands of people were chased into the swamps, followed by the pounding, lethal blasts of the gun. Pro-government fighters not only killed children but also mutilated their bodies as the means of slaying these infants.[51]

Revenge clearly did not explain all motivations and sometimes it was a thin veil over personal ambitions. Yet, the need to justify the violence and the discussions of the dead highlight the continued resonance of revenge. For example, in 2018, during the mobilisation of the *gojam* in Koch, the government county commissioner used the history of the prophets to justify the moral and spiritual obligation of the youth to fight and seek revenge against the entire Dok community of Ler. In his speeches to mobilise people to attack, he recited histories of Kolang Ket (discussed in this book's opening chapters) whose death in 1925 was perpetrated by a Nuer government official from Ler near the port of Adok. In 2018, the commissioner asked the *gojam* to attack IO

---

[50]   By 'extra-lethal' killings I mean physical violence against a person's body that goes beyond what is necessary to cause death. It is talking about acts such as crucifixion and bodily mutilation that result in death.

[51]   African Union Commission of Inquiry, *Final Report*.

areas around Ler as a way to take revenge for Kolang's death nearly a century before.[52] Although this was an attack in the national war between the government and SPLA-IO, for those fighting it was best justified as a feud amid prophetic histories. At the same time, for those who fought, their superior weaponry allowed them to return with significant loots of cattle and property.

A war made by peace?

As soon as the war started in December 2013, and before the SPLA-IO had even coalesced around Riek Machar's leadership, IGAD, with international support, initiated peace negotiations in Addis Ababa. The parties and issues in contention had yet to be clarified, and the parties were still gaining momentum. They were far from a stalemate and appetite to negotiate. Yet, from the eruption of violence in Juba, there was an instant international appetite for peace. As the international community watched events unfold in December 2013, many were confronted by a cognitive dissonance about the nature of the South Sudanese political system. The 'Troika' governments – the UK, the USA and Norway – plus the EU and the UN had increasingly discussed imperfections in South Sudan's governance systems. In 2012, the UK's Department for International Development had even started to tailor assistance in South Sudan accordingly. Yet, the speed, scale and urban focus of the way the conflict erupted in 2013 shocked people and brought immediate calls for peace. In this moment of dissonance and disbelief, international diplomats were relieved that the East African regional powers, notably Ethiopia, Kenya and Uganda were all eager to take a lead in brokering peace.

Control of the peace agreements by IGAD and the international community quickly meant that this new peace process mimicked those of the 2005 CPA and other peace settlements. It was assumed that the new peace agreement to deal with the post-December 2013 war would not only be a cessation of hostilities, but would include a new power-sharing government during a transition period that would end with an election. It would include elements promoting political and economic liberal systems. It would also have the same rituals that would help set up the process and make the peace-makings distinct.

There was irony in IGAD leading the peace negotiations. Uganda was a member of IGAD and was also actively fighting for the South Sudan government. In early 2014, its army played an active, visible role in securing for the government control of Juba, Bor, the oilfields and major roads, and deterring an SPLA-IO attack on the capital. The securing of these major government assets and transport routes was useful for a broader part of the international

[52] Observation and subsequent conversations among the Jagei, April and May 2018.

community. As the war escalated through 2014 and 2015, the negotiations seemed to be nothing more than noise. Maybe, at best, they were an attempt by foreign mediators to make a seemingly illegible, unreasonable war into a legible conflict. Many senior figures, especially in the cash-strapped SPLA-IO, were clearly using the negotiations as an opportunity to rest and recuperate on the budget of international donors.

At the same time, the peace negotiations had power to reshape the politics of the *hakuma*. The IGAD peace negotiations proved crucial in establishing the structure and hierarchies of the SPLA-IO. The CPA had made it clear that authority was established through peace and war. Through political settlements, international legitimacy could be bestowed on rebel groups. Therefore, by assuming leadership over the negotiations from the outset, Riek Machar also asserted himself as leader over the SPLA-IO. This was even visible in the name of the SPLA-IO. Many senior commanders in the armed opposition to government opposed the choice as they had fought the SPLA throughout the 1980s and 1990s. However, to appeal to a broader South Sudanese constituency, Machar wanted to keep the SPLA-IO name. The first IGAD cessation of hostilities was signed in the name of the SPLA-IO before the armed opposition had even met and selected a name. Yet, as it was now internationally recognised and used in legal text, the SPLA-IO name stuck.

Eventually, in 2015, Salva Kiir and Riek Machar signed the Agreement on the Resolution of Conflict in South Sudan (ARCSS). However, as Kiir signed it he was explicit that he did not want to. There was no deal with Machar and the SPLA-IO. The following months and years after the 2015 ARCSS saw no decline in fighting between the government and SPLA-IO. In April 2016, Machar flew to Juba to join the join the 'unity' government.

However, the signing of the 2015 ARCSS did result in the escalation and growing geographic spread of the war. The ARCSS and government responses to it both pushed war into the Equatorias and increased fighting in Bahr el Ghazal. In 2014, when the ARCSS was being negotiated, there was just one man behind one placard in the large negotiating room which read 'Equatorias'. The mediators focused on the SPLA-IO and government and saw the war as primarily about Bahr el Ghazal and Upper Nile. Fighting escalated and spread after the signing of the ARCSS. The Equatorias became a major theatre of war and a proliferation of armed groups emerged there. Their lack of involvement in the peace agreement, for many Equatorians, was indicative of their exclusion from power in the state.

Despite the ARCSS escalating the war, international diplomats were hesitant to accept its total failure in case this discouraged their governments' engagement. The pretence of peace was lost in July 2016 when violence erupted in Juba just two months after SPLA-IO leader Riek Machar returned to the city to form a Transitional Government of National Unity. On the 2 July

2016, unknown gunmen killed two SPLA-IO soldiers, increasing the nervousness of Machar's troops. A few days later, at the Presidential Palace, during a live news conference with both Kiir and Machar, fighting erupted outside between their bodyguards. The heavily armed bodyguards quickly killed each other in large numbers. Many of the bodyguards were close relatives of the elite, increasing their personal bitterness instantly. The peace fell apart and fighting spread across Juba 8–11 July while, government forces pursued Machar out of Juba as far as the Democratic Republic of the Congo.[53]

In the days when Riek Machar fled, Taban Deng declared himself leader of the SPLA-IO and Kiir quickly accepted this. Almost all the SPLA-IO refused Taban's leadership, but this created a divided opposition and ambiguities for the international community. Fighting again escalated in Koch and areas to the east of the Bilnyang. The splitting of the SPLA-IO divided counties and families even further, as well as allowing the government to use larger, local militia for raids into government-held areas. Their local knowledge increased the brutality and penetration of these attacks.

The 2018 Revitalised Agreement on the Resolution of Conflict in South Sudan

On the 26 June 2018, Kiir and Machar signed the Khartoum Declaration of the Peace Agreement on the instruction of then President Bashir of Sudan and President Museveni of Uganda. This was essentially a deal not between Kiir and Machar, but between Bashir and Museveni.[54] These two foreign presidents and close supporters of the warring parties were able to force an acceptance of a deal. Bashir's new interest in prioritising peace in South Sudan was connected to his need for revenue to protect his increasingly fragile government. The Sudan and South Sudan ministries of petroleum agreed to resume oil production in Heglig and Unity State, and for Sudan's army to provide protection for these fields.[55] Upholding the ARCSS framing, this deal was written into a 'revitalised' ARCSS agreement which was signed by the SPLM/A-IO, the government and the South Sudan Opposition Alliance on the 12 September 2018. 'It was the devil that misled us in the first place, hence we fought … I

53   Small Arms Survey, 'Spreading Fallout: The Collapse of the ARCSS and New Conflict along the Equatorias-DRC Border', HSBA Issue Brief (2017), www.smallarmssurvey.org/sites/default/files/resources/HSBA-IB28-Spreading-Fallout.pdf, accessed 17 July 2022.
54   Mahmood Mamdani, 'The Trouble with South Sudan's New Peace Deal: The Revitalized Agreement on the Resolution of the Conflict in South Sudan (R-ARCSS)', *The Zambakari Advisory*, Special Issue (2019), page 57.
55   Nyaba, 'The Fundamental Problems of South Sudan', page 21.

therefore ask that we take brooms and clean off the pain and bitterness the war had created in our hearts'.[56]

People in Unity State, who had experienced the brunt force of *hakuma* power, welcomed peace. At the same time, the peace of the Revitalised Agreement on the Resolution of Conflict in South Sudan (R-ARCSS) was also arbitrary and a further expression of the *hakuma*'s ability to rain favour. One of the most brutal, annual offensives into central Unity State took place in May 2018, just before the June 2018 deal.[57] As discussed, narratives of revenge, including for the death of Kolang Ket, were key parts of the cultural archive that was evoked to justify this violence. Yet, the peace deal now meant that, overnight, the politico-military leadership was demanding a lack of revenge and not compliance with its moral demands. Suddenly the demand was 'peace' and not 'war'.

A lack of justice

In contrast and in recognition of the failures of parts of the CPA, ARCSS included a Chapter V that outlined provisions for justice, accountability, reconciliation and healing. However, the details of these provisions were left unsettled. Their existence did prompt discussion in NGO meetings in Juba and between diplomats in foreign capital cities about what justice might look like. Yet, the written words of the whole agreement carried the same fictional, mystical character as much of the CPA. No-one believed that Chapter V would ever be implemented in a way that offered meaningful accountability through challenging the impunity of the *hakuma*. If anything, the peace agreement prompted the international community to champion a new state-building agenda that sought to enhance the divine, sovereign nature of the new government of national unity.

As discussed throughout this book, the inclusion of justice in the resolution of the conflict was not only important to appease contemporary hot, hurting hearts and demands for revenge, but to uphold moral and spiritual obligations to the living and the dead. It was also important as a way to re-establish relationships between citizens and the government, to re-establish a judicial form of peace (and war) and to limit the violence of government. Government elites, during the wars and peace of the last three decades, had interrupted the potential for judicial peace and created unending feuds. This lack of judicial redress of grievances provided elites with opportunities to mobilise support along populist,

---

[56]   SPLA-IO Commander, Malakal POC Peace Celebration, 1 December 2018.

[57]   UNMISS and UNHR, Indiscriminate Attacks Against Civilians in Unity State, April–May 2018 (2018), https://unmiss.unmissions.org/sites/default/files/unmissohchr_report_on_indiscriminate_attacks_against_civilians_in_southern_unity_april-may_2018.pdf, accessed 17 July 2022.

moral lines.[58] Justice was needed to remake government-citizen relations to the extent that citizens' demands for judicial peace could be realised.

The very nature of the ARCSS and R-ARCSS, like the CPA, even further cemented the negotiated nature of peace that enhanced government powers. The R-ARCSS was presented as a rupture and making of a new government and constitutional arrangements, and not continuity with the past. It was now presented as the new document to justify arrangements of power. It was performed as if it was a blank slate, even if this dissonance from reality reduced its meaning. Yet, the R-ARCSS was a continuity of the turbulent politics where elites could give and take life, and give and take war.

At the same time, compensation was demanded by fighters from the elites under whose aegis they fought. Political elites in South Sudan have had to use various tactics to recruit armed forces to fight on their behalf. They have used popular narratives of revenge and explicit promises of financial payments. Plus, both government and opposition forces have been recruited with the promise of future financial rewards for those who survive and compensation for those who do not.[59] Families on all sides of the Bilnyang are grappling with whether they should marry for relatives killed in these years of war. These expectations were entrenched after the CPA when many Southeern Sudanese married wives for those sons who had been lost in the wars.

The wartime dead were not settled by the peace agreements. While the *hakuma* demanded peace, there was ambiguity over the morality of not insisting upon revenge. These unsettlements and ambiguities meant that there was an easy potential for armed conflict to start again.

Peace that makes war

Craze and Marko argue that conflict in South Sudan after 2018 continued not despite the peace agreement, but because of it.[60] They argue that the R-ARCSS, by giving the parties the power to appoint all government positions, created 'a

---

[58] Pendle, "'The dead are just to drink from'".

[59] Peter Gadet, speech at funeral in Khartoum, 2015.

[60] Joshua Craze, 'The War They Call Peace', *Sidecar* (9 July 2021), https://new-leftreview.org/sidecar/posts/the-war-they-call-peace, accessed 10 July 2021; Joshua Craze and Ferenc David Marko, 'Death by Peace: How South Sudan's Peace Agreement Ate the Grassroots', *Debating Ideas* (6 January 2022), https://africanarguments.org/2022/01/death-by-peace-how-south-sudans-peace-agreement-ate-the-grassroots, accessed 16 July 2022; Joshua Craze, 'When Peace Produces War: The Case of South Sudan', Special Report, Risks of Peace in Post-War Yemen Series, https://static1.squarespace.com/static/535dcd87e4b08cab3cb3e421/t/61f9355bfe787d019f61b734/1643722075758/e6b9aed53703337d91b7c7946696764e61f8f68d857c6.pdf, accessed 17 July 2022.

centralized regime that appoints not only state governors, but even county commissioners, according to a political calculus determined in Juba'.[61] As many of the parties were 'briefcase' rebels they were easily controlled by the governing regime.[62] In order to control populations, especially when there is a lack of government funds, violence is used. This often involves a fragmentation that cements, and does not undermine, central control.[63] Yet, as Chapters 5 and 6 describe, these dynamics were nothing new and only entrenched a post-CPA system of governance and armed conflict. In such a context, the unsettled dead, as discussed above, can easily be evoked to justify violence.

Conclusion

The wars in South Sudan after 2013 brought widespread experiences of arbitrary violence from the government and SPLA-IO *hakuma*. This arbitrary violence without impunity again portrayed the *hakuma* as god-like. In these wars, power in the *hakuma* shifted seismically. The wars in South Sudan from 2013 radically reshaped the security arena in the country. Through years of deadly violence, armed opposition groups became visibly incapable of challenging Salva Kiir's leadership. The security arena has also been reconfigured to wither the SPLA and allow the rise of armed forces more directly controlled by the president and his cadre. Therefore, there have been seismic shifts in the *hakuma*.

At the same time, the wars of the *hakuma* were not devoid of the spiritual and cosmic logics. The government and armed opposition heavily relied upon rurally recruited forces which meant they had first-hand experience of witnessing conflicts in the post-CPA era. These recruits had long experience of these contestations to restrain *hakuma* violence by contesting its impunity, as well as the continuity and remaking of moral norms such as for revenge. For both government and opposition forces, armed conflict post-2013 often made moral sense because it satisfied the demand for revenge from past, and often recent, grievances.

Peace-making started almost as soon as the war began. Peace deals did not quieten the dead or provide judicial peace. Worse than this, they also reaffirmed structures that would create violence and armed conflict. The peace made by regional actors was to be incredibly violent. In the following two chapters we explore in more depth the consequences of the post-2013 wars and peace for the communities around the Bilnyang and connected rivers.

---

[61]   Joshua Craze, 'The War They Call Peace'.
[62]   Ibid.
[63]   Ibid.

CHAPTER 12

Prophets Making Peace: Peace-making in Unity State, post-2013

This chapter describes how the armed conflicts in Unity State from 2013 to 2022 repeatedly placed the Nuer prophets in competition with the *hakuma* and the unrestrained, supranatural power of the gun. Repeatedly the militarised power of the *hakuma* 'silenced' other authorities, including the prophets. Some prophets failed to protect lives, cattle and property during government offensives. In a system of divine authority reliant on empirically observed displays of power, these military defeats weakened prophets. Plus, in areas of armed opposition control, the emergence of the *gojam* (armed youth associated with the SPLA-IO) brought new levels of gun ownership and new pluralities of divine powers to kill with impunity. Additionally, the wars challenged the significance of *nueer* and the prophetic power to find solution.

At the same time, the silencing of the prophets was understood in cosmic terms and was repeatedly temporary. Even during these years of brutal armed conflict, the prophets still actively sought to create and enforce limits on *hakuma* violence, demanding moral restraint and a lack of impunity. Accounts of when prophetic power did challenge the *hakuma*'s brute force were lauded and told for reassurance that the *hakuma*'s power could be bounded. Prophetic defeat was still understood in cosmic terms; the lack of power of the prophets was seen as the result of pollution and cosmic confusions, and not simply as their subordination to the power of the *hakuma*.

This chapter provides an account of the 'silencing' of the prophets by the wars of the *hakuma*, and the resilience of the prophetic power despite this silencing. Prophets restored their authority even after rejection, and new divinities seized prophets. Repeatedly prophetic power is built to demand a limit to the violence of the *hakuma,* to insist on the continued existence of *nueer* and demand peace. Prophets are able to do this through their divine power to kill through the curse. Even those empowered by the gun are not empowered to commit arbitrary violence with impunity; they are still subject to the dangers of *nueer.* Soldiers still feared *nueer* (spiritual impurity), drinking bitter water from the cases of spent shells when the bitter bile of an ox was absent. Prophetic authority comes through limiting the plurality of god-like power by limiting the impunity of the gun. When figures in the *hakuma* are seen as partisan, using government power to arbitrarily rain favour on their own clans and communities, prophets repeatedly gain authority through their ability to be more set apart. The chapter draws on examples from the Prophetess Nyachol and Prophet Gatluak. It also describes the wartime seizure of Geng Mut Liah Wal by TILING, a divinity whose seizure made Geng a powerful guan kuoth (prophet). These prophets all resided among communities to the east of the Bilnyang, in central Unity State.

The silencing of the divinities

As described in Chapter 10, the post-CPA period saw the seizure of new Nuer prophets among the communities to the east of the Bilnyang. These prophets repeatedly drew on the cultural archive and evoked histories of previous Nuer prophets. By 2013, there were two significant, active prophets in central Unity State, in Ler and Mayendit Counties. Nyachol, who claimed to have been seized by MAANI, was residing in a large *luak* in the borderlands between Ler and Mayendit County. Another prophet – Gatluak Gatkuoth – was residing near Ler. Notably, there was still no prophet in Koch and no prophet of MAANI recognised by people in Koch. MAANI's absence was as striking as the others' presence.

The wars after 2013 challenged the power of the Nuer prophets in three ways. Firstly, the superior, asymmetrical military power of the government was so overwhelming that it threated to display the impossibility of restraint and make the *hakuma* as the supreme god-like being. Secondly, the SPLA-IO's formation of the *gojam* from the armed cattle guard proliferated guns and *hakuma* power, potentially bringing a plurality of little deities with the power to kill with impunity. Thirdly, the scale of death and killing threated to diminish the significance of *nueer.*

Government power

Repetitive displays of superior military power in the post-2013 wars appeared to place the *hakuma* at the top of the cosmic polity, silencing divine competitors. After 2013, the scale of violence perpetrated by the warring parties again challenged the prophets and their claims to power. Like the communities among whom they lived, the prophets had also to struggle to gain any foothold to push back against militarised forces whose violence was seemingly arbitrary. Prophets themselves have not been safe, and the large-scale displays of military might from government undermined the divine's ability to claim power of equivalence. As one *kuaar muon* (Nuer priest) described in 2018, 'The power of the gun has silenced everybody, including divinities'.[1]

For example, in 2014, during early government raids on Ler and Mayendit, many people brought their belongings to Nyachol's *luak* in anticipation that her divine authority over the *luak* would provide protection to the items even against government attacks. Someone informed government soldiers of the hoard, and they attacked the *luak* within a few days. They were even said to have brought a large truck to fill up with all the possessions that had been gathered together in the *luak*. Nyachol's *luak* offered no protection.

However, some accounts of Nyachol's brute power still abounded. In 2014, as government forces moved south, her armed youth were said to have stopped them from moving off the road and into rural areas to the west. Rumour has it that Nyachol's supporters even managed to capture a government tank.

In a different example, the 2015 government offensives on Ler dramatically reduced the authority of Gatluak Gatkuoth, another Nuer prophet who had been seized in the post-CPA period. Based in the SPLA-IO areas near Ler, Gatluak had a reputation for the protection of cattle. When people near Ler realised that government offensives were approaching, many chose to place their cattle with Gatluak's herd while they fled further into the swamps and islands. However, his divine powers of protection could not resist the pro-government forces. The attackers took all his cattle and all of those that he had been entrusted to protect. Gatluak himself ended up fleeing far away from Ler to the safer town of Nyal (Panyijar County) much further south.

Just over a year later, in June 2016, Gatluak returned by canoe from Nyal (southern Unity State) to the island of Kok, a then SPLA-IO-controlled area near Ler. When he arrived back to his area near Ler, he waited in the canoe for a goat to be found to sacrifice to him. He was attempting to be consistent with the cultural archive that suggested that prophets should not step onto new soil until an animal is sacrificed in recognition of their authority and to ensure there is a peaceful relationship. However, in 2016, no animal was immediately brought to Gatluak. Livestock were few and far between, and so an animal to sacrifice was hard to find. His failure to protect those herds and his flight to Nyal had weakened his authority and people did not fear him with the urgency he previously commanded. He had to wait in the canoe for three days before a goat was brought. His claims of divine authority had been trumped and undermined by the more successful claims of supranatural authority by the *hakuma*.

Despite Gatluak's failure to protect, his authority was not fully lost. Within a year, he had resumed significant authority and almost instantly re-acquired wealth in cattle, partly as people started to bring cattle to him to petition him for help. In interviews, descriptions of his wealth were used to demonstrate

---

[1]   *Kuaar muon* from Lang, Jagei, Bentiu PoC, Sector 2, July 2018.

that he still had power. Over the following years he remained a prominent local authority figure around Ler and was often consulted on illness, floods, conflict and other uncertainties.

The *gojam*

New assertions of divine-like power were not only manifest through government offensives, but also through the new guns and structures of authority in the armed opposition areas. From December 2013, in Ler, Mayendit and initially in Koch, there was widespread support for the armed opposition and emerging SPLA-IO, including from the armed cattle guard. As noted in the previous chapter, rom early 2014, the emerging SPLA-IO tried to co-opt the cattle guard and gave them the name '*gojam*', a term that vaguely references an Arabic word for army division. The *gojam* started using army-like ranks.[2]

In many ways, the armed cattle guard became part of the *hakuma* when they became *gojam* in that they became part of the armed forces of the formal armed opposition. In addition to their ranks, the SPLA-IO gave the *gojam* guns, or sent them on journeys to points there they could be collected. In large meetings, the SPLA-IO commanders also gave instructions to the *gojam* about conduct in battle and coordination with the more formal forces. When attacking the government, they were a joint force with SPLA-IO soldiers and were indistinguishable from this broad sphere of the *hakuma*. However, the *gojam* did not fall completely under SPLA-IO control. They remained attached to their communities and local public authorities, as opposed to the SPLA-IO army command.[3] There was still space for Nuer prophets to wrestle to demand authority over these *gojam*. Without clear structures and hierarchies of order, the arming of the *gojam* was potentially arming a plurality of minor deities, all with the power to kill with impunity through the guns they were given. Yet, the SPLA-IO, the prophets and other authority figures all sought to restrain them. Through restraining the *gojam*'s use of the gun they would no longer be divine.

Nueer

As discussed in Chapters 2, 3 and 10, among the Nuer, *nueer* is a potentially lethal pollution that arises after transgression of divinely sanctioned prohibitions, such as killing.[4] During the post-CPA period, increasingly the Nuer

[2]   Naomi Pendle, 'Competing Authorities and Norms of Restraint: Governing Community-Embedded Armed Groups in South Sudan', *International Interactions* 47:5 (2021): 873–897.

[3]   Pendle, 'Competing Authorities and Norms of Restraint'.

[4]   Edward Evans-Pritchard, *Nuer Religion* (Oxford University Press, 1956), pages 293–294; Sharon Hutchinson, *Nuer Dilemmas: Coping with Money, War and the*

prophets remoulded their function to include the detection and resolution of *nueer*. Prophet authority increasingly was entangled with a recognition of *nueer*. As previously described, Hutchinson has documented how the wars of the 1980s and 1990s challenged the existence of *nueer* as leaders from the SPLA and anti-SPLA *hakuma* questioned whether *nueer* applied in wars of the *hakuma* and whether *nueer* was a consequence if the slain was unknown to the slayer.[5] The wars after 2013 involved the same figures in the *hakuma* again demanding armed conflict, and often without restraint.

At the same time, soldiers remade cultural archives to make *nueer* relevant and solvable. In the battles after 2013, it was not clear to the young men who fought that *nueer* was irrelevant. Some soldiers give accounts of seeking battlefield cleansing from the dangers of *nueer*. Soldiers narrated the problem of the lack of *kuar muon* and prophets when the battles were raging. Therefore, to seek cleansing from *nueer* they would drink water from spent bullet cases.[6] Bitterness is a key aspect of the cultural archive's resolution to *nueer*. In the 1950s, Evans-Pritchard had written of a wild cucumber being used as an alternative sacrifice to an ox.[7] Kurimoto argues that it is the bitterness of the cucumber that allows its equivalence to an ox and, specifically, the bile of the ox which would be drunk by the warring parties.[8] For the soldiers, the bitterness of the gun power equated with the bitterness of the bile of the ox to make this gun-power-water adequate.[9] Yet, there was still ambiguity about the adequacy of this solution.[10]

A bigger challenge to the prophetic role in relation to the *nueer* was a new concern that *nueer* was beyond solution. The mass violence of the *hakuma* meant that killing and death was common. People described how people no longer mourned.[11] In such a situation, *nueer* was everywhere and additional *nueer* through additional killings made no difference when the dangers faced were already exponentially large. Therefore, people doubted if even the prophets had the power to ease the potential dangers of *nueer*.

State (University of California Press, 1996), pages 106–107; Sharon Hutchinson, '"Dangerous to Eat": Rethinking Pollution States among the Nuer of Sudan', *Africa: Journal of the International African Institute* 62:4 (1992): 490–504.

5   Hutchinson, *Nuer Dilemmas*, page 108.
6   Interviews in Koch County, March 2019.
7   Evans-Pritchard, *Nuer Religion*, page 128.
8   Eisei Kurimoto, 'An Ethnography of "Bitterness": Cucumber and Sacrifice Reconsidered'. *Journal of Religion in Africa* 22:1 (1992): 47–65.
9   Interviews in Koch County, March 2019.
10   Ibid.
11   Ibid.

Prophets, *nueer* and peace-making

Despite the asymmetrical military power of the *hakuma*, the prophets challenged the *hakuma*'s implicit god-like claims by pushing back against the immunity of the gun and the *hakuma*'s demand for war. They used their growing association with peace-making to demand peace, even when forces of the government and armed opposition were demanding war. The prophets sought to assert their divine power through their own command of peace even in the midst of war. In this way, the gun becomes entangled in spiritual and normative struggles that can temper the impunity.[12] The following example illustrates the prophets' ongoing authority to demand peace

Prophetic peace and the *gojam* in Tochriak

After large-scale government offensives into southern Unity State, people fled away from the main towns such as Ler to islands of highlands in the swamps to the east. These previously almost empty fishing islands quickly became bustling settlements of thousands of people where humanitarian aid was delivered. A presence in the form of a local system of governance was created by SPLA-IO forces among these communities.

In early 2018, a man defected from the government army in Ler to the SPLA-IO in these nearby islands. His defection brought much excitement as he brought with him to Tochriak island a PKM (a machine gun). Among the SPLA-IO, guns and ammunition were in desperately short supply. The commissioner claimed the defector and gun into his service as part of his coordination of the local SPLA-IO. However, the *gojam* of the defector's clan also wanted the man and his gun to be under their control and not directly under the control of the county-wide SPLA-IO government.

The commissioner released the defector and his gun to return to his clan, claiming that he released the gun to prevent conflict with the defector's clan.[13] However, a rival clan feared that this amounted to the commissioner favouring the defector's clan at a time of significant intra-clan tension. The commissioner was not seen as a detached government figure, but a member of his home community using the power of the *hakuma* to rain favour. Therefore, tensions between two *gojam* groups from different clans grew. The other clan was angry when the commissioner allowed the gun and man to be part of the other clan's *gojam*; they feared that the PKM could also be used in intra-*gojam* conflict and not just against the government's forces.

---

[12]   Sharon Hutchinson and Naomi Pendle, 'Violence, Legitimacy, and Prophecy: Nuer Struggles with Uncertainty in South Sudan', *American Ethnologist* 42:3 (2015): 415–430, page 425.

[13]   Commissioner, Tochriak (Ler County, Unity State), early 2018.

One day the *gojam* of the two clans happened to meet on the path to Thonjor. One *gojam* opened fire. The man who had defected ran, but one of his clan members was shot dead. Fighting broke out between the two groups. Large groups of *gojam* quickly mobilised and fighting rapidly escalated across the area. The commissioner quickly became involved to try to separate the parties, but he was seen as partisan. For the armed opposition, this clan fighting threatened to undermine their anti-government efforts. The father of the man who was killed also demanded that there not be revenge for his death, but not everyone would listen.

Nuer prophet Gatluak Gatkuoth stepped in to make peace by insisting on the recognition of *nueer*. Like Nyachol, as discussed in Chapter 10, Gatluak invoked and remade the cultural archive to stop the fighting by insisting that Nuer, even when associated with the *hakuma* was subject to *nueer*. Gatluak insisted that the *gojam*, with guns from the *hakuma* of the SPLA-IO, were subject to *nueer*. The context of large-scale killings and the pervading presence of *nueer* did not mean that for this specific killing it was immaterial. Alternatively, Gatluak cited the cultural archive to highlight the continuity of *nueer* and the consequences of the killing of this man. Although the gun could kill him, it was not without spiritual and moral consequences and restraint; there was not impunity.

Initially, Gatluak consulted the two groups separately. As the killing of the man had caused *nueer*, the two parties could not safely meet. Despite his humiliation in 2014–15, by 2018 he had built-up sizeable support again, as demonstrated through the remaking of his new, large herd comprised of gifts to thank him for his help. Once he had spoken to each party, then Gatluak oversaw the slaughter of two bulls and the drinking of the bile by each group. The slaughter of these two bulls allowed them to peacefully come into proximity with each other.

Gatluak then counselled the warring parties. He said 'you are fighting over what you don't know. These guns we have been working so hard to get. We have been working hard to get as many guns as we can from Ler'. He suggested that they should turn their focus on their war with the government, and discouraged them from fighting each other. Eventually people agreed, a bull was killed and all were invited to jump over it. Gatluak warned that the blood of the bull was not a joke as the blood of the bull is the same colour as their blood. The sacrifice evoked the cultural archive, but he also used the blood of the bull as a material reminder of their own mortality. The threat was explicit that whoever broke the peace and reopened the feud would also have his blood spilt. The prophet was able to threaten with his power to kill through the curse in order to provide a sanction against ending the peace. It was also agreed that compensation would be exchanged when the war had ended. Peace was still judicial and could be remade through this compliance with the Nuer laws.

A later event was interpreted by the clans as affirming Gatluak's power to enforce peace though the power to kill by the curse with impunity. Initially, even though Gatluak had tried to make peace, some people's hearts were still bitter and they were cautious about whether peace had been finally settled. A man from one of the clans was shot by an unknown gunman. Many of his kin interpreted this as an act of the feud and blamed the SPLA-IO local authorities for allowing it. On a Sunday soon after their kinsman was shot, two brothers went to church for prayers. The commissioner and commander were there. During the service, one of these brothers took out a gun to shoot the commissioner and division commander. His brother saw him before he could fire and grabbed the gun. As he grabbed the gun, his brother accidentally shot him in the leg. Many in these clans interpreted his failure to shoot in revenge and the injury to his brother as proof of the power of Gatluak's curse to protect the peace.

Gatluak has not just been involved in demanding an end to feuds but also in asserting the repertoires of violence that are acceptable during conflict and that make peace more possible. In July 2019, a revenge attack took place on a nutrition nurse who was working for a South Sudanese NGO. He had finished his day's work and returned home to his *tukal* to work on the day's reports. He was inside the *tukal* with one friend when a group of men came to his home intending to kill him in revenge for a previous killing in their own family. One of the group set fire to the rear of the *tukal* while the others stood in front of the door. One of the men had a PKM and started to shower the *tukal* with bullets. The *tukal* quickly caught fire and so the men inside were forced to flee. The nurse's friend had a gun and tried to exit the *tukal* while shooting. In this moment, he was killed. Somehow, in that commotion, the nurse managed to escape through the *tukal* door and to disappear among the high crops. By this stage, neighbours heard the shooting and approached to help. The attackers fled without a chance to pursue the nurse.

The commissioner quickly became involved to quieten the situation. His particular concern was the form of violence used. While revenge killings were not unusual, *tukals* were not normally burnt during family feuds. This was particularly dangerous as more people could easily be killed in such fires. With higher death tolls and possible deaths of women and children, peace would be harder to make. A senior commander from the SPLA-IO was called in to demand an end to the burning of homes. The commissioner also asked for Gatluak's support. Gatluak came and publicly condemned the burning of the *tukal*. He also interpreted the survival of the nurse of indicative of the moral problems with burning *tukals*. Killing was not morally unbounded, even with fires and guns, and so people might well be protected from attacks, even when their protection seems impossible, if the violence used violates the rules and norms of revenge.

Making peace in the UN Protection of Civilians sites

Even in the spaces of the UN Protection of Civilians sites (PoCs), prophetic powers were used to make peace. From the outset of the war in December 2013, people ran to the peace-keeping bases of the United Nations Mission in South Sudan (UNMISS) for protection. It had bases in all ten of the state capitals across South Sudan, and civilians demanded that they offer protection. Many who fled never felt safe to leave and so remained. These bases became an unprecedented, quasi-permanent, UN-guarded refuge for civilians fleeing attacks. Across South Sudan, in the years after December 2013, over 200,000 South Sudanese fled to these PoCs. In December 2013, a few thousand people from Bentiu town fled to the PoCs. In 2015, with the escalation of violence in rural areas, large numbers fled into the PoCs including from the communities to the east of the Bilnyang and connected rivers. For years, the population of the Bentiu PoC has consistently been over a hundred thousand.

The PoCs located within existing UNMISS premises have been beset by legal and operational ambiguities, and various figures with blurred authority. Humanitarian agencies have also been responsible for maintaining standards of living and basic services in PoCs. For many people, living inside the Bentiu PoCs has been a new experience of urban life and life in close proximity to humanitarian agencies.

The UN and PoC site residents have questioned the continued authority of prophets and chiefs. Life in the PoC sites was a radical reconfiguration of how homes and families were spatially arranged, and how resources were acquired. People now lived in close proximity to strangers, had their food and health care provided by humanitarians, and had a new structure of camp leadership designed around their PoC site living arrangements. In this new context, there was a question about the continuity of the cosmic and moral worlds of previous village life.

At the same time, prophetic ideas have been drawn upon to make peace in the PoC sites. For example, before 2013, a girl had been courted by a man named Gatkuoth. However, their relationship did not last and they split up. In 2014, this girl fled with her family to the PoC site in Bentiu. In Bentiu, she met a man named Tor and they married. Later on, Gatkuoth also moved to that PoC. He had not known of the girl's marriage and when he saw her washing a man's clothes, he questioned her about her marriage. She told him of her marriage to Tor and he immediately behaved violently. He hit her and she hurt him in retaliation. Tor was called to the fight and nearly joined in. Yet he took advice and instead called the Community Watch Group who intervened to stop the fighting. They were all taken to court and the court ruled in favour of Tor. His wife was sent for medical treatment and Gatkuoth was arrested by the UN police.

At the arrest of Gatkuoth, his brother and father violently protested. They went to Tor's house where he was taking dinner with friends. They attacked them while they were seated and three of Tor's friends were injured. Gatkuoth and Tor were both from the Jagei (based around the area of greater Koch) section of Kolang Ket but were from different sub-sections of the Bor and Jediet. As more people were drawn into the violence, concern grew that the conflict would be interpreted along sub-sectional lines. This identity politics could have quickly mobilised much larger numbers.

At this point, the situation was quickly escalated to the chairman of the Community High Committee of the camp. He called the Jagei community leader in the camp, who called together leaders from the conflicting sections. After four days of negotiations, it was agreed that the sides would pay compensation for injuries caused and the injured were sent for medical examination.

Divine authority helped make peace. The Jagei community leader explained that compensation alone was not adequate to make peace. He insisted that the warring parties greet each other. He also insisted that they go together to the home of Dingding Kuol Kolang. Dingding was not a prophet of MAANI but had authority over the *luak* of Nyaruac in the absence of a prophet of MAANI. Powers of his prophetic ancestors had been passed to him and he could still bless and curse with impunity. At the time, he was living in the PoC site in Bentiu. As the community leader explained the situation to Dingding, the latter threatened on behalf of MAANI that anyone who reopened the conflict between Bor and Jedeit would himself have a *bit* (curse) fall upon him. The threat of his power to kill gave force to the demand for peace.

Peace of the Nuer

The peace-making attempts of prophets have not just extended to the urban centres of the PoCs. They have also extended to attempts to make peace between government and SPLA-IO forces. Prophetess Nyachol has continued to pursue her political agenda of Nuer unity. While she has opposed the government, she has also adamantly opposed the political and military divisions between the Nuer in Unity State.

In 2017, the government forces controlled Rubkany – a market town in Mayendit on the road from Bentiu to Ler. The villages and grazing lands nearby were controlled by SPLA-IO forces. Nyachol invited both commissioners to visit her at the same time. Neither felt they could refuse her. In this way, she tricked the two commissioners into meeting and demanded that they make peace. Both were able to escape this demand by saying that they needed high levels of permission for such peace-making. Yet, Nyachol challenged their implicit claims to decide when war and peace should be conducted. There have been various incidences since, when, without the attention of

higher authorities, the government and SPLA-IO in Mayendit have cooperated to prevent the escalation of violence.

The seizure by TILING

Between June and August 2019, a South Sudanese NGO had chartered over
eighty planes to land food at the Thonyor airstrip on these SPLA-IO controlled
islands near Ler. A new food-aid warehouse had been built in January 2019 and
now there was a rush to fill it with adequate food to prevent extreme hunger.
Each day that a plane was scheduled to land, people would gather around the
small strip of dusty soil where the plane would land. Logisticians of the NGO
were there to coordinate the plane's landing and to formally receive the food.
They would also organise a sizeable team of local labour that would be paid
to move the food from the aircraft to the warehouse. Demand for that minimal
work prompted people to swarm the airstrip before the plane's arrival. Despite
the scale of the operation, the South Sudanese had no car in Thonyor and the
muddy nature of the land during the rains prevented a car from being useful.

Geng Mut was a school headteacher and nutrition assistant for this large
South Sudanese NGO in Thonyor. He was also an officer in the swelling ranks
of the SPLA-IO. In 2019, Geng fell seriously ill. His family repeatedly took
him to the clinic to diagnose and treat his sickness. People in the clinic could
not work out the cause of his sickness and had little hope for his survival. His
brothers still carried him between home and the clinic to receive injections in
hope that they would help.

In June 2019, while Geng was still ill, Gatluak Gatkuoth came to visit
Thonyor. With his followers in tow, he walked around Thonyor singing. Many
goats were also killed. In the midst of the excitement about Gatluak's visit,
Geng jumped up from his bed and ran to grab the spear and dang of his late
uncle, Nyuon Liah Wal. Having been unable to walk unaided a few moments
before, Geng joined the dancing around Gatluak.

Before his death in 2008, Nyuon Liah Wal was a prophet and seized by the
divinity TILING, who had FIRST seized Nyuon's father (and Geng's grand-
father), Liah Wal Reath in the 1930s. The divinity TILING first appeared near
Ler when Liah Wal had eaten dog meat – a food considered unnatural and usually expected to cause death. Liah did not die but announced himself seized by
a divinity. The chief opposed his seizure and the government briefly arrested
Liah, but it was the chief who ended up being removed from his position.
TILING quickly grew in popularity and Liah ended the practice of eating dog
meat. TILING focused on sacrifices and dances to invoke good crops, and
the bumper harvest of 1937 was credited to him.[14] By the time of Liah Wal's

[14]   Douglas Johnson, *Nuer Prophets: A History of Prophecy from the Upper Nile in*

death, TILING was established as one of the most powerful western Nuer divinities, and Liah a correspondingly powerful prophet.

In grabbing his uncle's spear, Geng evoked a century-old history and claimed to have also been seized by TILING. On seeing Geng and Nyuon's spear, Gatluak opened up the crowd. Those drumming for Gatluak started drumming a new song, 'as if inspired by *kuoth*' (spirit). To the sound of this drum, Geng started dancing on one leg, replicating the dance performed by Liah and Nyuon. At this, Gatluak and the crowd started to proclaim him as seized by TILING.

Gatluak then came to stay in Geng's home to perform a series of sacrifices of bulls and goats in order to evoke TILING to come. After this, Geng was taken to the swamps to test if TILING had seized him. TILING has always been able to safely call a certain type of long, black snake (*thol*). Geng's ability to do this confirmed his seizure.

TILING through Geng immediately sought to appeal to the armed youth of the *gojam*. Since the 1990s, commanders around the Bilnyang, including Riek Machar, had discouraged scarification.[15] Scarification had been associated with initiation into age groups who could participate in conflict. Yet, relying on the youth's military support, the SPLA, including Machar at the time, opposed scarification as it undermined the unity of the youth, causing divisions between those who were and who were not scarred. As Geng had attended school and become literate, there was less of an expectation to be initiated. Yet, the *gojam* were the main supporters of the prophets and TILING also needed to appeal to this constituency. Gatluak carried out Geng's initiation, and about ninety other young men also joined Geng to be scarred at this time.

The scarification of a large cohort of young men in 2019 marked a revolutionary moment in spiritual alliances and cosmological hierarchies. The *hakuma* was consistently bringing predatory, deadly violence and, for many young men, the prophets offered a more consistent understanding and powerful source of protection. As discussed in Chapter 1, control of initiation was an important way in which the prophets asserted their control over the armed youth. The claims of MAANI and Kolang Ket to power in the late nineteenth century were intimately tied to the martial youth as Kolang Ket demanded that the next cohort of youth should not be initiated into a new age set until he returns from a journey, and another prophet was cursed to death when

---

the Nineteenth and Twentieth Centuries (Clarendon Press, 1994), page 276.

15   Naomi Pendle, '"They Are Now Community Police": Negotiating the Boundaries and Nature of the Government in South Sudan through the Identity of Militarised Cattle-Keepers', *International Journal of Minority and Group Rights* 22:3 (2015): 410–434.

she failed to adhere to this instruction.[16] In 2019, over a century later, the prophets of Geng and Gatluak were remaking their authority over the youth by invoking these symbolic and bodily practices.

At the same time, the meaning was different and the cultural archive was remade. The 2019 initiations were not about asserting the power of one prophet over another, but about asserting the power of the prophets over the *hakuma*. Firstly, in the western Nuer historically, the prophets were competitive and rivalrous.[17] Kolang Ket had cursed his main rival to death when she initiated youth without his permission. In contrast, in 2019, Gatluak supported Geng. Secondly, the *hakuma* was now the main opposition. In order for Geng to have the power of the prophets he had to symbolically leave the group of the educated, who were associated with the broader sphere of the *hakuma*, and submit to the authority of the home community. This came through scarification. Thirdly, the youth were now heavily armed and carried the divine-like power of the *hakuma* through their guns. In their scarification, these young men still submitted to the divine power of the prophets. They sought to recognise in the prophets a power even greater than the guns of the government.

An immediate priority of TILING after his seizure of Geng was to establish compensation exchange and the settling of feuds through animal sacrifice in order to enforce a meaningful peace. As with Nyachol after her 2010 seizure, Geng quickly started hearing cases and settling feuds. From August 2019, TILING demanded that those who were feuding should come to him to make peace. At the same time, this was a significant remaking of the cultural archive to meet contemporary demand. Geng and the former prophets of TILING had not been associated with solving conflicts and bringing peace.[18]

For example, in August 2019, TILING heard a case between two families in one clan. In 2018, one man had shot another dead. The father of the deceased had initially discouraged revenge. In 2019, the brother of the deceased then killed the father of the killer. The father was an elderly trader and the killing left hearts hot for further revenge. Fearing revenge, the family of the brother who had taken revenge handed this brother over to the commissioner to be arrested. Geng ordered the SPLA-IO commissioner to bring him and other prisoners to him. This included those who had killed, as well as those who had committed other crimes. These prisoners have since remained in his *luak* in effective detention. He has warned them against committing further offences and has invited the warring parties to come to make peace. This power of

---

[16]   Jedeit J. Riek and Naomi Pendle, *Speaking Truth to Power in South Sudan: Oral Histories of the Nuer Prophets* (Rift Valley Institute, 2018).

[17]   Johnson, *Nuer Prophets.*

[18]   Interview with Nuer chief, Bentiu PoCs, 2018.

Geng, including other those detained by the *hakuma* displays his authority in the *hakuma*-prophet relationship.

Following Nyachol's previous attempts at SPLA-IO – government reconciliation, Geng also attempted to united the warring parties. In 2021, following the Revitalised Agreement on the Resolution of the Conflict in South Sudan (R-ARCSS), new transitional government commissioners were appointed. On the 10 April 2021, Geng invited the government commissioner, commanders, *gojam* and IO forces to his *luak* for a day of reconciliation.

Nuer prophets have continued to struggle to create political space to end feuds and create peace. This is despite elites often seeking division in order to more easily mobilise fighting forces. At the same time, the peace promoted by these contemporary prophets in central Unity States has repeatedly focused on an exclusive, ethnic peace. Dominated by intra-Nuer fighting, the prophets' peace-making activities have focused on intra-Nuer peace. Historically, the powers of the prophets were often to a broad range of people and not limited by ethnic lines. This was the case during the time of Nyaruac and as recently as Gatdeang's rule in Mayom.[19] At the same time, new prophetic figures in Unity State have increasingly been explicit that a 'cool' peace is only possible with other Nuer.[20] This is often a response to the lack of possibility of judicial redress for grievances, but it has re-created and reinforced identities that make elite interests into an easily mobilisable force.

Conclusion

The dominating, arbitrary violence of the *hakuma*, the pervasive presence of *nueer* after so much killing and the arming of the *gojam* all had consequences for the cosmic polity. While the large-scale offensives of the government demonstrated their superior god-like powers, the proliferation of guns again had the potential to spread this power, effectively turning the armed youth into a multiplicity of deities – of beings with the ability to kill with impunity. The irrelevance of *nueer* challenged the ability to demand restraint and impunity. However, as this chapter has shown, the cosmic consequences of the post-2013 wars were not conclusive. Instead, contestation has continued and the Nuer prophets have continued to play a significant role in the post-2013 cosmic polity. Nuer prophets have asserted their power to physically limit and challenge guns. Importantly, they have also demanded the continuity of the significance of *nueer* and the possibility of a solution to its deadly dangers. While soldiers drew on the cultural archive, and remade it, to use the bitterness

---

[19] Riek and Pendle, *Speaking Truth to Power*; Johnson, *Nuer Prophets*; Hutchinson and Pendle, 'Violence, Legitimacy, and Prophecy'.
[20] Ibid.

of spent bullet cases to solve *nueer*, the prophets offered a less ambiguous solution by again offering cattle sacrifices as a way to ease the demands of *nueer* and allow peace to be possible. This reinforcing of *nueer* was primarily popular with the armed youth who most brutally faced the consequences of unrestrained violence. The Nuer prophets continued to be popular with the armed youth and, therefore, also gained power through this military might. When TILING seized Geng, a key part of the making of his authority was a moment of collective scarification, invoking centuries-old histories of the prophets' controlling processes of initiation.

In 2022, government forces appeared to achieve their last major offensive against the SPLA-IO forces in Ler, Koch and Mayendit, ending the previous eight years of SPLA-IO presence in the area. The region was fully back under government control again. During the years of war, the prophets have remained oddly united, possibly brought together by the extreme opponent of the *hakuma* and the gun in the cosmic polity. If this is now a moment of *hakuma* unity through government victory, it is unclear the impact this will have. Maybe it is now that we will see the return of larger prophetic rivalries.

CHAPTER 13

Peace and Unending Wars in Warrap State post-2013

As described in Chapter 10, the post-2013 decade resulted in the cementing of national government power in the hands of a politico-military cadre close to Salva Kiir. From 2016, this included three of South Sudan's most powerful people in the security arena – the President, the Director of National Security and the Commander of the Presidential Guard – all having Warrap State as their home state. The sons of the communities to the west of the Bilynang and connected rivers had immense military power. However, as was the case after the the the Comprehensive Peace Agreement (CPA) and, as described in Chapter 6, an autochthonous *hakuma* mixed with ancestral claims and liberal shifts in land and resource rights brought ambiguity and conflict.

***

The peace meeting in February 2022 in a Warrap Town (Tonj North County, Warrap State) was coming towards the end of its second and final day. Participants were seated on UNMISS-funded chairs on three sides of the rectangle, and officials and the speaker were on the fourth side. Two, small white bulls were now tied to two *lɔc* (cattle pegs) in the middle of the rectangle. Most people had been there for the whole meeting and were slumped on their chairs in the heat of the afternoon. They were largely silent, and appeared to be almost in a state of slumber, as various bishops and local political figures got up to speak from the front. Then, suddenly, without warning, the approximately fifty people on the side where I sat spontaneously stood up and started running away. They did not run far, but they ran fast. They were afraid. My first thought was to think it was someone shooting, but there was no gun sound. Then I wondered if there was a snake that I could not see. Yet, in the vacated space, no snake was visible. I decided to move anyway; fifty residents of the area were bound to be a better judge of danger than me.

The panicked movement had been caused by the spear of a *bany e bith* who had started his invocations over the bull in the middle of the ground. He held the spear over the bull and spoke of how the bull would die to stop others dying in the conflict. He pointed the spear downwards but at an angle which meant that it sometimes pointed in the direction of where we had been seated. No-one wanted to be in the line of the spear as the *bany e bith* spoke words of death and curse. As the man next to me said, 'after all, that would be worse than a bullet'.

Before the invocations started, there had been disagreement over the positioning of the *lɔc*. Both communities had brought their *lɔc* with them. The numerically larger community had wanted their *lɔc* placed ahead; the government insisted the two *lɔc* be placed side-by-side. At the time, there was some popular support for the meeting; it was described as a peace of the home community and not the peace of the *hakuma*. People were excited that the peace had been prompted by a woman's group and backed by a local NGO, and was not just based on orders from the *hakuma*. People also said that this meeting differed from Wunlit as the cattle sacrifice concluded the meeting as opposed to opening it.

The peace meeting was held to end the 2020–22 fighting in Tonj North County. The peace only held for four months. In June 2022, cattle were raided. They were raided as part of a series of tit-for-tat raids between communities. However, on this occasion, political figures in Juba commanded the intervention of certain army divisions. Soldiers were sent in to reclaim the cattle. The soldiers themselves divided along communal lines, smudging the distinction between the *hakuma* and the home communities. The peace-meeting curse of the *baany e biith* was feared in the moment but was not enough to stop fatal violence. Nearly ninety people were killed that June.[1]

Peace and unending wars in Tonj North

Craze and Marko attribute the conflicts in Warrap State after the 2018 Revitalised Agreement on the Resolution of Conflict in South Sudan (R-ARCSS) to the agreement's new centralised control over state and county appointments. As much as this caused conflict, it was nothing new. As described in Chapters 5 and 6, the CPA had radically reformed rights over land, labour, property and resources. In the ambiguities around land, this had increased the importance of the appointment of the governor and commissioners, and communities feared when they suspected that these appointees would not recognise their rights. At the same time, these appointments in practice were almost wholly made by Juba, allowing centralised control. This was particularly the case in areas like Warrap State where the presidency had an intimate knowledge and

---

[1]   Two eye-witness accounts from opposing sides of the community.

private interest. Chapters 6 and 7 intentionally trace conflicts, post the CPA, through periods of war, and after R-ARCSS, to show this continuity.

Yet, in Warrap State there was a radical change to political dynamics post-2013. This was most visible in Tonj North. The radical shift after 2013 was the cementing of control of the security arena by Salva Kiir and a Warrap State cadre. While Kiir had been president before, others in the government and SPLA had restrained his control over the security forces. The post-2013 wars changed this. As described in Chapter 11, the years of war provided an opportunity for Kiir to wither the power of the SPLA and develop more directly loyal forces. Initially this included the Mathiang Anyoor under the leadership of Paul Malong. Recruitment in Dinka-speaking areas of Bahr el Ghazal in 2012 created this force which fought the Sudan government, and then for the government in Juba. In 2014, Paul Malong was appointed SPLA Chief of Staff. However, by 2016, Paul Malong's power threatened Kiir – and Kiir feared his rebellion. This encouraged Kiir's further support of Akol Koor Kuc (from Tonj North, Warrap State) who had been Director of Internal Security Bureau (ISB) of the National Security Service (NSS) from 2013. According to Craze, 'under Kuc's leadership, the NSS transformed from an intelligence gathering agency into one of the most efficient military organizations in the country'.[2] In 2017, there was a new commander from Warrap State appointed to head the Presidential Guard, replacing Marital Ciennoung Yol (from Lakes State). The post-2013 period, and especially post-2016, saw the rise of national power in the hands of sons of Warrap State and the communities to the west of the Bilnyang. Initially there was close cooperation between the leadership of National Security and the new leadership of the Presidential Guard.

The growing power of the Warrap State leaders, mixed with land and military labour regimes built on autochthony, caused increased conflict. Some of this, especially in relation to Greater Gogrial, is already documented in Chapter 6. The rise of these Warrap State leaders put particular strains on the martial youth as these leaders sought to recruit armed forces from this shared but limited pool. From 2012, there were repeated, often forced, recruitment campaigns, with chiefs both assisting and resisting. For example, Craze suggests that as many as 10,000 men were recruited between September 2018 and August 2019.[3] Chapter 6 focused on conflict and peace in Gogrial after the CPA into the post-2013 period. Here, instead, we consider Tonj North County.

In 2020, there was a controversial disarmament campaign in Warrap State. The heavy-handed disarmament in some communities was understood as certain army leaders contesting the power of Akol Koor Kuc through attacks

2   Joshua Craze, '"And Everything Became War": Warrap State Since the Signing of the R-ARCSS', HSBA Briefing Paper (Small Arms Survey, 2022).
3   Ibid.

on this community. In clashes that followed, forces of the National Security Service and the national army supported different sides.[4] Armed conflict has sliced across communities in Tonj North ever since. Lots of these conflicts were based on histories of past grievances such as elopement, cattle theft or individual killings, and escalated to conflicts that killed hundreds.

Destructive, new patterns of violence have been a constant concern. There was not only cattle raiding, but also numerous targeted assassinations, the burning of *tukals*, the killing of children, the blockading of access to aid and markets, and the cutting of fruit trees. Dinka norms of war suggest that women and children should not be the targets of armed conflict.[5] Beyond this, targets that could also harm children and women, such as the domestic space of the *tukal*, are also out-of-bounds in legitimate warfare. The violation of such norms in the 2020–22 conflicts was often interpreted as a declaration that peace was no longer imaginable or possible; as norms of war were violated, there was no process in the cultural archive that could resolve the conflict to make peace. The patterns of violence themselves also imagined long-term harm and antagonism. For example, the cutting of fruit trees was unprecedented and seemingly designed to create hunger for years into the future. It was an act of violence that imagined a long war.

Unending wars had their utility. Craze makes the astute observation that these armed conflicts in Warrap State incorporated the patterns of violence from the national civil war into the wars of the home.[6] The wars may have introduced new imaginings of what violence was possible, but the making of unending wars was also instrumental for those who wanted to claim land and labour through imagined communities. Unending armed conflicts, or the imagining of such, not only divided communities but remade these boundaries as static and inter-generational. These newly made bounded communities could justify greater claims on land and labour.

Throughout these ongoing wars people kept trying or claiming to make peace. Warrap State governors repeatedly carried out 'peace tours'. These peace tours included a series of summary executions; their peace was physically very violent. Governors showed that they had the power to kill with impunity and to step outside of the law. People perceived some governors' interventions as partisan, and subsequent armed conflict was partly defensive against such power. During these years, government-initiated peace meetings were also held. Yet, people often had little confidence in these gatherings. Armed conflict continued.

---

[4]   Ibid.

[5]   Naomi Pendle, 'Competing Authorities and Norms of Restraint: Governing Community-Embedded Armed Groups in South Sudan', *International Interactions* 47:5 (2021): 873–897.

[6]   Ibid.

The peace of Mayen Jur

The peace of Mayen Jur appears to provide a counter example to stories of unending war. The years of relative peace in Mayen Jur (Warrap State, near Unity State) since 2013 appear to contradict the narrative of the proliferation of conflict by the *hakuma*. Yet, importantly, the peace of Mayen Jur was also a manifestation of the will of the *hakuma*. After decades of hostility, the peace was itself an arbitrary act of the god-like *hakuma*.

If you travel in one of the few vehicles that regularly journeys on the road to the north-west of Wau, you can continue on the straight but deteriorating murram road for about five hours during which you pass occasional settlements and by-pass others that are hidden further from the road's edge. The landscape is scattered with trees, including many that are large and mature. Along the way, you pass cattle being herded to market and, occasionally, other commercial vehicles carrying people and their goods. After about five hours (if the road is dry), you will reach the Gogrial East County capital, Lietnhom, and the bend in the River Jur. At this point, you are about halfway to Mayen Jur. Along this axis of the road, the river marks the division between the south-western unbroken, sandier, higher land that is covered with scattered trees, and the north-eastern lower, swampier land of the *toc*. Beyond the river in the *toc*; there are only dry-season tracks over these muddied plains and no all-season roads. These lower, richer flood plains host dry-season cattle camps. The *toc* also historically hosted permanent settlements that were on higher islands of dry land dotted through the swamp. This swamp is fed by the River Jur and also the Bilnyang and connected river systems, as well as the Bahr el Ghazal to the north. Mayen Jur (Warrap State) sits in the middle of these swamp lands. Located among a criss-crossing confluence of rivers, settlements are on a grid of higher, drier land. Mayen Jur is known for its abundance of milk, honey and crops as the land is regularly replenished by the flooding waters.

Since the 1980s, Mayen Jur has been a significant node in national political confrontations. Since the 1980s, forces with a rivalrous relationship to the SPLA, such as those of Matip, Puljang and Gadet (see Chapter 11) have been stationed to the north-east of Mayen Jur in Mayom County (Unity State), while areas to the south-west of Mayen Jur in Gogrial have largely had SPLA sympathies. This has militarised and polarised the relationship, and remade Mayen Jur into a frontline in the wars between Southern rebels. Mayen Jur experienced two decades of violent conflict and militarised landscapes.[7] During the 1990s, settlements in Mayen Jur had been abandoned after deadly raids. The post-CPA era had not seen a confident resettling of Mayen Jur and,

---

[7]   Naomi Pendle, 'Contesting the Militarization of the Places Where They Met: The Landscapes of the Western Nuer and Dinka (South Sudan)'. *Journal of Eastern African Studies* 11:1 (2017): 64–85.

episodically, nearby settlements were also displaced. Mayen Jur was effectively a barracks for SPLA soldiers and defensive forces such as the *titweng* (armed cattle guards with extended responsibilities).

The wars across Mayen Jur were made to be unending wars.[8] Historically, communities had met and intermarried across the Unity-Warrap border. Yet, the killing of women and children in attacks in the 1990s violated previous norms of war and, as more recently in Tonj North, made the wars unending. By the 2000s, people could not imagine peace between the Dinka and Nuer. Most of the Nuer in Mayom County did not attend the Wunlit Peace Meeting, and cross-border courts seemed unfathomable.

Then 2014 brought a new peace. Despite these decades of militarisation, and despite a sense of crisis in South Sudan in the years after December 2013, Mayen Jur started to experience a nascent end to violent conflict and signs of a more long-lasting peace. From the outset of the war in December 2013, the government relied on an alliance with forces from Mayom. These commanders were strategically important because of their proximity to the oilfields and their ability to act as a check against the rapidly emerging opposition. They also had historic grievances with the leadership of the Sudan People's Liberation Army – In Opposition (SPLA-IO), Taban Deng and Riek Machar, and so continued this rivalry through an alliance with government.[9] Puljang cemented his leadership during this period and became well known for taxing cattle and income in Mayom, and for using raids into southern Unity State to build the herds of his supporters.[10]

In this context of the Juba government's reliance on Puljang's forces and new political space for peace between Mayom and Gogrial, Puljang took the opportunity to instigate peace between the *titweng* (armed cattle guard) of Gogrial East (Warrap State) and Mayom (Unity State). For Puljang, peaceful relationships with the *titweng* carried various benefits. After the successful 2015 raids into southern Unity State, his forces had larger herds for which they needed adequate pasture. The lush grazing lands of the *toc* around Mayen Jur were an obvious source of grazing that was then almost unused because of the ongoing relationships of conflict – and could be made accessible through peace. Friendship with Gogrial East also offered Puljang increased chances to benefit from cattle trade. Herders from Mayom gained peaceful access to Wau in order to take cattle for sale. Some traders from Mayom did themselves herd cattle as far as Wau. Most instead only brought cattle to cattle markets in the *toc* or to

8   Ibid.

9   See Chapter 11 and Joshua Craze, Jérôme Tubiana and Claudio Gramizzi, 'A State of Disunity: Conflict Dynamics in Unity State, South Sudan, 2013–15', HSBA Working Paper 42 (Small Arms Survey, 2016).

10   Craze et al., 'A State of Disunity'.

Lietnhom where they were bought by Dinka traders who took them on to Wau for sale. As Bentiu grew back as a market, those in Gogrial East could travel to Mayom to sell bulls there. They would be taken on by herders from Mayom for sale in Bentiu. The necessity of permits ensured that the trade happened in sight of these government authorities and that it could be taxed.

In 2015, President Kiir re-divided the states in South Sudan and appointed Gum Makuac as the first governor of the new Gogrial State. While Gum was from Gogrial East, his mother had been from Mayom and Gum had maintained close relations with his maternal kin. This further facilitated peace negotiations.[11] The new 2016 peace in Mayen Jur could easily be interpreted as a deal in the elite political marketplace. In reward for Puljang's loyalty, Kiir made peace possible to allow him to benefit from the *toc*.

Initially, communities were tentative about this arbitrary peace. Despite the leaders' military might, these figures initially failed to persuade the communities to accept peace, which was only eventually made through the interventions of Nuer prophet Gatdeang of Mayom and Dinka *bany e bith* Mangong Madut. Mangong Madut's home is in Mayen Jur. At the time, he also had another home in Warabeyi as did many from Mayen Jur who fled during fighting. While there were free divinities in Gogrial at the time, it was the *baany e biith* who was seen as the established, peace-making authority figure and an equivalent to the increasingly priestly role of the prophet. When Puljang and Gum's initial attempts to enact an elite deal failed, they sought support from these divine leaders. Mangong Madut was invited to Mayen Jur. There he slaughtered a bull as a sign of peace. Once the bull was slaughtered and Gatdeang learnt of the sacrifice, he interpreted it as a sign of welcome and he also came to Mayen Jur to start the process of peace-making.

In 2016, people finally gathered to make the peace. Alongside government officials, two further *baany e biith* from Gogrial East – Akol Deng and Thik Arop Riiny – also joined the meeting. For the prophet and *bany e bith*, at the heart of the meeting was an attempt to reassert the spiritual significance of war and, therefore, the lack of spiritual impunity for arbitrary violence. This manifested itself in attempts to reshape patterns of violence and attempts to remake times of conflict as a law-governed space.

Firstly, patterns of violence over the previous decades had violated norms of war and enacted god-like claims to power. This had increased the deadly nature of battles in ways that breached previous expectations of restraint during conflict. Raids would often take place at the break of dawn, when light was still limited. These dawn raids in limited light had the strategic benefit of allowing attackers to approach with an element of surprise.[12] However,

---

11   Interviews with people from Gogrial, in Juba and by telephone, 2019.
12   Observations of chiefs' meetings, 2012, Lietnhom.

this surprise provides no opportunity for an equal defence, and the lack of light makes accidental killings very easy. The killing of women had such high spiritual consequences and resulted in demands for endless feuds. Attacking in a way that risked killing women signalled that those attacking could not imagine a time of peace, but instead only an endless feud. Previously, attacks would intentionally not be made at dawn to prevent the accidental killing of women.[13] Therefore, the Gogrial-Mayom attacks at dawn conspicuously showed no care to avoid killing even women and children. They also indicated an image of an unending war without peace. Because of these dangers, many of the cattle camps in the *toc* had long been devoid of women and children. However, these dawn attacks still highlighted the lack of respect for these norms of war.

In 2016, the prophet and *bany e bith* pushed for this issue to be explicitly addressed at the peace meeting. In so doing they sought to reinstate a lack of impunity for arbitrary killing by the *hakuma* and the gun. They offered peace despite the spiritual dangers and consequences of the twenty-year war. Their combined spiritual authority made this unlikely healing more imaginable. Yet, their healing also came with the strong demand for such raiding patterns to halt. The troubles of dawn raids dominated discussions.[14]

Secondly, the prophet and *bany e bith* pushed for the war years to be seen as a time when laws still applied. A significant question that arose in attempts to make peace was the question of wives in inter-ethnic marriages. Those from Gogrial East and Mayom had historically intermarried and there were many Nuer wives living in the Dinka lands, and vice versa. When conflict had erupted in the 1990s, many of these wives fled to their father's homeland in fear that they might be targeted as part of the inter-ethnic revenge. Many had lived back home with their fathers for years or occasionally even decades. Among both the Dinka and Nuer, when a daughter returns from her marital home to her father's home on a long-term basis, this would usually indicate the wife has her father's permission to divorce her husband. For this to be done legally and to not cause conflict, the wife's father would have to repay the bride-price to the husband and his family. However, when these wives fled across ethnic lines during conflict, the cattle were not returned to their husbands. Therefore, according to Nuer and Dinka customary law, the husbands of these wives still had a legitimate grievance against families across these ethnic lines. These grievances could only be dissolved by returning either the bride wealth or the wives themselves.

[13]   Interviews with paramount chiefs, 2012 and 2014, Kuajok and Addis Ababa.
[14]   Interview with local church leader who attended the peace meeting, 2018.

The prophet and *bany e bith* enforced the return of the wives to their husbands and oversaw this throughout 2016 and 2017.[15] Many of these women also had children with them. Some of the wives had assumed the war would last indefinitely and had taken another husband in their father's community. A normal interpretation of the Dinka and Nuer laws would consider the first husband, who had paid the bride-price, to be the legal father of all the children that the wife had borne. In this situation, the prophet and *bany e bith* took on a role as interpreters and enforcers of the customary law. They assumed this authority and built their power by the ability to make these rulings. This role was not questioned by the governing authorities, who were eager for them to end the violent conflict.

Some of the wives who were returned had been estranged from the husbands for decades. The children were neither the biological children of these legal fathers, nor did they have any relationship with them. Yet, the choice for these wives and children was removed from them and even from their families. This was a violent decision that felt unjust for many. The prophet and *bany e bith* insisted on them for the sake of the good of the wider community and for peace, so these returns were enforced.

Crucially, the prophets and the *baany e biith* were enforcing a logic of peace that complied with law and judicial logics. These priests remade the social insignificance of war by making wartime choices still subject to previous laws. They were not an exception or a rupture. It was not that all was fair in war, but war times were still governed by the continuity of the customary law. Therefore, even in times of war, impunity could not be expected.

The peace meeting also insisted on the creation of the *wanth tong* court. '*Wanth tong*' literally means the place of fighting, and the court was set up to sit in this place where the communities had historically fought in Mayen Jur. The name of the court both referred to this physical location but also the court's intention to replace the fighting. The court was both backed by the government and the religious leaders, giving the court the backing of both divine and *hakuma* powers. The court had the power to try cases of raiding, as well as to grant compensation after killings. It was not a new initiative but re-created a previous border court that dated back to the Anglo-Egyptian Condominium period.[16], Elders remember that, at the time of the Condominium government, there were laws in the land of Wanth Tong that governed the relationship of the Nuer in Mayom County and the Dinka in Gogrial East County.

---

[15]   Interview with sub-chief and member of the Mayenjur peace committee, Mayendjur, July 2018.

[16]   Interview with second member of the Mayenjur peace committee, Mayenjur, July 2018, in Dinka.

From 2016, the new court was headed by Dinka Chief Mapuol Wol. The court's deputy was Nuer Chief Gil Nyanteer. The court also included commissioners, the Gogrial governor, Puljang, other chiefs and *majokwut* (leaders of the cattle camp) and women. Plus, Gatdeang (until his death) and Mangong Madut also sat on this court. Most of the cases heard by the court have involved accusations of stolen cattle. Importantly, this court allowed the peaceful redress of grievances and did not force people to seek violent, self-help justice framed in ethnic terms. Relationships between families could be peacefully restored, and a feud was not necessary. For the court to operate, agreements were made to make common the substantive law of the two groups. For example, after elopement the Nuer expected to be paid three cattle but now accepted to be paid just one. After adultery, Dinka were normally paid four cattle as compensation but now accepted to receive only three.[17]

The government had wanted to enforced execution by firing squad against anyone who threatened the peace, such as by stealing cattle. Punitive executions are an expression of the government's power and their assertion of their power to kill with impunity. However, chiefs and religious leaders contested this government assertion that executions were necessary. Part of the fear of summary executions is the scale of deaths it could cause without any legal check on this violence. As one chief explained in June 2018, '[m]en will all be finished if this rule is applied'. The government forces could not ignore this unified pressure and agreed to soften their stance. Instead, it was agreed that a perpetrator who broke the peace would be fined six cows and imprisoned in Mayen Jur for three years.

The peace agreement was concluded with the slaughter and cutting in half of bulls. The feuding parties walked between the two halves as a sign of the ending of the feud.[18] The ritual ending of impurity and the re-creation of community was crucial.

As a sign of confidence in this peace, in 2016, some people returned to Mayen Jur. In 2017, more people returned and even started to cultivate in the *toc*. This investment of labour implied a confidence that the *toc* would be secure enough to make harvest possible. Yet, the *toc* remained heavily armed and people kept their families at second homes further away. Women only went to the *toc* for the months of the harvest.

To cement the peace, an Episcopal Church of Sudan (ECS) priest also started a school in Mayen Jur. As elsewhere, this school opening was driven by this priest whose family were in Mayen Jur. The explicit aim in opening the school was to allow the Nuer and Dinka communities to come together and

---

[17]   Interview with sub-chief and member of the Mayenjur peace committee, Mayenjur, July 2018, in Dinka.

[18]   Interview with peace monitor, Mayenjur, July 2018, in Dinka.

interact peacefully. Through this act of school building, the clergyman wanted to explicitly remake identities and again naturalise the meeting of Nuer and Dinka in these contested borderlands. The school would embody the lack of spiritual and physical danger in these communities meeting together. These dangers had been made through years of war.

However, in the end, this 2016–19 peace in Mayen Jur was only temporary, based on negotiation and ultimately vulnerable to the temporary authority of various leaders. In 2018, Gatdeang died in Mayom, thus removing his guarantee of the peace. In April 2020, President Kiir, through the national army command, called Puljang to Juba. While in Juba he effectively came under house arrest. His power was quickly curtailed by his physical distance from Mayom and his inability to return. Deadly raids occurred between Mayon and Gogrial, with peace easily shattered by shifting politics.

Yet, the profitability of peace had become visible. Again in 2021, commissioners from Mayom and Gogrial East tried to cement peace through trade. A cattle market was established in Gum Mac, on a piece of high land between the nine rivers near Mayen Jur. Here cattle could be bought and traded, with the local governments benefiting from the collection of significant taxes. Yet, the peace was a government peace with significant economic benefits for political leaders. For the cattle keepers and traders, peace felt tentative. In May 2022, when a Dinka trader refused to pay tax, Nuer officials restrained him. He responded with gun fire in the tax office in Gum Mac. Almost instantly, people in Gum Mac divided along ethnic lines and fought. Some saw this as motivated by internal Warrap State politics. Yet, the long unending wars meant that peace was incredibly fragile. The future of peace in Mayen Jur remains unclear.

Conclusion

In both Tonj North and Mayen Jur, peace was violent. Divine authority figures with the power to threaten a lethal curse were crucial for making the possibility of peace imaginable. The *hakuma* demanded peace, but it repeatedly turned to other divine authorities in order to support their demand for peace. People feared the power of the curse in the moment and took seriously not only the ritual performances but the possibility of lethal punishment. In Tonj North, people fled the *bany e bith*'s spear. In Mayen Jur, a prophet and *bany e bith* managed to bring communities together. They also insisted on a reimagining of wartime relations as law- governed, forcing the war to not be a period devoid of moral norms.

Despite the power of the curse, the peace was not able to resist political interference and competing demands, driven by shifting political economies to reimagine wars as unending. Fears of being politically disempowered and others' political interests intermingled to produce new armed conflict. The wars in both Tonj North and Mayen Jur had used patterns of violence that violated all norms and codes of war, and that, therefore, made peace less possible. The wars had been fought as if they were unending, and armed conflict was easily aggravated when people's cosmological expectations were not met. In this context of the making of unending wars, peace was not only violent in that it was enforced through violence, but also because it often demonstrated the *hakuma*'s arbitrary inclinations to switch between demands for war and demands for peace.

CHAPTER 14

The Problems of Forgiveness, 2013–2020

During these years of war, churches continued to assert their divine authority through their ability to demand peace. In the cosmic polity, for churches, peace was a key way to assert legitimate power. This chapter first discusses this demand for peace at the national level. Churches used their histories and divine authority to contest the unrestrained power of the *hakuma*, to push back against arbitrary displays of violence and to demand peace. This involved church leaders' engagement in the Intergovernmental Authority on Development (IGAD) peace meetings, and their willingness to make statements against the *hakuma* in churches and in public statements.

The chapter then discusses how church leaders also tried to assert their authority through peace-making among South Sudanese communities, including in communities surrounding the Bilnyang and connected rivers. These assertions of authority came during a period of the proliferation of churches and new intra-church competition. However, the church's peace alienated, and even offended, many.[1] Their insistence on forgiveness was seen by some as immoral; it not only ignored the judicial model of peace, but rejected moral obligations to the dead. While the Christian understanding of forgiveness is bound up in sacrifice and punishment, this entails a reformulation of understandings of life post-death which is not commonplace. For many in the communities around the Bilnyang, the church's peace was for the educated alone, excluding many of those who implemented violence. The temporality of the church was also different, offering no immediate curse and sanction for the violation of peace agreements.

At the same time, church leaders have managed to make peace when they can confront the war-makers in the *hakuma* itself. They have also shown that there is potential to support rituals that have promoted more inclusive communities and that have encouraged peace by dampening divisions. How to understand the wartime dead is an ongoing contestation and church leaders

---

[1]   There is no, single, united 'church' in South Sudan. At the same time, South Sudanese, often when being critical, speak of 'the peace of the church'. For all churches in South Sudan there is a shared conviction in the importance of forgiveness.

Figure 5.   A soldier waves a cross as people gather in the county headquarters to celebrate the day of South Sudan's independence from Sudan, Warrap State, 9 July 2011 (Naomi Ruth Pendle).

have not been absent from these debates. A dispute near Ler about how to treat the bodies of captured spies provides an example that ends this chapter. Christian ideals did allow a more inclusive treatment of those who had died. Yet, these practices needed enforcing through military power and were really made possible through the proximity of the church to the *hakuma* and its guns, showing displays of the power of God himself.

The national churches – speaking truth to power

Among the politicians, the smart-suited lobbyists and occasional foreign diplomat, there were also senior bishops staying in the Radisson Blu Hotel in 2014 during the IGAD-led peace negotiations. In their long, purple robes, they could be spotted from afar. Church leaders were present throughout the peace negotiations. Almost all these senior church leaders had been educated and had lived abroad for extended periods, and their senior clerical status had given them opportunities to travel the world and to attend conferences. In contrast to the chiefs, whose authority had been dampened by being in Addis Ababa (see the Introduction), their authority, linked to a worldwide church, was nurtured in those hotel lobbies and conference rooms.

At a national level, church leaders continued to assert authority to demand peace. As discussed in Chapter 4, the church had a long history in the Sudans of being involved in peace-making. In the 1970s, international church bodies had mediated the Addis Ababa Peace Agreement between the Sudan government and Anya-Nya rebels. In the late 1990s, the church gained a reputation for their role in local peace initiatives, through meetings such as Wunlit. After fighting erupted in 2013, church leaders continued to demonstrate their authority and demanded peace.

From the outset of the conflict in December 2013, national church leaders in the South Sudan Council of Churches were vocal in demanding peace. In the days before conflict erupted on 15 December, church leaders had addressed the SPLM leadership meeting in the Nyakuron Centre in Juba to urge them to settle differences peacefully. Within two days of the conflict erupting in December 2013, the South Sudan Council of Churches (SSCC) had issued its first statement of many, calling for peace.

Church leaders repeatedly asserted their peace-making authority through assertions of neutrality. This was not only useful to establish them as potential mediators, but it also set them outside of the intra-*hakuma* politics and, therefore, distinct from them. In 2014, IGAD had asked a cross-denominational group of church leaders to select representatives to participate in the talks. Instead, church leaders agreed to only act as observers to the talks. Also, in 2014, in IGAD's push for inclusivity, representatives of civil society, just like chiefs, were invited to a symposium connected to the peace talks. The warring parties argued over whether they were adequately represented, politically, among these groups, despite them being meant to be independent voices.[2] At this time, Riek Machar complained about the lack of representation of the Presbyterian Church among the church leaders observing the talks. The Presbyterian Church has its largest congregations in Nuer areas that, at the time, were largely assumed to be aligned to the SPLA-IO. The church leaders themselves pushed back. They highlighted that the Presbyterian Church had been involved in the selection of the church observers at the talks. More bluntly, they also emphasised that the church was not subsumed within the polarising politics of the warring parties. Rebuked, Riek apologised to the church representatives.[3]

[2]   Observations while in Addis Ababa, April and May 2014.
[3]   Interview with senior church leader, Radison Blu Hotel, Addis Ababa, May 2014.

Evoking cultural archives, some church leaders explicitly drew on prophetic idioms to claim the divine authority needed to contest the *hakuma*'s war. Zink's work in Bor has highlighted the importance of prophetic traditions to South Sudanese understandings of Christianity.[4] In relation to the post-2013 conflict, church leaders described themselves as having been 'appointed watchmen and women by divine authority'.[5] The South Sudan Council of Churches was interpreting the prophetic as the literal duty 'to see and to speak'. Being prophetic was not simply about foreseeing the future, but about seeing and speaking truth to power. Their call was not just to bring an immediate peace but to take a broader prophetic stance against the *hakuma*'s violent form of authority. Again, like the Nuer prophets and Nuer and Dinka priests, they were challenging the *hakuma*'s ability to live beyond the moral order and without spiritual sanction. This church-leader recall of the prophetic resonated with the 1990s growth of the church through its perceived connection to existing idioms of the prophetic, as well as with the continued power of prophetic figures.

From the outset, national church leaders were critical of the warring parties; the SSCC was critical of the way government leaders waged war and were not committed to a real peace.[6] Specific church leaders gained reputations for being incredibly vocal against the government. For example, Bishop Santo Loku Pio Doggale gained a reputation for publicly criticising the government. After the Equatorias entered the conflict in 2015, the church became even more critical, especially of the government itself. This reflected the significant authority of the church in the Equatorias. As the SSCC described itself, at this time, they went from being like guide dogs that 'lead you away from trouble' to watchdogs 'that bark'.[7]

This speaking of truth to power was also visible from church leaders in Gogrial, Ler and the surrounding areas. Moses Deng had been appointed Bishop of Wau (covering Gogrial) in 2009. He was vocally in favour of peace and sometimes publicly critical of government. For example, in 2015 in an article of a Diocese magazine, Bishop Moses wrote:

> The politicians are usually quick to divide the community but later on fail to unite them. This is how they behave and we don't want our community to remain the same. Some of the politicians cause the war for personal interest, to gain the wealth and top position in the government.[8]

---

[4]   Jesse Zink, *Christianity and Catastrophe in South Sudan* (Baylor Press, 2018).

[5]   The Rt Rev. Peter Gail Lual Marrow, Chairman South Sudan Council of Churches, 'A Statement From Kigali' during church leaders' retreat, Kigali, Rwanda, 1–7 July 2015.

[6]   Ibid.

[7]   Ibid.

[8]   Bishop Moses Deng, 'A Word from the Diocesan Bishop of Wau: Renewal:

This bishop has also spoken of the broad spiritual cost of the war:

> We very much need to be healed from blind hatred and the ignorance of using violence to get our own way. What I would like to say to both President Kiir and Dr Riek Machar is that if you love our nation, you will make the necessary sacrifice to bring peace to it now. Continuing to fail and carry-on fighting shames us all, but to bring peace would be a great gift that would secure the future of South Sudan.[9]

The outspoken nature of the church leaders and the SSCC near the Bilnyang and across South Sudan is striking because of the lack of space for free speech by others. During these years of war, the South Sudan government was further limiting freedom of expression including through the arrest and disappearance of outspoken journalists and civil society leaders. Academics were being exiled for discussing political visions, and newspapers were often confiscated. In continuing to challenge government and its assumptions of impunity, church leaders represented the rarity of such.

As you drive through Juba, you are constantly attentive to the bustle of overtaking cars and swerving motorbikes. Your car traces a wiggled line along the wide, tarmac road as it avoids obstacles to stay safe. Occasionally, as you drive, you start to hear the distant sound of a multiplicity of sirens. These collective sirens demand that you pull over to the side of the road as a VIP zooms through the city. Every Sunday morning, through the years of the conflict, a collection of such cars rushed to various churches across Juba.

At the national level, the proximity to and not distance of the *hakuma* from the church gave it the political space to be prophetic. Leaders of the *hakuma* kept attending church as they feared the divine, or because they could use time at church to build their networks among other leaders or to rally support from their constituencies. Their presence in the church has made many critical of the church's intimacy with the *hakuma*, but it did give it space to challenge the *hakuma* and to claim a superior divine power. For example, on one Sunday morning when President Kiir was attending a cathedral in Juba, the sermon was so critical that Kiir refused to attend church again for months afterwards.

Around the Bilnyang and connected rivers

Alongside these national interventions, church leaders in the communities around the Bilnyang also tried to assert their divine authority to demand peace. Often explicitly evoking the success of Wunlit and their role in this

---

Informing, Enlightening and Transforming Lives' (Wau Diocesan newsletter, September 2015).

9   Ibid.

process, church leaders worked with local government authorities or got NGO funding to convene and host peace meetings between communities. This came during a period of significant intra-church competition, and church leaders also struggled to make peace meaningful to the competing cosmic ontologies and understandings of peace in these Nuer and Dinka communities.

Intra-church competition

In the 2010s, churches were changing in the lands of the Bilnyang. In Gogrial, the post- Comprehensive Peace Agreement (CPA) period had intensified inter-denominational competition and challenged the Catholic monopolies on Christianity in the region that dated to the Anglo-Egyptian Condominium era eighty years earlier. In the 1980s, as discussed above, young men were recruited into the SPLA from Nuer and Dinka areas around the Bilnyang and sent to Ethiopia for training. In Ethiopia, the influence of figures like Anglican Bishop Nathaniel Garang Anyieth, resulted in the conversion to Christianity of tens of thousands of young men, especially from Dinka areas.[10] They joined the Episcopalian Church (part of the Anglican Communion) and were discipled by the church leaders while in the refugee and training camps. When the SPLA was forced out of Ethiopia in the 1990s, some of these young converts returned to Gogrial as Episcopalian evangelists.[11] By the 2010s, these early evangelists had risen to the leadership of a sizeable church and many had been appointed as bishops in the ECS church, giving them the authority to ordain clergy. In contrast to the Catholic Church whose priests were often recruited abroad, the Anglican church offered a local and more present clergy. On a weekly basis in rural areas, the Catholic Church was still dominantly led by catechists, with Mass only being offered by visiting priests a few times a year.

From 2009, the ECS Bishop of Wau was himself originating from Gogrial. As the bishop established his authority, he drew on cultural archives around priestly and political power. Bishop Moses was from the same village as President Kiir and from the family of one of the longest serving chiefs in Gogrial – Nyal Chan. The bishop's training in the SPLA's child soldier army (the Red Army) and his connections to Kiir gave him authority through the *hakuma*. His links to Nyal Chan connected him to histories of government and divine authority in Gogrial. As a bishop, he presented a different interpretation of authority and was able to build on and revise these previous connections with power and the divine. Personal histories of church leaders that allow

---

[10]   Zink, *Christianity and Catastrophe in South Sudan.*
[11]   For a more detailed discussion of Christianity in refugee camps in Ethiopia, see ibid.

connections to cultural archives of divinity have been key in building authority, as Zink records in his history of the church in Jonglei State.[12]

The closeness of the ECS leadership to the people was further strengthened through the proliferation of new dioceses from 2015. As discussed, in 2015 Kiir increased the administrative states of South Sudan from ten to twenty-eight. Shortly afterwards, and in the run-up to the selection of a new ECS Primate to lead the South Sudan Anglican church from Juba, the ECS also started to proliferate its dioceses. The Diocese of Wau became eight dioceses and, therefore, eight bishops could be appointed. The ECS church could now offer to the people of Gogrial a unique, unprecedented closeness to the clergy.

At the same time, the Catholic Church remained dominant in much of Gogrial. The government elite from Gogrial still largely attended Catholic Churches in Wau, Kuajok and Juba. They had been educated at the Catholic schools in Gogrial decades before and many had continued to attend church through the years of war. Kiir himself has been explicit about his close mentorship by some Catholic priests. This leadership support for the Catholic Church helped maintain its popularity in Gogrial. Furthermore, to an extent, the distance of the Catholic Church from the people helped keep them divine by adding a layer of power and mysticism to the clergy. The fact that the ECS leadership were autochthonous allowed them to understand the cosmic battles but, like the *hakuma*, it became hard to set themselves apart. Many discussions about why people doubted the church in Gogrial did not highlight their distance, but events during their proximity, such as when Catholic clergy visited the village and sourced 'holy water' from the local borehole.[13]

Government leaders even used church construction in their home villages to try to build authority among these constituents.[14] For example, in a market village in Gogrial one government leader significantly funded and organised the erection of a large church building. For years, the church had met under a large tree near the market and the home of the paramount chief. The politician had first promised to build the large, brick church building after the CPA was signed. He promised to raise funds among Catholics in Juba in order to build this church back at home. After years of promises, he eventually produced the initial funding for a fence to demarcate the land. Then, by November 2015, the church itself was erected. The politician had managed to raise funds for cement and iron sheets. The members of the church also gave their labour and

[12] Ibid.
[13] Discussions in Gogrial, May 2022.
[14] Naomi Pendle, 'Commanders, Classrooms, Cows and Churches: Accountability and the Construction of a South Sudanese Elite', in Wale Adebanwi and Roger Orock (eds), *Elites and the Politics of Accountability in Africa* (Michigan University Press, 2021).

time to make and fire the bricks that would be used for its walls. The church was massive and a rival in size to the Cathedral in Wau, the centre of the Diocese. After its construction, one friend commented: 'Now our village is a city'.[15] However, by 2022, the unfinished church was already falling into disrepair, with the iron sheets often pulled apart in times of strong winds.

There was also church competition in Koch, Ler and Mayendit to the east of the Bilnyang. This took a different shape partly because of different patterns of community migration. As people came and went and found new places of safety, old churches were remade and new churches appeared. For example, the first Seventh Day Adventist (SDA) Church in Tochriak only emerged when people came to Tochriak from the SDA Church in the Bentiu Protection of Civilians (PoC) sites.[16] The temporary urbanisation in the Bentiu PoCs was introducing new religious ideas. While new churches were established, old churches were challenged. The scale of the conflict that hit Ler and Mayendit meant that more established churches saw this as a period of decline and uncertainty. 'Due to the wars, the people are tempted not to believe in their God but to believe in earthly things'.[17]

The problem of the peace of the church

For many people in the communities around the Bilnyang, the peace of the church is itself arbitrary and not compliant with the logics of peace in the cultural archive. For many, this means that the peace of the church is meaningless, rejected or even violent. Three significant problems were often cited: firstly, the demand for forgiveness is seen as immoral; secondly, the church is part of an educated sphere and discrete from most people who implement violence around the Bilnyang; thirdly, the temporalities of the church for breaking the peace of the church were too long-term.

Forgiveness

The SSCC, as well as international and local church leaders, have constantly offered forgiveness as the solution to conflict and a means to peace.[18] In the South Sudan Council of Churches Action Plan for Peace Vision 2023, the document asserts: 'There is a long history in South Sudan of using healing and reconciliation tools to build relationships where past actions have damaged

---

[15]   Ibid.

[16]   Interview with evangelist in the Seventh Day Adventist Church, Tochriak, 20 April 2020.

[17]   Presbyterian Church Elder, Tochriak, April 2020.

[18]   Archbishop Justin Bada Arama speaking to the Anglican Communion News Service, September 2018.

social cohesion, and of communal apologies, public forgiveness, and reconciliation, often led or supported by the Church'. Wunlit is often still cited as
the archetypal example of peace negotiations that can be offered by a church
leadership. In Gogrial, the ECS has been active in preaching forgiveness. For
example, after trainings in Kuajok in April and May 2015, 'Peace Mobilisers'
for the Committee for National Healing, Peace and Reconciliation conducted
thirty-nine *payam* consultations in Warrap State. People expressed grievances
that they were told would be contributed to the national agenda. Forgiveness
was encouraged.

For those living around the Bilnyang, the church's demand for forgiveness
was often cited as part of the problem with church peace. It was problematic as
it did not offer a judicial peace in which obligations to the dead are upheld. In
his frustration with discussion of the 2018 Ajiep Peace Conference in Gogrial,
one chief critically equated this peace meeting with the peace of the church.

> This peace meeting should not just like peace-making in the church. What
> about huge loss to the victims? How will their children be fed? Better you
> judge the issue first and exchange the cows if you really want peace. The lead-
> ers are just saying peace.[19]

Church leaders' demand for forgiveness after conflict in the Bilnyang is
asking for a revolutionary re-conception of peace, of the relations between
the governed and the *hakuma* and of life after death itself. Forgiveness is
presented as an 'ideal type',[20] – an ideal type that feels far from morally
inappropriate for many, and that can often be accused of creating an ugly
disregard for the dead.[21] To forgive your brother's killer implies that you have
authority to forgive for your dead brother. Alternatively, people have shown
ongoing concern to provide a wife (through compensation) for the dead to
give them as ongoing social life through their children (as discussed in earlier chapters). Chiefs in Gogrial and prophets in Mayendit and Ler have built
their authority on being able to protect and evolve a system of judicial peace
despite contradictory demands from other warring parties. The church's focus
on forgiveness, and not compensation or revenge for the dead, appears to have
left the dead forgotten. Forgiveness is feared as it could condemn the deceased
to a final death and remain morally unpalatable.[22]

---

[19]   Chief from Gogrial East, speech at Ajiep Peace Conference, 20 April 2018.

[20]   Anna Macdonald, 'Transitional Justice and Political Economies of Survival in
       Post-conflict Northern Uganda', *Development and Change* 48:2 (2017): 286–311,
       page 299.

[21]   Interviews with people in Gogrial, 2019; interview with people in Juba, March
       2020.

[22]   Conversation with researcher from Ler, Nairobi, 2019.

South Sudanese church leaders have themselves recognised the complexity of forgiveness.[23] Yet, biblical forgiveness is not without sacrifice. In the Old Testament, biblical sacrifice was used to rid people of pollution from wrong against God and the community that could harm the whole community.[24] Jesus explicitly equates his death with the death of a sacrificial animal. In so doing, the sacrifice for healing no longer comes from an animal but from God himself who alone can offer a once-and-for-all healing. Yet, this healing is bound up with alternative ideas of immortality that do not give the dead a second chance at life through a posthumous wife. Immortality is instead based on faith in Christ's sacrifice. Without a belief in Christ's divinity and the cost of his sacrifice, the demand for forgiveness becomes empty.

Another problem with forgiveness is that it has been used towards *hakuma* impunity. Some church leaders highlight that forgiveness does not necessarily equate with a lack of punishment. Yet, in South Sudan, church leaders have often praised *hakuma* leaders for forgiving each other and reconciling. This reiterates the *hakuma*'s ability to act with impunity as they can just be forgiven. Ironically, as the church seeks to build its power over peace, they end up also supporting the god-like nature of the *hakuma*. As one long-time South Sudanese observer noted,

> Absolutely horrible. I know exactly, because I saw it many times, what this kind of South Sudanese peace and reconciliation will look like, a big fat platform for people already in power to tell people with none that it's over and done with and they better just forgive. No one should have any trust in these two people who do not even take on any accountability for what they have done, let alone apologise, when they join 'as brothers' for the New York Times.[25]

Leaders of the *hakuma* have often explicitly sought forgiveness from each other and from their citizens. For example, in November 2018, President Kiir said on Machar's return to Juba, 'Dr. Riek Machar and I and all the opposition leaders who signed the agreement have forgiven each other. We have consciously decided to move this country forward'.[26]

---

[23]   Rt Rev. Peter Gail Lual Marrow, Chairman South Sudan Council of Churches, 'A Statement From Kigali' during church leaders' retreat, Kigali, Rwanda, 1–7 July 2015.

[24]   Mary Douglas, *Jacob's Tears: The Priestly Work of Reconciliation* (Oxford University Press, 2004).

[25]   Skye Wheeler, Facebook, 7 June 2016.

[26]   Salva Kiir quote in Radio Tamazuj, 'Kiir: "I and Machar have forgiven each other"', 1 November 2018, https://radiotamazuj.org/en/news/article/kiir-i-and-machar-have-forgiven-each-other, accessed 11 December 2022.

Across the country, after this reunion between Kiir and Machar, there were further peace rallies that brought together government and IO elites. Speaking at one such rally in Malakal in December 2018, the government's deputy governor said,

> I greet my brother from the IO who joined us in Malakal after so long an absence. My special greetings go to you, our citizens, here in the POC. Before I proceed, I would like to ask for forgiveness from you, my people. If I am forgiven, I can then speak freely.[27]

The crowd was initially perplexed and quietly started discussing this, before the IO leadership prompted their reply of 'yes'.

The church has demanded forgiveness and this often seemed to echo the demands of government. In April 2019, the Pope surprised politicians and observers by kissing the feet of Salva Kiir, Riek Machar and others during their visit to the Vatican. South Sudan's leaders had been in Rome on an 'ecumenical retreat' hosted by the heads of the Catholic Church and the Anglican Communion.[28] In kissing their feet, the Pope upturned the system of the hierarchies of power. He used his authority to demand humility. At the same time, many South Sudanese were offended by the Pope's actions. Nuer prophets in the last decade had remade their authority or justified the absence of the divine because of the polluted nature of the land after war and extreme acts of violence.[29] This involved the divine physically excluding himself from those in government and those who killed. Here, instead, the Pope had welcomed them to his palace and shared intimacy with them through kissing their feet. Even the Pope's forgiveness to some seemed abhorrent as acts of *hakuma* violence had been against their families and not against the Pope. It was unclear why people should be forgiven and why the Pope had the right to forgive.

Recognising the concern with forgiveness, some clergy have been explicit that forgiveness does not include impunity. The SSCC stated that 'forgiveness is not the same as impunity; accountability, particularly through restorative justice, can still be pursued'.[30] They argue that forgiveness can be conceptualised in a way that allows punishment and accountability while also allowing the more emotional response of forgiveness. Yet, in this interpretation of

27 Government Deputy Governor of Malakal, Malakal POC Peace Celebration, 1 December 2018.
28 Inés San Martín, 'From Conversion Therapy to Immigration, Church Draws Fire in Spain', *Crux: Taking the Catholic Pulse* (11 April 2019).
29 Discussions in Koch, 2018; interviews about Nyachol in Mayendit, 2013.
30 Rt Rev. Peter Gail Lual Marrow, Chairman South Sudan Council of Churches, 'A Statement From Kigali' during church leaders' retreat, Kigali, Rwanda, 1–7 July 2015.

'forgiveness', it is unclear if peace and not war will always follow. After all, as discussed throughout this book, much armed mobilisation happens in South Sudan to try to challenge the *hakuma*'s impunity and establish restraint and accountability when it is absent.

A peace of the educated

The peace of the church is also seen as the peace of the educated. All churches near the Bilnyang and connected river systems have remained closely associated with the class of the educated. For example, many people in rural Gogrial only start attending church when they start attending school or if they are from a family with educated parents. Plus, church leaders across denominations in Gogrial and Ler often linked their own testimonies of Christian conversation to education. The ECS Bishop (now Archbishop) of Wau first learnt about Jesus and heard biblical teaching while at school in Ethiopian refugee camps in the 1980s. An evangelist at the SDA Church in Ler first learnt about Jesus from a classmate at school.

Catholic and Anglican churches have continued to prioritise education and run schools.[31] Some interpret the written nature of the Bible as highlighting how Christianity is being primarily for the educated.

> Also, the reason why the Bible was written and bought was for the educated people to use because they are the ones who respect its laws and regulations meanwhile those who are not educated do not respect it, they only respect the laws and regulations of the spear master.[32]

The extent to which the church in Gogrial and Ler is still seen as synonymous with education limits the church's authority over those who implement violence. Many of those who are armed and mobilised to conflict are not formally educated. Parents around the Bilnyang still often divide the labour of their sons between those in the cattle camp and those in school. While there is movement between the two, sons often specialise over time.[33] Those who go to the cattle camp have a reputation for being well trained in military labour and defence. It is often these young men who implement the armed conflicts of the community. However, as their time in the cattle camp usually excluded them from going to school, they usually see themselves as discrete from the sphere of formal education, which includes the church. The context loses influence and this dichotomy does become blurred, especially when cattle are kept closer to churches. For example, in 2017 and 2018, armed cattle keepers

---

31   Deng, 'A Word from the Diocesan Bishop of Wau'.
32   Interview with man in Gogrial, June 2018, in Dinka.
33   Observations in Tonj, Gogrial, Ler and Mayendit from 2010-22.

in SPLA-IO areas near Ler were attending the local Presbyterian Church, especially when they were given t-shirts for singing in the choir.[34]

The temporality of the curse

Another significant concern with the peace of the church is the power of the church to guarantee the peace. *Baany e biith*, *kuar muon* and Nuer prophets relied on the power of the curse to guarantee the peace; people could face spiritual pollution, illness and death if they reopened the feud. The power of the God of the churches was also capable of deadly punishment.

For example, after Salva Kiir's visit to the Pope in Rome, he returned to South Sudan. On Kiir's return, and while addressing Parliament, he shared: 'I was shocked and trembled when His Holiness, the Pope, kissed our feet. It was a blessing and can be a curse if we play games with the lives of our people'.[35] Kiir was explicit that God could also bring punishment if the peace was broken and there was no adherence to the boundaries of violence.

At the same time, people have discussed concern about the long-term temporalities of the curses of the Bible. As a man near Ler explained in 2019, 'the Nuer prophets' curse comes true immediately and this helps many people believe. However, the curse of God only comes true in the distant future, after we die. Only educated people believe this. Others want to experience the power of God now'.

Without the power of the curse of God having immediate implications, the church has often ended up working closely with the *hakuma* to guarantee peace. While church leaders often go to significant lengths to show that they are unarmed and un-militarised, they often still have to rely on *hakuma* support to make peace likely.

Inclusive communities and protecting the dead

Some of the most powerful actions of the church in the Bilnyang towards peace have not been through peace meetings themselves. Instead, they have come when the church has been able to challenge and remake the cultural archive to be more inclusive. Rituals of burial, as with rituals of peace, can make communities more exclusive or inclusive. Backed with the power of the gun, through their proximity to government, churches have been able to enforce rituals that are more inclusive and that dampen divisions.

[34]   Interview with man from Ler, June 2019.
[35]   Paul Samasumo, 'Salva Kiir: I trembled when the Pope kissed our feet', *Vatican-news.va* (16 May 2019), www.vaticannews.va/en/africa/news/2019-05/salva-kiir-i-trembled-when-the-pope-kissed-our-feet.html, accessed 19 October 2022.

An incident in Tochriak in 2015 provides an example. In Tochriak, along-side temporary shelters and NGO compounds, is a football pitch. When teams play, they attract a crowd. Yet, if you look carefully, one area of the football pitch has grass that grows a more vivid green than the rest of the pitch. People avoid running here.

In 2015, the government commander in Ler sent out six local government soldiers to scout out the area in preparation for an attack on Tochriak. They had been captured by SPLA-IO-aligned *gojam* and brought to the SPLA-IO general in a *luak* at the administrative centre. While waiting for the IO general to question them, a man had run into the *luak* and stabbed one of them. He demanded revenge as his son had recently been killed by government soldiers. However, the IO general stopped the man from killing the captured soldier. After the general had finished his questioning of the soldiers, other *gojam* (cattle guards) joined the father's demand for the death of the soldiers to sat-isfy their demand for revenge. They dragged the six men out to kill them. Some of the local NGO workers tried to object. Yet, as the soldiers tried to flee, they were shot dead on the football ground.

The deaths of these soldiers and the continued presence of their bodies raised new spiritual dilemmas. Once they had fallen, they were not touched. The *gojam* talked to each other of a fear of burying them. Knowing that many from their community had died without burial fighting government soldiers, for many, burial seemed too dignified, and neglectful of the revenge demanded by their own dead. People also spoke about a fear that burial would bring a *bit* (curse) into the land that would increase their own vulnerability to death.[36] They drew on cultural archives about the potential to pollute the land to cement their concerns about their burial.

The following day was a Sunday and people gathered in the local church. In Tochriak many of those who attend church are the more educated and also associated with the *hakuma* – the IO commanders and generals, and those who have jobs with the NGOs. Some *gojam* also attend to sing in the choir.

That morning one NGO worker stood up and spoke against the refusal to bury the government soldiers. He highlighted the public health dangers and his concerns that hyenas would gain a taste for human blood. He also chal-lenged any fears of a *bit* and argued that there was a duty to bury the dead. The IO general was attending church and briefly said that he agreed with the speech of the NGO worker. He was arguing for a shared moral community that was not limited to the IO supporters. He argued that government and SPLA-IO supporters shared a common humanity before God and that they should not be excluded from post-death rituals.[37]

---

[36] Interview with NGO worker working near Ler who witnessed these events, Juba, 2018.

[37] Interview with church attendee, 2016, by telephone.

That day the NGO worker and other church attendees went from church to bury the dead. The IO general went with them to stop the *gojam* violently protesting and to make it clear that he supported the initiative for the good of the Tochriak community. They dug a shallow grave and buried the six soldiers together. The *gojam* continued to petition the general and threatened to dig up the bodies, but the general's insistence and their appreciation of the problem of having bodies so central in the community encouraged them to accept the decision. In this instance, the church's notions of burial and treatment of the dead had prevailed. At the same time, it had highlighted their reliance on the might of the powers of the *hakuma* and their connection with it.

Conclusion

Churches are part of the cosmic polity; they assert the divinity of God and their divine power. Their claims to be able to demand peace, from the 1970s and into recent years, is a significant part of how they have established their authority among local and international communities, and with the *hakuma*. Church leaders at a national level have spoken truth to power and demanded accountability and peace from the leaders of the *hakuma*. They have been publicly outspoken even when free speech generally has been heavily restrained.

Church leaders around the Bilnyang have also tried to establish their authority through peace-making. This came in the context of growing inter-church competition. However, many people have pushed back against this. The peace of the church has been seen as arbitrary and even morally abhorrent for its relinquishing of moral responsibilities to the dead. Forgiveness also brings the dangers of accepting *hakuma* impunity. The peace of the church is often seen as only for the educated, excluding many of those who implement violence, while the lack of immediate curse from violating the peace of the church leaves its power as ambiguous.

While the church has heavily invested in peace meetings, some of the churches' most powerful pro-peace actions have been through more daily remakings of the cultural archive, including sometimes with the backing of the militarised power of the *hakuma*. Through these remakings, church leaders have been able to challenge exclusive communities and have tried to leave space for peace. Church leaders have been able to do this best when they are autochthonous and know the cultural archive well. An example of this is through the church's control and contestation over a key, wartime burial. There is more to understand about how the church is influencing daily wartime practice in favour of a less violent peace, including through activities such as burial and posthumous care.

Conclusion: The Cosmic Politics of Peace in South Sudan

Peace remains violent in the context of South Sudan's unsettled cosmic polity. In South Sudan, the *hakuma* has long been akin to the divine, both in how it acts and how it is understood, claiming the authority to decide with impunity whether to assert favour or destruction, life or death, war or peace. Divine rivalries have long and violent histories in South Sudan that overlap with and cut across periods of colonial rule, war, peace and 'no war, no peace'. Peace for people in South Sudan has long been about a renegotiation of the relationship not just between warring parties, but between South Sudanese people and the *hakuma*. Peace does not simply involve a re-arranging of individuals in the *hakuma* or a new collection of amicable government elites, but instead involves hedging in the *hakuma* – whether the *hakuma* is government, formal opposition or other armed men. The *hakuma* needs to be restrained and kept within legal and morally bounded limits so that it cannot arbitrarily decide if there should be peace or war, and so that its claims to divinity can be clipped. When the *hakuma*'s brute force is too much to restrain, its moral and spiritual impunity can at least be challenged. At the same time, many peace meetings, agreements and peace-making activities in South Sudan since the late 1800s have not restrained the *hakuma* but have instead set the *hakuma* beyond moral bounds and made it like the divine. Such peace is often violent.

The rivalries of the cosmic polity pre-date the coming of the *hakuma*, but the god-like nature has made the *hakuma* a dominant player in this arena. This book has highlighted how, since the coming of the *hakuma* in the mid-nineteenth century, the ability to rain arbitrary favour and destruction, including war and peace, with impunity, has been a key feature of what the *hakuma* is in South Sudan. Therefore, for those living around the Bilnyang and connected rivers, from the coming of the social and political sphere of the *hakuma* in the mid-nineteenth century, the *hakuma* has been god-like. The various forms of *hakuma* have not explicitly claimed to be divine, but their ability to rain favour or destruction, life or death, peace and war, with arbitrariness and impunity, place them in the cosmic polity. In the cosmologies of the Nuer and

Dinka, this was enough to make the *hakuma* appear to be divine – or at least claiming to be divine. This tallies with Graeber and Sahlin's descriptions of all global governments being god-like because of the contingent histories of our world. Therefore, by the late nineteenth century in Southern Sudan, in the political imaginary, the *hakuma* were established as part of the cosmic polity.

The *hakuma*'s ability to demand peace, as much as its ability to kill or demand war, can also be arbitrary, violent and an assertion of divine-like powers. Peace meetings and agreements often lead to upsurges in physical violence in the everyday lives of South Sudanese. Yet, in addition, since the colonial period, peace-making in South Sudan has often involved *hakuma* demands over the logics, terms and conditions of peace. Peace meetings and peace-making have often been a space to remake and reinterpret the cultural archive. The terms of *hakuma*-backed peace often demand the impunity of the *hakuma* and demand compliance with the peace through military threat. Peace then becomes violent not only because of any direct physical violence, but because it entrenches the power of the *hakuma* to demand its own impunity for killing, war and peace. The *hakuma* is not restricted, and its potential for violence remains.

The god-like nature of the *hakuma* is not indicative of its distance or absence. Nilotic cosmologies often place God at a distance,[1] but in prophets, for example, divinities can seize nearby people. Proximity does not negate divinity in Nuer and Dinka cosmologies. The *hakuma*, since the colonial era, has been entangled in the everyday and intimate, as well as the seismic negotiations of power, even in the most rural areas that appear at a distance from government centres. There is no absence of government. Instead, the *hakuma*-god dwells close to, and rains favour and destruction, in the most intimate parts of life. Over time, the presence of the *hakuma* has been part of the re-crafting of the cultural archive. This is both because the archive incorporates ideas of the *hakuma* and bends to creatively refuse it.

With the *hakuma* part of the gods, it is in the cosmic polity that war and peace are ultimately made. Peace involves demands to suspend and constrain violence – to limit the power of the warring parties to carry out arbitrary violence. Yet, power is constructed by sitting outside of this, being able to demand war and peace, and not being subject to the suspension of arbitrary violence. For over a century, the wars of Southern/South Sudan have also been the wars of the *hakuma*. Since the nineteenth century, these have been linked to the country's deep connections to global networks of trade and exploitation. In contemporary South Sudan it is impossible to find a war that is not entangled with the broad *hakuma* sphere. In this context, stopping war and making peace is about limiting the divine-like nature of the *hakuma* and asserting that

---

[1]   David Graeber and Marshall Sahlins, *On Kings* (HAU Books, 2017), page 89.

the *hakuma* is still subject to moral and spiritual restraints. Stopping war is about restraining the arbitrary power of the government both to declare war or peace. From the perspective of the cosmic polity, peace-making is about limiting the power of the *hakuma* to, with impunity, rain favour or destruction, to demand lethal killing or a refrain from lethal killing.

This book documents the long struggle by divine authorities from communities around the Bilnyang and connected rivers to limit the power of the *hakuma* and to make it morally and legally bounded. Throughout the history of the *hakuma* in South Sudan, and especially in recent decades, some of the main struggles for power have been about either limiting the god-like power of the *hakuma,* or challenging their god-like nature by ending their impunity. Officials in the Anglo-Egyptian Condominium government were killed by elephants, recent *baany e biith* who came too close to the *hakuma* died when they used money of the *hakuma* to kill with the curse, and Nuer prophets have barred entry to their *luaks* based on Nuer government officers being culpable for their actions as *hakuma*. Repeatedly, divine authorities have sought to limit the *hakuma*'s claims of impunity. Nuer prophets, even in the years of post-2013 wars, remade and re-insisted on the existence of spiritual pollution such as *nueer*, as well as their power to offer solutions. Divine authorities have remade rituals, moral understandings and practices as a form of protest, intentional rejection and creative refusal. Religious leaders have often taken a leading role in pushing back against the *hakuma* in attempts to keep them morally bounded. This has included seeing wars not only as wars of the *hakuma* but also as wars of revenge and subject to the moral norms that govern revenge and allow a lasting peace.

Therefore, political debates in South Sudan are happening, in part, through the remaking of rituals, the reshaping of ideas of purity and pollution and the retelling of histories. Much armed conflict in recent years, including national wars, has been understood as wars of revenge. Claims that wars are wars of revenge are not assertions of primordial understandings of war. Instead, they are attempts to culturally refuse wars of the *hakuma* as morally discrete and exceptional. They are attempts to assert logics of war and peace that are not based on money, markets, secular relations or individual deals. Revenge and associated notions of peace draw on rich archives of ideas and histories that limit the *hakuma* and that reimagine that the control of whether peace and war occur could be returned to the South Sudanese people.

At the same time, the peace of these other cosmic authorities and moral logics are not non-violent. These remade rituals have been used to mobilise support for war, as happened in December 2013. For many priests and prophets, confronted by such continuous violence, their logics of peace have increasingly entrenched exclusive ethnic communities that can ultimately be instrumentalised by elites. Increasingly pollution and ritual have been remade to only offer peace to mono-ethnic communities. This carries the danger of entrenching, cosmologically, these current political divides.

Plus, the overwhelming and ever-growing military might of the *hakuma* makes the *hakuma* incredibly *bitter.* When there are large offences by the government or armed opposition groups, few South Sudanese even expect the local divine authorities to be able to push back. However, for some, the *hakuma*'s power is not only overwhelming because of military might. The wars of the *hakuma* have brought spiritual pollution. Therefore, the lack of divine power in the land is as much a manifestation of divinities' exclusion by this spiritual pollution, as it is by being overwhelmed by military power.

International peace-making efforts, such as the 2005 Comprehensive Peace Agreement (CPA) and the 2018 Revitalised Agreement on the Resolution of Conflict in South Sudan (R-ARCSS), have been implicitly built not only on commitments to economic and political liberalism, but also to the underlying secular assumptions of contemporary European and North American political orders. Whether Europe and North America are secular, and devoid of gods and god-like governments, is not clear and is an empirical question for another space. Yet, what is clear is that this image of liberalism being entangled with secularism means that international peace-meeting efforts have claimed to be devoid of divine power. They have not paid attention to the cosmic politics at play in wars and peace in South Sudan, including the power of divine authorities and the South Sudanese *hakuma*, but also the cosmic implications of their own actions. This blindness to the cosmic hierarchies allows international actors to ignore the real politics, anxieties and struggles at play. It also allows them to be blind to their own (probably unintentional) actions that are akin to being divine.

For international diplomats and humanitarians, the danger of blindness to the cosmic polity is that they engage in policies that undermine efforts to maintain a moral order and lack of impunity, even in the midst of war. The danger is that they undermine the only authorities who might have the power to make peace that is cosmologically consistent and less violent. Much focus of international attention in South Sudan, including UN Security Council mandates for the UN Mission in South Sudan, have highlighted the need to protect civilians. The UN, NGOs and donor governments have seen the South Sudan government compliance to international humanitarian law as a key way to do this. Pursuing a Protection of Civilians agenda ultimately aspires to restrain government and prevent them being god-like; if governments are hedged in by international humanitarian law, they can no long carry out destruction with impunity. Without knowing, these international actors are engaging with the cosmic politics of South Sudan. Without being more cognisant of this politics, their involvement is more likely to have unintended consequences. The UN, NGOs and donor governments share with many South Sudanese divine authorities the aspiration to restrain the *hakuma*. They both seek to provide frameworks – moral or legal – that provide a boundary around the legitimate actions of the *hakuma*. They also use the threat of lethal power to encourage compliance. Some divine authorities can threaten the deadly power of the curse, while the UN displays deadly powers through the gun.

The international community has welcomed the role of some divine authorities in their efforts to restrain the South Sudanese *hakuma*. Church leaders and organisations have been key actors in peace-making at the national level. Local peace meetings have also often included invited Nuer and Dinka priests. However, as discussed in this book, this has often resulted in the hedging in to custom of these other divine authorities, reducing their power, including their power to restrain the *hakuma*. Peace meetings have not only prevented accountability for their past violence, they have also asserted their authority to determine when arbitrary violence is morally acceptable and to recode their violence as legitimate.

When non-government divine authorities have used violence to create peace or limit the *hakuma*, the UN and donor governments have seen them as an obstacle to peace.[2] However, for many South Sudanese, limiting lethal power to the *hakuma* amounts to an increase, not decrease, in the potential for arbitrary violence and destruction as the *hakuma* is then unrestrained. Divine authorities appeal to the South Sudanese as they ensure that, even when communities are disarmed or outgunned by the *hakuma*, there is still the power to curse. There is a need for international actors to better appreciate the anxieties and aspirations they share with these divine authorities about the unrestrained power of the *hakuma*.

At the same time, divine authorities are far from inherently benign or necessarily supportive of inclusive, non-violent peace. International actors cannot just lean on some imagined, static notion of tradition, but must be politically savvy in their dealings with divine powers, as much as they are in their dealings with government and opposition officials. Many divine authorities have been involved in the slow remaking of norms of revenge and spiritual pollution, with many enforcing these remade cultural archives through the power to curse with impunity. These remade norms can create new divisions between social groups, ethnicising divisions and entrenching the cultural archive as politicised histories. There is a need for an appreciation not of the momentary instrumentalisation of history and 'tradition', but of an awareness of how this slowly changes over time and absorbs divisive narratives that potentially make peace impossible.

[2]   See, for example, 'Incidents of Intercommunal Violence in Jonglei State' (UNMISS 2012), https://unmiss.unmissions.org/sites/default/files/june_2012_jonglei_report.pdf, accessed 18 October 2022.

The future violence of peace

Peace often induces violent conflict in South Sudan. It is not just a state of 'no war, no peace' – people are not just resting in limbo between wars. Peace often, itself, generates violence and conflict. South Sudanese responses to peace do not make sense and cannot be understood unless we recognise this propensity for peace to be violent and produce conflict.

Most of this book was written after the signing of the 2018 R-ARCSS. On the 12 September 2018, peace apparently started again as the warring parties signed this long document. The Troika refrained from signing the agreement after the failures of ARCSS, but for international actors this comprehensive peace agreement quickly became the only framework for 'long-term stability and durable peace' to be achieved in South Sudan.[3] Diplomats lauded the warring parties when they finally filled government positions in the transitional government as prescribed by the peace agreement, and the UN talked as if there would be a peaceful election in South Sudan in the coming years.[4]

This book has illustrated how the periods after such peace agreements have continued to be violent in the communities around the Bilnyang and connected rivers. The experiences of these communities are not discrete from broader experiences in South Sudan. Other parts of South Sudan have also seen episodic deadly upsurges in violence including after peace agreements. Even where parties to R-ARCSS declined in their explicit fighting with each other, there was an 'increase in sub-national violence'.[5]

Yet, peace is not only violent when it produces an upsurge in armed conflict. Declarations of war and demands for mobilisation can amount to raining death both on those who fight and those caught in the conflicts. Peace can also be morally and spiritually abhorrent when peace leaves hearts hot, creating more demands for revenge and more moral confusion.

At the time of writing, Salva Kiir's government has defeated armed opposition across South Sudan, including in the communities around the Bilnyang. Yet, this government victory against armed groups such as the SPLA-IO means that the national leadership is dominated by an autochthonous leadership from the west of the Bilnyang. If there are now powerful, rivalrous relationships that are shaping national politics, they are from within the *hakuma* from these communities. In enacting these rivalries, figures in the *hakuma* are mobilising based

---

3   Nicholas Haysom, 'Briefing to the UN Security Council by the Secretary-General's Special Representative for South Sudan', https://unmiss.unmissions.org/briefing-un-security-council-secretary-general's-special-representative-south-sudan-nicholas-0, accessed 17 October 2021.

4   Discussion with UNMISS employee, 10 October 2021, online.

5   Haysom, 'Briefing to the UN Security Council by the Secretary-General's Special Representative for South Sudan'.

on identities that evoke shared family histories. Ancestors are a significant part of the cosmic polity, and such narratives bring them to life. At the same time, the instrumentalisation of ancestors by the living has limits; ancestors often end up as rivals to the living.[6] As the *hakuma* is drawn into these cosmic games, there is potential to hedge them in by custom and seek limits to their power to kill with impunity. The ancestors and the divinities continue to limit the divine power of the *hakuma*, and peace-making must not close the space for this.

[6]   Graeber and Sahlins, *On Kings*, page 10.

Bibliography

Archival sources

South Sudan National Archive, Juba (SSNA)
The Sudan Archive, Durham (SAD)
Sudan Open Archive, available at www.sudanarchive.net

Books and journal articles

6, Perri and Paul Richards. *Mary Douglas: Understanding Social Thought and Conflict* (New York: Berghahn Books, 2017).

Abbink, Jon and Tijo Salverda. *The Anthropology of Elites: Power, Culture, and the Complexities of Distinction* (New York: Palgrave Macmillan, 2013).

African Union Commission of Inquiry on South Sudan. *Final Report of the African Union Commission of Inquiry on South Sudan* (Addis Ababa, Ethiopia: The Commission of Inquiry on South Sudan, 2014).

Agamben, Giorgio. *Homo Sacer: Sovereign Power and Bare Life*. Translated by Daniel Heller-Roazen (Stanford: Stanford University Press, 1998).

Akoi, Abraham Diing and Naomi Pendle. '"I Kept My Gun": Remaking and Reproducing Social Distinctions during Return in South Sudan'. *Journal of Refugee Studies* 33:4 (2020): 791–812.

Allen, Tim. 'The Violence of Healing'. *Sociologus* 47:2 (1997): 101–128.

Allen, Tim. 'Vigilantes, Witches and Vampires: How Moral Populism Shapes Social Accountability in Northern Uganda'. *International Journal on Minority and Group Rights* 22:3 (2015): 360–386.

Allen, Tim. 'Witchcraft, Sexuality and HIV/AIDS among the Azande of Sudan'. *Journal of Eastern African Studies* 1:3 (2007): 359–396.

Allen, Tim, and Kyla Reid. 'Justice at the Margins: Witches, Poisoners, and Social Accountability in Northern Uganda'. *Medical Anthropology* 34:2 (2015): 106–123.

Allen, Tim and Mareike Schomerus, *A Hard Homecoming: Lessons Learned from the Reception Center Process in Northern Uganda – An Independent Study* (Washington, DC: United States Agency for International Development, 2006).

Arjona, Ana, Nelson Kasfir, and Zachariah Mampilly, *Rebel Governance in Civil War* (Cambridge: Cambridge University Press, 2015).

Anai, Anai Mangong. 'Warrap State Peace and Reconciliation Conference – Mayen Rual' Report of Warrap State Peace and Reconciliation Conference. PACT, Mayen Rual, Southern Sudan, 17 June 2005.

Anderson, David and Douglas Johnson. *Revealing Prophets: Prophecy in Eastern African History* (London and Athens, OH: James Currey and Ohio University Press, 1995).

Arendt, Hannah. *On Revolution* (London: Penguin, 1990 [1963]).

Arnold, Matthew B. and Chris Alden. '"This Gun is our Food": Disarming the White Army Militias of South Sudan'. *Conflict, Security & Development* 7:3 (2007): 361–385.

Ashworth, John and Maura Ryan. '"One Nation from Every Tribe, Tongue, and People": The Church and Strategic Peacebuilding in South Sudan'. *Journal of Catholic Social Thought* 10:1 (2013): 47–67.

Ashworth, John. 'Wunlit Peace Conference (1999)'. In John Akec, Lam Akod, John Ashworth, Oliver Albino, Paride Taban, et al. (eds), *We Have Lived Too Long to Be Deceived: South Sudanese Discuss the Lessons of Historic Peace Agreements* (London: Rift Valley Institute, 2014): 33–36.

Autesserre, Séverine. *Peaceland: Conflict Resolution and the Everyday Politics of International Intervention* (Cambridge: Cambridge University Press, 2014).

Bompani, Barbara and Maria Frahm-Arp. *Development and Politics from Below: Exploring Religious Spaces in the African State.* Non-governmental Public Action Series (Houndmills and New York: Palgrave Macmillan, 2010).

Chirrilo Madut Anei and Naomi Pendle, *Wartime Trade and the Reshaping of Power in South Sudan: Learning from the Market of Mayen-Rual* (Nairobi: Rift Valley Institute, 2018).

Jan Bachmann, Naomi Pendle and Leben Moro, 'The Longue Durée of Short-lived Infrastructure – Roads and State Authority in South Sudan'. *Geoforum* 133 (2022).

Baczko, Adam, Giles Dorronsoro and Arthur Quesnay. *Civil War in Syria: Mobilization and Competing Social Orders* (Cambridge: Cambridge University Press, 2017).

Baczko, Adam. 'Legal Rule and Tribal Politics: The US Army and the Taliban in Afghanistan (2001–13)'. In Christian Lund and Michael Eilenberg (eds), *Rule and Rupture: State Formation Through the Production of Property and Citizenship* (Chichester: Wiley, 2017): 213–234.

Bagayoko, Nassem. 'Introduction: Hybrid Security Governance in Africa'. *IDS Bulletin* 43:4 (2012): 1–13.

Bayoumi, Ahmed. 'The History and Traditional Treatment of Smallpox in the Sudan'. *Journal of Eastern African Research and Development* 6:1 (1976): 1–10.

Bell, Catherine. *Ritual Theory, Ritual Practice* (Oxford: Oxford University Press, 1992).

Bell, Christine. *On the Law of Peace: Peace Agreements and the Lex Pacificatoria* (Oxford: Oxford University Press, 2008).

Bell, Christine. 'Peace Agreements: Their Nature and Legal Status'. *American Journal of International Law* 100 (2006): 373–412.

Bell, Christine. 'Peace Settlements and Human Rights: A Post-Cold War Circular History'. *Journal of Human Rights Practice* 9:3 (2017): 358–378.

Bell, Christine and Jan Pospisil. 'Navigating Inclusion in Transitions from Conflict: The Formalised Political *Un*settlement'. *Journal of International Development* 29:5 (2017): 576–593.

Bellamy, Alex J. and Charles T. Hunt, 'Twenty-First Century UN Peace Operations: Protection, Force and the Changing Security Environment'. *International Affairs* 91:6 (2015): 1277–1298.

Berry, Sara. 'Chieftaincy, Land, and the State in Ghana and South Africa'. In John Comaroff and Jean Comaroff (eds), *The Politics of Custom: Chiefship, Capital and the State in Contemporary Africa* (Chicago, IL: University of Chicago Press, 2018): 79–109.

Berry, Sara. *No Condition is Permanent: The Social Dynamics of Agrarian Change in Sub-Saharan Africa* (Madison: University of Wisconsin Press, 1993).

Boege, Volker, Anne Brown, Kevin Clements and Anna Nolan. *On Hybrid Political Orders and Emerging States: State Formation in the Context of 'Fragility'* (Berlin: Berghof Research Center for Constructive Conflict Management, 2008).

Boehm, Christopher. *Blood Revenge: The Enactment and Management of Conflict in Montenegro and other Tribal Societies* (Philadelphia: University of Pennsylvania Press, 1984).

Boone, Catherine. 'Land Regimes and the Structure of Politics: Patterns of Land-related Conflict'. *Africa* 83:1 (2013): 188–203.

Boone, Catherine. 'Property and Constitutional Order: Land Tenure Reform and the Future of the African State'. *African Affairs* 106:425 (2007): 557–586.

Boone, Catherine. *Property and Political Order in Africa: Land Rights and the Structure of Politics* (Cambridge: Cambridge University Press, 2014).

Boone, Catherine. 'Sons of the Soil Conflict in Africa: Institutional Determinants of Ethnic Conflict Over Land'. *World Development* 96 (2017): 276–293.

Boswell, Alan. 'Insecure Power and Violence: The Rise and Fall of Paul Malong and the Mathiang Anyoor'. Briefing Paper (Geneva: Small Arms Survey, 2019).

Bourdieu, Pierre and Passeron, Jean-Claude, *Reproduction in Education, Society and Culture* (London: Sage 1990).

Bourdieu, Pierre. 'Rethinking the State: Genesis and Structure of the Bureaucratic Field'. *Sociological Theory* 12:1 (1994): 1–18.

Bourdieu, Pierre. *Distinction: A Social Critique of the Judgement of Taste* (New York: Routledge, 1984).

Bourdieu, Pierre. 'The Social Space and the Genesis of Groups'. *Theory and Society* 14:6 (1985): 723–744.

Bradbury, Mark, John Ryle, Michael Medley and Kwesi Sansculotte-Greenidge. *Local Peace Processes in Sudan: A Baseline Study* (London: Rift Valley Institute, 2006).

Branch, Adam. 'The Violence of Peace: Ethno-justice in Northern Uganda'. *Development and Change* 45:3 (2014): 608–630.

Burton, John W. 'When the North Winds Blow: A Note on Small Towns and Social Transformation in the Nilotic Sudan'. *African Studies Review* 31:3 (1988): 49–60.

Caroll, Stuart. *Blood and Violence in Early Modern France* (Oxford: Oxford University Press, 2006).

Chandler, D. *Empire in Denial: The Politics of State-Building* (London: Pluto Press, 2006).

Checchi, Francesco, Adrienne Testa, Abdihamid Warsame, Le Quach and Rachel Burns, 'Estimates of Crisis-attributable Mortality in South Sudan, December 2013–April 2018'. London School of Hygiene and Tropical Medicine, 2018, www.lshtm.ac.uk/south-sudan-full-report (accessed 7 December 2020).

Chinn, P. L. and A. Falk-Rafael, 'Peace and Power: A Theory of Emancipatory Group Process'. *Journal of Nursing Scholarship* 47:1 (2015): 62–69.

Cleveland, William L. and Martin Bunton. 'A History of the Modern Middle East', 4th edn (Boulder, CO: Westview Press, 2009).

Collins, Robert O. *The Land Beyond the Rivers: The Southern Sudan, 1898–1918* (New Haven, CT: Yale University Press, 1971).

Cooper, Neil. 'Review Article: On the Crisis of the Liberal Peace'. *Conflict, Security & Development* 7:4 (2007).

Comaroff, Jean and John Comaroff. 'Occult Economies and the Violence of Abstraction: Notes from the South African Postcolony'. *American Ethnologist* 26:2 (1999): 279–303.

Comaroff, John and Jean Comaroff. 'Chiefs, Capital, and the State in Contemporary Africa: An Introduction'. In John Comaroff and Jean Comaroff (eds), *The Politics of Custom: Chiefship, Capital, and the State in Contemporary Africa* (Chicago, IL: University of Chicago Press, 2018): 1–48.

Comaroff, John and Jean Comaroff. *The Politics of Custom: Chiefship, Capital and the State in Contemporary Africa* (Chicago, IL: University of Chicago Press, 2018).

Cooper, Frederick. 'Conflict and Connection: Rethinking Colonial African History'. *The American Historical Review* 99:5 (1994): 1516–1545.

Cooper, Frederick. *Africa Since 1940: The Past of the Present* (Cambridge: Cambridge University Press, 2002).

Copnall, James. *A Poisonous Thorn in Our Hearts: Sudan and South Sudan's Bitter and Incomplete Divorce* (London: C. Hurst & Co., 2014).

Cormack, Zoe. 'Borders are Galaxies: Interpreting Contestations over Local Aministrative Boundaries in South Sudan'. *Africa* 86:3 (2016): 504–527.

Cormack, Zoe. 'The Making and Remaking of Gogrial: Landscape, History and Memory in South Sudan' (PhD diss., Durham University, 2014).

Craze, Joshua. '"And Everything Became War": Warrap State Since the Signing of the R-ARCSS'. HSBA Briefing Paper (Geneva: Small Arms Survey, 2022).

Craze, Joshua. 'Displaced and Immiserated: The Shilluk of Upper Nile in South Sudan's Civil War, 2014–2019'. Geneva: Small Arms Survey, 2019, www.smallarmssurveysudan.org/fileadmin/docs/reports/HSBA-Report-South-Sudan-Shilluk.pdf (accessed 5 April 2020).

Craze, Joshua. *The Politics of Numbers: On Security Sector Reform in South Sudan, 2005–2020* (London School of Economics, 2021), www.lse.ac.uk/africa/assets/Documents/Politics-of-Numbers-Joshua-Craze.pdf (accessed 6 December 2020).

Craze, Joshua. 'The War They Call Peace', *Sidecar*, 9 July 2021, https://newleftreview.org/sidecar/posts/the-war-they-call-peace (accessed 10 July 2021).

Craze, Joshua. 'When Peace Produces War: The Case of South Sudan'. Special Report, Risks of Peace in Post-War Yemen Series, https://static1.squarespace.com/static/535dcd87e4b08cab3cb3e421/t/61f9355bfe787d019f61b734/1643722075758/e6b9aed53703337d91b7c7946696764e61f-8f68d857c6.pdf (accessed 17 July 2022).

Craze, Joshua. 'Unclear Lines: State and Non-State Actors in Abyei'. In Christopher Vaughan, Mareike Schomerus and Lotje De Vries (eds), *The Borderlands of South Sudan: Authority and Identity in Contemporary and Historical Perspectives* (New York: Palgrave Macmillan, 2013): 45–66.

Craze, Joshua and Ferenc David Marko. 'Death by Peace: How South Sudan's Peace Agreement Ate the Grassroots', *Debating Ideas* (6 January 2022), https://africanarguments.org/2022/01/death-by-peace-how-south-sudans-peace-agreement-ate-the-grassroots (accessed 16 July 2022).

Craze, Joshua, Jérôme Tubiana and Claudio Gramizzi. 'A State of Disunity: Conflict Dynamics in Unity State, South Sudan, 2013–15'. HSBA Working Paper 42 (Geneva: Small Arms Survey, 2016).

De Boeck, Filip. 'Postcolonialism, Power and Identity: Local and Global Perspectives from Zaire'. In Richard Werbner and Terence Ranger (eds), *Postcolonial Identities in Africa* (Atlantic Highlands, NJ: Zed Books, 1996): 75-106.

de Waal, Alex. 'Peace and the Security Sector in Sudan, 2002–11'. *African Security Review* 26:2 (2017): 180–198.

de Waal, Alex. 'Sudan'. In Alpaslan Özerdem and Roger Mac Ginty (eds), *Comparing Peace Processes* (Abingdon: Routledge, 2019): 303–318.

de Waal, Alex. 'When Kleptocracy Becomes Insolvent: Brute Causes of the Civil War in South Sudan'. *African Affairs* 113:452 (2014): 347–369.

de Waal, Alex. *Somalia's Disassembled State: Clan Formation and the Political Marketplace* (Boston: World Peace Foundation, 2019).

de Waal, Alex and Naomi Pendle. 'South Sudan: Decentralization and the Logic of the Political Marketplace'. In L. Biong, and S. Logan (eds), *The Struggle for South Sudan* (London, I.B. Tauris, 2018).

Deng, David K. '"Land Belongs to the Community": Demystifying the "Global Land Grab" in Southern Sudan'. LDPI Working Paper no. 4 (Rotterdam: Land Deal Politics Initiative 2011).

Deng, Francis Mading and M.W. Daly. *Bonds of Silk: Human Factor in the British Administration of the Sudan* (East Lansing: Michigan State University Press, 1990).

Deng, Francis Mading. *Customary Law in the Modern World: The Crossfire of Sudan's War of Identities* (Abingdon: Routledge, 2010).

Deng, Francis Mading. *Tradition and Modernization: A Challenge for Law among the Dinka of Sudan* (New Haven, CT: Yale University Press, 1971).

Deng, Luka Biong. 'The Sudan Famine of 1998'. IDS Bulletin (Brighton: Institute of Development Studies, 1984).

Dezalay, S. 'Wars on Law, Wars through Law?' *Journal of Law and Society* 47:S1 (2020).

Dijk, Rijk van and Emile van Rouveroy van Nieuwaal. 'Introduction: The Domestication of Chieftaincy in Africa: From the Imposed to the Imagined'. In Emile van Rouveroy van Nieuwaal and Rijk van Dijk (eds), *African Chieftaincy in a New Socio-Political Landscape* (Hamburg: Lit Verlag, 1999): 1–20.

Dodge, Toby. '"Bourdieu Goes to Baghdad": Explaining Hybrid Political Identities in Iraq'. *Journal of Historical Sociology* 31:1 (2018): 25–38.

Dodge, Toby. 'The Ideological Roots of Failure: The Application of Kinetic Neo-Liberalism to Iraq'. *International Affairs* 86:6 (2010): 1269–1286,

Douglas, Mary. *Implicit Meanings: Selected Essays in Anthropology* (London: Routledge, 1975).

Douglas, Mary. *Jacob's Tears: The Priestly Work of Reconciliation* (New York, Oxford University Press: 2004).

Douglas, Mary. *Leviticus as Literature* (Oxford: Oxford University Press, 2000).

Douglas, Mary and Gerald Mars. 'Terrorism: A Positive Feedback Game'. *Human Relations* 56:7 (2003): 763–786.

Duffield, Mark. *Development, Security and Unending War: Governing the World of Peoples* (Cambridge: Polity Press, 2007).

Duffield, Mark. *Global Governance and the New Wars: The Merging of Development and Security* (London: Zed Books, 2001).

Džuverović, N. 'To Romanticise or Not to Romanticise the Local'. *Conflict, Security & Development* 21:1 (2021): 21–24.

Eggers, Nicole. 'Authorities that are Customary'. *Journal of Eastern African Studies* 14:1 (2020): 24–42.

Elfversson, Emma. 'Peace From Below: Governance and Peacebuilding in Kerio Valley, Kenya', *The Journal of Modern African Studies* 54:3 (2016): 469–493.

Ellis, Stephen and Gerrie Ter Haar. *Worlds of Power: Religious Thought and Political Practice in Africa* (London: C. Hurst & Co., 2004).

Evans-Pritchard, Edward. *Nuer Religion* (Oxford: Oxford University Press, 1956).

Evans-Pritchard, Edward. *The Nuer: A Description of the Modes of Livelihood and Political Institutions of a Nilotic People* (Oxford: Clarendon Press, 1940).

Evans-Pritchard, Edward. 'The Sacrificial Role of Cattle among the Nuer'. *Africa: Journal of the International African Institute* 23:3 (1953): 181–198.

Darby, John, and Roger Mac Ginty. *Contemporary Peacemaking Conflict, Violence, and Peace Processes* (Houndmills and New York: Palgrave Macmillan, 2003).

Elwert, Georg and Thomas Bierschenk. 'Development Aid as Intervention in Dynamic Systems', *Sociologia Ruralis* 28:2/3 (1988): 99–112.

Feierman, Steve. 'Colonizers, Scholars, and the Creation of Invisible Histories'. In Victoria E. Bonnell and Lynn Hunt (eds), *Beyond the Cultural Turn: New Directions in the Study of Society and Culture* (London: University of California Press, 1999): 182–216.

Feyissa, Dereje. 'The Religious Framing of the South Sudanese Civil Wars: The Enduring Legacy of Ngundeng's Prophecy'. *Journal for the Study of the Religions of Africa and its Diaspora* 3:1 (2017): 60–77.

Fields, Karen. *Revival and Rebellion in Colonial Central Africa*. Princeton, NJ: Princeton University Press, 1985.

Fortna, Virginia Page. *Does Peacekeeping Work? Shaping Belligerents' Choices after Civil War* (Princeton, NJ: Princeton University Press, 2008).

Fortna, Virginia. *Peace Time: Cease-Fire Agreements and the Durability of Peace* (Princeton, NJ: Princeton University Press, 2004).

Foucault, Michel. *The Birth of Biopolitics: Lectures at the Collège de France 1978–79* (Basingstoke: Palgrave Macmillan, 2010).

Fountain, Philip. 'Toward a Post-secular Anthropology'. *The Australian Journal of Anthropology* 24:3 (2013): 310–328.

Fukuyama, Francis. *The End of History and the Last Man* (London: Hamish Hamilton, 1992).

Gagnon, Georgette and John Ryle. 'Report of an Investigation into Oil Development in Western Upper Nile'. Canadian Auto Workers Union; Steelworkers Humanity Fund; Simons Foundation; United Church of Canada, Division of World Outreach; World Vision Canada, 2001.

Gaonkar, Dilip Parameshwar. 'Toward New Imaginaries: An Introduction'. *Public Culture* 14:1 (2002): 1–19.

Gallagher, John and Ronald Robinson. 'The Imperialism of Free Trade'. *The Economic History Review* 6:1 (1953): 1–15.

Garang, John. 'Identifying, Selecting and Implementing Rural Development Strategies for Sudan' (PhD diss., Iowa State University, 1981).

Geschiere, P. *The Modernity of Witchcraft: Politics and the Occult in Postcolonial Africa / Sorcellerie et politique en Afrique: la viande des autres* (Charlottesville, VA: University Press of Virginia 1997).

Gessi, Romolo. *Seven Years in the Soudan* (London: Sampson Low, Marston & Company, 1892).

Gluckman, Max. 'The Peace in the Feud'. *Past and Present* 8:1 (1955): 1–14.

Graeber, David. 'Culture as Creative Refusal'. *Cambridge Anthropology* 31:2 (2013): 1–19.

Graeber, David. 'Dead Zones of the Imagination: On Violence, Bureaucracy, and Interpretive Labour'. *Journal of Ethnographic Theory* 2:2 (2012): 105–128.

Graeber, David. *Lost People: Magic and the Legacy of Slavery in Madagascar* (Indiana, University of Indiana Press, 2007).

Graeber, David. 'On the Moral Grounds of Economic Relations: A Maussian Approach' (Chicago, IL: Open Anthropology Cooperative Press, 2010).

Graeber, David. 'The Sword, the Sponge, and the Paradox of Performativity: Some Observations on Fate, Luck, Financial Chicanery, and the Limits of Human Knowledge'. *Social Analysis* 56:1 (2012): 25–42.

Graeber, David and Marshall Sahlins. *On Kings* (Chicago, IL: HAU Books, 2017).

Gray, Richard. *A History of the Southern Sudan 1839–1889* (Oxford: Oxford University Press, 1961).

Gready, Paul and Simon Robins. 'From Transitional to Transformative Justice: A New Agenda for Practice'. *International Journal of Transitional Justice* 8:3 (2014): 341–342.

Hansen, Thomas B. and Finn Stepputat. 'Introduction: States of Imagination'. In Thomas B. Hansen and Finn Stepputat (eds), *States of Imagination: Ethnographic Explorations of the Postcolonial State* (Durham, NC: Duke University Press, 2001): 1–40.

Hansen, Thomas B. and Finn Stepputat (eds). *Sovereign Bodies: Citizens, Migrants, and States in the Postcolonial World* (Princeton, NJ: Princeton University Press, 2005).

Healy, Sally. 'Peacemaking in the Midst of War: An Assessment of IGAD's Contribution to Regional Security'. Crisis States Working Papers Series 2, no. 59 (London: LSE, 2009).

Hellweg, Joseph. 'Sacrifice, Ethics, and Alinesitoué: Human Rights and Ritual Discourse in a Revolutionary Prophetic Movement'. *Journal of Africana Religions* 6:1 (2018): 134–142.

Hennings, Jan. *Russia and Courtly Europe: Ritual and the Culture of Diplomacy, 1648–1725* (Cambridge: Cambridge University Press, 2016).

Herbst, Jeffrey. *States and Power in Africa: Comparative Lessons in Authority and Control* (Princeton, NJ: Princeton University Press, 2014).

Herzfeld, Michael. 'Meaning and Morality: A Semiotic Approach to Evil Eye Accusations in a Greek Village'. *American Ethnologist* 8: 3 (1981): 560–574.

Hoffmann, Kasper. 'Myths Set in Motion: The Moral Economy of Mai Mai Governance'. In Ana Arjona, Nelson Kasfir and Zachariah Mampilly (eds), *Rebel Governance in Civil War* (Cambridge: Cambridge Univeristy Press, 2015): 158–179.

Kasper Hoffmann, Koen Vlassenroot and Emery Mudinga, '*Courses au pouvoir*: The Struggle Over Customary Capital in the Eastern Democratic Republic of Congo', *Journal of Eastern African Studies* 14:1 (2020): 125–144.

Howell, Paul Philip. *Manual of Nuer Law* (Oxford: Oxford University Press, 1954).

Howell, Paul Philip. 'Notes on the Ngork Dinka of Western Kordofan'. *Sudan Notes and Records* 32:2 (1951): 239–293.

Howell, Paul Philip. 'Observations on the Shilluk of the Upper Nile: Customary Law – Marriage and the Violation of Rights in Women'. *Journal of the International African Institute* 23:2 (1953): 94–109.

Hunt, Charles T. 'Analyzing the Co-Evolution of the Responsibility to Protect and the Protection of Civilians in UN Peace Operations'. *International Peacekeeping* 26:5 (2019): 630–659.

Hunt, Nancy Rose. *A Nervous State: Violence, Remedies, and Reverie in Colonial Congo* (Durham, NC: Duke University Press, 2016).

Hutchinson, Sharon. 'A Curse from God? Religious and Political Dimensions of the Post-1991 Rise of Ethnic Violence in South Sudan'. *The Journal of Modern African Studies* 39:2 (2001): 307–331.

Hutchinson, Sharon. '"Dangerous to Eat": Rethinking Pollution States among the Nuer of Sudan'. *Africa: Journal of the International African Institute* 62:4 (1992): 490–504.

Hutchinson, Sharon. *Nuer Dilemmas: Coping with Money, War and the State* (Berkeley: University of California Press, 1996).

Hutchinson, Sharon. 'Nuer Ethnicity Militarized'. *Anthropology Today* 16:3 (2000): 6–13.

Hutchinson, Sharon. 'The Cattle of Money and the Cattle of Girls among the Nuer, 1930–83'. *American Ethnologist* 19:2 (1992): 294–316.

Hutchinson, Sharon and Naomi Pendle. 'Violence, Legitimacy, and Prophecy: Nuer Struggles with Uncertainty in South Sudan'. *American Ethnologist* 42:3 (2015): 415–430.

Hutton, Lauren, *South Sudan: From Fragility at Independence to a Crisis of Sovereignty* (The Hague: Clingendael Institute, 2014).

International Bank for Reconstruction and Development. *Appraisal of the Development Program of the Sudan Railways* (Washington, DC: World Bank Documents, 1958).

International Crisis Group. *South Sudan: Compounding Instability in Unity State* (Brussels: International Crisis Group, 2011).

'Itinerary of the Bahr el Ghazal River'. In Count Gleichen (ed.), *The Anglo-Egyptian Sudan: A Compendium Prepared by Officers of the Sudan Government*, Volume 1 (London: Harrison and Sons for HMSO, 1905).

James, Wendy. *The Listening Ebony: Moral Knowledge, Religion and Power among the Uduk of Sudan* (Oxford: Clarendon, 1988).

James, Wendy and Douglas Johnson. *Vernacular Christianity: Essays in the Social Anthropology of Religion* (Oxford: Lilian Barber Press, 1988).

Janzen, John. *Ngoma: Discourses of Healing in Central and Southern Africa* (Berkeley: University of California Press, 1992).

Johnson Douglas. 'Briefing: The Crisis in South Sudan'. *African Affairs* 113:451 (2014): 300–309.

Johnson, Douglas. *Empire and the Nuer: Sources on the Pacification of the Southern Sudan, 1898–1930* (Oxford: Oxford University Press for the British Academy, 2016).

Johnson, Douglas. 'Judicial Regulation and Administrative Control: Customary Law and the Nuer, 1898–1954'. *The Journal of African History* 27:1 (1986): 59–78.

Johnson, Douglas. 'New Sudan or South Sudan? The Multiple Meanings of Self-Determination in Sudan's Comprehensive Peace Agreement'. *Civil Wars* 15:2 (2013): 141–156.

Johnson, Douglas. *Nuer Prophets: A History of Prophecy from the Upper Nile in the Nineteenth and Twentieth Centuries* (Oxford: Clarendon Press, 1994).

Johnson, Douglas. 'Prophecy and Mahdism in the Upper Nile: An Examination of Local Experiences of the Mahdiyya in Southern Sudan'. *British Journal of Middle Eastern Studies* 20:1 (1993): 42–56.

Johnson, Douglas. *South Sudan: A New History for a New Nation* (Athens: Ohio University Press, 2016).

Johnson, Douglas. 'The Great Famine in the Sudan'. In Douglas Johnson and David Anderson (eds), *Ecology of Survival: Case Studies from Northeast African History* (London: Lester Crook Academic, 1988): 63–64.

Johnson Douglas. 'The Political Crisis in South Sudan'. *African Studies Review* 57:3 (2014): 167–174.

Johnson, Douglas. 'The Return of Ngundeng's *Dang*', *Sudan Studies Journal* (Sudan Studies Association, 2009).

Johnson, Douglas. *The Root Causes of Sudan's Civil Wars: Peace or Truce* (Oxford: James Currey, 2003).

Jok, Jok Madut. *Breaking Sudan: The Search for Peace* (London: Oneworld Publications, 2017).

Jok, Jok Madut. 'Lessons in Failure: Peacebuilding in Sudan/South Sudan'. In T. McNamee and M. Muyangwa (eds), *The State of Peacebuilding in Africa* (Cham: Palgrave Macmillan, 2021).

Jok Madut Jok, *Sudan: Race, Religion and Violence* (Oxford: Oneworld Publications, 2007).

Jok, Jok Madut. 'The Political History of South Sudan'. In Timothy McKulka (ed.), *A Shared Struggle: The People and Cultures of South Sudan* (Kingdom of Denmark/ Government of South Sudan/ UN, 2013): 85–144.

Jok, Jok Madut and Hutchinson, Sharon. 'Sudan's Prolonged Second Civil War and the Militarization of Nuer and Dinka Ethnic Identities'. *African Studies Review* 42:2 (1999): 125–145.

Kaldor, Mary. 'In Defence of New Wars'. *Stability: International Journal of Security and Development* 2:1 (2013): 1–16.

Kane, Ross. 'Ritual Formation of Peaceful Publics: Sacrifice and Syncretism in South Sudan (1991– 2005)'. *Journal of Religion in Africa* 44:3–4 (2014): 386–410.

Kaplan, Robert. D. 'The Coming Anarchy: How Scarcity, Crime, Overpopulation, Tribalism, and Disease are Rapidly Destroying the Social Fabric of our Planet'. *The Atlantic Monthly* (February 1994).

Kuper, Adam. 'The Return of the Native'. *Current Anthropology* 44:3 (2003): 389–402.

Keen, David. *Complex Emergencies* (Cambridge: Polity Press, 2007).

Khan, Mushtaq H. 'Political Settlements and the Analysis of Institutions'. *African Affairs* 117:469 (2018): 636–655.

Kindersley, Nicki. 'Rule of Whose Law? The Geography of Authority in Juba, South Sudan'. *The Journal of Modern African Studies* 57:1 (2019): 61–83.

Kindersley, Nicki and Joseph Diing Majok. *Monetized Livelihoods and Militarized Labour in South Sudan's Borderlands* (London: Rift Valley Institute, 2019).

Kleinfield, Rachel and Robert Muggah. 'No War, No Peace: Healing the World's Violent Societies'. In Edward de Waal (ed.), *Think Peace: Essays for an Age of Disorder* (Washington, DC: Carnegie Endowment for International Peace, 2019).

Kratz, Corinne A. '"We've Always Done It Like This … Except for a Few Details": "Tradition" and "Innovation" in Okiek Ceremonies'. *Comparative Studies in Society and History* 35:1 (1993): 30–65.

Kuol, Luka Biong Deng. 'Dinka Youth in Civil War: Between Cattle, Community and Government'. In Victoria Brereton (ed.), 'Informal Armies: Community Defence Groups in South Sudan's Civil War'. Report. London: Saferworld, 2017.

Kuol, Luka Biong Deng. 'Political Violence and the Emergence of the Dispute over Abyei, Sudan, 1950–1983', *Journal of Eastern African Studies* 8:4 (2014): 573–589.

Kurimoto, Eisei. 'An Ethnography of "Bitterness": Cucumber and Sacrifice Reconsidered'. *Journal of Religion in Africa* 22:1 (1992): 47–65.

Kuyok, Kuyok Abol. *South Sudan: The Notable Firsts* (Milton Keynes: AuthorHouse UK, 2015).

Kyed, Helene Maria and Lars Buur. 'Introduction: Traditional Authority and Democratization in Africa'. In Lars Buur and Helene Maria Kyed (eds), *State Recognition and Democratization in Sub-Saharan Africa: A New Dawn for Traditional Authorities?* (New York: Palgrave Macmillan, 2007): 1–30.

Lentz, Carola. *Ethnicity and the Making of History in Northern Ghana* (Edinburgh: Edinburgh University Press, 2006).

Leonardi, Cherry. *Dealing with Government in South Sudan: History of Chiefship, Community and State* (Woodbridge: James Currey, 2013).

Leonardi, Cherry. '"Liberation" or Capture: Youth in between "Hakuma" and "Home" during Civil War and its Aftermath in Southern Sudan'. *African Affairs* 106:424 (2007): 391–412.

Leonardi, Cherry. 'Paying "Buckets of Blood" for the Land: Moral Debates over Economy, War and State in Southern Sudan'. *The Journal of Modern African Studies* 49:2 (2011): 215–240.

Leonardi, Cherry. 'Points of Order? Local Government Meetings as Negotiation Tables in South Sudanese History'. *Journal of East African Studies* 9:4 (2015): 650–668.

Leonardi, Cherry, Leben Moro, Martina Santschi and Deborah Isser. *Local Justice in South Sudan* (London: Rift Valley Institute, 2010).

Leonardsson, Hanna and Gustav Rudd. 'The "Local Turn" in Peacebuilding: A Literature Review of Effective and Emancipatory Local Peacebuilding'. *Third World Quarterly* 36:5 (2015): 825–839.

Lewis, B.A. 'The Nuer Political Problem', SSNA UNP 66.G.3 (Province Archives, Malakal, December 1944), 44–47.

Lewis, B.A. *The Murle – Red Chiefs & Black Commoners* (Oxford: Oxford University Press, 1972).

Lienhardt, Godfrey. *Divinity and Experience: The Religion of the Dinka* (Oxford: Clarendon Press, 1961).

Lienhardt, Godfrey. 'Religion'. In Harry L. Shapiro (ed.), *Man, Culture, and Society* (New York: Oxford University Press, 1956).

Lonsdale John. 'Moral & Political Argument in Kenya'. In Bruce Berman, Will Kymlicka and Dickson Eyoh (eds), *Ethnicity & Democracy in Africa* (Oxford: James Currey, 2004): 73–95.

Lowrey, William. O. 'A Flicker of Hope in Sudan' (Washington, DC: Sudan Open Archive, 1998).

Lowrey, William O. Dinka-Nuer Reconciliation Conference (Washington, DC: Sudan Open Archive, 2002), www.sudanarchive. net/?a=d&d=SLPD19990200-01 (accessed 11 December 2022).

Lowrey, William O. 'Passing the Peace … People to People: The Role Of Religion in an Indigenous Peace Process among the Nuer People of Sudan' (PhD diss., Union Institute Graduate School, 1995).

Lubkemann, Stephen. *Culture in Chaos: An Anthropology of the Social Condition in War* (Chicago, IL: University of Chicago Press, 2008).

Lugard, Frederick. *The Dual Mandate in British Tropical Africa* (Abingdon: Frank Case & Co, 1922).

Lupton, Frank and Malcolm Lupton. 'Mr. Frank Lupton's (Lupton Bey) Geographical Observations in the Bahr-el-Ghazal Region: With Introductory Remarks by Malcolm Lupton' *Proceedings of the Royal Geographical Society and Monthly Record of Geography* 6:5 (1884): 245–255.

Mac Ginty, Roger. 'Hybrid Peace: The Interaction between Top-Down and Bottom-Up Peace'. *Security Dialogue* 41:4 (2010): 391–412;

Mac Ginty, Roger. 'Indicators: A Proposal for Everyday Peace Indicators'. *Evaluation and Program Planning* 36:1 (2013): 56–63.

Mac Ginty, Roger. 'Indigenous Peace-Making versus the Liberal Peace'. *Cooperation and Conflict* 43:2 (2008): 139–163.

Mac Ginty, Roger and Oliver Richmond. 'The Local Turn in Peace Building: A Critical Agenda for Peace'. *Third World Quarterly* 34:5 (2013): 763–783.

Macdonald, Anna. 'Transitional Justice and Political Economies of Survival in Post-conflict Northern Uganda'. *Development and Change* 48:2 (2017): 286–311.

Maine, Henry. *Ancient Law* (J.M. Dent & Sons, 1861).

Mamdani, Mahmood. *Citizen and Subject: Contemporary Africa and the Legacy of Late Colonialism* (Princeton, NJ: Princeton University Press, 1996).

Mamdani, Mahmood. 'The Trouble with South Sudan's New Peace Deal: The Revitalized Agreement on the Resolution of the Conflict in South Sudan (R-ARCSS)'. *The Zambakari Advisory*, Special Issue (2019): 58–60.

Marriage, Zoe. *Formal Peace and Informal War: Security and Development in Congo* (Abingdon: Routledge, 2013).

Massoud, Mark Fathi. *Law's Fragile State: Colonial, Authoritarian, and Humanitarian Legacies in Sudan* (New York: Cambridge University Press, 2013).

Massoud, Mark Fathi. 'Theology of the Rule of Law', *Hague Journal on the Rule of Law, HJRL* 11:2/3 (2019): 485–491.

Matthew, Arnold and Matthew LeRiche. *South Sudan: From Revolution to Independence* (London: C. Hurst and Co., 2012).

Mawson, Andrew. 'The Triumph of Life: Political Dispute and Religious Ceremonial Among the Agar Dinka of the Southern Sudan' (PhD diss., Darwin College, 1989).

Mawut, L. L. 'The Southern Sudan Under British Rule 1898–1924: The Constraints Reassessed' (PhD diss., Durham University, 1995).

McCall, Storrs. 'Unpublished Manuscript on the History of the First Civil War in South Sudan (Anya-Nya)' (Sudan Open Archive, 1972).

McCallum, Judith. 'Wunlit Conference (1999)'. In John Akec et al. (eds), *We Have Lived Too Long to Be Deceived: South Sudanese Discuss the Lessons of Historic Peace Agreements* (London: Rift Valley Institute, 2014): 29–30.

McEvoy, Claire and Gergely Hideg. 'Global Violent Deaths 2017: Time to Decide' (Geneva: Small Arms Survey, 2017).

Meierhenrich, J. *The Remnants of the Rechtsstaat: An Ethnography of Nazi Law* (Oxford: Oxford University Press, 2018).

Menkhaus, Kenneth, 'International Peacebuilding and the Dynamics of Local and National Reconciliation in Somalia'. *International Peacekeeping* 3:1 (1996): 42–67.

Merry, Sally Engle. 'The Rule of Law and Authoritarian Rule: Legal Politics in Sudan'. *Law and Social Inquiry* 41:2 (2016): 465–470.

Meyer, Birgit and Peter Geschiere (eds). *Globalization and Identity: Dialectics of Flow and Closure* (Oxford: Wiley-Blackwell, 1999).

Millar, Gearoid. 'For Whom do Local Peace Processes Function? Maintaining Control through Conflict Management'. *Cooperation and Conflict* 52:3 (2017): 293–308.

Migiro, Katy. 'Aid Groups Raise Fears of Escalating Violence in South Sudan'. *Reuters* (21 May 2015).

Moodie, Ellen. *El Salvador in the Aftermath of Peace: Crime, Uncertainty, and the Transition to Democracy* (Philadelphia: University of Pennsylvania Press, 2010).

Moore, Sally Falk. *Law as Process: An Anthropological Approach* (Oxford: James Currey, 2000).

Morrice, H. A. 'The Development of Sudan Communications'. *Sudan Notes and Records* 30:1 (1949): 1–38.

Munive, Jairo. 'Disarmament, Demobilisation and Reintegration in South Sudan: The Limits of Conventional Peace and Security Templates'. DIIS Report no. 2013:07. Danish Institute for International Studies, 2013, www.econstor.eu/handle/10419/97057 (accessed 17 July 2022).

Nadarajah, Suthaharan. '"Conflict-Sensitive" Aid and Making Liberal Peace'. In Mark Duffield and Vernon Hewitt (eds), *Empire, Development & Colonialism: The Past in the Present* (Woodbridge: James Currey, 2009): 59–73.

Nafziger, Wayne and Juha Auvinen. *Economic Development, Inequality, and War: Humanitarian Emergencies in Developing Countries* (New York: Palgrave Macmillan, 2003).

New Sudan Council of Churches. *The Story of People-to-People Peacemaking in Southern Sudan* (Nairobi: NSCC, 2002).

Newman, Edward, Roland Paris and Oliver Richmond (eds). *New Perspectives on Liberal Peace-building* (Tokyo: UN University Press, 2009)

Nhial, Nhial Deng, Wunlit – Dinka-Nuer West Bank Peace and Reconciliation Conference (Wunlit: NSCC, February 1999), page 8, www.sudanarchive.net/?a=d&d=SLPD19990200-01 (accessed 11 December 2022).

Nikkel, Mark R. *Dinka Christianity: The Origins and Development of Christianity among the Dinka of Sudan with Special Reference to the Songs of Dinka Christians* (Nairobi: Paulines Publications Africa, 2001).

Nyaba, Peter Adwok. *The Disarmament of the Gel-Weng of Bahr El Ghazal and the Consolidation of the Nuer – Dinka Peace Agreement 1999* (Rotterdam: Pax Christi for New Sudan Council of Churches, 2001).

Nyaba, Peter Adwok. 'The Fundamental Problems of South Sudan: How to Sustain Peace and Conditions of Socio-economic Development', *The Zambakari Advisory: Special Issue* (2019): 20–24.

Nyaba, Peter Adwok. *The Politics of Liberation in South Sudan: An Insider's View* (Kampala: Fountain Publishers, 1997).

Ong, Lynette. '"Thugs-for-Hire": Subcontracting of State Coercion and State Capacity in China'. *Perspectives on Politics* 16:3 (2018): 680–695.

Ong'ondi, Tinega and Simon Simonse. 'Conflict in the Greater Gogrial: Report of the Fact Finding Mission to Assess the Possibility of a Church led Mediation Process'. Unpublished, 2008.

Oppenheim, Naomi. 'Popular History in the Black British Press: Edward Scobie's Tropic and Flamingo, 1960–64', *Immigrants & Minorities* 37:3 (2019): 136–162.

Paffenholz, T. 'Unpacking the Local Turn in Peacebuilding', *Third World Quarterly* 36:5 (2015): 857–874.

Page, C. H. 'Inland Water Navigation of the Sudan'. *Sudan Notes and Records* 2:4 (1919): 293–306.

Pankhurst, Richard and Douglas Johnson. 'The Great Drought and Famine of 1888–1892 in Northeast Africa'. In Douglas Johnson and David Anderson (eds), *Ecology of Survival: Case Studies from Northeast African History* (London: Lester Crook Academic, 1988).

Paris, Roland. *At War's End: Building Peace after Civil Conflict* (Cambridge: Cambridge University Press, 2004).

Paris, Roland. 'International Peacebuilding and the "Mission Civilisatrice"'. *Review of International Studies* 28:4 (2002): 637–656.

Parry, Jonathan and Maurice Bloch. *Money and the Morality of Exchange* (Cambridge: Cambridge University Press, 1989).

Pendle, Naomi. 'Commanders, Classrooms, Cows and Churches: Accountability and the Construction of a South Sudanese Elite'. In Wale Adebanwi and Roger Orock (eds), *Elites and the Politics of Accountability in Africa* (Ann Arbor: Michigan University Press, 2021).

Pendle, Naomi, 'Competing Authorities and Norms of Restraint: Governing Community-Embedded Armed Groups in South Sudan'. *International Interactions* 47:5 (2021): 873–897.

Pendle, Naomi. 'Contesting the Militarization of the Places Where they Met: The Landscapes of the Western Nuer and Dinka (South Sudan)'. *Journal of Eastern African Studies* 11:1 (2017): 64–85.

Pendle, Naomi 'Politics, Prophets and Armed Mobilizations: Competition and Continuity over Registers of Authority in South Sudan's Conflicts'. *Journal of Eastern African Studies* 14:1 (2020): 43–62.

Pendle, Naomi. '"The Dead Are Just To Drink From": Recycling Ideas of Revenge among the Western Dinka, South Sudan'. *Africa* 88:1 (2018): 99–121.

Pendle, Naomi. 'The "Nuer of Dinka Money" and the Demands of the Dead: Contesting the Moral Limits of Monetised Politics in South Sudan'. *Conflict,Security & Development* 20:5 (2021): 587–605.

Pendle, Naomi. '"They Are Now Community Police": Negotiating the Boundaries and Nature of the Government in South Sudan through the Identity of Militarised Cattle-Keepers'. *International Journal of Minority and Group Rights* 22:3 (2015): 410–434.

Pinaud, Clémence, 'South Sudan: Civil War, Predation and the Making of a Military Aristocracy'. *African Affairs* 113:451 (2014): 192–211.

Pinaud, Clémence, *War and Genocide in South Sudan* (Ithaca, NY and London: Cornell University Press, 2021).

Pospíšil, Jan, *Peace in Political Unsettlement : Beyond Solving Conflict* (Cham: Palgrave Macmillan, 2019).

Power, Thomas and Eve Warburton (eds), *Democracy in Indonesia: From Stagnation to Regression?* (Singapore: ISEAS – Yusof Ishak Institute, 2020): 303–325.

Prunier, Gérard and Rachel M. Gisselquist. 'The Sudan: A Successfully Failed State'. In Robert Rotberg (ed.), *State Failure and State Weakness in a Time of Terror* (Washington, DC: Brookings Institution, 2003): 101–127.

Pugh, Michael. 'Local Agency and Political Economies of Peacebuilding'. *Studies in Ethnicity and Nationalism* 11:2 (2011): 308–320.

Pugh, Michael. 'The Political Economy of Peacebuilding: A Critical Theory Perspective'. *International Journal of Peace Studies* 10:2 (2005): 23–42.

Ranger, Terence. 'The Invention of Tradition in Colonial Africa'. In Eric Hobsbawm and Terence Ranger (eds), *The Invention of Tradition* (Cambridge: Cambridge University Press, 1983): 211–262.

Rappaport, Roy. *Ritual and Religion in the Making of Humanity* (Cambridge: Cambridge University Press, 1999).

Richards, Paul. 'To Fight or to Farm? Agrarian Dimensions of the Mano River Conflicts (Liberia and Sierra Leone)'. *African Affairs* 104:417 (2005): 571–590.

Richmond, Oliver P. 'The Problem of Peace: Understanding the "Liberal Peace"'. *Conflict, Security & Development* 6:3 (2006): 291–314.

Richmond, Oliver P. 'A Post-liberal Peace: Eirenism and the Everyday'. *Review of International Studies* 35:3 (209): 557–580.

Richmond, Oliver P. and Audra Mitchell. *Hybrid Forms of Peace from Everyday Agency to Post-liberalism* (Houndmills: Palgrave Macmillan, 2012).

Riek, Jedeit J. and Naomi Pendle. *Speaking Truth to Power in South Sudan: Oral Histories of the Nuer Prophets* (London: Rift Valley Institute, 2018).

Roelofs, Portia. 'Contesting Localisation in Interfaith Peacebuilding in Northern Nigeria'. *Oxford Development Studies* 48:4 (2020): 373–386.

Rolandsen, Øystein. 'A False Start: Between War and Peace in the Southern Sudan, 1956–62'. *The Journal of African History* 52:1 (2011): 105–123.

Rolandsen, Øystein. 'Civil War Society? Political Processes, Social Groups and Conflict Intensity in the Southern Sudan, 1955–2005' (PhD diss., University of Oslo, 2010).

Rolandsen, Øystein. 'The Making of the Anya-Nya Insurgency in the Southern Sudan 1961–64'. *Journal of Eastern African Studies* 5:2 (2011): 211–232.

Rolandsen, Øystein and Nicki Kindersley. *South Sudan: A Political Economy Analysis* (Oslo: Norwegian Institute of International Affairs, 2017).

Rowe, John A. and Kjell Hødnebø. 'Rinderpest in the Sudan 1888–1890: The Mystery of the Missing Panzootic'. *Sudanic Africa* 5 (1994): 149–178.

Rt Rev. Peter Gail Lual Marrow, Chairman South Sudan Council of Churches. 'A Statement From Kigali' during church leaders' retreat, Kigali, Rwanda, 1–7 July 2015.

Sahlins, Marshall. *Culture and Practical Reason* (Chicago, IL and London: University of Chicago Press, 1976).

San Martín, Inés. 'From Conversion Therapy to Immigration, Church Draws Fire in Spain'. *Crux: Taking the Catholic Pulse* (11 April 2019).

Sanderson, L. P. and N. Sanderson. *Education, Religion and Politics in Southern Sudan, 1899–1964* (London and Khartoum: Ithaca Press, 1981).

Santschi, Martina. 'Encountering and "Capturing" Hakuma: Negotiating Statehood and Authority in Northern Bahr-El-Ghazal State, South Sudan' (PhD diss., University of Bern, 2013).

Schierup, Carl-Ulrik (ed.). *Scramble for the Balkans: Nationalism, Globalism and the Political Economy of Reconstruction* (Basingstoke: Macmillan, 1999).

Schmitt, Carl. *Political Theology: Four Chapters on the Concept of Sovereignty*. Translated by George Schwab (Chicago, IL: University of Chicago Press, 2005 [1922]).

Schweinfurth, Georg. *The Heart of Africa: Three Years' Travels and Adventures in the Unexplored Regions of Central Africa, From 1868 to 1871*, Volume 1 (New York: Harper, 1874).

Scott, James C. *Seeing Like a State: How Certain Schemes to Improve the Human Condition Have Failed*. Yale Agrarian Studies (New Haven, CT and London: Yale University Press, 1998).

Shore, Chris and Stephen Nugent. *Elite Cultures: Anthropological Perspectives* (London: Routledge, 2002).

Sikainga, Ahmad Alawad. *City of Steel and Fire – A Social History of Atbara, Sudan's Railway Town (1906–1984)* (Oxford: James Currey, 2002).

Small Arms Survey, 'Spreading Fallout: The Collapse of the ARCSS and New Conflict along the Equatorias-DRC Border', HSBA Issue Brief (2017), www.smallarmssurvey.org/sites/default/files/resources/HSBA-IB28-Spreading-Fallout.pdf (accessed 17 July 2022).

Snowden, John. 'Work in Progress: Security Force Development in South Sudan through February 2012'. Working Paper no. 27 (Geneva: Small Arms Survey, 2012).

Spiegel, Samuel, Hazel Gray, Barbara Bompani, Kevin Bardosh and James Smith. 'Decolonising Online Development Studies? Emancipatory aspirations and critical reflections – a case study'. *Third World Quarterly* 38:2 (2017): 270–290.

Spear, Thomas. 'Neo-traditionalism and the Limits of Invention in British Colonial Africa'. *The Journal of African History* 44:1 (2003): 3–27.

Srinivasan, Sharath. *When Peace Kills Politics: International Intervention and Unending Wars in the Sudans* (London: Hurst & Company, 2021).

Stewart, Pamela J. and Andrew J. Strathern. *Violence: Theory and Ethnography* (London: Continuum, 2002).

Summers, Marc and Stephanie Schwartz. *Dowry and Division: Youth and State Building in South Sudan* (Washington DC: USIP, 2011).

Swartz, David. *The Sociology of Pierre Bourdieu* (London: The University of Chicago Press, 1997).

Tapscott, Rebecca. *Arbitrary States* (Oxford: Oxford UP, 2021).

Tapscott, Rebecca. 'Vigilantes and the State: Understanding Violence through a Security Assemblages Approach'. *Perspectives on Politics* (June 2021): 1–16.

The Carter Center. *Observing Sudan's 2010 National Elections* (Atlanta, GA: The Carter Center, 2010).

Thomas, Edward. *South Sudan: A Slow Liberation* (London: Zed Books, 2015).

Thompson, Edward Palmer. *Whigs and Hunters: The Origin of the Back Act* (London: Breviary Stuff Publications, 2013 [1975]).

Tinné, John. 'A Communication from Mr. Tinné Relative to the Dutch Ladies' Expedition from Khartùm up the River Bahr-el-Ghazal, Commencing 26 February, at a Point on the White Nile'. *Proceedings of the Royal Geographical Society of London* 8:1 (1863–1864): 12–18.

Titherington, G. W. 'The Riak Dinka of Bahe El Ghazal Province'. *Sudan Notes and Records* 10 (1927): 159–209.

Tounsel, Christopher. *Chosen Peoples: Christianity and Political Imagination in South Sudan* (Durham, NC: Duke University Press, 2021).

Tounsel, Christopher. 'Khartoum Goliath: SPLM/SPLA Update and Martial Theology during the Second Sudanese Civil War'. *Journal of Africana Religions* 4:2 (2016): 129–153.

Tvedt, Terje. *The River Nile in the Age of the British: Political Ecology and the Quest for Economic Power* (London: I.B. Tauris, 2016).

Uvin, Peter. *Aiding Violence: The Development Enterprise in Rwanda* (Williamsburg, MA: Kumarian Press, 1998).

Van Bockhaven, Vicky. 'Anioto and Nebeli: Local Power Bases and the Negotiation of Customary Chieftaincy in the Belgian Congo (ca. 1930–1950)'. *Journal of Eastern African Studies* 14:1 (2020): 63–83.

Van Bockhaven, Vicky. 'Anioto: Leopard-men Killings and Institutional Dynamism in Northeast Congo, c. 1890–1940'. *The Journal of African History* 59:1 (2018): 21–44.

Venugopal, Rajech. *Nationalism, Development and Ethnic Conflict in Sri Lanka* (Cambridge: Cambridge University Press, 2018).

Verweijen, Judith & Vicky Van Bockhaven. 'Revisiting Colonial Legacies in Knowledge Production on Customary Authority in Central and East Africa'. *Journal of Eastern African Studies* 14:1 (2020): 1–23.

Vezzadini, Elena. 'Setting the Scene of the Crime: The Colonial Archive, History, and Racialisation of the 1924 Revolution in Anglo-Egyptian Sudan'. *Canadian Journal of African Studies* 49:1 (2015): 67–93.

Vick, Karl. 'A New Peace in Sudan'. *Washington Post* (7 July 1999), www.washingtonpost.com/archive/politics/1999/07/07/a-new-peace-in-sudan/7c064da9-d5d2-4b17-84cc-03ef04c4a36c (accessed 19 October 2022).

Vlassenroot, Koen. 'Citizenship, Identity Formation & Conflict in South Kivu: The Case of the Banyamulenge'. *Review of African Political Economy* 29:93–94 (2007): 499–516.

Walzer, Michael. 'Can There Be a Decent Left?' *Dissent* (Spring 2002).

Werner, Roland, William Anderson and Andrew Wheeler. *Day of Devastation, Day of Contentment: The History of the Sudanese Church across 2000 years* (Nairobi: Paulines Publications Africa, 2000).

Wheeler, Andrew. 'Finding Meaning Amid the Chaos: Narratives of Significance in the Sudanese Church'. In Niels Kastfelt (ed.), *Religion and African Civil Wars* (New York: Palgrave Macmillan, 2005): 54–81.

Wheeler, Skye. 'South Sudan's New War: Abuses by Government and Opposition Forces' (New York: Human Rights Watch, 2014).

Wheeler, Skye and Samer Muscati. '"They Burned It All": Destruction of Villages, Killings, and Sexual Violence in Unity State, South Sudan' (New York: Human Rights Watch, 2015).

White, L. *Speaking with Vampires: Rumor and History in Colonial Africa.* Studies on the History of Society and Culture (Berkeley: University of California Press, 2000).

Wickens, G. E. 'Dr. G. Schweinfurth's Journeys in the Sudan'. *Kew Bulletin* 27:1 (1972): 129–146.

Willems, Rens and David Deng. 'Justice and Conflict in South Sudan: Observations from a Pilot Study' (The Hague: University for Peace, 2015).

Willis, Charles A. with Arthur H. Alban, *The Upper Nile Province Handbook: A Report on Peoples and Government in the Southern Sudan*, edited by Douglas H. Johnson (Oxford: Oxford University Press for the British Academy, 1995 [1931]).

Willis, Justin. 'Hukm: The Creolization of Authority in Condominium Sudan'. *The Journal of African History* 46:1 (2005): 29–50.

Wilson, Jacqueline. 'Local Peace Processes in Sudan and South Sudan'. Peaceworks (Washington, DC: US Institute for Peace, 2014).

Wilson, Salim. *I Was a Slave* (London: Stanley Paul, 1939).

Woodward, Peter. 'Review of *City of Steel and Fire – A Social History of Atbara, Sudan's Railway Town (1906–1984)* by Ahmad Alawad Sikainga'. *Annales d'Éthiopie* 20 (2004): 281–283.

Woodward, Susan. *Balkan Tragedy: Chaos and Dissolution after the Cold War* (Washington, DC: Brookings Institution, 1995).

Young, John. *Isolation and Endurance: Riek Machar and the SPLM-IO in 2016–17* (Geneva: Small Arms Survey, 2017).

Young, John. *South Sudan's Civil War: Violence, Insurgency, and Failed Peacemaking* (London: Zed Books, 2019).

Young, John. 'Sudan People's Liberation Army Disarmament in Jonglei and its Implications'. Paper no. 137 (Pretoria: Institute for Security Studies, 2007), https://journals.co.za/doi/abs/10.10520/EJC48795 (accessed 17 July 2022).

Young, John. *The Fate of Sudan: The Origins and Consequences of a Flawed Peace Process* (London: Zed Books, 2012).

Young, John. 'The South Sudan Defence Forces in the Wake of the Juba Declaration'. Working Paper no. 1 (Geneva: Small Arms Survey, 2006).

Zink, Jesse A. *Christianity and Catastrophe in South Sudan* (Waco, TX: Baylor Press, 2018).

Index

Previously published titles in the series

Violent Conversion: Brazilian Pentecostalism and Urban Women in Mozambique, Linda Van de Kamp (2016)

Beyond Religious Tolerance: Muslim, Christian & Traditionalist Encounters in an African Town, edited by Insa Nolte, Olukoya Ogen and Rebecca Jones (2017)

Faith, Power and Family: Christianity and Social Change in French Cameroon, Charlotte Walker-Said (2018)

Contesting Catholics: Benedicto Kiwanuka and the Birth of Postcolonial Uganda, Jonathon L. Earle and J. J. Carney (2021)

Islamic Scholarship in Africa: New Directions and Global Contexts, edited by Ousmane Oumar Kane (2021)

From Rebels to Rulers: Writing Legitimacy in the Early Sokoto State, Paul Naylor (2021)

Sacred Queer Stories: Ugandan LGBTQ+ Refugee Lives and the Bible, Adriaan Van Klinken and Johanna Stiebert, with Sebyala Brian and Fredrick Hudson (2021)

Labour & Christianity in the Mission: African Workers in Tanganyika and Zanzibar, 1864–1926, Michelle Liebst (2021)

The Genocide against the Tutsi, and the Rwandan Churches: Between Grief and Denial, Philippe Denis (2022)

Competing Catholicisms: The Jesuits, the Vatican & the Making of Postcolonial French Africa, Jean Luc Enyegue, SJ (2022)

Islam in Uganda: The Muslim Minority, Nationalism & Political Power, Joseph Kasule (2022)